THE CRAFT OF GENERAL MANAGEMENT

The Practice of Management Series

Harvard Business School Publications

The Craft of General Management
Readings selected by Joseph L. Bower

The Entrepreneurial Venture
Readings selected by William A. Sahlman and Howard H. Stevenson

Managing People and Organizations
Readings selected by John J. Gabarro

Strategic Marketing Management
Readings selected by Robert J. Dolan

THE CRAFT OF GENERAL MANAGEMENT

READINGS SELECTED BY

Joseph L. Bower

Harvard Business School

HARVARD BUSINESS SCHOOL PUBLICATIONS
Boston, Massachusetts

Library of Congress Cataloging-in-Publication Data

The Craft of general management / edited by Joseph L. Bower.
p. cm. — (The Practice of management series)
Includes index.
ISBN 0-87584-313-1 (paperback)
1. Industrial management. 2. Management. I. Bower, Joseph L.
II. Series.
HD31.C67 1991
658—dc20 91-31671
CIP

The Harvard Business School Publications Practice of Management Series is distributed in the college market by McGraw-Hill Book Company. The readings in each book are available individually through PRIMIS, the McGraw-Hill custom publishing service. Instructors and bookstores should contact their local McGraw-Hill representative for information and ordering.

Printed in the United States of America.

95 94 93 92 5 4 3 2 1

JOSEPH L. BOWER

Professor Joseph L. Bower, a leading expert in the fields of corporate strategy and public policy, has devoted his research and teaching to the problems top managers face as they deal with the rapidly changing political and competitive circumstances of the world economy. Since joining the faculty of Harvard University Graduate School of Business Administration in 1963, he has taught, researched, and published on the development of strategy and organizations, resource allocation, the study of business environment, and the working relations of business and government here and abroad.

Currently Chairman of Doctoral Programs, Director of Research, and Donald Kirk David Professor of Business Administration at Harvard, Professor Bower's research interests include the work of top management in formulating strategy and developing organizations for today's competitive global environment. He has completed a study of the strategic problems posed by the restructuring of major industries and is the author of a book on the subject entitled *When Markets Quake* (Harvard Business School Press, 1986). Another book, *The Two Faces of Management: An American Approach to Leadership in Business and Government,* was published by Houghton Mifflin in 1983. His many articles deal with corporate strategy and public policy.

Professor Bower has consulted widely on problems of strategy and organization with companies here and abroad as well as with the U.S. government.

CONTENTS

PART FOUR MANAGING COMPLEXITY

PART FIVE
LEADERSHIP

SERIES PREFACE

The Harvard Business School has a long and distinguished publishing history. For decades, the School has furnished original educational materials to academic classrooms and executive education programs worldwide. Many of these publications have been used by individual managers to update their knowledge and skills. The Practice of Management Series, developed by Harvard Business School Publications, continues this tradition.

The series addresses major areas of the business curriculum and major topics within those areas. Each of the books strikes a balance between broad coverage of the area and depth of treatment; each has been designed for flexibility of use to accommodate the varying needs of instructors and programs in different academic settings.

These books also will serve as authoritative references for practicing managers. They can provide a refresher on business basics and enduring concepts; they also offer cutting-edge ideas and techniques.

The main objective of the Practice of Management Series is to make Harvard Business School's continuing explorations into management's best practices more widely and easily available. The books draw on two primary sources of material produced at the School.

Harvard Business School is probably best known for its field research and cases. Faculty members prepare other material for their classrooms, however, including essays that define and explain key business concepts and practices. Like other classroom materials produced at Harvard Business School, these "notes," as they are called at the School, have a consistent point of view—that of the general manager. They have a common purpose—to inform the actual practice of management as opposed to providing a theoretical foundation. The notes are an important source of selections for the books in this series.

The *Harvard Business Review* has long been recognized by professors and managers as the premier management magazine. Its mix of authors—academics, practicing executives and managers, and consultants—brings to bear a blend of research knowledge and practical intelligence on a wide variety of business topics. *Harvard Business Review* articles challenge conventional wisdom with fresh approaches and often become a part of enlightened conventional wisdom. The magazine speaks primarily to the practice of management at the level of the general manager. *Harvard Business Review* articles are another essential source of selections for this series.

Finally, this series includes selections published by other distinguished institutions and organizations. In instances where there were gaps in coverage or viewpoint, we have taken the opportunity to tap books and other journals besides the *Harvard Business Review*.

ACKNOWLEDGMENTS

The books in this series are the products of a collaborative effort. Joseph L. Bower, the Harvard Business School faculty member who wrote the introduction to *The Craft of General Management*, worked closely with a Harvard Business School Publications editor, Sarah Conner, to select and arrange the best available materials. Professor Bower's content expertise, teaching experience, and diligence, together with Ms. Conner's editorial skill and commitment, have been crucial to the development of the book.

The Harvard Business School faculty whose work is represented in the books have generously taken the time to review their selections. Their cooperation is much appreciated.

Each of the books has been evaluated by practitioners or by professors at other institutions. We would like to thank the following individuals for their careful readings of the manuscript for the collection on general management: John Francis Lubin, The Wharton School, University of Pennsylvania; Edward Zajac, Kellogg Graduate School of Management, Northwestern University; Ari Ginsberg, New York University; and Carolyn Woo, Krannert Graduate School of Management, Purdue University. Their evaluations and many useful suggestions have helped us develop and shape this book into a more effective teaching instrument.

We would like to thank Maria Arteta, former Director of Product Management for Harvard Business School Publications; Bill Ellet, Editorial Director of Harvard Business School Publications; and Benson P. Shapiro, Malcolm P. McNair Professor of Marketing and former faculty adviser to Harvard Business School Publications. The Practice of Management Series would not have materialized without their support, guidance, and insight.

INTRODUCTION

Learning about management requires mastering a considerable body of knowledge and skills. First, it is necessary to master accounting, the language by which the economic performance of a firm is measured. We must also understand the basic functions of the firm: production, marketing, and finance. Because people are what make companies go, we study human behavior in organizations and the design of systems for information and control, planning, and budgeting. Beyond these basics of the firm, we can study international business and the business environment. Recently, attention has focused on business ethics and the need to take account of personal values and social responsibility when making decisions. These studies often are supplemented by work in economics, psychology, and business history.

Is the result of all this work a comprehensive picture of what is involved in managing a company? Clearly not; for the list just presented leaves out the most basic activity of all—the work of leading the firm. Someone has to set goals for the firm, motivate the activities of its members, and integrate their efforts so that they are cohesive. Most managers take some part in these activities, but only the general manager has all these responsibilities in his or her job description.

In large firms, the general manager's role often is so complex that attempts are made to divide the work. A chief executive's office with three or four members often is the result. Many multi-business firms have several divisional general managers as well as group managers for clusters of divisions. The challenges of dealing with this kind of complexity are discussed in some of these readings, but the authors here have focused their analysis on the work of the top manager in whatever form the organization takes, the manager President Harry Truman had in mind when he said, "The buck stops here."

The following true story provides an interesting way of illustrating what general management is all about. The fact that it takes place in a collective, that most unusual of social experiments, is particularly interesting, for it illustrates the generality of the problems discussed here. In a sense, the men and women who formed this collective thought they could escape many of the problems that tax general managers. The fact that they could not reveals that general management problems exist in all organizations, in all cultures, at all times. Those problems are worth studying.

In the 1960s there was a radical newspaper in Boston called the *Phoenix*. Its politics were anti-war, and it was very successful. Its audience was the huge number of college students and young adults in the Boston area. Theaters, clothing stores, Budweiser, and Marlboro found it an excellent vehicle for reaching the audience of affluent young adults through their ads.

Eventually, some of the members of the *Phoenix* staff came to the conclusion that the paper was "selling out." They left to found a new paper that would be true to their ideals. They called it *The Real Paper*. The group of four or five that set up the new publication agreed to run it as a pure cooperative.

The Real Paper succeeded. It grew. The staff grew. As the paper grew, the staff found it useful to specialize in order to effectively carry out the tasks of running the new paper. The individuals became good at their functional tasks, and one of their number found that he was spending a lot of his energy keeping the group coordinated. He was good at it, and he found that the members asked him to perform that function more and more often. From that perspective, he also noted that the situation was changing. With the ending of the Vietnam war, the aging of the passionately anti-government crowd, and their move to the suburbs, the market was changing, growing, and shifting location. Major questions about product and market were facing the paper.

When he tried to get his fellow members to focus on the problem, the unofficial coordinator discovered that they were tired of long cooperative meetings. They had jobs to attend to—sales, production, or reporting—and they had families to go home to.

The organization had developed a general manager who perceived the need for a change in strategy, but he couldn't succeed because the organization didn't provide for a general manager. The paper had to be sold.

All but temporary organizations pass through this cycle of shared vision, growth, specialization, local vision, loss of coherence, diffusion of resources, loss of fit with the environment, and decline. Whatever internal arrangements worked to give the market what it wanted eventually lose their effectiveness as the organization, its members, or its customers, change.

In nineteenth-century companies, dealing with this problem of changing circumstances was the owner's responsibility. But as organizations became larger and owners became anonymous shareowners, it became clear that someone had to keep the organization and its members aligned with each other and with the markets. For example, at General Motors, Alfred Sloan, Jr., took over the reins from entrepreneur-founder William Durant after Durant proved unable to organize in an economic fashion the many properties he had assembled. At DuPont, Pierre DuPont moved the family's concerns out of the center of the company to a finance committee so that the most talented professionals available could work unhindered on the company's problems. In each instance, though the scale was vast, the problems echoed those of *The Real Paper*. Business historian Alfred D. Chandler, Jr., has described the way most American companies passed through this sequence, almost always with an individual rising to deal with a crisis in a way that involved bringing new people to the forefront and developing a new organization.

The craft of general management is usually difficult. There are no formulas to follow. The many textbooks and casebooks on the subject provide considerable insight and guidance, but each general manager faces a unique set of circumstances that must be dealt with in real time. In addition, as circumstances change, so must the general manager.

General managers must play many roles. Perhaps most important, they are responsible for the results of their organization's behavior—good or bad. Subject to social and legal restraints, they must achieve acceptable economic results, however they are defined. This is the role of the organization leader.

Where an organization's capability is inadequate in relation to its objectives, the general manager must be an organization builder. By recruiting new members and strengthening existing members, designing useful working relationships, and encouraging team effort, the general manager makes the organization a more effective economic actor. In doing the work of building, a general manager often finds himself or herself playing the role of teacher or coach.

It is not enough to be an architect, designing an organization's structure and supervising construction. Individuals seldom have the skills required for the new positions as they are laid out on paper, and they are not always happy to work closely with their colleagues. Making new organizational arrangements work is a key part of the general manager's job. At times when results have been poor and crisis threatens, the general manager must act as a surgeon, cutting away ineffective parts of an organization. In recent times, the simple term "restructuring" has been used to describe absolutely traumatic shifts in the size and positioning of an organization's resources. At General Electric in the early 1980s for example, the new general manager, Jack Welch, laid off more than 100,000 workers and managers to restore the competitive capability of the company. As unpleasant as this was (Welch acquired the nickname "Neutron Jack"), it proved an essential step in General Electric's return to the levels of effectiveness and profitability demanded by intensely competitive markets.

To keep from merely reacting to the moves of competitors or shifts in markets, the general manager bears principal responsibility for developing an effective strategy for the organization. The role of strategist is particularly demanding, because it requires comprehending the substance of the business and how it is changing. This means the general manager must understand relevant technology and how it is changing products and processes, assess customer needs, and develop organizational capability measured against the competition.

What is particularly hard about developing strategy is that it almost always requires members of the organization to change in fundamental ways. This often upsets social relationships among individuals and groups, and often requires people to develop new skills. Perhaps the most crucial thing a general manager does, therefore, is motivate people. A general manager's ability to inspire executives and workers to take on the personal and organizational challenges of change has a great deal to do with whether the firm is able to implement strategy successfully.

Leader, organization builder, teacher, coach, surgeon, strategist, and motivator: these roles do not always fit together easily. A manager whose experience, personality, and style make some tasks easy often finds other tasks difficult. At times, several roles must be performed simultaneously, challenging even the most seasoned managers.

This book provides some two dozen perspectives on general management. Its five sections cover the nature of the work of general managers, the task of formulating corporate strategy, building an organization, managing complexity, and the challenge of leading an organization. It may help to sketch these sections in a little more depth.

THE WORK OF GENERAL MANAGEMENT

The opening piece examines the tool kit that a general manager needs. Andrall Pearson's scheme reflects his experience as president of a major multinational corporation. His tough-minded view of the role is an appropriate opening. It is complemented by Ed Wrapp's classic *Harvard Business Review* article, which paints a more subtle picture of how a general manager leads. The careful reader will note that Pearson and Wrapp do not really disagree. The first lays out the domain of general management; the second shows how general management is accomplished over time. James Brian Quinn goes further, providing a flexible framework for managing constant change and its effects. Peter Drucker's article suggests just how much of a general manager's work deals with issues that lie outside of the company. If the day existed when a manager could focus only on the company and its customers, that day has passed. Drucker lays out an agenda for contemporary managers.

MAKING STRATEGY

The job of making effective corporate strategy calls for vision and creativity, aided by careful analysis of what is happening in one's industry and how corporate competence can be turned to competitive advantage. Michael Porter's work has illuminated this process, and the second section opens with two of his articles. The first lays out a framework for industry and competitive analysis that provides a strong basis for understanding the potential profitability of individual markets. The second examines multi-business firms and the problems that have developed where firms tried to diversify through mergers and acquisitions. Porter's analytic approach, emphasizing microeconomics, has been challenged, however. The next two articles describe the role played in strategy by manufacturing capability and the critical role played by a CEO's rough-cut sense of what he or she wants the organization to accomplish.

The Wheelwright and Hayes article on manufacturing relates directly to Pearson's view of general management work that emphasizes building operating capability. On the other hand, Prahalad and Hamel have a view of how goals ought to be developed that is more consistent with Wrapp and Quinn than with Porter. You will find both approaches illuminating, but ask yourself how Porter's view of strategy can be integrated with Prahalad's and Hamel's view of how a general manager ought to formulate the purposes of the corporation.

BUILDING THE ORGANIZATION

This section focuses on the hard work of developing managers, designing useful organizational structures, developing a work environment in which people are committed to what they are doing, and paying people so that their motivation remains congruent with organizational strategy. The last two pieces examine how the way an organization functions influences the way resources are allocated and operations are managed.

The opening article by Andrall Pearson provides a clear view of the work involved in recruiting, training, evaluating, and selecting managers. The role of teacher and coach is laid out with considerable clarity. Henry Mintzberg's piece offers a broad view of organization structure and suggests how to design one that offers the best fit.

Compensation is critical to making any organization work. For a general manager the task of constructing a compensation scheme is complicated because people are paid for past, present, and future contributions, and they focus on far more than money. Michael Beer's piece lays out how a general manager ought to take into account the multiple dimensions of compensation. The Walton article shows the vital connection between motivation and systems of compensation and control. To achieve the power of a fully committed, highly motivated organization, a completely different management mindset is required.

Bower's piece on resource allocation and the Bower and Hout article on fast-cycle organizations make it clear how people and organization issues are linked to strategy. Far from being mere add-ons, incentives and structure tell most members of a complex organization what top management expects of them.

MANAGING COMPLEXITY

The first three sections address the variety that characterizes the work of general management. This fourth section probes a bit deeper, exploring the complexity that general managers must engage. The first two articles deal with the fundamental differences between business and government, as well as with the challenges posed by government involvement in business. The third examines the particular general management structures that are necessary for a multinational company. The section ends with a careful look at the moral problems connected with general management work. Andrews and Friedman present radically different views, reflecting the deep division that characterizes the issue. It is important to think through the profound differences in these two approaches to social responsibility, for they bear directly on the craft of general management.

LEADERSHIP

Peter Drucker and Abraham Zaleznik have written about what the future holds for general management. They are especially concerned with the unique contribution that intelligent, courageous leaders can make. We use their work to close this collection because they emphasize the substantial contribution made by great leaders. The philosopher Alfred North Whitehead, Jr., said that "a great society is one in which business managers think greatly of their calling." Drucker and Zaleznik make the point clear.

The work of general management, done well, has a transforming effect on an organization and society. When it is done poorly, the effects can be disastrous. These are the stakes that make the study of general management worthwhile.

JOSEPH L. BOWER

PART ONE

THE WORK OF GENERAL MANAGEMENT

Six Basics for General Managers 1

ANDRALL E. PEARSON

The general manager's job is varied and complex. Their responsibilities are broad, encompassing every aspect of an organization—finance, personnel, operations, organization design, and so on. But whatever the leadership style or company setting, argues Andrall Pearson, successful GMs stress fundamentals. In this reading, he uses a variety of examples to show how they perform the six tasks that lay the foundation for effective performance: shaping the work environment, setting strategy, allocating resources, developing managers, building the organization, and overseeing operations. Together, these tasks are key to setting priorities and achieving corporate goals.

Great coaches stress fundamentals—the basic skills and plays that make a team a consistent winner. Great general managers do the same thing. They know that sustained superior performance can't be built on one-shot improvements like restructurings, massive cost reductions, or reorganizations. Sure, they'll take such sweeping actions if they're in a situation where that's necessary or desirable. But their priority is avoiding that kind of situation. And they do that by focusing on the six key tasks that constitute the foundations of every general manager's job: shaping the work environment, setting strategy, allocating resources, developing managers, building the organization, and overseeing operations.

This list shouldn't be surprising; the fundamentals of a general manager's job should sound familiar after all. What makes it important is its status as an organizing framework for the vast majority of activities general managers perform. It helps you define the scope of the job, set priorities, and see important interrelationships among these areas of activity.

SHAPING THE WORK ENVIRONMENT

Every company has its own particular work environment, its legacy from the past that dictates to a considerable degree how its managers respond to problems and opportunities. But whatever the environment a general manager inherits from the past, shaping—or reshaping—it is a critically important job. And that's as true in small- and medium-sized companies as it is in giants like General Motors and General Electric.

Three elements dictate a company's work environment: (1) the prevailing performance standards that set the pace and quality of people's efforts; (2) the business concepts that define what the company is like and how it operates; and (3) the people concepts and values that prevail and define what it's like to work there.

Of these three, performance standards are the single most important element because, broadly speaking, they determine the quality of effort the organization puts out. If the general manager sets high standards, key managers will usually follow suit. If the GM's standards are low or vague, subordinates aren't likely to do much better. High standards are thus the principal means by which top general managers exert their influence and leverage their talents across the entire business.

For this reason, unless your company or division already has demanding standards—and very few do—the single biggest contribution you can make to immediate results and long-term success is to raise your performance expectations for every manager, not just for yourself. This means making conscious decisions about what tangible measures constitute superior performance; where your company stands now; and whether you're prepared to make the tough calls and take the steps required to get from here to there.

Clearly one of the most important standards a GM sets is the company's goals. The best GMs establish goals that force the organization to stretch to achieve them. This doesn't mean arbitrary, unrealistic goals that are bound to be missed and motivate no one, but rather goals that won't allow anyone to forget how tough the competitive arena is.

I vividly remember one general manager who astonished subordinates by rejecting a plan that showed nice profits on a good sales gain for the third year in a row. They thought the plan was demanding and competitive. But the GM told them to come back with a plan that kept the same volumes but cut base cost levels 5% below the prior year's, instead of letting them rise with volume. A tough task, but he was convinced the goal was essential because he expected their chief competitor to cut prices to regain market share.

During the next few years, the company dramatically changed its cost structure through a series of innovative cost reductions in production, distribution, purchasing, corporate overhead, and product-mix management. As a result, despite substantial price erosion, it racked up record profits and share-of-market gains. I doubt the company would ever have achieved those results without that tangible goal staring management in the face every morning.

The same kind of thinking is apparent in the comments of a top Japanese CEO who was asked by a U.S. trade negotiator how his company would compete if the yen dropped from 200 to the dollar to 160. "We are already prepared to compete at 120 yen to the dollar," he replied, "so 160 doesn't worry us at all."

High standards come from more than demanding goals, of course. Like top coaches, military leaders, or symphony conductors, top general managers set a personal example in terms of the long hours they work, their obvious commitment to success, and the consistent quality of their efforts. Moreover, they set and reinforce high standards in small ways that quickly mount up.

They reject long-winded, poorly prepared plans and "bagged" profit targets instead of complaining but accepting them anyway. Their managers have to know the details of their business or function, not just the big picture. Marginal performers don't stay long in pivotal jobs. The best GMs set tight deadlines and enforce them. Above all, they are impossible to satisfy. As soon as the sales or production or R&D department reaches one standard, they raise expectations a notch and go on from there.

One general manager, for instance, asks key managers to rank subordinates yearly on a scale from one to nine. Then he reminds everyone that the same performance it took to get a six this year will earn only a five next year. Sure, this approach creates extra stress, possibly even frustration. It also reduces complacency, encourages personal growth, and yields better results.

The second element of the work environment that GMs consistently influence is the basic business concepts the company adopts. Whether they've written it down or not, top-notch GMs have a broad overview of the fields they want to compete in and the way the company will succeed in those chosen fields—the balance between centralization and decentralization, the role of line and staff, the kinds of rewards that will motivate people to achieve their goals, the skills needed to become an industry leader. In short, this overview defines how the company is going to be different—and better—from a collection of totally independent businesses.

Moreover, because every business environment changes over time, the best general managers constantly ask: What kind of business do we want to run? Are we in the right fields? Do we still have viable positions in each? How should we be reshaping the business? The result of this process is a set of business concepts that shift in small ways *in a consistent direction.*

Johnson & Johnson is an excellent example. The company, which has a fine corporate track record over several decades, wants to be the leader in the lower-tech growth segments of health care, so it has a broad-based business, facing diverse smaller competitors all around the globe. To remain a leader, CEO James Burke feels that he and his managers have to excel at spotting promising new market segments early, tailoring products to serve them, and getting those products to market quickly. They do this through a network of roughly 100 tightly focused, freestanding operating companies.

This highly decentralized organization is skilled at marketing and product innovation and supported by a corporate credo that glues everything together into a very humane yet competitive company. Managers throughout J&J know exactly what they're trying to do and how they are to do it. This carefully crafted corporate overview gives J&J a significant competitive edge virtually everywhere it operates.

Despite its overall success, J&J now faces a new set of competitive conditions that are forcing managers to rethink long-standing business concepts. In several major parts of the business, customers have decided they want fewer suppliers and better integrated distribution and administrative services. So J&J is figuring out how to maintain its traditional decentralized divisions—and all they stand for—yet compete with companies that offer broader coordinated product lines and services.

The third element in shaping the work environment—the company's people concepts—is closely related to the other two. Fast-paced, innovative businesses require different managers than companies in slow-growth, grind-it-out businesses where the emphasis is on cost control and high volume. For example, one aggressive, growth-oriented company decided it needed: a mix of high-potential managers, not a few good managers at the top with implementers below; innovative managers who act like owners, not administrators content to pass decisions up the line; and ambitious quick learners, not people content to move slowly up the corporate ladder.

Naturally, that same pattern won't apply to every company. To determine what does apply, a GM focuses on two questions: What kind of managers do we need to compete effectively, now and in the foreseeable future? What do we have to do to attract, motivate, and keep these people? GMs who ask these questions consistently and act on the answers end up with more high-impact managers than those who haven't given much attention to the mix of skills and styles it takes to win their particular battles.

The best GMs also get deeply involved in determining their company's values—"what it's like to work here." Henry Schacht, the CEO of Cummins Engine, is a good example. He has a keen sense of the kind of organization he wants Cummins to be. Even as he reduced the company's work force by 50%, he carefully thought through how to make cuts in a way people would understand and consider fair. Moreover, this deep concern for fellow employees and high ethical standards permeate Cummins—just as they did when Irwin Miller was CEO. So employees don't need policy manuals or rule books to act ethically and fairly—they just do it.

While this may sound obvious, I've known many general managers who end up with conflicting cultural values and inconsistent norms of behavior because they haven't consciously decided what's important to them. And of course, there are always a few whose own values are flawed or expedient, but who are nonetheless successful in the short run. In time, however, character flaws or even shortcomings like inconsistency do catch up with people—causing serious problems for both the GM and the company.

CRAFTING A STRATEGIC VISION

Since the general manager is the only executive who can commit the entire organization to a particular strategy, the best GMs are invariably involved in strategy formulation, spearheading the effort, not just presiding over it. To begin with, they have a strategic vision for each business, or they develop one quickly when they're appointed to a new job.

When Ned Johnson took over Fidelity Management & Research, for example, he decided there were two things wrong with the mutual fund industry: competition was based on who had performed best lately, so fund managers lived or died on the basis of each quarter's or year's performance; and customers were constantly shifting funds because of poor performance or poor service. To avoid these problems, Johnson envisioned a supermarket of 50 to 60 funds that offer customers every conceivable investment focus plus superior service. That way, if a particular fund doesn't have a record year, customers usually blame themselves, not the fund manager. And the company's superior service makes it easy for customers to switch to another Fidelity fund. Moreover, with so many funds operating, Fidelity always has four or five winners to brag about.

When David Farrell took over May Department Stores, several "experts" advised him to diversify out of the "dying" department store business. But Farrell saw an opportunity in the fact that competitors like Sears were diversifying into financial services, while others were moving into specialty stores. Instead of following the crowd, he focused his company on becoming the merchandising and operating leader in the department store business in each of its markets. He centralized merchandising concepts, priced aggressively, eliminated loser departments, built strong execution-driven local managements, and got control of costs. The result: while former key competitors like Allied, ADG, and Federated were stumbling, May emerged as the largest, best run publicly held company in its chosen field. Not in every market, of course; but overall, it's the best—which is a long way from the medium-sized, lackluster performer Farrell inherited.

In both cases, the GM's strategic vision, which took into account the industry, the customer, and a specific competitive environment, led to innovation targeted at a particular competitive position. That's what distinguishes a useful vision from the bunch of meaningless generalities some GMs use to describe their business strategies.

Next, high-impact GMs regard competitiveness gaps—in products, features, service—as crises. Closing those gaps becomes their overriding priority, not just another important business problem. Implicit in achieving that is something most GMs don't do well, namely understanding in detail how their costs, products, services, and systems stack up against their competitors'. How many GMs, for instance, would have disassembled a competitor's entire car to show production people what they were up against, as Honda's U.S. president did? Too many GMs—not just the ones in Detroit—build their strategies around unsupported assumptions and wishful thinking about their comparative performance.

Recently, for example, I saw a consultant's report comparing the cost structure of a major U.S. electronics components producer with its Japanese competitor. The Japanese company had spent more money and a higher percentage of sales in just two areas—R&D and quality. In return, it got fewer rejects, better products, more market share, and higher earnings per share.

Guess who changed his views—five years too late—about where his company stood and what was required to regain market leadership?

Today you cannot write about strategy without talking about giving customers better value than your competitors do. Yet talking about the concept and making it live are two different things. Outstanding GMs seem to be personally committed to serving customers better and to producing better performing products. Instead of just looking inward, they get their competitive information first-hand by talking to knowledgeable customers and distributors. And that knowledge gives them the conviction they need to make things happen and gain a competitive edge.

Recognizing that lasting competitive edges are hard to generate, the best GMs build on existing strengths while searching out new sources of advantage. First, they improve sales and profits of their strongest products, in their strongest markets, with their strongest distributors. Then they use the resulting faster payoffs to help fund the search for future edges. Moreover, building on strength keeps competitors so busy responding to your initiatives that they have less time to launch their own.

Finally, the best GMs expect their competition to retaliate to any strategic move that works, and they plan for the worst-case response. They also get out of games they cannot win. For years, for example, Heinz prided itself on introducing more new soups than Campbell did. Then its managers discovered they were playing Campbell's game, not their own, since Campbell would routinely copy their new product and use its superior brand acceptance and distribution muscle to overwhelm them at the point of sale. Consequently, Heinz shifted its focus from "beating Campbell" to making money in soup; it cut costs and concentrated on the low-price niche that didn't interest Campbell.

MARSHALING RESOURCES

All general managers say they allocate resources to support competitive strategies, keep the company economically healthy, and produce high returns. Yet if you analyze the way the process works in most companies, you find excessive support for marginal businesses, low payout projects, and operating necessities. In short, no strategic focus.

The best GMs concentrate more resources on situations that provide the opportunity to gain an important competitive edge, or at least improve on one they already enjoy. Long before restructuring came into vogue, they were prepared to shift emphasis to get more bounce for their bucks.

Another difference is the way the top GMs treat money. Sounds humorous until you reflect on one of the cardinal weaknesses of most professional managers: they spend company cash as though it belonged to someone else. Even one-time owners often invest in marginal projects they'd never have dreamed of financing when the business belonged to them. In contrast, outstanding GMs think like owners. They avoid projects where everything has to work 110% to get a decent return. To marshal resources for winning strategies, they're willing to postpone or rethink high-risk investments or shortchange low-return businesses. They're also tough-minded about who gets what because they realize outstanding returns don't come from parceling out money to subordinates who promise the best numbers (despite low odds) or to key managers to keep them happy. This doesn't mean they are risk-averse—far from it. But by focusing on fewer bets and backing them aggressively, they improve the odds.

Moreover, top GMs carefully protect the downside on major investments. Everyone knows that promising ideas often fail in the marketplace. Yet many GMs are perfectly willing to bet the company before they know if a new strategy will work. They plunge ahead and build a factory, hire lots of overhead, and launch new products quickly and aggressively—presumably to beat competitors to the punch. But when the idea doesn't succeed right away, this flat-out approach produces nothing but a big write-off.

The best GMs also do lots of little things—like farming out pilot runs and renting plants and machinery—that limit their front-end exposure. They try to avoid processes that can't be converted to other uses. They add overhead grudgingly. They do regional rollouts to test the market and control costs. Then, when they're sure the idea will work, they go to war for it.

Finally, top GMs are always searching for unproductive assets to get them up to par or off the books. To do this, they follow up on big capital expenditures to be sure the projected benefits are realized. They charge each business unit with managing its balance sheet and carefully measure its return. And they put constant pressure on the organization to improve productivity.

James Robison, the former GM of Indian Head, expressed this perspective in a colorful way. "Every Friday evening we start a whole new ball game," he'd say. "That means every business, plant, machine, and job is open to question. If it's not producing an adequate return, it's on our hit list. If we can't figure out how to improve the situation promptly, we start to look for ways to get rid of it."

DEVELOPING STAR PERFORMERS

Everyone knows how important it is to attract talented managers, develop them quickly, and keep them challenged and effectively deployed. Yet not everyone does what's required to achieve this. In fact, very few companies do. Lack of management talent ranks right behind low standards as a cause of poor performance.

The best GMs willingly make the tough calls it takes to upgrade an organization. They don't try to rationalize inaction by hoping that more experience will somehow transform a weak manager into a strong one or a solid performer into an outstanding one. As a result, each year they have better managers in critical spots instead of a group that's merely one year longer in the tooth.

Making tough people decisions has to start at the top. Otherwise, managers will postpone action, rationalize marginal performance, or mistake the recruitment of one or two outsiders for real upgrading. For this reason, the best GMs lead annual personnel reviews instead of delegating that job to department heads or division presidents.

They use challenging job assignments to speed high-potential managers' development and eliminate blockages to open up spots. They also understand how critically important job rotation is and break down functional empires that get in the way. Finally, they directly influence important appointments by exercising a veto or offering subordinates a slate of candidates to choose from.

Above all, they get line managers deeply involved in the upgrading process by forcing periodic, tough-minded appraisals of individuals and groups. They constantly ask how their high-potential people are performing and how managers are solving their people problems. But action, not questions, is the key, especially against the bottom quartile performers. To that end, they make sure the process produces better results each year and that it gets pushed farther down in the organization.

The best GMs also know that compensation is a means to an end, not an end in itself. Rewards are linked to performance. They pay their best performers considerably more, even if that means paying the average performers less than they expect. They're also willing to take the heat by cutting bonuses in a poor year instead of pretending the bad year never happened and rewarding everyone for "trying hard."

Finally, the best GMs invariably surround themselves with good people—achievers, not cronies or loyalists. They don't hire only in their own image but rather tolerate, even encourage, a variety of styles. Every year their talent pool gets deeper and better because they're constantly building critical mass on the theory that you never have enough good people. That way, when opportunities arise, they don't have to create a hole in one part of the business to fill an opening in another.

ORGANIZATIONAL BODYBUILDING

One of the most innovative GMs I know once proudly told me about his plan to reorganize and decentralize his business in order to make faster decisions, improve execution in local markets, and reduce costs. Great objectives *if* they're realistic. In his business, however, fast, local decisions aren't particularly important—and his company was already regarded as a fast mover, not a laggard. The company's local execution was already superior to its main competitor's by a wide margin. The new decentralized organization would cost roughly what the old one did—in the early stages, before it had a chance to grow. In short, he was planning a major reorganization for generic problems that didn't apply to his company. The moral of this story: before you reorganize, be sure of what you're trying to do better and why.

The best GMs seem to look for the simplest ways to do things, which usually means fewer layers, bigger jobs, and broader responsibilities. They also get personally involved in solving important problems, regardless of what the organization chart says. Academic organizational concepts won't keep them from intruding on someone else's territory if the stakes are crucial to the company's success. To reduce hurt feelings, they make sure—in advance—that subordinates understand how the system works and why intrusion is sometimes required. But they don't use that prerogative as an excuse to dabble in everyone else's territory.

Another organizational bias worth noting is that the best GMs organize around people rather than concepts or principles. When they have a strategy or business problem or a big opportunity, they turn to the individual who has the right skills and style for that job. Then, having made the match, they delegate responsibility without hemming the person in with a tight job description or organizational constraints. Then managers feel more responsible for results simply because they are more responsible.

I've seen many GMs who thought they were solving major problems with logical sounding reorganizations that left out the most essential ingredient—the appropriate leader. Naturally, those reorganizations accomplished very little. You can't ignore organizational logic or strategic fit, to be sure. But people are usually the dominant consideration.

Trite as it may sound, somewhere along the line, the best GMs have learned the value and impact of teamwork. With so much emphasis today on financial restructuring, strategy formulation, and technology, it's not surprising that many executives get ahead by spearheading successful projects in their particular functional areas. They learn to push their ideas through a small, narrowly based group of subordinates and peers but not how to manage a diverse team of executives from several areas. And they learn almost nothing about the problems of implementing their ideas in other functional areas or integrating the efforts of a disparate, often geographically dispersed group of managers.

In contrast, the best GMs routinely bring managers together to talk about the business, to get multiple inputs on important projects, and to line up their support.

Finally, the best GMs use staff people well and expect them to make positive contributions, not to nitpick or "gotcha." They appoint strong functional leaders (not line-manager rejects, politicians, or tired old pros) who can provide innovative, idea-driven leadership (not just ask good questions) and can transfer ideas across the organization. As a result, line managers respect and use the staff instead of writing unfriendly memos or playing unproductive political games.

UP AND RUNNING

The sixth and last area of responsibility for a GM is supervising operations and implementation. That means running the business day-to-day by producing sound plans, spotting problems and opportunities early, and responding aggressively to them.

Top GMs are usually very results-oriented. Their operating plans are commitments, not just something they're trying hard to achieve. They know the numbers and what's required to meet them. But they also know that surprises will occur, so they keep enough flexibility in their spending to allow for competitive threats, good new ideas, or softer volume. Unlike less resourceful GMs, they don't miss their profit plan every year because of *expected* unexpected events.

At the same time, they don't wreck the business to "make plan" in a serious downturn. If business drops off sharply, they move faster than others to scale back costs, cut discretionary expenditures, and eliminate losers. But they don't sacrifice competitiveness just to look good in a bad year.

Next, they push for functional excellence all across the business. In contrast to the GM who is satisfied to have one or two high-performing departments only, they demand superior execution in every function. They also refuse to let weakness in one or two areas (like control, R&D, or engineering) neutralize their strong departments. As a result, they get more out of every strategy and every program than their competitors do.

A keen sense of the organization's capabilities separates top GMs from less able executives. They don't commit the company to more things than it can handle or—at the other extreme—to a pace that falls short of its capacity. They also understand the impact of concentrating on a few things at one time. At May Department Stores, for instance, David Farrell achieved almost miraculous improvements in shrinkage, inventory levels, labor costs, and store-level merchandising simply by focusing the entire organization's efforts on these mundane operating problems.

These managers are also bugs on costs. They understand the "money mechanics" of their business: how costs behave as volumes shift. And they don't let cost percentages get out of control however "reasonable" the explanation may be. For example, they simply won't permit overhead to rise from 12% of sales to 14% no matter what. They continually search for ways to do things better at lower cost. And they don't settle for vague answers, wishful thinking, or lack of follow-up when new departments or programs are proposed.

Finally, top GMs use information better than their colleagues do to spot problems early and to identify potential competitive edges. It isn't a question of more information; they simply use information better. Partly it's because the best GMs are that rare combination of fine operator and fine conceptualizer. But it goes beyond that. Figures and facts mean something to them because they know their customers, products, and competitors so well. And they never stop trying to read those facts and figures for clues to an edge in the marketplace.

They train themselves to ask "so what" and "why." Field visits to plants and offices provide them with firsthand information. They demand reports on what's important, not sheets and sheets of data from MIS. Above all, they've learned to listen, to be genuinely interested in what people think about the business, the competitive environment, strategy, other people, the organization—the works. Lawrence Bossidy, vice chairman of GE, put it well: "If your subordinates don't have good ideas, get rid of them and get some who do. But when you have good people, make darned sure you listen to what they have to say."

To sum up, outstanding GMs affect their companies in six important ways. They develop a distinctive work environment; spearhead innovative strategic thinking; manage company resources productively; direct the people development and deployment process; build a dynamic organization; and oversee day-to-day operations. Individually, none of these things is totally new or unique. But successful GMs are better at seeing the interrelationships among these six areas, setting priorities, and making the right things happen. As a result, their activities in these areas make a coherent and consistent pattern that moves the business forward.

These six responsibilities don't tell the whole story, of course. Leadership skills and the GM's personal style and experience are important pieces of the whole. But focusing effort in these six areas will help any GM become more effective. And that should mean making the right things happen faster and more often—which is what all of us want to achieve as general managers.

DISCUSSION QUESTIONS

1. Inventory your skills and strengths according to the "six basics for general managers." In which areas are you most comfortable or experienced? Which are most problematic for you, and why?
2. Does the author overstate the influence a general manager can have on an organization? Does he adequately account for the impact of economic forces, competitor moves, incompetent managers, etc., on a company's competitiveness?
3. How do GMs develop a strategic vision, as the author says they must? Choose a firm with which you are familiar and identify the components of its strategic vision.
4. According to the author, "the best GMs also get deeply involved in determining their company's values." How do GMs communicate a company's values and ethics? Should a company be patterned on the ethical standards of the GM alone?
5. General managers, in order to be effective, must understand all levels of their firm's operations. Is it necessary for employees at all levels of the organization to understand the general manager's job?

2 Good Managers Don't Make Policy Decisions

H. EDWARD WRAPP

According to popular belief and many management textbooks, general managers spend most of their time setting policy, communicating precise goals and objectives, and making decisions. In this reading, Edward Wrapp takes a different view, based on his many close working relationships with general managers. To be successful, says Wrapp, senior executives need to cultivate five skills. First, they need to develop a network of information sources in order to keep informed about operating decisions being made at different levels in the company. Second, they need to marshal their energies and time to concentrate on a limited number of significant issues. Third, they need to cultivate sensitivity to the power structure in the company. Fourth, they need to know how to indicate a sense of direction without publicly committing themselves to a specific set of objectives. Finally, and most important, they need to be skillful at developing opportunities. In essence, the effective senior manager is an opportunist who tries to piece together parts that appear to be incidental into a program that moves toward his or her objectives.

The upper reaches of management are a land of mystery and intrigue. Very few people have ever been there, and the present inhabitants frequently send back messages that are incoherent both to other levels of management and to the world in general.

This absence of firsthand reports may account for the myths, illusions, and caricatures that permeate the literature of management—for example, such widely held notions as these:

- Life gets less complicated as a manager reaches the top of the pyramid.
- Managers at the top level know everything that's going on in the organization, can command whatever resources they may need, and therefore can be more decisive.
- The general manager's day is taken up with making broad policy decisions and formulating precise objectives.
- The top executive's primary activity is conceptualizing long-range plans.
- In a large company, the top executive may meditate about the role of his or her organization in society.

I suggest that none of these versions alone, or in combination, is an accurate portrayal of what a general manager does. Perhaps students of the management process have been overly eager to develop a theory and a discipline. As one executive I know puts it, "I guess I do some of the things described in the books and articles, but the descriptions are lifeless, and my job isn't."

What common characteristics, then, do successful executives exhibit in reality? I shall identify five skills or talents which, in my experience, seem especially significant.

KEEPING WELL INFORMED

First, each of my heroes has a special talent for keeping informed about a wide range of operating decisions being made at different levels in the company. As they move up the ladder, they develop a network of information sources in many different departments. They cultivate these sources and keep them open no matter how high they climb in the organization. When the need arises, they bypass the lines on the organization chart to seek more than one version of a situation.

In some instances, especially when they suspect a manager would not be in total agreement with their decision, subordinates will elect to inform him or her in advance, before they announce a decision. In these circumstances, the manager may defer the decision, redirect it, or even block further action. However, the manager does not insist on this procedure. Ordinarily the members of the organization will decide at what stage to inform the manager.

Top-level managers are frequently criticized by writers, consultants, and lower management for continuing to enmesh themselves in operating problems rather than withdrawing to the "big picture." Without doubt, some managers do get lost in a welter of detail and insist on making too many decisions. Superficially, the good manager may seem to make the same mistake—but for different purposes. Only by keeping well informed about the decisions being made can the good manager avoid the sterility so often found in those who isolate themselves from operations. If she or he follows the advice to free her or himself from operations, the general manager may soon subsist on a diet of abstractions, leaving the choice of food in the hands of subordinates. As Kenneth Boulding put it, "The very purpose of a hierarchy is to prevent information from reaching higher layers. It operates as an information filter, and there are little wastebaskets all along the way."[1]

What kinds of action does a successful executive take to ensure that information is live and accurate? One company president that I worked with, for example, sensed that his vice presidents were insulating him from some of

1. From a speech at a meeting sponsored by the Crowell Collier Institute of Continuing Education in New York, as reported in *Business Week*, February 18, 1967, p. 202.

the vital issues being discussed at lower levels. He accepted a proposal for a formal management development program primarily because it afforded him an opportunity to discuss company problems with middle managers several layers removed from him in the organization. By meeting with small groups of these men in an academic setting, he learned much about their preoccupations, and also about those of his vice presidents. And he accomplished his purposes without undermining the authority of line managers.

FOCUSING TIME AND ENERGY

The second skill of the good manager is knowing how to save energy and hours for those few particular issues, decisions, or problems which require personal attention. He or she knows the fine and subtle distinction between keeping fully informed about operating decisions and allowing the organization to force him or her into participating in these decisions or, even worse, making them. Recognizing that special talents can only bear on a limited number of matters, the good manager chooses issues that will have the greatest long-term impact on the company, and on which he or she can be most productive. Under ordinary circumstances, the limit is three or four major objectives during any single period of sustained activity.

To *not* become involved as a decision maker they best make sure that the organization keeps them informed at various stages; they don't want to be accused of indifference to such issues. They train subordinates not to look for a decision. The communication from below becomes essentially one of: "Here is our sizeup, and here's what we propose to do."

Reserving hearty encouragement for those projects which hold superior promise of a contribution to total corporate strategy, the superior manager acknowledges receipt of information on other matters. When a problem comes from the organization, he or she finds a way to transmit know-how short of giving orders—usually by asking perceptive questions.

PLAYING THE POWER GAME

To what extent do successful top executives push their ideas and proposals through the organization? The common notion that the "prime mover" continually creates and forces through new programs, like a powerful majority leader in a liberal Congress, is in my opinion very misleading.

The successful manager is sensitive to the power structure in the organization. In considering any major current proposals he can plot the position of various individuals and units in the organization on a scale ranging from complete, outspoken support down to determined, sometimes bitter, and often well-cloaked opposition. In the middle of the scale is indifference. Usually, several aspects of a proposal will fall into this area, and here the manager operates. By assessing the depth and nature of blocks in the organization, the manager can move through what I call corridors of comparative indifference. He or she seldom challenges a blocked corridor, preferring to pause until it has opened up.

Related to this particular skill is the ability to recognize when a few trial balloon launches are needed in the organization. The organization will tolerate only a certain number of proposals which emanate from the apex of the pyramid, so no matter how great the temptation to stimulate the organization with a flow of personal ideas, the good manager knows he must work through others in different parts of the organization. Studying the reactions of key individuals and groups to the trial balloons these persons send up, the manager can better assess how to limit the emasculation of proposals. There is seldom a proposal which is supported by all quarters of the organization. The emergence of strong support in certain quarters is almost sure to evoke strong opposition in others.

A SENSE OF TIMING

Circumstances like these mean that a good sense of timing is a priceless asset for a top executive. For example, a vice president had for some time been convinced that her company lacked a sense of direction and needed a formal long-range planning activity to fill the void. Up to the time in question, her soft overtures to other top executives had been rebuffed. And then she spotted an opening.

A management development committee proposed a series of weekend meetings for second-level officers in the company. After extensive debate, but for reasons not announced, the president rejected this proposal. The members of the committee openly resented what seemed to them an arbitrary rejection.

The vice president, sensing a tense situation, suggested to the president that the same officers who were to have attended the weekend management development seminars be organized into a long-range planning committee. The timing was perfect. The president, looking for a bone to toss to the committee, acquiesced immediately, and the management development committee in its next meeting enthusiastically endorsed the idea.

This vice president had been conducting a kind of continuing market research to discover how to sell her long-range planning proposal. Her previous probes of the "market" had told her that the president's earlier rejections of the proposal were not so final as to preclude an eventual shift in the "corridors of attitude."

The vice president caught the committee in a conciliatory mood, and her proposal rode through with flying colors.

CAUTIOUS PRESSURE

As good managers stand at a point in time, they can identify a set of goals, albeit pretty hazy. Their timetables, also pretty hazy, suggest that some goals must be accomplished sooner than others, and that others may be safely postponed for several months or years. They have a still hazier notion of how to reach these goals. They assess key individuals and groups. They know that each has its own set of goals, some of which they thoroughly understand and others about which they can only speculate. They know also that these individuals and groups represent blocks to certain programs or projects, and that as points of opposition, they must be taken into account. As day-to-day operating decisions are made, and as both individuals and groups respond to proposals, it is more clear where the corridors of comparative indifference are. The manager takes action accordingly.

APPEARING IMPRECISE

The fourth skill of the successful manager is knowing how to satisfy the organization that it has a sense of direction without ever actually committing publicly to a specific set of objectives. This is not to say that he does not have better objectives—personal and corporate, long-term and short-term. They are significant guides to thinking, and the successful manager modifies them continually while gaining a better understanding of the resources, the competition, and the changing market demands. But as the organization clamors for statements of objectives, these are samples of what it gets back:

"Our company aims to be number one in its industry."

"Our objective is growth with profit."

"We seek the maximum return on investment."

"Management's goal is to meet its responsibilities to stockholders, employees, and the public."

In my opinion, statements such as these provide almost no guidance to the various levels of management. Yet they are quire readily accepted as objectives by large numbers of intelligent people.

MAINTAIN VIABILITY

Why does the good manager shy away from precise statements of objectives for the organization? The main reason is that specific objectives will not be relevant for any reasonable period into the future. Conditions in business change continually and rapidly, and corporate strategy must be revised to take the changes into account. The more explicit the statement of strategy, the more difficult it becomes to persuade the organization to turn to different goals when needs and conditions shift.

The public and the stockholders, to be sure, must perceive the organization as having a well-defined set of objectives and a clear sense of direction. But in reality the good top manager is seldom so certain of the direction which should be taken. Better than anyone else, he or she senses many, many threats to the company—threats which lie in the economy, in the actions of competitors, and, not least, within the organization.

The good manager also knows that it is impossible to state objectives clearly enough so that everyone in the organization understands what they mean. Objectives only get communicated over time by consistency or pattern in operating decisions. Such decisions are more meaningful than words. When precise objectives are spelled out, the organization tends to interpret them so they fit its own needs.

Subordinates who keep pressing for more precise objectives are working against their own best interests. Each time objectives are stated more specifically, a subordinate's range of possibilities for operating are reduced. The narrower field means less room to roam and to accommodate the flow of ideas coming up from his or her part of the organization.

AVOID POLICY STRAITJACKETS

The successful manager's reluctance to be precise extends into the area of policy decisions. He or she seldom makes a forthright statement of policy, aware perhaps that in some companies executives spend more time arbitrating disputes caused by stated policies than in moving the company forward. Management textbooks contend that well-defined policies are the sine qua non of a well-managed company. My research does not bear this out.

For example, the president of one company with which I am familiar deliberately leaves assignments of his top officers vague and refuses to define policies for them. He passes out new assignments seemingly with no pattern in mind and consciously sets up competitive ventures among his subordinates. His methods, though they would never be sanctioned by a classical organization planner, are deliberate—and, incidentally, quite effective.

Since able managers do not make policy decisions, does this mean that well-managed companies operate without policies? Certainly not. But their policies evolve over time from an indescribable mix of operating decisions. A pattern of guidelines for various levels of the organization comes from a series of decisions.

The skillful manager resists the urge to write a company creed or to compile a policy manual. Preoccupation with detailed statements of corporate objectives, departmental goals, and comprehensive organization charts and job descriptions is often the first symptom of atrophy.

The "management by objectives" school, so widely heralded in recent years, suggests that detailed objectives be spelled out at all levels in the corporation. This method is feasible at lower levels of management, but it becomes unworkable at the upper levels. The top manager must think out objectives in detail, but withhold some or at least communicate them to the organization in modest doses. It may take months or years to prepare the organization for radical departures from what it is currently striving to attain.

Suppose, for example, that a president is convinced the company must phase out of the principal business it has been in for 35 years. Although making this change is one of his objectives, he may well feel that he cannot disclose the idea to even his vice presidents, whose total know-how is in the present business. A blunt announcement that the company is changing horses would be too great a shock, so he begins moving toward this goal without a full disclosure to his management group.

Spelling out objectives in detail may only complicate the task of reaching them. Specific statements give the opposition an opportunity to organize its defenses.

MUDDLING WITH A PURPOSE

The fifth and most important skill I shall describe bears little relation to the doctrine that management is (or should be) a comprehensive, systematic, logical, well-programmed science. Of all the heresies set forth here, this should strike doctrinaires as the rankest!

The successful manager recognizes the futility of trying to push total packages or programs through the organization. He or she is willing to take less than total acceptance in order to achieve modest progress toward goals. Avoiding debates on principles, he or she tries to piece together parts that may appear to be incidental into a program that moves at least part of the way toward the objectives. Optimistic and persistent, the good manager says over and over, "There must be some parts of this proposal on which we can capitalize."

Relationships among different proposals present opportunities for combination and restructuring. It follows that the manager has wide-ranging interests and curiosity. The more things she knows about, the more opportunities she will have to discover parts which are related. This process does not require great intellectual brilliance or unusual creativity. This wide range of interests makes it more likely that she will tie together several unrelated proposals. The good manager is skilled as an analyst, but even more talented as a conceptualizer.

If the manager has built or inherited a solid organization, it will be difficult to come up with an idea which no one in the company has ever thought of before. The most significant contribution may be to see relationships that no one else has seen.

A division manager, for example, had set as one objective at the start of a year, an improvement in product quality. At the end of the year, reviewing progress toward this objective, she could identify three significant events which had brought about a perceptible improvement.

First, the head of the quality control group, a veteran manager who was doing only an adequate job, had asked early in the year for assignment to a new research group. The division manager installed a promising young engineer in this key spot.

A few months later, opportunity number two came along. The personnel department proposed a continuous program of checking the effectiveness of training methods for new employees. The proposal was acceptable to the manufacturing group. The division manager's only contribution was to suggest that the program should include a heavy emphasis on employees' attitudes toward quality.

A third opportunity arose when one of the division's best customers discovered that the wrong material had been used for a large lot of parts. The heat this generated made it possible to institute a completely new system of procedures for inspecting and testing raw materials.

As the division manager reviewed the year's progress on product quality, these were the three most important developments. None of these developments could have been predicted at the start of the year, but she was quick to see the potential in each when it popped up in the day-to-day operating routines.

EXPLOITING CHANGE

The good manager can function effectively only in an environment of continual change. A *Saturday Review* cartoonist caught the idea when he pictured an executive seated at a massive desk instructing his secretary to "send in a deal; I feel like wheelin'." Only the manager with many changes in the works can discover new combinations of opportunities and open up new corridors of comparative indifference. His or her creative stimulation comes from trying to make something useful of the proposal or idea on the desk. He will try to make strategic change a way of life in the organization and continually review the strategy even though current results are good.

Charles Lindblom wrote an article with an engaging title, "The Science of Muddling Through."[2] He described what he called "the rational comprehensive method" of decision making. The essence of this method is that for every problem the decision maker proceeds deliberately, one step at a time, to collect complete data; to analyze the data thoroughly; to study a wide range of alternatives, each with its own risks and consequences; and, finally, to formulate a detailed course of action. Lindblom immediately dismissed "the rational comprehensive method" in favor of what he called "successive limited comparisons." He saw a decision maker comparing the alternatives in order to learn which most closely meets the objectives he or she has in mind. Since this is an

2. Harold J. Leavitt and Louis R. Pondy, ed., *Readings in Managerial Psychology* (Chicago: University of Chicago Press, 1964), p. 61.

opportunistic process, he saw the manager as a muddler, but a muddler with a purpose.

H. Igor Ansoff, in his book, *Corporate Strategy*, espoused a similar notion in what he described as the "cascade approach."[3] In his view, possible decision rules are formulated in gross terms and are successively refined through several stages as the emergence of a solution proceeds. This process gives the appearance of solving the problem several times over, but with successively more precise results.

Both Lindblom and Ansoff moved us closer to an understanding of how managers really think. The process is not abstract; rather, the manager searches for a means of drawing into a pattern the thousands of incidents which make up the day-to-day life of a growing company.

CONTRASTING PICTURES

It is interesting to note, in the writings of students of managment, the emergence of the concept that, rather than making decisions, the leader's principal task is to maintain operating conditions that permit the various decision-making systems to function effectively. Supporters of this theory, it seems to me, overlook the subtle turns of direction which the leader can provide. The leader cannot add purpose and structure to the balanced judgments of subordinates by simply rubber-stamping their decisions. He or she must weigh the issues and reach his or her own decisions.

Richard M. Cyert and James G. March contend that real-life managers do not consider all possible courses of action, that their search ends with one satisfactory alternative. In my sample, good managers are not guilty of such myopic thinking. Unless they mull over a wide range of possibilities, they cannot come up with the imaginative combinations of ideas which characterize their work.

Many of the articles about successful executives picture them as great thinkers who sit at their desks drafting master blueprints for their companies. The successful top executives I have seen at work do not operate this way. Rather than produce a full-grown decision tree, they start with a twig, help it grow, and ease themselves out on the limbs only after they have tested to see how much weight the limbs can stand.

In my picture, the general manager sits in the midst of a continuous stream of operating problems. The organization presents a flow of proposals to deal with the problems. Some of these proposals are contained in voluminous, well-documented, formal reports; some are as fleeting as the walk-in visit from a subordinate whose latest inspiration came during the morning's coffee break. Knowing how meaningless it is to say, "This is a finance problem," or, "That is

---

3. H. Igor Ansoff, *Corporate Strategy* (New York: McGraw-Hill, 1965).

a communications problem," the manager feels no compulsion to classify them. As Gary Steiner, in one of his speeches, put it, "He has a high tolerance for ambiguity."

In considering each proposal, the general manager tests it against at least three criteria:

1. Will the total proposal—or, more often, will some part of the proposal—move the organization toward the objectives in mind?
2. How will the whole or parts of the proposal be received by the various groups and subgroups in the organization? Where will the strongest opposition come from, which group will furnish the strongest support, and which group will be neutral or indifferent?
3. How does the proposal relate to programs already in process or currently proposed? Can some parts of the proposal under consideration be added on to a program already under way, or can they be combined with all or parts of other proposals in a package which can be steered through the organization?

THE MAKING OF A DECISION

As another example of a general manager at work, consider the train of events which led to a parent company president's decision to attempt to consolidate two of his divisions.

Let us call the executive Mr. Brown. One day the manager of Division A came to him with a proposal that Division A acquire a certain company. That company's founder and president—let us call him Mr. Johansson—had a phenomenal record of inventing new products, but earnings had been less than phenomenal. Johansson's asking price for his company was high when evaluated against the earnings record.

Not until Brown began to speculate on how Johansson might supply fresh vigor for new products in Division A did it appear that perhaps a premium price could be justified. For several years, Brown had been unsuccessful in stimulating the manager of that division to see that she must bring in new products to replace those that were losing their place in the market.

The next idea that came to Brown was that Johansson might invent not only for Division A but also for Division B. As Brown analyzed how this could work out organizationally, he began to think about the markets being served by Divisions A and B. Over the years, several basic but gradual changes in marketing patterns had occurred, and the marketing considerations that had dictated the establishment of separate divisions no longer prevailed. Why should the company continue to support duplicated overhead expenses in the two divisions? As Brown weighed the issues, he concluded that by consolidating the two divisions he could also shift responsibilities in the management groups in ways that would strengthen them overall.

If we were asked to evaluate Brown's capabilities, how would we respond? Putting aside the objection that the information is too sketchy, our tendency might be to criticize Brown. Why did he not identify the changing market patterns in his continuing review of company position? Why did he not force the issue when the division manager failed to do something about new product development? Such criticism would reflect "the rational comprehensive method" of decision making.

But, as I analyze the gyrations in Brown's thinking, one characteristic stands out. He kept searching for follow-on opportunities from the original proposal, opportunities that would stand up against the three criteria earlier mentioned. In my book, Brown rates as an extremely skillful general manager.

If this analysis of how skillful general managers think and operate has validity, then it should help us see several problems in a better light. For instance, the investment community is increasingly interested in sizing up the management of a company being appraised. Thus far, the analysts rely mainly on results or performance rather than on probes of management skills. But current performance can be affected by many variables, both favorable and unfavorable, and is a dangerous base for predicting what the management of a company will produce in the future. Testing the key managers of a company against the five skills described holds promise for evaluating the caliber of a management group. The manager who is building a company and the one who is moving up through the hierarchy of a larger organization require essentially the same capabilities for success.

DISCUSSION QUESTIONS

1. The article encourages general managers to keep well-informed about decisions at all levels of the company by maintaining a broad network of information sources. Is it possible for a GM to have too much information, or can you never have enough when making decisions?
2. The author has observed that effective GMs concentrate their time and resources on a few major objectives and stay well-informed about the rest. At any given time, do you tend to focus on more rather than on fewer projects? How do you choose the projects to which you will devote the most time?
3. Does the author's description of operating in the "corridors of comparative indifference" challenge your conception of how managerial authority is exercised?
4. Do you agree that, more often than not, corporate objectives should not be communicated concretely? What are some advantages to making explicit a company's strategy? In what situa-

tions would you seek to publicly define corporate objectives and strategy?

5. Is your business education training you to see relationships and opportunities in "the continuous stream of operating problems and decisions"? Are you learning to recognize patterns in the constant flow of information and to use them to further corporate goals?

3 Strategic Change: "Logical Incrementalism"

JAMES BRIAN QUINN

By virtue of their position, general managers are responsible for planning strategy for their corporations or businesses. The literature strongly suggests that strategic change and strategy formation are accomplished through formal planning and following a logical series of steps. In reality, argues Quinn, strategic change is rarely achieved solely by rational means; rather than prescribing a systematic strategy, general managers rely on intuition, monitoring the way a strategy evolves and making adjustments to it in light of new information and changing events. Quinn provides an insightful look at this process, which he calls "logical incrementalism." Emphasizing the inherent flexibility of this process, he illustrates how it enables general managers to use rational analysis as well as to respond to new and changing data when charting and implementing strategy.

When I was younger I always conceived of a room where all these [strategic] concepts were worked out for the whole company. Later I didn't find any such room. . . . The strategy [of the company] may not even exist in the mind of one man. I certainly don't know where it is written down. It is simply transmitted in the series of decisions made.

– *Interview quote*

When well-managed major organizations make significant changes in strategy, the approaches they use frequently bear little resemblance to the rational-analytical systems so often touted in the planning literature. The full strategy is rarely written down in any one place. The processes used to arrive at the total strategy are typically fragmented, evolutionary, and largely intuitive. Although one can usually find embedded in these fragments some very refined *pieces* of formal strategic analysis, the real strategy tends to evolve as internal decisions and external events flow together to create a new, widely shared consensus for action among key members of the top management team. Far from being an abrogation of good management practice, the rationale behind this kind of strategy formulation is so powerful that it perhaps provides the normative model for strategic decision making—rather than the step-by-step "formal systems planning" approach so often espoused.

THE FORMAL SYSTEMS PLANNING APPROACH

A strong normative literature states what factors should be included in a systematically planned strategy and how to analyze and relate these factors step-by-step. The main elements of this formal planning approach include:

1. Analyzing one's own ***internal situation***: strengths, weaknesses, competencies, problems;
2. ***Projecting*** current product lines, profits, sales, investment needs into the future;
3. Analyzing selected ***external environments*** and opponents' actions for opportunities and threats;
4. Establishing ***broad goals*** as targets for subordinate groups' plans;
5. ***Identifying the gap*** between expected and desired results;
6. Communicating ***planning assumptions*** to the divisions;
7. Requesting ***proposed plans*** from subordinate groups with more specific target goals, resource needs, and supporting action plans;
8. Occasionally asking for ***special studies of alternatives, contingencies***, or longer-term opportunities;
9. Reviewing and approving divisional plans and summing these for corporate needs;
10. Developing ***long-term budgets*** presumably related to plans;
11. ***Implementing*** plans;
12. ***Monitoring and evaluating*** performance (presumably against plans, but usually against budgets).

While this approach is excellent for some purposes, it tends to focus unduly on measurable quantitative factors and to underemphasize the vital qualitative, organizational, and power-behavioral factors which so often determine strategic success in one situation versus another. In practice, such planning is just one element in a continuous stream of events that really determine corporate strategy.

THE POWER-BEHAVIORAL APPROACH

Other investigators have provided important insights on the crucial psychological, power, and behavioral relationships in strategy formulation. Among other things, they have enhanced understanding about: the **multiple goal structures** of organizations, the **politics** of strategic decisions, executive **bargaining** and **negotiation** processes, **satisficing** (as opposed to maximizing) in decision making, the role of **coalitions** in strategic management, and the practice of "**muddling**" in the public sphere. Unfortunately, however, many power-behavioral studies have been conducted in settings far removed from the realities of strategy formulation. Others have concentrated solely on human dynamics, power relationships, and organizational processes and ignored the ways in which systematic data analysis shapes and often dominates crucial aspects of strategic decisions. Finally, few have offered much normative guidance for the strategist.

THE RESEARCH

Recognizing the contributions and limitations of both approaches, I attempted to document the dynamics of actual strategic change processes in ten major companies as perceived by those most knowledgeably and intimately involved. Cooperating companies included: General Motors Corp., Chrysler Corp., Volvo (AB), General Mills, Pillsbury Co., Xerox Corp., Texas Instruments, Exxon, Continental Group, and Pilkington Brothers. The companies varied with respect to products, markets, time horizons, technological complexities, and national versus international dimensions.

Several important findings emerged from the investigation.

- Neither the "power-behavioral" nor the "formal systems planning" paradigm adequately characterizes the way successful strategic processes operate.
- Effective strategies tend to emerge from a series of "strategic subsystems," each of which attacks a specific class of strategic issues (e.g., acquisitions, divestitures, or major reorganizations) in a disciplined way, but which is blended incrementally and opportunistically into a cohesive pattern that becomes the company's strategy.
- The logic behind each "subsystem" is so powerful that, to some extent, it may serve as a normative approach for formulating these key elements of strategy in large companies.
- Because of cognitive and process limits, almost all of these subsystems—and the formal planning activity itself—must be managed and linked together by an approach best described as "logical incrementalism."
- Such incrementalism is not "muddling." It is a purposeful, effective, proactive management technique for improving and integrating both the analytical and behavioral aspects of strategy formulation.

This reading will document these findings, suggest the logic behind several important "subsystems" for strategy formulation, and outline some of the management and thought processes executives in large organizations use to synthesize them into effective corporate strategies. Such strategies embrace those patterns of high leverage decisions (on major goals, policies, and action sequences) which affect the viability and direction of the entire enterprise or determine its competitive posture for an extended time period.

CRITICAL STRATEGIC ISSUES

Although certain "hard data" decisions (e.g., on product-market position or resource allocations) tend to dominate the analytical literature, executives identified other "soft" changes that have at least as much importance in shaping their concern's strategic posture. Most often cited were changes in the company's:

1. Overall organizational structure or its basic management style;
2. Relationships with the government or other external interest groups;
3. Acquisition, divestiture, or divisional control practices;
4. International posture and relationships;
5. Innovative capabilities or personnel motivations as affected by growth;
6. Worker and professional relationships reflecting changed social expectations and values;
7. Past or anticipated technological environments.

When executives were asked to "describe the processes through which their company arrived at its new posture" vis-à-vis each of these critical domains, several important points emerged. First, few of these issues lent themselves to quantitative modeling techniques or perhaps even formal financial analyses. Second, successful companies used a different "subsystem" to formulate strategy for each major class of strategic issues, yet these "subsystems" were quite similar among companies even in very different industries. Finally, no single formal analytical process could handle all strategic variables simultaneously on a planned basis. Why?

PRECIPITATING EVENTS

Often external or internal events over which managements had essentially no control would precipitate urgent, piecemeal, interim decisions that inexorably shaped the company's future strategic posture.

Analyses from earlier formal planning cycles did contribute greatly, as long as the general nature of the contingency had been anticipated. No organization—no matter how brilliant, rational, or imaginative—could possibly foresee the timing, severity, or even the nature of all precipitating events. Further, when these events do occur there might be neither time, resources, nor information enough to undertake a full formal strategic analysis of all possible options and their consequences. Yet early decisions made under stress conditions often meant new thrusts, precedents, or lost opportunities that were difficult to reverse later.

AN INCREMENTAL LOGIC

Recognizing this, top executives usually consciously tried to deal with precipitating events in an incremental fashion. Early commitments were kept broadly formative, tentative, and subject to later review. In some cases neither the company nor the external players could understand the full implications of alternative actions. All parties wanted to test assumptions and have an opportunity to learn from and adapt to the others' responses. Such behavior recurred frequently in other widely different contexts. For example:

Neither the potential producer nor user of a completely new product or process (like xerography or float glass) could fully conceptualize its ramifications without interactive testing. All parties benefited from procedures which purposely delayed decisions and allowed mutual feedback. Some companies, like IBM or Xerox, have formalized this concept into "phase program planning" systems. They make concrete decisions only on individual phases (or stages) of new product developments, establish interactive testing procedures with customers, and postpone final configuration commitments until the last possible moment.

Similarly, even under pressure, most top executives were extremely sensitive to organizational and power relationships and consciously managed decision processes to improve these dynamics. They often purposely delayed initial decisions, or kept such decisions vague, in order to encourage lower-level participation, to gain more information from specialists, or to build commitment to solutions. Even when a crisis atmosphere tended to shorten time horizons and make decisions more goal oriented than political, perceptive executives consciously tried to keep their options open until they understoodhow thc crisis would affect the power bases and needs of their key constituents. . . .

INCREMENTALISM IN STRATEGIC SUBSYSTEMS

One also finds that an incremental logic applies in attacking many of the critical subsystems of corporate strategy. Those subsystems for considering diversification moves, divestitures, major reorganizations, or government-external relations are typical and will be described here. In each case, conscious incrementalism helps to: (1) cope with both the cognitive and process limits on each major decision, (2) build the logical-analytical framework these decisions require, and (3) create the personal and organizational awareness, understanding, acceptance, and commitment needed to implement the strategies effectively.

THE DIVERSIFICATION SUBSYSTEM

Strategies for diversification, either through R&D or acquisitions, provide excellent examples. The formal analytical steps needed for successful diversification are well documented. However, the precise directions that R&D may project the company can only be understood step-by-step as scientists uncover new phenomena, make and amplify discoveries, build prototypes, reduce concepts to practice, and interact with users during product introductions.

Similarly, only as each acquisition is sequentially identified, investigated, negotiated for, and integrated into the organization can one predict its ultimate impact on the total enterprise.

A step-by-step approach is clearly necessary to guide and assess the strategic fit of each internal or external diversification candidate. Incremental processes are also required to manage the crucial psychological and power shifts that ultimately determine the program's overall direction and consequences. These processes help unify both the analytical and behavioral aspects of diversification decisions. They create the broad conceptual consensus, the risk-taking attitudes, the organizational and resource flexibilities, and the adaptive dynamism that determine both the timing and direction of diversification strategies. Most important among these processes are:

- ***Generating a genuine, top-level psychological commitment to diversification.*** General Mills, Pillsbury, and Xerox all started their major diversification programs with broad analytical studies and goal-setting exercises designed both to build top-level consensus around the need to diversify and to establish the general directions for diversification. Without such action, top-level bargaining for resources would have continued to support only more familiar (and hence apparently less risky) old lines, and this could delay or undermine the entire diversification endeavor.
- ***Consciously preparing to move opportunistically.*** Organizational and fiscal resources must be built up in advance to exploit candidates as they randomly appear. And a "credible activist" for ventures must be developed and backed by someone with commitment power. All successful acquirers created the potential for "profit-centered" divisions within their organizational structures, strengthened their financial-controllership capabilities, took action to create low-cost capital access, and maintained the shortest possible communication lines from the "acquisitions activist" to the resource-committing authority. All these actions integrally determined which diversifications actually could be made, the timing of their accession, and the pace they could be absorbed.
- ***Building a "comfort factor" for risk taking.*** The perception of risk is largely a function of knowledge about a field. Hence well-conceived diversification programs should anticipate a trial-and-error period during which top managers reject early proposed fields or opportunities until they have analyzed enough trial candidates to "become comfortable" with an initial selection. Early successes tend to be "sure things" close to the companies' past (real or supposed) expertise. After a few successful diversifications, managements tend to become more confident and accept other candidates—farther from traditional lines—at a faster rate. Again the way this process is handled affects both the direction and pace of the actual program.
- ***Developing a new ethos.*** If new divisions are more successful than the old—as they should be—they attract more resources and their political power grows. Their most effective line managers move into

> corporate positions, and slowly the company's special competence and its ethos change. Finally, the concepts and products which once dominated the company's culture may decline in importance or even disappear. Publicly acknowledging these consequences to the organization at the beginning of a diversification program would clearly be impolitic, even if the manager both desired and could predict the probable new ethos. These factors must be handled adaptively, as opportunities present themselves and as individual leaders and power centers develop.

Each of the above processes interacts with all others (and with the random appearance of diversification candidates) to affect action sequences, elapsed time, and ultimate results in unexpected ways. Few diversification programs end up as initially envisioned. Consequently, wise managers recognize the limits to systematic analysis in diversification, and use formal planning to build the "comfort levels" executives need for risk taking and to guide the program's early directions and priorities. They then modify these flexibly, step-by-step, as new opportunities, power centers, and developed competencies merge to create new potentials.

THE DIVESTITURE SUBSYSTEM

Similar practices govern the handling of divestitures. Divisions often drag along for years before they can be strategically divested. In some cases, ailing divisions might have just enough yield or potential to offer hoped-for viability. In others, they might represent the company's vital core from earlier years, the creations of a powerful person nearing retirement, or the psychological touchstones of the company's past traditions.

Again, in designing divestiture strategies, top executives had to reinforce vaguely felt concerns with detailed data, build up managers' comfort levels about issues, achieve participation in and commitment to decisions, and move opportunistically to make actual changes. In many cases, the precise nature of the decision was not clear at the outset. Executives often made seemingly unrelated personnel shifts or appointments which changed the value set of critical groups, or started a series of staff studies which generated awareness or acceptance of a potential problem. They might then instigate goal assessment, business review, or "planning" programs to provide broader forums for discussion and a wider consensus for action. Even then they might wait for a crisis, a crucial retirement, or an attractive sale opportunity to determine the timing and conditions of divestiture. In some cases, decisions could be direct and analytical. But when divestitures involved the psychological centers of the organization, the process had to be much more oblique and carefully orchestrated. For example:

When General Rawlings became president at General Mills, he had his newly developed Staff (Corporate Analysis) Department make informal presentations to top management on key issues. Later these were expanded to formal Management Operating Reviews (MORs) with all corporate and divisional top managers and controllers present. As problem operations were identified (many "generally known for a long time"), teams of corporate and divisional people were assigned to investigate them in depth. Once needed new data systems were built and studies came into place, they focused increasing attention on some hasty post-World War II acquisitions. . . .

Careful incrementalism is essential in most divestitures to disguise intentions yet create the awareness, value changes, needed data, psychological acceptance, and managerial consensus required for such decisions. Early, openly acknowledged, formal plans would clearly be invitations to disaster.

THE MAJOR REORGANIZATION SUBSYSTEM

It is well recognized that major organizational changes are an integral part of strategy. Sometimes they constitute a strategy themselves, sometimes they precede and/or precipitate a new strategy, and sometimes they help to implement a strategy. However, like many other important strategic decisions, macro-organizational moves are typically handled incrementally *and* outside of formal planning processes. Their effects on personal or power relationships preclude discussion in the open forums and reports of such processes.

In addition, major organizational changes have timing imperatives (or "process limits") all their own. In making any significant shifts, the executive must think through the new roles, capabilities, and probable individual reactions of the many principals affected. He may have to wait for the promotion or retirement of a valued colleague before consummating any change. He then frequently has to bring in, train, or test new people for substantial periods before he can staff key posts with confidence. During this testing period he may substantially modify his original concept of the reorganization, as he evaluates individuals' potentials, their performance in specific roles, their personal drives, and their relationships with other team members.

Because this chain of decisions affects the career development, power, affluence, and self-image of so many, the executive tends to keep close counsel in his discussions, negotiates individually with key people, and makes final commitments as late as possible in order to obtain the best matches between people's capabilities, personalities, and aspirations and their new roles. Typically, all these events do not come together at one convenient time, particularly the moment annual plans are due. Instead the executive moves opportunistically, step-by-step, selectively moving people toward a broadly conceived organizational goal, which is constantly modified and rarely articulated in detail until the last pieces fit together.

Major organizational moves may also define entirely new strategies the guiding executive cannot fully foresee. For example:

When Exxon began its regional decentralization on a worldwide basis, the Executive Committee placed a senior officer and board member with a very responsive management style in a vaguely defined "coordinative role" vis-à-vis its powerful and successful European units. Over a period of two years this man sensed problems and experimented with voluntary coordinative possibilities on a pan-European basis. Only later, with greater understanding by both corporate and divisional officers, did Exxon move to a more formal "line" relationship for what became Exxon Europe. Even then the move had to be coordinated in other areas of the world. All of these changes together led to an entirely new internal power balance toward regional and non-U.S. concerns and to a more responsive worldwide posture for Exxon. . . .

In such situations, executives may be able to predict the broad direction, but not the precise nature, of the ultimate strategy which will result. In some cases, such as Exxon, the rebalance of power and information relationships *becomes* the strategy, or at least its central element. In others, organizational shifts are primarily means of triggering or implementing new strategic concepts and philosophies. But in all cases, major organizational changes create unexpected new stresses, opportunities, power bases, information centers, and credibility relationships that can affect both previous plans and future strategies in unanticipated ways. Effective reorganization decisions, therefore, allow for testing, flexibility, and feedback. Hence, they should, and usually do, evolve incrementally.

THE GOVERNMENT-EXTERNAL RELATIONS SUBSYSTEM

Almost all companies cited government and other external activist groups as among the most important forces causing significant changes in their strategic postures during the periods examined. However, when asked "How did your company arrive at its own strategy vis-à-vis these forces?" it became clear that few companies had cohesive strategies (integrated sets of goals, policies, and programs) for government-external relations, other than lobbying for or against specific legislative actions. To the extent that other strategies did exist, they were piecemeal, ad hoc, and had been derived in a very evolutionary manner. Yet there seemed to be very good reasons for such incrementalism. . . .

> We are a very large company, and we understand that any massive overt action on our part could easily create more public antagonism than support for our viewpoint. It is also hard to say in advance exactly what public response any particular action might create. So we tend to test a number of different approaches on a small scale with only limited or local company identification. If one approach works, we'll test it further and amplify its use. If another bombs, we try to keep it from being used again. Slowly we find a series of advertising, public relations, community relations actions that seem to help. Then along

comes another issue and we start all over again. Gradually the successful approaches merge into a pattern of actions that becomes our strategy. We certainly don't have an overall strategy on this, and frankly I don't think we devote enough [organizational and fiscal] resources to it. This may be our most important strategic issue. . . .

In this realm, uncontrollable forces dominate. Data are very soft, can often be only subjectively sensed, and may be costly to quantify. The possible responses of individuals and groups to different stimuli are difficult to determine in advance. The number of potential opponents with power is very high, and the diversity in their viewpoints and possible modes of attack is so substantial that it is physically impossible to lay out probabilistic decision diagrams that would have much meaning. Results are unpredictable and error costs extreme. Even the best intended and most rational-seeming strategies can be converted into disasters unless they are thoroughly and interactively tested. . . .

For such reasons, companies will probably always have to derive major portions of their government-external relations strategies in an experimental, iterative fashion. But such incrementalism could be much more proactive than it often has been in the past. Favorable public opinion and political action take a long time to mold. There is a body of knowledge about how to influence political action. There are also methods of informal and formal analyses which can help companies anticipate major political movements and adjust their goals or policies in a timely fashion. Once potential approaches are experimentally derived (without destroying needed flexibilities), more cohesive planning can ensure that the resources committed are sufficient to achieve the desired goals, that all important polities are included in plans, and that rigorous and adaptive internal controls maintain those high performance, attitude, service, and image qualities that lend credibility to the strategy. But again, one sees logical incrementalism as the essential thread linking together information gathering, analysis, testing, and the behavioral and power considerations in this strategic subsystem.

FORMAL PLANNING IN CORPORATE STRATEGY

What role do classical formal planning techniques play in strategy formulation? All companies in the sample do have formal planning procedures embedded in their management direction and control systems. These serve certain essential functions. In a process sense, they:

- Provide a discipline forcing managers to take a careful look ahead periodically;
- Require rigorous communications about goals, strategic issues, and resource allocations;
- Stimulate longer-term analyses than would otherwise be made;
- Generate a basis for evaluating and integrating short-term plans;
- Lengthen time horizons and protect long-term investments such as R&D;

- Create a psychological backdrop and an information framework about the future against which managers can calibrate short-term or interim decisions.

In a decision-making sense, they:

- Fine tune annual commitments;
- Formalize cost reduction programs;
- Help implement strategic changes once decided on (for example, coordinating all elements of Exxon's decision to change its corporate name).

Finally, "special studies" had high impact at key junctures for specific decisions.

FORMAL PLANS ALSO "INCREMENT"

Although individual staff planners were often effective in identifying potential problems and bringing them to top management's attention, the annual planning process itself was rarely (if ever) the initiating source of really new key issues or radical departures into new product/market realms. These almost always came from precipitating events, special studies, or conceptions implanted through the kinds of "logical incremental" processes described above.

In fact, formal planning practices actually institutionalize incrementalism. There are two reasons for this. **First,** in order to utilize specialized expertise and to obtain executive involvement and commitment, most planning occurs "from the bottom up" in response to broadly defined assumptions or goals, many of which are longstanding or negotiated well in advance. Of necessity, lower-level groups have only a partial view of the corporation's total strategy, and command only a fragment of its resources. Their power bases, identity, expertise, and rewards also usually depend on their existing products or processes. Hence, these products or processes, rather than entirely new departures, should and do receive their primary attention. **Second,** most managements purposely design their plans to be "living" or "ever green." They are intended only as "frameworks" to guide and provide consistency for future decisions made incrementally. To act otherwise would be to deny that further information could have a value. Thus, properly formulated formal plans are also a part of an incremental logic.

SPECIAL STUDIES

Formal planning was most successful in stimulating significant change when it was set up as a "special study" on some important aspect of corporate strategy. For example:

When it became apparent that Pilkington's new flat glass process would work, the company formed a Directors Flat Glass Committee consisting of all internal directors associated with flat glass "to consider the broad issues of flat glass [strategy] in both the present and the future." The committee did not attempt detailed plans. Instead, it tried to deal in broad concepts, identify alternate routes, and think through the potential consequences of each route some ten years ahead. Of some of the key strategic decisions Sir Alastair later said, "It would be difficult to identify an exact moment when the decision was made. . . . Nevertheless, over a period of time a consensus crystallized with great clarity.". . .

In each case there were also important precursor events, analyses, and political interactions, and each was followed by organizational, power, and behavioral changes. But interestingly, such special strategic studies also represent a "subsystem" of strategy formulation distinct from both annual planning activities and the other subsystems exemplified above. Each of these develops some important aspect of strategy, incrementally blending its conclusions with those of other subsystems, and it would be virtually impossible to force all these together to crystallize a completely articulated corporate strategy at any one instant.

TOTAL POSTURE PLANNING

Occasionally, however, managements do attempt very broad assessments of their companies' total posture. An example follows:

Shortly after becoming CEO of General Mills, Mr. James McFarland decided that his job was "to take a very good company and move it to greatness," but that it was up to his management group, not himself alone, to decide what a great company was and how to get there. Consequently he took some 35 of the company's topmost managers away for a three-day management retreat. On the first day, after agreeing to broad financial goals, the group broke up into units of six to eight people. Each unit was to answer the question "What is a great company?" from the viewpoints of stockholders, employees, suppliers, the public, and society. Each unit reported back at the end of the day, and the whole group tried to reach a consensus through discussion.

On the second day the groups, in the same format, assessed the company's strengths and weaknesses relative to the defined posture of "greatness." The third day focused on how to overcome the company's weaknesses and move it toward a great company. This broad consensus led, over the next several years, to the surveys of fields for acquisition, the building of management's initial "comfort levels" with certain fields, and the acquisition-divestiture strategy that characterized the McFarland era at General Mills. . . .

Yet even such major endeavors were only portions of a total strategic process. Values which had been built up over decades stimulated or constrained alternatives. Precipitating events, acquisitions, divestitures, external relations, and organizational changes developed important segments of each strategy incrementally. Even the strategies articulated left key elements to be defined as new information became available, polities permitted, or particular opportunities appeared (like Pilkington's Electro-float invention or Xerox's Daconics acquisition). Major product thrusts (like Pilkington's TV tubes or Xerox's computers) proved unsuccessful. Actual strategies therefore evolved as each company overextended, consolidated, made errors, and rebalanced various thrusts over time. And it was both logical and expected that this would be the case.

LOGICAL INCREMENTALISM

All of the above suggest that strategic decisions do not lend themselves to aggregation into a single massive decision matrix where all factors can be treated relatively simultaneously in order to arrive at a holistic optimum. Many have spoken of the "cognitive limits" which prevent this. Of equal importance are the "process limits"—i.e., the timing and sequencing imperatives necessary to create awareness, build comfort levels, develop consensus, select and train people, and so on—which constrain the system, yet ultimately determine the decision itself. Unlike the preparation of a fine banquet, it is virtually impossible for the manager to orchestrate all internal decisions, external environmental events, behavioral and power relationships, technical and informational needs, and actions of intelligent opponents so that they come together at any precise moment.

CAN THE PROCESS BE MANAGED?

Instead, executives usually deal with the logic of each "subsystem" of strategy formulation on its own merits and usually with a different subset of people. They try to develop or maintain a consistent pattern among the decisions made in each subsystem. Knowing their own limitations and the unknowability of events, they consciously try to tap the minds and psychic drives of others. They often purposely keep questions broad and decisions vague in early stages to avoid creating undue rigidities and to stimulate others' creativity. Logic, of course, dictates that they make final commitments *as late as possible* consistent with the information they have.

Consequently, many successful executives will initially set only broad goals and polices which can accommodate a variety of specific proposals from below yet give a sense of guidance to the proposers. As they come forward the proposals automatically attract the support of sponsors. Being only proposals, executives can treat these at less politically charged levels, as specific projects rather than as larger goal or policy precedents. Therefore, they can encourage, discourage, or kill alternatives with considerably less political exposure. As events and opportunities emerge, they can guide the pattern of escalated or accepted proposals to suit their own purposes without committing prematurely to any rigid solution set that unpredictable events might prove wrong or that opponents might find threatening enough to counter.

A STRATEGY EMERGES

Successful executives link together and bring order to a series of strategic processes and decisions spanning years. At the beginning of the process it is literally impossible to predict all the shape of the company's future. The best executives can do is to forecast the most likely forces that will impinge on the company's affairs and the ranges of their possible impact. They then attempt to build a resource base and a corporate posture that are so strong in selected areas that the enterprise can survive and prosper. They consciously select market/technological/product segments which the concern can "dominate" given its resource limits, and place some "side bets" in order to decrease the risk of catastrophic failure or to increase the company's flexibility for future options.

They then proceed to handle urgent matters incrementally, to start longer-term sequences whose futures are perhaps murky, to respond to unforeseen events as they occur, to build on successes, and to brace up or cut losses on failures. They constantly reassess the future, find new congruencies as events unfurl, and blend the organization's skills and resources into new balances of dominance and risk aversion as various forces intersect to suggest better—but never perfect—alignments. The process is dynamic, with neither a real beginning nor end. . . .

Strategy deals with the unknowable, not the uncertain. It involves forces of such great number, strength, and combinatory powers that one cannot predict events in a probabilistic sense. Hence logic dictates that one proceed flexibly and experimentally from broad concepts toward specific commitments, making the latter concrete as late as possible in order to narrow the bands of uncertainty and to benefit from the best available information. This is the process of "logical incrementalism."

"Logical incrementalism" is not "muddling," as most people use that word. It is conscious, purposeful, proactive, good management. Properly managed it allows the executive to bind together the contributions of rational systematic analyses, political and power theories, and organizational behavior concepts. It helps the executive achieve cohesion and identity with new directions. It allows him to deal with power relationships and individual behavioral needs, and permits him to use the best possible informational and analytical inputs in choosing his major courses of action. . . .

DISCUSSION QUESTIONS

1. What are the implications for lower-level employees of top management's tendency to delay decisions or keep them vague during a crisis? Does that confuse or demoralize employees?
2. What are the disadvantages to allowing strategy to evolve incrementally?
3. Are logical incrementalism and formal systems planning incompatible?

Management and the World's Work 4

PETER F. DRUCKER

Less than 150 years ago, when Marx was working on Das Kapital, *the concept of "management" was unknown. Since then, according to Peter Drucker, management has transformed the economic and social fabric of the world's developed countries. Drucker traces the path this transformation has taken, showing how management has created a global economy and set new rules for countries that seek to participate in that economy as equals. He then describes the challenges now facing managers in developing and developed countries, emphasizing how the essential principles of management can help them build successful, productive, and achieving enterprises all over the world.*

When Marx was beginning work on *Das Kapital* in the early 1850s, the phenomenon of management was unknown. So were the enterprises that managers run. The largest manufacturing company around was a Manchester, England cotton mill employing fewer than 300 people, owned by Marx's friend and collaborator Friedrich Engels. And in Engels's mill—one of the most profitable businesses of its day—there were no "managers," only first-line supervisors, or charge hands, who were workers themselves, each enforcing discipline over a handful of fellow "proletarians."

Rarely in human history has any institution emerged as fast as management or had as great an impact as quickly. In less than 150 years, management has transformed the social and economic fabric of the world's developed countries. It has created a global economy and set new rules for countries that would participate in that economy as equals. And it has itself been transformed.

To be sure, the fundamental risk of management remains the same: to make people capable of joint performance by giving them common goals, common values, the right structure, and the ongoing training and development they need to perform and to respond to change. But the very meaning of this task has changed, if only because the performance of management has converted the work force from one composed largely of unskilled laborers to one of highly educated knowledge workers.

Few executives are aware of the tremendous impact management has had. Indeed, a good many are like M. Jourdain, the character in Moliere's *Le Bourgeois Gentilhomme* who did not know that he spoke prose. They barely realize that they practice—or mispractice—management. As a result, they are ill-prepared for the tremendous challenges that come upon them. For the truly important problems managers face do not come from technology or politics. They do not originate outside of management and enterprise. They are problems caused by the very success of management itself.

Eighty years ago, on the threshold of World War I, when a few people were just becoming aware of management's existence, most people in developed countries (perhaps four out of every five) earned their living in three occupations. There were domestic servants—in Great Britain, the largest single occupation (a full third of all workers), but a very large group everywhere, even in the United States. There were farmers—usually family farmers, who accounted for more than half the working population in every country except England and Belgium. And finally, there were blue-collar workers in manufacturing industries—the fastest growing occupation and the one that by 1925 would embrace almost 40% of the U.S. labor force.

Today domestic servants have all but disappeared. Full-time farmers account for only 3%–5% of the working population in the non-Communist, developed countries, even though farm production is four to five times what it was 80 years ago. Blue-collar manufacturing employment is rapidly moving down the same path as farming. Manual workers employed in manufacturing in the United States now make up only 18% of the total work force; by the end of the century, they are likely to account for 10% or so in the United States and elsewhere—with manufacturing production steadily rising and expected to be at least 50% higher. The largest single group, more than one-third of the total, consists of workers whom the U.S. Bureau of the Census calls "managerial and professional." And a larger proportion of the total adult population than ever before—almost two-thirds in the United States, for instance—is now gainfully employed in every developed, non-Communist country.

Management has been the main agent of this unprecedented transformation. For it is management that explains why, for the first time in human history, we can employ large numbers of knowledgeable, skilled people in productive work. No earlier society could do this. Indeed, no earlier society could support more than a handful of such people because, until quite recently, no one knew how to put people with different skills and knowledge together to achieve common goals. Eighteenth-century China was the envy of contemporary Western intellectuals because it supplied more jobs for educated people than all of Europe did—some 20,000 per year. Yet today, the United States with a roughly comparable population produces nearly one million college graduates a year, most of whom have little difficulty finding well-paid employment. What enables us to employ them is management.

Knowledge, especially advanced knowledge, is always highly specialized. By itself it produces nothing. Yet a modern large business can usefully employ up to 10,000 highly knowledgeable people who possess up to 60 different fields of knowledge. Engineers of all sorts, designers, marketing experts, economists, statisticians, psychologists, planners, accountants, human resources people—all work together in a joint venture, and none would be effective without the managed enterprise that is business.

The question of which came first—the educational explosion of the last 100 years or the management that could put this knowledge to productive use—is moot. Modern management and modern enterprise clearly could not exist without the knowledge base that developed societies have built. But equally, it is management and management alone that makes all this knowledge and these knowledgeable people effective. The emergence of management has converted knowledge from a social ornament and luxury into what we now know to be the true capital of any economy.

And knowledge, in turn—instead of bricks and mortar—has become the center of capital investment. Japan invests a record 8% of its annual GNP in plant and equipment. But Japan invests at least twice as much in education, two-thirds in schools for the young, the rest in the training and teaching of adults (largely in the organizations that employ them). And the United States puts an even larger share—roughly 20%—of its much larger GNP into education and training. In the modern society of enterprise and management, knowledge is the primary resource and society's true wealth.

Not many business leaders could have predicted this development back in 1870, when large enterprises like those we know today were beginning to take shape. The reason was not so much lack of foresight as lack of precedent. At that time, the only large permanent organization around was the army. Not surprisingly, therefore, its command-and-control structure became the model for the men who were putting together transcontinental railroads, steel mills, modern banks, and department stores.

The command model, with a very few at the top giving orders and a great many at the bottom obeying them, remained the norm for nearly 100 years. But it was never as static as its longevity might suggest. On the contrary, it began to change almost at once, as specialized knowledge of all sorts poured into enterprise. The first university-trained engineer in manufacturing industry was hired in Germany in 1867, and within five years he had built a research department. Other specialties followed suit, and by World War I the familiar typical functions of a manufacturer had been developed: research and engineering, manufacturing, sales, finance and accounting, and a little later, human resources.

Even more important for its impact on enterprise—and on the world economy in general—was another management-directed development that took place at this time. That was the application of management to manual work in the form of training. The child of wartime necessity, training has propelled the transformation of the world economy in the last 30 years because it allows low-wage countries to do something that traditional economic theory had said could never be done: to become efficient—and yet still low-wage—competitors almost overnight.

Until World War I, it was axiomatic that it took a long time (Adam Smith said several hundred years) for a country or region to develop a tradition of labor and the expertise in manual and organizational skills needed to produce and market a given product, whether cotton textiles or violins. But during World War I, large numbers of totally unskilled, preindustrial people had to be made productive in practically no time. To meet this need, businesses in the United States and the United Kingdom began to apply Frederick Taylor's principles of "scientific management," developed between 1885 and 1910, to the systematic training of blue-collar workers on a large scale. They analyzed tasks and broke them down into individual, unskilled operations that could then be learned quite quickly. Further developed in World War II, training was then picked up by the Japanese and, 20 years later, by the South Koreans, who made it the basis for their countries' phenomenal development.

During the 1920s and 1930s, management was applied to many more areas and aspects of manufacturing business. Decentralization, for instance, arose to combine the advantages of bigness and the advantages of smallness within one enterprise. Accounting went from "bookkeeping" to analysis and control. Planning grew out of the "Gantt charts" designed in 1917 and 1918 to plan war production, and so did the use of analytical logic and statistics, which used quantification to convert experience and intuition into definitions, information, and diagnosis. Marketing similarly evolved as a result of applying management concepts to distribution and selling.

Moreover, as early as the mid-1920s and early 1930s, some management pioneers (Thomas Watson, Sr. at the fledgling IBM, General Robert E. Wood at Sears, Roebuck, and Elton Mayo at the Harvard Business School among them) began to question the way that manufacturing was organized. Eventually, they concluded that the assembly line was a short-term compromise despite its tremendous productivity: poor economics because of its inflexibility, poor use of human resources, even poor engineering. And so they began the thinking that eventually led to "automation" as the way to organize the manufacturing process, and to "Theory Y," teamwork, quality circles, and the information-based organization as the way to manage human resources.

Every one of these managerial innovations represented the application of knowledge to work, the substitution of system and information for guesswork, brawn, and toil. Every one, to use Frederick Taylor's terms, replaced "working harder" with "working smarter."

The powerful effect of these changes became apparent during World War II. To the very end, the Germans were by far the better strategists. And because they had the benefit of much shorter interior lines, they needed far fewer support troops and could match their opponents in combat strength. Yet the Allies won—their victory achieved by management.

The United States, with one-fifth the population, had almost as many men in uniform as all the other belligerents together. Yet it still produced more war material than all the others taken together. And it managed to get that material to fighting fronts as far apart as China, Russia, India, Africa, and Western Europe. No wonder, then, that by the war's end almost all the world had become management conscious. Or that management emerged as a recognizably distinct kind of work, one that could be studied and developed into a discipline—as happened in each of the countries that has exercised economic leadership during the postwar period.

But also, after World War II we began slowly to see that management is not business management. It pertains to every human effort that brings together in one organization people of diverse knowledge and skills. And it can be powerfully applied in hospitals, universities, churches, arts organizations, and social service agencies of all kinds. These "third sector" institutions have grown faster than either business or government in the developed countries since World War II. And their leaders are becoming more and more management conscious. For even though the need to manage volunteers or raise funds may differentiate nonprofit managers from their for-profit peers, many more of their responsibilities are the same—among them, defining the right strategy and goals, developing people, measuring performance, and marketing the organization's services.

This is not to say that our knowledge of management is complete. Management education today is on the receiving end of a great deal of criticism, much of it justified. What we knew about management 40 years ago—and have codified in our systems of organized management education—does not necessarily help managers meet the challenges they face today. Nevertheless, that knowledge was the foundation for the spectacular expansion the world economy has undergone since 1950, in developed and developing countries alike. And what has made that knowledge obsolete is, in large measure, its own success in hastening the shift from manual work to knowledge work in business organizations.

To take just one example, we now have a great need for new accounting concepts and methods. Experts like Robert Kaplan have pointed out that many of the assumptions on which our system is based are no longer valid. For example, accounting conventions assume that manufacturing industry is central; in fact, service and information industries are now more important in all developed countries. They also assume that a business produces just one product, whereas practically all modern businesses produce a great many different products. But above all, cost accounting, that proud invention of the mid-1920s, assumes that 80% of all costs are attributable to direct manual labor. In reality, manual labor in advanced manufacturing industries today accounts for no more than 8%–12% of all costs. And the processes used in industries like automobiles and steel, in which labor costs are higher, are distinctly antiquated.

Efforts to devise accounting systems that will reflect changes like these—and provide accurate managerial information—are under way. But they are still in the early stages. So are our efforts to find solutions to other important management challenges: structures that work for information-based organizations; ways to raise the productivity of knowledge workers; techniques for managing existing businesses and developing new and very different ones at the same time; ways to build and manage truly global businesses; and many more.

Management arose in developed countries. How does its rise affect the developing world? Perhaps the best way to answer this question is to start with the obvious: management and large enterprise, together with our new communications capacity, have created a truly global economy. In the process, they have changed what countries must do to participate effectively in that economy and to achieve economic success.

In the past, starring roles in the world's economy were always based on leadership in technological innovations. Great Britain became an economic power in the late eighteenth and early nineteenth centuries through innovation in the steam engine, machine tools, textiles, railroads, iron making, insurance, and international banking. Germany's economic star rose in the second half of the nineteenth century on innovation in chemistry, electricity, electronics, optics, steel, and the invention of the modern bank. The United States emerged as an economic power at the same time through innovative leadership in steel, electricity, telecommunications, electronics, automobiles, agronomy, office equipment, agricultural implements, and aviation.

But the one great economic power to emerge in this century, Japan, has not been a technological pioneer in any area. Its ascendancy rests squarely on leadership in management. The Japanese understood the lessons of America's managerial achievement during World War II more clearly than we did ourselves—especially with respect to managing people as a resource rather than as a cost. As a result, they adapted the West's new "social technology," management, to make it fit their own values and traditions. They adopted (and adapted) organization theory to become the most thorough practitioners of decentralization in the world. (Pre-World War II Japan had been completely centralized.) And they began to practice marketing when most American companies were still only preaching it.

Japan also understood sooner than other countries that management and technology together had changed the economic landscape. The mechanical model of organization and technology came into being at the end of the seventeenth century when an obscure French physicist, Denis Papin, designed a prototypical steam engine. It came to an end in 1945, when the first atomic bomb exploded and the first computer went on line. Since then, the model for both technology and organizations has been a biological one—interdependent, knowledge intensive, and organized by the flow of information.

One consequence of this change is that the industries that have been the carriers of enterprise for the last 100 years—industries like automobiles, steel, consumer electronics, and appliances—are in crisis. And this is true even where demographics seem to be in their favor. For example, countries like Mexico and Brazil have an abundant supply of young people who can be trained easily for semiskilled manual work. The mechanical industries would seem to be a perfect match. But as competitors in every industrial nation have found, mechanical production is antiquated unless it becomes automated—that is, unless it is restructured around information. For that reason alone, education is perhaps the greatest "management" challenge developing countries face.

Another way to arrive at the same conclusion is to look at a second fact with which developing countries must reckon: the developed countries no longer need them as they did during the nineteenth century. It may be hyperbole to say, as Japan's leading management consultant, Kenichi Ohmae, has said, that Japan, North America, and Western Europe can exist by themselves without the two-thirds of humanity who live in developing countries. But it is a fact that during the last 40 years the countries of this so-called triad have become essentially self-sufficient except for petroleum. They produce more food than they can consume—in glaring contrast to the nineteenth century. They produce something like three-fourths of all the world's manufactured goods and services. And they provide the market for an equal proportion.

This poses an acute problem for developing countries, even very big ones like China and India. They cannot hope to become important economic powers by tracking the evolution of enterprise and management—that is, by starting with nineteenth and early twentieth-century industries and productive processes based mainly on a manual work force. Demographically they may have no choice, of course. And maybe they can even begin to catch up. But can they ever get ahead? I doubt it.

During the last 200 years, no country has become a major economic power by following in the footsteps of earlier leaders. Each started out with what were, at the time, advanced industries and advanced production and distribution processes. And each, very fast, became a leader in management. Today, however, in part because of automation information and advanced technology, but in much larger part because of the demand for trained people in all areas of management, development requires a knowledge base that few developing countries possess or can afford. How to create an adequate managerial knowledge base fast is the critical question in economic development today. It is also one for which we have no answer so far.

The problems and challenges discussed so far are largely internal to management and enterprise. But the most important challenge ahead for management in developed countries is the result of an external change that I call "pension fund socialism." I am referring, of course, to the shift of the titles of ownership of public companies to the institutional trustees of the country's employees, chiefly through their pension funds.

Socially this is the most positive development of the twentieth century because it resolves the "Social Question" that vexed the nineteenth century—the conflict between "capital" and "labor"—by merging the two. But it has also created the most violent turbulence for management and managers since they arose a century ago. For pension funds are the ultimate cause of the explosion of hostile takeovers in the last few years; and nothing has so disturbed and demoralized managers as the hostile takeover. In this sense, takeovers are only a symptom of the fundamental questions pension fund socialism raises about the legitimacy of management: To whom are managers accountable? For what? What is the purpose and rationale of large, publicly owned enterprises?

In 1986, the pension funds of America's employees owned more than 40% of U.S. companies' equity capital and more than two-thirds of the equity capital of the 1,000 largest companies. The funds of large institutions (businesses, states, cities, public service and nonprofit institutions like universities, school districts, and hospitals) accounted for three-quarters of these holdings. The funds of individuals (employees of small businesses and the self-employed) accounted for the other fourth. (Mutual funds, which also represent the savings of wage earners rather than of "capitalists," hold another 5%–10% of the country's equity capital.)

These figures mean that pension funds are now the primary suppliers of capital in the United States. Indeed, it is almost impossible to build a new business or expand an existing one unless pension-fund money is available. In the next few years, the funds' holdings will become even larger, if only because federal government employees now have a pension fund that invests in equity shares. Thus, by the year 2000, pension funds will hold at least two-thirds of the share capital of all U.S. businesses except the smallest. Through their pension funds, U.S. employees will be the true owners of the country's means of production.

The same development, with a lag of about ten years, is taking place in Great Britain, Japan, West Germany, and Sweden. It is also starting to appear in France, Italy, and the Netherlands.

This startling development was not foreseen, but it was inevitable—the result of several interdependent factors. First is the shift in income distribution that directs 90% or so of the GNP in non-Communist, developed countries into the wage fund. (The figure varies from 85% in the United States to 95% or more in the Netherlands and Denmark.) Indeed, economically the "rich" have become irrelevant in developed countries, however much they dominate the society pages and titillate TV viewers. Even the very rich have actually become much poorer in this century if their incomes are adjusted for inflation and taxation. To be in the same league as the "tycoon" of 1900, today's "super-rich" person would need a net worth of at least $50 billion—perhaps $100 billion—and income to match. A few Arab oil sheiks may qualify, but surely no one in a developed country.

At the same time, wage earners' real incomes have risen dramatically. Few employees in turn-of-the-century America could lay aside anything beyond their mortgage payments or the premiums on funeral insurance. But since then, the American industrial worker's real income and purchasing power have grown more than 20 times larger, even though the number of hours worked has dropped by 50%. The same has occurred in all the other industrially developed countries. And it has happened fastest in Japan, where the real income of industrial workers may now be as much as 30 times what it was 80 years ago.

Demand for this income is essentially limitless because we are again in the midst of an intensively creative period. In the 60 years between 1856 and World War I, a technical or social innovation that led almost immediately to a new industry appeared, on average, once every 14 months. And this entrepreneurial explosion underlay the rise of the tycoons. We needed people like J. P. Morgan, John D. Rockefeller, Sr., Andrew Carnegie, Friedrich Krupp, and the Mitsui family who could finance whole industries out of their private pockets. Technical and social innovations are coming just as fast today. And the effect of all this energy is that companies and countries require enormous amounts of capital just to keep up, let alone move ahead—amounts that are several orders of magnitude larger than those the tycoons had to supply 80 years ago.

Indeed, the total pretax incomes of America's 1,000 highest income earners would be barely adequate to cover the capital needs of the country's private industry for more than three or four days. This holds true for all developed countries. In Japan, for instance, the pretax incomes of the country's 2,000 highest income earners just about equals what the country's private industry invests every two or three days.

These economic developments would have forced us in any event to make workers into "capitalists" and owners of productive resources. That pension funds became the vehicle—rather than mutual funds or direct individual investments in equity as everyone expected 30 years ago—is the result of the demographic shift that has raised life expectancies in developed countries from age 40 to the mid- and late-70s. The number of older people is much too large, and the years during which they need an income too many, for them to depend on support from their children. They must rely on monies they themselves have put aside during their earning years—and these funds have to be invested for long stretches of time.

That modern society requires an identity of interest between enterprise and employee was seen very early, not only by pre-Marxist socialists like Saint-Simon and Fourier in France and Robert Owen in Scotland but also by classical economists like Adam Smith and David Ricardo. Attempts to satisfy this need through worker ownership of business thus go back more than 150 years. Without exception, they have failed.

In the first place, worker ownership does not satisfy the workers' basic financial and economic needs. It puts all the workers' financial resources into the business that employs them. But the workers' needs are primarily long-term, particularly the need for retirement income many years hence. So to be a sound investment for its worker-owners, a business has to prosper for a very long time—and only one business out of every 40 or 50 ever does. Indeed, few even survive long enough. But worker ownership also destroys companies in the end because it always leads to inadequate capital formation, inadequate investment in research and development, and stubborn resistance to abandonment of outmoded, unproductive, and obsolete products, processes, plants, jobs, and work rules.

Zeiss Optical Works, the oldest worker-owned business around, lost its leadership position in consumer optics to the Americans and the Japanese for just this reason. Time and again, Zeiss's worker-owners preferred immediate satisfaction—higher wages, bonuses, benefits—to investing in research, new products, and new markets. Worker ownership underlies the near collapse of industry in contemporary Yugoslavia. And its shortcomings are so greatly hampering industry in China that the country's leaders are trying to shift to "contract management," which will expand managerial autonomy and check the power of "work councils" and worker-owners.

And yet, worker ownership of the means of production is not only a sound concept, it is also inevitable. Power follows property, says the old axiom. Both James Madison, in the Federalist Papers, and Karl Marx took it from the seventeenth century English philosopher, James Harrington, who in turn took it from Aristotle. It can be found in early Confucian writings as well. And since property has shifted to the wage earners in all developed countries, power has to follow. Yet unlike any other worker ownership of the means of production, pension fund socialism maintains the autonomy and accountability of enterprise and management, market freedom, competition, and the ability to change and to innovate.

But pension fund socialism does not function fully as yet. We can solve the financial and economic problems it presents. We know, for instance, that a pension fund must invest no more than a small fraction of its assets, 5% perhaps, in the shares of its own company or of any one company altogether. We know quite a bit, though not nearly enough, about how to invest pension fund money. But we still have to solve the basic sociopolitical problem: how to build the accomplished fact of employee ownership into the governance of both pension funds and businesses.

Pension funds are the legal owners of the companies in which they invest. But they not only have no "ownership interest;" as trustees for the ultimate beneficiaries, the employees, they also are legally obligated to be nothing but "investors," and short-term investors at that. That is why it is worker ownership that has made the hostile takeover possible. For as trustees, the pension funds must sell if someone bids more than the market price.

Whether hostile takeovers benefit shareholders is a hotly debated issue. That they have serious economic side effects is beyond question. The fear of a hostile takeover may not be the only reason American managements tend to subordinate everything—market standing, research, product development, service, quality, innovation—to the short term. But it is surely a major reason. Moreover, the hostile takeover is a frontal attack on management and managers. Indeed, what makes the mere threat of a takeover so demoralizing to managers (especially the middle managers and professionals on whom a business depends for its performance) is the raiders' barely concealed contempt, which management sees as contempt for wealth-producing work, and their work's subordination to financial manipulation.

For their part, the raiders and their financial backers maintain that management is solely accountable to the shareholders whatever their wishes, even if those represent nothing more than short-term speculative gains and asset stripping. This is indeed what the law says. But the law was written for early nineteenth-century business conditions, well before large enterprise and management came into being. And while every free-market country has similar laws, not all countries hold to them. In Japan, for instance, custom dictates that larger companies exist mainly for the sake of their employees except in the event of bankruptcy; and Japanese economic performance and even Japanese shareholders have surely not suffered as a result. In West Germany too, large enterprises are seen as "going concerns," whose preservation is in the national interest and comes before shareholders' gains.

Both Japan and Germany have organized an extra-legal but highly effective way to hold business managements accountable, however, in the form of the voting control exercised by the big commercial banks of both countries. No such system exists in the United States (or the United Kingdom), nor could it possibly be constructed. And even in Japan and Germany, the hold of the banks is weakening fast.

So we must think through what management should be accountable for; and how and through whom its accountability can be discharged. The stockholders' interest, both short- and long-term, is one of the areas, to be sure. But it is only one.

One thing is clear to anyone with the slightest knowledge of political or economic history: the present-day assertion of "absolute shareholder sovereignty" (of which the boom in takeovers is the most spectacular manifestation) is the last hurrah of nineteenth century, basically preindustrial capitalism. It violates many people's sense of justice—as the upsurge of "populism" and anti-Wall Street rhetoric in the 1988 presidential campaign attest.

But even more important, no economy can perform if it puts what Thorstein Veblen, some 70-odd years ago, called "the acquisitive instinct" ahead of the "instinct of workmanship." Modern enterprise, especially large enterprise, can do its economic job—including making profits for the shareholders—only if it is being managed for the long run. Investments, whether in people, in products, in plants, in processing, in technology, or in markets, require several years of gestation before there is even a "baby," let alone full-grown results. Altogether far too much in society—jobs, careers, communities—depends on the economic fortunes of large enterprises to subordinate them completely to the interests of any one group, including shareholders.

How to make the interests of shareholders—and this means pension funds—compatible with the needs of the economy and society is thus the big issue pension fund socialism has to resolve. And it has to be done in a way that makes managements accountable, especially for economic and financial performance, and yet allows them to manage for the long term. How we answer this challenge will decide both the shape and place of management and the structure, if not the survival, of the free-market economy. It will also determine America's ability to compete in a world economy in which competitive long-range strategies are more and more the norm.

Finally, what is management? Is it a bag of techniques and tricks? A bundle of analytical tools like those taught in business schools? These are important, to be sure, just as the thermometer and a knowledge of anatomy are important to the physician. But what the evolution and history of management—its successes as well as its problems—teach is that management is, above all else, a very few, essential principles. To be specific:

1. Management is about human beings. Its task is to make people capable of joint performance, to make their strengths effective and their weaknesses irrelevant. This is what organization is all about, and it is the reason that management is the critical, determining factor. These days, practically all of us are employed by managed institutions, large and small, business and nonbusiness—and that is especially true for educated people. We depend on management for our livelihoods and our ability to contribute and achieve. Indeed,

our ability to contribute to society at all usually depends as much on the management of the enterprises in which we work as it does on our own skills, dedication, and effort.

2. Because management deals with the integration of people in a common venture, it is deeply embedded in culture. What managers do in West Germany, in Britain, in the United States, in Japan, or in Brazil is exactly the same. How they do it may be quite different. Thus one of the basic challenges managers in a developing country face is to find and identify those parts of their own tradition, history, and culture that can be used as building blocks. The difference between Japan's economic success and India's relative backwardness, for instance, is largely explained by the fact that Japanese managers were able to plant imported management concepts in their own cultural soil and make them grow. Whether China's leaders can do the same—or whether their great tradition will become an impediment to the country's development—remains to be seen.
3. Every enterprise requires simple, clear, and unifying objectives. Its mission has to be clear enough and big enough to provide a common vision. The goals that embody it have to be clear, public, and often reaffirmed. We hear a great deal of talk these days about the "culture" of an organization. But what we really mean by this is the commitment throughout an enterprise to some common objectives and common values. Without such commitment there is no enterprise; there is only a mob. Management's job is to think through, set, and exemplify those objectives, values, and goals.
4. It is also management's job to enable the enterprise and each of its members to grow and develop as needs and opportunities change. This means that every enterprise is a learning and teaching institution. Training and development must be built into it on all levels—training and development that never stop.
5. Every enterprise is composed of people with different skills and knowledge doing many different kinds of work. For that reason, it must be built on communication and on individual responsibility. Each member has to think through what he or she aims to accomplish—and make sure that associates know and understand that aim. Each has to think through what he or she owes to others—and make sure that others understand and approve. Each has to think through what is needed from others—and make sure that others know what is expected of them.
6. Neither the quantity of output nor the bottom line is by itself an adequate measure of the performance of management and enterprise. Market standing, innovation, productivity, development of people, quality, financial results—all are crucial to a company's performance and indeed to its survival. In this respect, an enterprise is like a human being. Just as we need a diversity of measures to assess the health and performance of a person, we need a diversity of measures for an enterprise. Performance has to be built into the enterprise and its management; it has to be measured—or at least judged—and it has to be continuously improved.

7. Finally, the single most important thing to remember about any enterprise is that there are no results inside its walls. The result of a business is a satisfied customer. The result of a hospital is a healed patient. The result of a school is a student who has learned something and puts it to work ten years later. Inside an enterprise, there are only cost centers. Results exist only on the outside.

About management, as about any other area of human work, much more could be said. Tools must be acquired and used. Techniques and any number of processes and procedures must be learned. But managers who truly understand the principles outlined above and truly manage themselves in their light will be achieving, accomplished managers—the kind of managers who build successful, productive, and achieving enterprises all over the world and who establish standards, set examples, and leave as a legacy both greater capacity to produce wealth and greater human vision.

DISCUSSION QUESTIONS

1. "Every enterprise . . . must be built on communication and individual responsibility. Each member has to think through what he or she aims to accomplish. . . . Each has to think through what he or she owes to others. . . ." What are the limits of individual responsibility in a firm? Should employees at certain levels in the hierarchy be given more direction than others? Or should managers have consistent levels of personal responsibility and freedom throughout the firm?
2. Is Drucker's assertion of the pervasive influence of management convincing?
3. Is Drucker's definition of management plausible? Do you find it workable?
4. Cite examples of firms in which strong corporate commitment to training and development has had an impact on corporate success. Explain the connection between training and the company's success.
5. Drucker says that "management is about human beings." Do you think general managers are responsible primarily for managing people, for making them "capable of joint performance"? Or are GMs responsible first and foremost for managing a company's bottom line? Are these two orientations compatible?

5 General Managers in the Middle

HUGO UYTERHOEVEN

With the emergence of the divisional form of corporate organization, general managers are increasingly found at the middle management level. They direct, not entire corporations, but rather a group, a division, or a department. The "general manager in the middle" faces challenges that are different from, and sometimes more difficult than, those faced by the general manager at the head of the firm. They must manage up as well as down, translate abstract goals from superiors into concrete results, accept full responsibility for their units without having full authority to carry out their plans, and make the transition from being a functional specialist to a generalist. In this reading, Hugo Uyterhoeven describes the challenges—and the rewards—of the "general manager in the middle."

Traditionally, the job of general manager has been equated with that of a company's chief executive. General manager and boss have been thought of synonymously. Yet, increasingly, corporate organizations are providing for general management positions at levels below the chief executive; and, as a result, the number of general managers at the middle level is rising.

The middle-level general manager phenomenon (i.e., a general manager who is responsible for a particular business unit at the intermediate level of the corporate hierarchy) is a direct outgrowth of the movement toward a divisional form of organization. For example, while the functional organization requires only one general manager, the divisional organization provides for a variety of business units, each requiring a general manager. Often the process of divisionalization extends several levels down in the organization (into the group, the division, the department), further increasing the need for general managers at lower levels.

The shift from functional to divisional organization began to occur in the United States during the 1970s and is now taking place in Europe. It is a worldwide phenomenon necessitated by the greater product-line diversity as well as by the growing international operations of most big corporations.

Although the divisional organization is now a familiar phenomenon, little attention has been directed at defining the middle-level general manager. Of course, one approach would be to refer to what is known about the top-level general manager, but this knowledge is not really applicable; the two positions are significantly different. Furthermore, general management at the middle organizational level is, in many respects, more difficult.

I shall attempt here to (1) define the characteristics and responsibilities of the middle-level general manager and (2) draw the implications for the individual assigned to it (hereafter called the "middle manager") as well as for the organization.

MANAGING RELATIONSHIPS

Middle managers, like most managers, accomplish their goals largely by managing relationships. There are few things that managers can do alone; they must usually rely on the support, cooperation, or approval of a large number of people. As the textbooks say, they "get things done through others."

Managing relationships at that level in the organization, however, is a threefold task, requiring middle managers to act as subordinate, equal, and superior: upward, they relate to their bosses as subordinates—they take orders; downward, they relate to their teams as superiors—they give orders; laterally, they often relate to peers in the organization as equals—for example, they may have to secure cooperation from a pooled sales force or solicit assistance from corporate staff services.

Thus the middle manager wears three hats in fulfilling the general management role. In contrast, the top-level general manager acts primarily as a superior—this alone is a significant difference between the two positions.

Managing the triple set of relationships is most demanding; it is analogous to a baseball player having to excel simultaneously in hitting, fielding, and pitching. The middle manager must be able not only to manage all three relationships but also to shift quickly and frequently from one to another.

In view of these conflicting and changing demands, it is often difficult for middle managers to arrive at consistent patterns of behavior. Moreover, in the process of satisfying the requirements of one set of relationships, they may reduce their effectiveness in managing another. For instance, a middle manager who follows orders from headquarters to the letter may thereby, in the eyes of subordinates, either weaken his or her authority or appear to be unreasonable and unresponsive. Consider this illustration taken from an internationally divisionalized company:

Headquarters restricted the freedom of one division manager to purchase from the outside, an order that threatened to undermine his authority as a general manager. He was torn between the dilemma of (1) asserting his authority with his subordinates by ignoring or fighting headquarters' orders, or (2) weakening his image as a superior by following headquarters' orders. Being a good subordinate would have weakened him as a superior; yet, by being a strong superior, he would have been a disloyal subordinate. As it turned out, the general manager held prolonged negotiations with a peer in the pooled sales force to arrive at a mutually satisfactory solution, but this made the general manager appear inconclusive and indecisive to his subordinates.

To successfully manage such multiple relationships, and their often conflicting and changing demands, a middle manager should recognize the full scope of the job. For instance, he or she should:

1. Make the network of relationships explicit. To whom does the manager have to relate? What are the key relationships?
2. Identify, in each specific situation, the triple set of requirements. What is required to be a good subordinate? What is required to be an effective colleague? And what does it take to provide leadership as a superior? This analysis should force a middle manager to focus not only on his or her own goals but also on those of "opposite numbers" at all three levels.
3. Recognize the difficulty of achieving consistent behavior in view of conflicting demands and be willing to wear three hats at the same time. Success will come from balancing all three roles. Sometimes it requires trade-offs. Under such complex circumstances, it helps to proceed explicitly.
4. Communicate his or her understanding of the job to others in the organization. (In turn, these others should bear in mind that, individually, they are each part of a multiple relationship; their expectations and responses should take this into account.)

A Playing Coach In some respects, middle managers are the leaders of their units who delegate, guide, and plan; in other respects, however, they have specific operating responsibilities and must "roll up their sleeves" to achieve output and meet targets. Therefore, they are both delegators and doers, both strategists and operators, or, to use another sports analogy, both coaches and players. In contrast, their superiors are usually coaches and their subordinates are normally players.

Continuing the analogy, sports experience indicates that it is easier to excel either as a coach or as a player and that the playing-coach job is clearly the most difficult—the skills of a successful player are different from those of a successful coach, but the playing coach must have the skills of both. Likewise, the dual role of middle managers combines different skills and actions. On the one hand, they need a broad overview, detachment, and a long-run perspective. On the other hand, they need detailed knowledge and experience, the ability to be involved directly and deeply, and a sense of urgency.

Acting both as player and as coach, middle managers must constantly balance the two roles and sometimes make trade-offs. Is he going to be too much of a player, too involved in operating details and in doing things himself? Or is he becoming too much of a coach by staying aloof, by delegating too much, by not getting sufficiently involved? It is easy to misperceive one's role, especially in regard to the latter. For example:

Top management in a large divisionalized corporation assigned a promising middle manager to a recent acquisition. Charged with enthusiasm for her new position, the manager saw herself as primarily a delegator, an organization builder whose job was to oversee the installation of parent company procedures and guide the acquisition's integration with staff services of the parent. She had not considered becoming directly involved in operating details or concentrating attention on increasing sales, both of which her immediate superior, the former owner-manager, saw as primary responsibilities of the middle management position.

This question of balance—of asking oneself, "To what extent do I get involved in actual operations and to what extent do I delegate?"—is most delicate. And the balancing of the two roles is, of course, also influenced by the demands, expectations, and abilities of the middle manager's superiors and subordinates. The choice is not entirely free.

THE BILINGUAL MANAGER

In keeping with their dual role, middle managers usually receive abstract guidance from superiors in the form of goals that must be translated into concrete action.

If, for example, a company's chief executive sets the goal of a certain percentage increase in earnings per share (and mentions it to financial analysts, thereby making it an even stronger commitment), how does he go about achieving this goal? He will communicate it to his group vice president, who will salute and then pass it on to the divisional general manager, who, in turn, will salute and pass it on to the middle manager. The latter will salute, turn around, and find nobody to pass the goal on to. To use Harry Truman's famous dictum, this is where the buck stops.

The buck stops at the middle manager, who must assume the "bilingual" role of translating the strategic language of his or her superiors into the operational language of subordinates in order to get results. He or she must turn the abstract guidance of, say, more earnings per share or meeting the budget into the concrete action required to achieve the results.

Often the middle manager is presented these abstract goals carrying the label, "difficult but achievable." While such labels may have a motivating purpose, they are basically a euphemism for the following proposition: top management knows the results it wants to see, has no idea how to achieve them, and assigns the middle manager the twofold duty of figuring out how to perform the task and then getting it done.

Strategy Considerations There are several reasons for the foregoing results-oriented procedure. One explanation is that middle managers are closest to the action; therefore, they have most of the data and hence are in the best position to make the decisions relevant to translating goals into action. A second explanation states that it is a superior's privilege to push decision making down and let the subordinates sweat it out.

The implications of top management's approach, however, are more important than the explanations. First of all, middle-level general managers have much broader *de facto* responsibility than is usually codified in job descriptions or organization charts. Consequently, they must often be more like strategists than they realize. It is important, therefore, that they go beyond their formal job definition, functioning broadly enough so that they deal explicitly with the full scope of their real responsibilities. A narrow understanding of their roles, by contrast, may cause them to ignore critical tasks; they cannot assume a responsibility they do not recognize.

But with responsibility goes risk, particularly where the goals are abstract and the charter is unclear. The risk is further compounded by the many constraints, external as well as organizational, within which the middle manager operates. Along with risk, however, goes opportunity. To be a strategist rather than just an order taker is exciting, even without the job's ceremonial attributes.

Formulating strategy for translating abstract goals into concrete action requires the ability to develop plans. In doing so, middle managers must take into account external factors of an economic, political, marketing, technological, or competitive nature. Moreover, in line with their dual role, they must achieve congruence between the goals of subordinates (whose commitment is essential) and the goals imposed by superiors (whose approval they seek).

This strategic task is both intellectual and administrative in nature, and the communication of plans is as critical as their development. Often, communication is most effectively accomplished not through proclamation but, rather, through "teaching" the general management point of view during day-to-day activities.

Summing up, to translate goals into action, middle-level general managers must:

1. Define their jobs realistically and broadly.
2. Assume full responsibility for translating the abstract goals into concrete action through strategic decision making and planning, taking into account both external and organizational factors.
3. Effectively communicate their decisions and plans to both their superiors and subordinates.

From Action to Measurement Middle managers must be able to translate not only from abstract guidance into concrete action but also from concrete action into abstract measurement. Their superiors measure success in terms of results and are less interested in *how* it has been accomplished. Consequently, middle managers' performance is most often appraised by matching the abstract results of their actions with the abstract guidance that they have been given.

This fact of organizational life sometimes leads to misunderstanding. In one company, for example, a middle manager was unable to meet her goals and invoked her actions to show why. Top management, however, perceived the explanations as excuses. Concrete action was not part of its measurement system.

In terms of the total equation, there can be real problems when the signals from abstract measurement contradict those from abstract guidance. Where this occurs, the translation process frequently gets reversed. Instead of starting with the abstract guidance (goals) to develop specific action, the middle manager starts with the abstract measurement (required results) and translates backward to his or her plan of action. Here are two illustrations:

- In one company, top management emphasized the need for its divisions to have ample productive capacity. In the measurement of performance, however, excess capacity was looked on unfavorably. As a result, division managers added capacity very cautiously, achieving high plant-utilization ratios at the expense of lost sales (which did not show up in the measurement system).
- In another company, top management stressed the need for new product and market development; yet the middle managers were measured on the basis of short-term profitability. With R&D and marketing expenses reducing short-term profitability, pressures to achieve the latter created an obvious reluctance to incur the former.

Translating action into measurement involves the same skills as translating goals into action. One language is operational and involves a variety of dimensions, whereas the other is abstract and is often in terms of a single dimension. The required ability is to relate these two different languages. And when measurement and goals are contradictory, middle managers must be able to tread a thin line between the two, sometimes making trade-offs.

Furthermore, they must cope with an additional problem: the language of corporate measurement is sometimes inadequate for measuring and guiding the activities of subordinates. While top management typically measures middle managers on the basis of profit and loss, the middle manager has to evaluate subordinates using different quantitative measures (like costs, production and sales volume, number of rejects) as well as qualitative judgments (like adequacy of the plant layout, effectiveness of the R&D effort, comprehensiveness of the marketing activities). These measures not only are different in kind and more numerous but also require greater expertise and more intimate knowledge of specifics.

RESPONSIBILITY AND AUTHORITY

The middle manager typically assumes full responsibility for his or her other units and is evaluated on the results of the total operation. There is no way to shift the blame as might be done in a functionally organized setup, where marketing could claim that production did not deliver on time or production could point the finger at marketing for not bringing in enough orders.

Like the chief executive, middle managers have to account for the performance of others. Unlike the chief executive, however, they have only limited authority in the pursuit of their goals. They often need cooperation from equals, say, in a centralized research and development department; and they receive solicited, or unsolicited, guidance from superiors. Thus responsibility and authority do not overlap. The former exceeds the latter.

While textbooks state categorically that such an imbalance is wrong and that responsibility should be backed up with the necessary authority, the responsibility-authority discrepancy is an inevitable fact of life where divisionalization penetrates the organization. To function effectively in this imperfect world, middle managers must meet two requirements:

1. In spite of the limited authority, they must be willing to accept full responsibility and take action accordingly. At the same time, they should recognize that they cannot do everything themselves, that they must cooperate and coordinate with others. The ability to manage multiple relationships is critical here.
2. While they always have the opportunity to appeal to superiors when cooperation from equals is not forthcoming, they should rely on this route only as a last resort or when the issue is clear-cut—preventive settlements, even if they involve compromises, may be preferable. By going to court, they are asking people higher up to stick their necks out. The fact that these people have attained higher positions probably means that they are good at *not* sticking their necks out and are unlikely to be receptive unless middle managers pick their fights wisely, carefully, and infrequently.

Inevitable Politics Discrepancies between responsibility and authority, coupled with all of the previously discussed factors—multiple relationships, the playing-coach role, translation from goals to action and back to results—necessarily result in a structure that requires managers to coexist in a political atmosphere. There are different interests and interest groups, conflicting goals and ambitions, and positions of power and weakness.

Moreover, this coexistence is not necessarily peaceful. Career objectives and prestige, as well as positions of influence, are at stake, and the general manager in the middle is an easy and accessible target—malcontent soldiers do not pick on the general directly; they go for the general's officers.

The position of the middle manager is further exposed by a measurement system requiring direct and frequent responses. To meet their goals, they need cooperation and assistance and are therefore vulnerable to sabotage. In a political sense, they are up for reelection continuously. Thus they must possess political sensitivity as well as the constitution to stomach pressures and conflicts. They have to be aware of the configuration of the power structure and the direction of political winds. Unfortunately, in this potentially volatile atmosphere, managers often fail to ask an obvious but key question: "Who are my friends and who are my enemies?"

A MAJOR TRANSITION

The middle manager's job is usually an individual's first try at general management. Typically, he or she has been selected on the basis of outstanding achievement as a functional specialist; hence, previous experience is not transferable to this new terrain. The new position represents a major transition. Fred Borch, General Electric's chairman of the board and chief executive officer, considers the step from functional to general management to be the greatest challenge of a manager's entire career.

Indeed, the skills and activities that lead to success in a manager's functional career—whether marketing, manufacturing, engineering, R&D, control, or finance—are usually those of specialization, of deep involvement in a narrow area. The specialist knows more and more about less and less.

In the medical and legal professions, specialization is the usual route to excellence and eminence. The manager, too, during the early phases of his or her career, follows this pattern, establishing a track record by excelling in a particular specialty. But unlike the doctor and the lawyer, the career progression pattern is brutally shifted.

Having earned the proper stripes as a specialist, the manager is given a new and drastically different challenge, that of excelling as a generalist. Instead of knowing more and more about less and less, the manager now shifts to knowing less and less about more and more.

This transition, in turn, represents a big risk. Previously, each step up the functional specialization ladder led to familiar challenges that required proven skills. Now the challenges are new and the skills unproven. Not all managers will be able to make this transition; not all will possess the required general management skills; and in spite of earlier successes, not all will successfully meet the new challenge.

Overcoming Resentment In making their major and risky transition, middle managers, as noted earlier, do not always face a friendly working environment; rather, they may find that their promotions have caused resentment. Some who were not promoted may consider themselves better qualified because of age or seniority; they may view the new middle managers' capabilities and backgrounds as insufficient for the job. Others may resent the promoted individuals because they represent an "educated elite."

Yet new middle managers need the support of those very people who may resent their appointments. Their cooperation is essential and they will face constant obstacles until they have it. In overcoming this possible handicap of resentment, administrative skills and experience are of utmost importance. Unfortunately, however, these skills are typically the new middle manager's short suit; he or she is more often long on technical abilities and experience, which are obviously less relevant to the task.

Acclimating to New Terrain Since promotions do not always occur within the same department, the middle manager often comes from another segment of the organization. As a newcomer, he or she will probably be unfamiliar with the unit's history, opportunities, and problems. And obtaining facts or information to accurately diagnose the situation will not be easy, for the following reasons:

- While superiors have assessed the unit's performance in terms of its abstract results, the middle manager has to evaluate performance in terms of concrete action. The latter is much harder to determine than the former.
- The middle manager will have to become acquainted with not only the "formal" organization of the unit but its "informal" structure as well. While the formal structure can be found in manuals and organization charts, the informal one has to be discovered through daily activities and interpersonal relationships.
- Politics may color the facts given. Certain information may be deliberately withheld, while other aspects may be overemphasized.

In summary, the newcomer's fact-finding mission is difficult and hazardous, and he or she will be required to sift through information that is often contradictory, tough to evaluate, and not always obvious.

Furthermore, he or she will be dealing with a new set of people and thus will have to establish new relationships. This is a particularly difficult challenge to the manager who not only is undertaking his or her first general management job but also is possibly resented as a newcomer. Since relationships cannot be ordered from above, the middle manager will have to earn his or her own way and will have to gain the confidence and respect of counterparts not by virtue of the uniform worn, but instead by the quality of daily activities.

Without essential facts and established relationships, it is difficult for middle managers to get off to a fast start. Yet they often walk into situations that require quick and decisive action. In this event, they will have to walk a tightrope between (1) an early commitment based on inadequate facts and nonexisting relationships and (2) indecision while they establish facts and relationships.

The first course of action is often preferred, since it establishes a manager's authority and image. He or she may also be responding to pressures that are pushing in this direction. The risks, however, are great. Before proceeding on such a path, it is worthwhile to pause and consider the long-run implications of action that precede the establishment of facts and relationships. What, for example, are the chances of making major mistakes? While it is often argued that the wrong action is preferable to no action at all, it is important for the middle manager to get off to a good start, not just a fast one. Things that start badly usually get worse.

Experimental Leadership In making their transition, middle managers often function as agents of change. They may have received their assignments from top management in order to bring about changes in their new units, or ambition may push them to develop new approaches. This implies experimentation and a process of learning through trial and error. Experimentation, however, means vulnerability. The middle manager's unit, for instance, may have been chosen as the experimental laboratory for the entire organization; and, since an experiment is easier to defeat than a long-established policy, the forces of resistance mentioned earlier may be encouraged to mount opposition, or even sabotage. Where the agent of change is an inexperienced newcomer, it is particularly easy to shift blame to the newcomer's shoulders.

Experimental leadership rarely permits one to move ahead at great speed in a single direction. It involves slow testing and occasional backtracking that may be viewed by subordinates as indecision and defeat. Thus they may interpret experimental leadership as lack of leadership, withholding their support and blaming their leader for inexperience or ignorance.

Under this handicap, success may be difficult to achieve. Top executives, in such circumstances, may not always come to the rescue. They may be watching rather than supporting the experiment. This is their privilege. From their vantage point, why should they stake their reputations, possibly their careers, on the uncertain outcome of an experiment?

Thus it is unrealistic to expect rescue from above. More important, to judge the soundness and results of an experimental change, whether initiated from above or by the middle manager, an objective or neutral superior is needed. He or she can also act as a mutually acceptable arbiter where conflicts arise, as in situations of limited authority.

The middle manager may be better served in the long run by having such a neutral arbiter above, rather than a prejudiced ally. In the former instance, cooperation and support can be obtained through candid and open negotiation; the availability of an objective judge encourages reasonable attitudes from all parties concerned.

In the latter instance, resistance from others is likely to go "underground," which obviously makes the task of obtaining cooperation and support more difficult. A case from one large company illustrates this point:

One of the divisions had to rely heavily on a centralized R&D department for its custom-made product innovations. Conflicts arose between the market-oriented division and the technology-oriented R&D department, so the division manager took his case to superiors. A new, marketing-oriented group vice president overwhelmingly ruled in favor of the division. Subsequently, the R&D department's contributions declined because of alleged "technical difficulties" and "conflicting demands from other divisions."

CHALLENGE AND OPPORTUNITY

This description of the middle-management position portrays it as a great challenge, as indeed it is. Why would anyone want to accept such an ill-defined, open-ended, risky assignment? Yet, as I pointed out earlier, with risk comes opportunity; and with open-endedness comes a job of considerably broader scope than the formal job description indicates.

Why is it not possible, then, to design this job by including all the positive elements and eliminating all the drawbacks? The answer is that the drawbacks are inherent in a divisional organizational structure—they can be excluded only by eliminating the structure itself.

A divisional structure, however, is essential to the conduct of large-scale operations for a diverse range of products in a variety of countries. It also permits a large number of managers to assume general management responsibilities early in their careers, sometimes in their early or middle thirties after less than 10 years of business experience. In contrast, the functional organization usually offers an individual a general management position only during his or her middle fifties, after some 25 to 30 years of business experience.

The choice, then, is between having a broad opportunity to assume an imperfect general management job at an early age and having a very limited opportunity to hold a "perfect" general management job late in one's career. To put it in the context of Churchill's famous statement: early in a person's career, the middle-management job is the worst assignment except for all the others. Moreover, the advantages and opportunities are many, both for the company and for the aspiring executive:

- The chance to run one's own show at a young age, rather than having to wait for a quarter of a century, should increase the probability of advancement, as well as make a business career more exciting.
- The shift from specialist to generalist early in one's career is less perilous, and failure is less painful, than if the shift occurs later. If a manager has spent some 25 years as a specialist, he or she is apt to be firmly set in his or her ways and will find it difficult to make a major change. A younger manager, on the other hand, should still be flexible and able to adapt more easily to a different set of job requirements. Failure is also easier to take—and to overcome—early in one's career than it is later on. (Putting a 25-year track record on the line is a big risk and one that might well destroy a person's entire career.)
- The early shift from specialist to generalist is also less risky from the company's viewpoint. When a manager who has been a specialist for a quarter of a century is selected for the president's job, the total conduct of the company is entrusted to someone with no record in general management. It is not at all certain that a successful engineering, marketing, manufacturing, or finance vice president will turn into a first-rate general manager. In the divisional organization, however, the middle manager typically manages one of several profit centers. Thus risk is greatly reduced by entrusting to an unproven general manager only a small segment of the total enterprise.
- A large number of general management slots in an organization enables a corporation to attract and retain many capable managers and avoids an elimination contest for a company's single general management position. This large reservoir of general managers can be transferred and promoted as new opportunities arise. Since the scarcest resource of a company is usually competent management, overcoming this hurdle may eventually constitute a real competitive advantage.

- The middle-management phenomenon is conducive to management development and training. A manager can start in a small profit center, establish a track record there, transfer to a larger unit, and so on. Thus both the breadth and the challenge of the general management job can be increased as he or she moves up in the ranks. Confidence and versatility will also be enhanced, fostering personal career development as well as strengthening corporate competence.
- Middle managers are close to the action. Leadership and coordination, therefore, take place on the battlefield rather than from distant headquarters. Decisions are made more quickly by better informed people who can more closely monitor an action's impact and ensure its proper implementation.

There are some important implications that can be drawn from the characteristics of the middle-level general management job; and they affect not only the person who holds it but also his or her superiors.

One common pitfall is that superiors tend to judge middle managers in terms of their own jobs. They believe that middle managers have the same opportunities, prerogatives, and power that they do and therefore should shoulder similar responsibility. This belief is frequently shared by the middle managers themselves.

As I have attempted to show, however, the middle manager's job is quite different from that of the top-level general manager. The job itself is demanding enough. It should not be made more difficult by an incorrect understanding of its scope and characteristics.

Top management often fails to recognize that imperfection is a fact of life in the middle-management job. Furthermore, formal job descriptions frequently reflect sacred dogmas like overlapping authority and responsibility. Such ostrichlike attitudes create unrealistic expectations among all parties involved. Unrealistic expectations inevitably produce disenchantments and failures. Reality, even though it may not correspond to the demands of theoretical elegance, must be faced. If reality imposes imperfection, as it does, then imperfection must be recognized and accepted, rather than swept under the rug.

Need for Ratification Given the job's characteristics, middle managers can govern effectively only with the consent of those being governed. While they are formally promoted or demoted by superiors, the jury usually consists of their subordinates and peers. By giving or withholding support, that jury greatly influences the middle manager's career.

This need for ratification is easily overlooked or underestimated by middle managers. They may approach the job with supreme confidence in their abilities, viewing the new appointment as evidence of their importance and talents. Where change is required, they may see themselves as the new leaders destined to bring order out of chaos and turn failure into success.

At the same time, they may see subordinates as old-timers who have failed in the past to meet the challenge. Hence they may doubt subordinates' abilities and downgrade their importance. Middle managers who approach their jobs by overestimating their own importance and underestimating that of their subordinates are erecting self-imposed barriers to ratification. They are creating the conditions for a self-fulfilling prophecy—with themselves as the ultimate victims.

Accommodation and Compromise Another important implication for middle managers is the necessity of finding their way in a maze of accommodation and compromise. They cannot always make quick decisions, take a straightforward course of action, or follow completely rational and logical solutions. They must bring what they judge as necessary within the realm of what is possible.

Often it is difficult to adjust to such a complex challenge. While they may have made their mark as technical experts whose previous successes were based on purely rational solutions to technical problems, optimization may not be the most successful approach in their new roles. Rarely do perfect solutions exist for middle managers. There are *viable* solutions, however, and they require constant accommodation and compromise.

Job Strategy Given the difficulty and challenge of general management at middle organizational levels, the job should be approached as explicitly as possible. Middle managers must attempt to define the following:

- The scope of their multiple relationships within the organizational structure as well as the specific people to whom they must relate;
- The "playing coach" role;
- The "bilingual" task of translating goals to action and action to measurement;
- The implications of having full responsibility while holding limited authority;
- The "political" environment in which they have to survive from a position of limited power and great vulnerability.

Just as companies formulate corporate strategy by matching their resources to their environment, so can middle managers formulate their job strategies—they can identify their total organizational environment and match these with their strengths and weaknesses as well as their personal values.

Looking at their jobs in strategic terms should help them face varied daily challenges, overcome frustrations, and develop consistent patterns of behavior. Obviously, a job strategy should not be a ceremonial proclamation but, instead, a plan of action that middle managers carry with them to guide them in their daily actions.

A managerial record, like a judicial one, is established through the cumulative impact of a series of decisions, many of which set precedents. If these decisions can be related not only to the specific demands of each separate issue but also to an overall philosophy and master plan, their internal consistency and cumulative impact will establish a strong and cohesive organizational fabric. This is the landmark of an effective and successful manager.

DISCUSSION QUESTIONS

1. Middle managers must act as both superior and subordinate. In which role are you most comfortable, and why?
2. What attributes does a middle manager need in order to translate superiors' abstract goals into concrete action?
3. Discuss the political sensitivities that a general manager in the middle must cultivate. Explain how these sensitivities would help her or him to do the job.
4. If you begin your business career as a functional specialist, what strategies will you use to acquire the administrative experience necessary for general management?
5. Do you think the author has overstated or understated the risks and pitfalls of middle management?

PART TWO

MAKING STRATEGY

How Competitive Forces Shape Strategy

6

MICHAEL E. PORTER

To plan effective strategies, general managers must understand their company's strengths and weaknesses, the nature of their industry, and their competitors' characteristics. In this reading, Michael Porter provides general managers with a framework for positioning a company and for capitalizing on industry changes by detailing the five forces that govern competition in an industry: the threat of new entrants, the bargaining power of customers, the bargaining power of suppliers, the threat of substitute products or services, and jockeying among current contestants. Understanding how these forces work in an industry and how they affect the company's particular situation enables general managers to stake out a position in their industry that is less vulnerable to attack.

The essence of strategy formulation is coping with competition. Yet it is easy to view competition too narrowly and too pessimistically. While one sometimes hears executives complaining to the contrary, intense competition in an industry is neither coincidence nor bad luck.

Moreover, in the fight for market share, competition is not manifested only in the other players. Rather, competition in an industry is rooted in its underlying economics, and competitive forces exist that go well beyond the established combatants in a particular industry. Customers, suppliers, potential entrants, and substitute products are all competitors that may be more or less prominent or active depending on the industry.

The state of competition in an industry depends on five basic forces, which are diagrammed in the *Exhibit*. The collective strength of these forces determines the ultimate profit potential of an industry. It ranges from intense in industries like tires, metal cans, and steel, where no company earns spectacular returns on investment, to mild in industries like oil field services and equipment, soft drinks, and toiletries, where there is room for quite high returns.

In the economists' "perfectly competitive" industry, jockeying for position is unbridled and entry to the industry very easy. This kind of industry structure, of course, offers the worst prospect for long-run profitability. The weaker the forces collectively, however, the greater the opportunity for superior performance.

Whatever their collective strength, the corporate strategist's goal is to find a position in the industry from which his or her company can best defend

EXHIBIT
Forces Governing Competition in an Industry

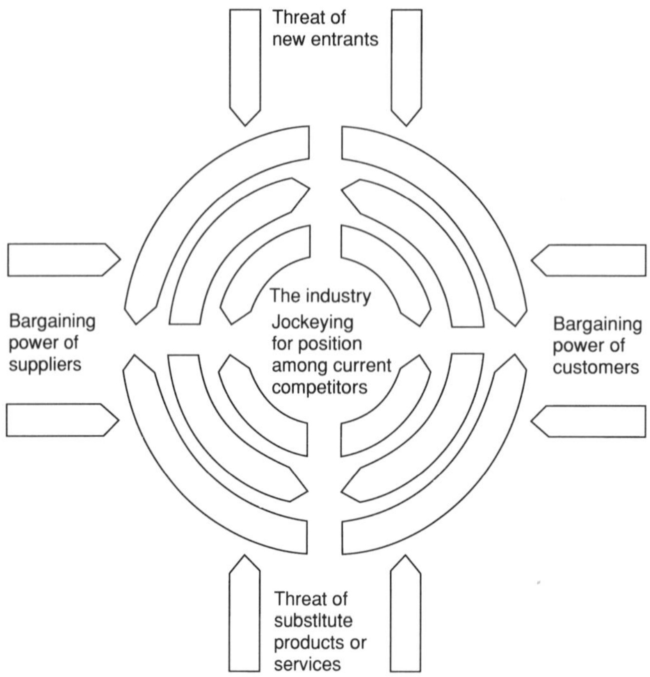

itself against these forces or can influence them in its favor. The collective strength of the forces may be painfully apparent to all the antagonists; but to cope with them, the strategist must delve below the surface and analyze the sources of each. For example, what makes the industry vulnerable to entry? What determines the bargaining power of suppliers?

Knowledge of these underlying sources of competitive pressure provides the groundwork for a strategic agenda of action. They highlight the critical strengths and weaknesses of the company, animate the position of the company in its industry, clarify the areas where strategic changes may yield the greatest payoff, and highlight the places where industry trends promise to hold the greatest significance as either opportunities or threats. Understanding these sources also proves to be of help in considering areas for diversification.

CONTENDING FORCES

The strongest competitive forces determine the profitability of an industry and so are of greatest importance in strategy formulation. For example, even a company with a strong position in an industry unthreatened by potential entrants will earn low returns if it faces a superior or a lower-cost substitute product—as the leading manufacturers of vacuum tubes and coffee percolators have learned to their sorrow. In such a situation, coping with the substitute product becomes the number one strategic priority.

Different forces take on prominence, of course, in shaping competition in each industry. In the ocean-going tanker industry the key force is probably the buyers (the major oil companies), while in tires it is powerful OEM buyers coupled with tough competitors. In the steel industry the key forces are foreign competitors and substitute materials.

Every industry has an underlying structure, or a set of fundamental economic and technical characteristics, that gives rise to these competitive forces. The strategist, wanting to position his or her company to cope best with its industry environment or to influence that environment in the company's favor, must learn what makes the environment tick.

This view of competition pertains equally to industries dealing in services and to those selling products. To avoid monotony in this article, I refer to both products and services as "products." The same general principles apply to all types of business.

A few characteristics are critical to the strength of each competitive force. I shall discuss them in this section.

THREAT OF ENTRY

New entrants to an industry bring new capacity, the desire to gain market share, and often substantial resources. Companies diversifying through acquisition into the industry from other markets often leverage their resources to cause a shake-up, as Philip Morris did with Miller beer.

The seriousness of the threat of entry depends on the barriers present and on the reaction from existing competitors that entrants can expect. If barriers to entry are high and newcomers can expect sharp retaliation from the entrenched competitors, obviously the newcomers will not pose a serious threat of entering.

There are six major sources of barriers to entry:

1. ***Economies of scale.*** These economies deter entry by forcing the aspirant either to come in on a large scale or to accept a cost disadvantage. Scale economies in production, research, marketing, and service are probably the key barriers to entry in the mainframe computer industry, as Xerox and GE sadly discovered. Economies of scale can also act as hurdles in distribution, utilization of the sales force, financing, and nearly any other part of a business.
2. ***Product differentiation.*** Brand identification creates a barrier by forcing entrants to spend heavily to overcome customer loyalty. Advertising, customer service, being first in the industry, and product differences are among the factors fostering brand identification. It is perhaps the most important entry barrier in soft drinks, over-the-counter drugs, cosmetics, investment banking, and public

accounting. To create high fences around their businesses, brewers couple brand identification with economies of scale in production, distribution, and marketing.

3. ***Capital requirements.*** The need to invest large financial resources in order to compete creates a barrier to entry, particularly if the capital is required for unrecoverable expenditures in up-front advertising or R&D. Capital is necessary not only for fixed facilities but also for customer credit, inventories, and absorbing start-up losses. While major corporations have the financial resources to invade almost any industry, the huge capital requirements in certain fields, such as computer manufacturing and mineral extraction, limit the pool of likely entrants.
4. ***Cost disadvantages independent of size.*** Entrenched companies may have cost advantages not available to potential rivals, no matter what their size and attainable economies of scale. These advantages can stem from the effects of the learning curve (and of its first cousin, the experience curve), proprietary technology, access to the best raw materials sources, assets purchased at preinflation prices, government subsidies, or favorable locations. Sometimes cost advantages are legally enforceable, as they are through patents.
5. ***Access to distribution channels.*** The newcomer on the block must, of course, secure distribution of its product or service. A new food product, for example, must displace others from the supermarket shelf via price breaks, promotions, intense selling efforts, or some other means. The more limited the wholesale or retail channels are and the more that existing competitors have these tied up, obviously the tougher that entry into the industry will be. Sometimes this barrier is so high that, to surmount it, a new contestant must create its own distribution channels, as Timex did in the watch industry in the 1950s.
6. ***Government policy.*** The government can limit or even foreclose entry to industries with such controls as license requirements and limits on access to raw materials. Regulated industries like trucking, liquor retailing, and freight forwarding are noticeable examples; more subtle government restrictions operate in fields like ski-area development and coal mining. The government also can play a major indirect role by affecting entry barriers through controls such as air and water pollution standards and safety regulations.

The potential rival's expectations about the reaction of existing competitors also will influence its decision on whether to enter. The company is likely to have second thoughts if incumbents have previously lashed out at new entrants or if:

- The incumbents possess substantial resources to fight back, including excess cash and unused borrowing power, productive capacity, or clout with distribution channels and customers.

- The incumbents seem likely to cut prices because of a desire to keep market shares or because of industrywide excess capacity.
- Industry growth is slow, affecting its ability to absorb the new arrival and probably causing the financial performance of all the parties involved to decline.

Changing Conditions From a strategic standpoint there are two important additional points to note about the threat of entry.

First, it changes, of course, as these conditions change. The expiration of Polaroid's basic patents on instant photography, for instance, greatly reduced the absolute cost entry barrier built by its proprietary technology. It is not surprising that Kodak plunged into the market. Product differentiation in printing has all but disappeared. Conversely, in the auto industry, economies of scale increased enormously with post-World War II automation and vertical integration—virtually stopping successful new entry.

Second, strategic decisions involving a large segment of an industry can have a major impact on the conditions determining the threat of entry. For example, the actions of many U.S. wine producers in the 1960s to step up product introductions, raise advertising levels, and expand distribution nationally surely strengthened the entry roadblocks by raising economies of scale and making access to distribution channels more difficult. Similarly, decisions by members of the recreational vehicle industry to vertically integrate in order to lower costs greatly increased the economies of scale and raised the capital cost barriers.

POWERFUL SUPPLIERS AND BUYERS

Suppliers can exert bargaining power on participants in an industry by raising prices or reducing the quality of purchased goods and services. Powerful suppliers can thereby squeeze profitability out of an industry unable to recover cost increases in its own prices. Customers likewise can force down prices, demand higher quality or more service, and play competitors off against each other—all at the expense of industry profits.

The power of each important supplier or buyer group depends on a number of characteristics of its market situation and on the relative importance of its sales or purchases to the industry compared with its overall business.

A *supplier* group is powerful if:

- It is dominated by a few companies and is more concentrated than the industry it sells to.
- Its product is unique or at least differentiated, or if it has built up switching costs. Switching costs are fixed costs buyers face in changing suppliers. These arise because, among other things, a buyer's product specifications tie it to particular suppliers, it has invested heavily in specialized ancillary equipment or in learning how to operate a supplier's equipment (as in computer software),

or its production lines are connected to the supplier's manufacturing facilities (as in some manufacture of beverage containers).
- It is not obliged to contend with other products for sale to the industry. For instance, the competition between the steel companies and the aluminum companies to sell to the can industry checks the power of each supplier.
- It poses a credible threat of integrating forward into the industry's business. This provides a check against the industry's ability to improve the terms on which it purchases.
- The industry is not an important customer of the supplier group. If the industry is an important customer, suppliers' fortunes will be closely tied to the industry, and they will want to protect the industry through reasonable pricing and assistance in activities like R&D and lobbying.

A *buyer* group is powerful if:

- It is concentrated or it purchases in large volumes. Large-volume buyers are particularly potent forces if heavy fixed costs characterize the industry—as they do in metal containers, corn refining, and bulk chemicals, for example—which raise the stakes to keep capacity filled.
- The products it purchases from the industry are standard or undifferentiated. The buyers, sure that they can always find alternative suppliers, may play one company against another, as they do in aluminum extrusion.
- The products it purchases from the industry form a component of its product and represent a significant fraction of its costs. The buyers are likely to shop for a favorable price and purchase selectively. Where the product sold by the industry in question is a small fraction of buyers' costs, buyers are usually much less price-sensitive.
- The industry's product is unimportant to the quality of the buyers' products or services. Where the quality of the buyers' products is very much affected by the industry's product, buyers are generally less price-sensitive. Industries in which this situation obtains include oil field equipment, where a malfunction can lead to large losses, and enclosures for electronic medical and test instruments, where the quality of the enclosure can influence the user's impression about the quality of the equipment inside.
- The industry's product does not save the buyer money. Where the industry's product or service can pay for itself many times over, the buyer is rarely price-sensitive; rather, he is interested in quality. This is true in services like investment banking and public accounting, where errors in judgment can be costly and embarrassing, and in businesses like the logging of oil wells, where an accurate survey can save thousands of dollars in drilling costs.
- The buyers pose a credible threat of integrating backward to make the industry's product. The Big Three auto producers and major buyers of cars have often used the threat of self-manufacture as a bargaining lever. But sometimes an industry engenders a threat to buyers that its members may integrate forward.

Most of these sources of buyer power can be attributed to consumers as a group as well as to industrial and commercial buyers; only a modification of the frame of reference is necessary. Consumers tend to be more price-sensitive if they are purchasing products that are undifferentiated, expensive relative to their incomes, and of a sort where quality is not particularly important.

The buying power of retailers is determined by the same rules, with one important addition. Retailers can gain significant bargaining power over manufacturers when they can influence consumers' purchasing decisions, as they do in audio components, jewelry, appliances, sporting goods, and other goods.

Strategic Action A company's choice of suppliers to buy from or buyer groups to sell to should be viewed as a crucial strategic decision. A company can improve its strategic posture by finding suppliers or buyers who possess the least power to influence it adversely.

Most common is the situation of a company being able to choose whom it will sell to—in other words, buyer selection. Rarely do all the buyer groups a company sells to enjoy equal power. Even if a company sells to a single industry, segments usually exist within that industry that exercise less power (and that are therefore less price-sensitive) than others. For example, the replacement market for most products is less price-sensitive than the overall market.

As a rule, a company can sell to powerful buyers and still come away with above-average profitability only if it is a low-cost producer in its industry or if its product enjoys some unusual, if not unique, features.

If the company lacks a low cost position or a unique product, selling to everyone is self-defeating because the more sales it achieves, the more vulnerable it becomes. The company may have to muster the courage to turn away business and sell only to less potent customers. Of course, some industries do not enjoy the luxury of selecting "good" buyers.

As the factors creating supplier and buyer power change with time or as a result of the company's strategic decisions, naturally the power of these groups rises or declines. In the ready-to-wear clothing industry, as the buyers (department stores and clothing stores) have become more concentrated and control has passed to large chains, the industry has come under increasing pressure and suffered falling margins. The industry has been unable to differentiate its product or engender switching costs that lock in its buyers enough to neutralize these trends.

SUBSTITUTE PRODUCTS

By placing a ceiling on prices it can charge, substitute products or services limit the potential of an industry. Unless it can upgrade the quality of the product or differentiate it somehow (as via marketing), the industry will suffer in earnings and possibly in growth.

Manifestly, the more attractive the price-performance trade-off offered by substitute products, the firmer the lid placed on the industry's profit potential. Sugar producers confronted with the large-scale commercialization of high-fructose corn syrup, a sugar substitute, learned this lesson. Substitutes not only limit profits in normal times; they also reduce the bonanza an industry can reap in boom times.

Substitute products that deserve the most attention strategically are those that (a) are subject to trends improving their price-performance trade-off with the industry's product, or (b) are produced by industries earning high profits. Substitutes often come rapidly into play if some development increases competition in their industries and causes price reduction or performance improvement.

JOCKEYING FOR POSITION

Rivalry among existing competitors takes the familiar form of jockeying for position—using tactics like price competition, product introduction, and advertising slugfests. Intense rivalry is related to the presence of a number of factors:

- Competitors are numerous or roughly equal in size and power. Foreign contenders, of course, have become part of the competitive picture in many U.S. industries.
- Industry growth is slow, precipitating fights for market share that involve expansion-minded members.
- The product or service lacks differentiation or switching costs, which lock in buyers and protect one combatant from raids on its customers by another.
- Fixed costs are high or the product is perishable, creating strong temptation to cut prices. Many basic materials businesses, like paper and aluminum, suffer from this problem when demand slackens.
- Capacity is normally augmented in large increments. Such additions, as in the chlorine and vinyl chloride businesses, disrupt the industry's supply-demand balance and often lead to periods of over-capacity and price cutting.
- Exit barriers are high. Exit barriers, like very specialized assets or management's loyalty to a particular businesses, keep companies competing even though they may be earning low or even negative returns on investment. Excess capacity remains functioning, and the profitability of the healthy competitors suffers as the sick ones hang on.[1] If the entire industry suffers from overcapacity, it may seek government help—particularly if foreign competition is present.
- The rivals are diverse in strategies, origins, and "personalities." They have different ideas about how to compete and continually run head-on into each other in the process.

---

1. For a more complete discussion of exit barriers and their implications for strategy, see my article, "Please Note Location of Nearest Exit," *California Management Review*, Winter 1976, p. 21.

As an industry matures, its growth rate changes, resulting in declining profits and (often) a shakeout. In the booming recreational vehicle industry of the early 1970s, nearly every producer did well; but slow growth since then has eliminated the high returns, except for the strongest members, not to mention many of the weaker companies. The same profit story has been played out in industry after industry—snowmobiles, aerosol packaging, and sports equipment are just a few examples.

An acquisition can introduce a very different personality to an industry, as has been the case with Black & Decker's takeover of McCullough, the producer of chain saws. Technological innovation can boost the level of fixed costs in the production process, as it did in the shift from batch to continuous-line photo finishing in the 1960s.

While a company must live with many of these factors—because they are built into industry economics—it may have some latitude for improving matters through strategic shifts. For example, it may try to raise buyers' switching costs or increase product differentiation. A focus on selling efforts in the fastest-growing segments of the industry or on market areas with the lowest fixed costs can reduce the impact of industry rivalry. If it is feasible, a company can try to avoid confrontation with competitors having high exit barriers and can thus sidestep involvement in bitter price cutting.

FORMULATION OF STRATEGY

Once having assessed the forces affecting competition in an industry and their underlying causes, the corporate strategist can identify the company's strengths and weaknesses. The crucial strengths and weaknesses from a strategic standpoint are the company's posture vis-à-vis the underlying causes of each force. Where does it stand against substitutes? Against the sources of entry barriers?

Then the strategist can devise a plan of action that may include (1) positioning the company so that its capabilities provide the best defense against the competitive force; and/or (2) influencing the balance of the forces through strategic moves, thereby improving the company's position; and/or (3) anticipating shifts in the factors underlying the forces and responding to them, with the hope of exploiting change by choosing a strategy appropriate for the new competitive balance before opponents recognize it. I shall consider each strategic approach in turn.

POSITIONING THE COMPANY

The first approach takes the structure of the industry as given and matches the company's strengths and weaknesses to it. Strategy can be viewed as building defenses against the competitive forces or as finding positions in the industry where the forces are weakest.

Knowledge of the company's capabilities and of the causes of the competitive forces will highlight the areas where the company should confront competition and where avoid it. If the company is a low-cost producer, it may choose to confront powerful buyers while it takes care to sell them only products not vulnerable to competition from substitutes.

The success of Dr Pepper in the soft drink industry illustrated the coupling of realistic knowledge of corporate strengths with sound industry analysis to yield a superior strategy. Coca-Cola and Pepsi-Cola dominate Dr Pepper's industry, where many small concentrate producers compete for a piece of the action. Dr Pepper chose a strategy of avoiding the largest-selling drink segment, maintaining a narrow flavor line, forgoing the development of a captive bottler network, and marketing heavily. The company positioned itself so as to be the least vulnerable to its competitive forces while it exploited its small size.

In the $11.5 billion soft drink industry, barriers to entry in the form of brand identification, large-scale marketing, and access to a bottler network are enormous. Rather than accept the formidable costs and scale economies in having its own bottler network—that is, following the lead of the Big Two and of Seven-Up—Dr Pepper took advantage of the different flavor of its drink to "piggyback" on Coke and Pepsi bottlers who wanted a full line to sell to customers. Dr Pepper coped with the power of these buyers through extraordinary service and other efforts to distinguish its treatment of them from that of Coke and Pepsi.

Many small companies in the soft drink business offer cola drinks that thrust them into head-to-head competition against the majors. Dr Pepper, however, maximized product differentiation by maintaining a narrow line of beverages built around an unusual flavor.

Finally, Dr Pepper met Coke and Pepsi with an advertising onslaught emphasizing the alleged uniqueness of its single flavor. This campaign built strong brand identification and great customer loyalty. Helping its efforts was the fact that Dr Pepper's formula involved lower raw-materials cost, which gave the company an absolute cost advantage over its major competitors.

There are no economies of scale in soft drink concentrate production, so Dr Pepper could prosper despite its small share of the business (6%). Thus Dr Pepper confronted competition in marketing but avoided it in product line and in distribution. This artful positioning combined with good implementation has led to an enviable record in earnings and in the stock market.

INFLUENCING THE BALANCE

When dealing with the forces that drive industry competition, a company can devise a strategy that takes the offensive. This posture is designed to do more than merely cope with the forces themselves; it is meant to alter their causes.

Innovations in marketing can raise brand identification or otherwise differentiate the product. Capital investments in large-scale facilities or vertical integration affect entry barriers. The balance of forces is partly a result of external factors and partly in the company's control.

EXPLOITING INDUSTRY CHANGE

Industry evolution is important strategically because evolution, of course, brings with it changes in the sources of competition I have identified. In the familiar product life-cycle pattern, for example, growth rates change, product differentiation is said to decline as the business becomes more mature, and the companies tend to integrate vertically.

These trends are not so important in themselves; what is critical is whether they affect the sources of competition. Obviously, the trends carrying the highest priority from a strategic standpoint are those that affect the most important sources of competition in the industry and those that elevate new causes to the forefront.

The framework for analyzing competition that I have described can also be used to predict the eventual profitability of an industry. In long-range planning the task is to examine each competitive force, forecast the magnitude of each underlying cause, and then construct a composite picture of the likely profit potential of the industry.

The outcome of such an exercise may differ a great deal from the existing industry structure. Today, for example, the solar heating business is populated by dozens and perhaps hundreds of companies, none with a major market position. Entry is easy, and competitors are battling to establish solar heating as a superior substitute for conventional methods.

The potential of this industry will depend largely on the shape of future barriers to entry, the improvement of the industry's position relative to substitutes, the ultimate intensity of competition, and the power captured by buyers and suppliers. These characteristics will in turn be influenced by such factors as the establishment of brand identities, significant economies of scale or experience curves in equipment manufacture wrought by technological change, the ultimate capital costs to compete, and the extent of overhead in production facilities.

The framework for analyzing industry competition has direct benefits in setting diversification strategy. It provides a road map for answering the extremely difficult question inherent in diversification decisions: "What is the potential of this business?" Combining the framework with judgment in its application, a company may be able to spot an industry with a good future before this good future is reflected in the prices of acquisition candidates.

MULTIFACETED RIVALRY

Corporate managers have directed a great deal of attention to defining their businesses as a crucial step in strategy formulation, to avoid the myopia of narrow, product-oriented industry definition. Numerous authorities have stressed the need to look beyond product to function in defining a business, beyond national boundaries to potential international competition, and beyond the ranks of one's competitors today to those that may become competitors tomorrow. As a result of these urgings, the proper definition of a company's industry or industries has become an endlessly debated subject.

One motive behind this debate is the desire to exploit new markets. Another, perhaps more important motive is the fear of overlooking latent sources of competition that someday may threaten the industry. Many managers concentrate so single-mindedly on their direct antagonists in the fight for market share that they fail to realize that they are also competing with their customers and their suppliers for bargaining power. Meanwhile, they also neglect to keep a wary eye out for new entrants to the contest or fail to recognize the subtle threat of substitute products.

The key to growth—even survival—is to stake out a position that is less vulnerable to attack from head-to-head opponents, whether established or new, and less vulnerable to erosion from the direction of buyers, suppliers, and substitute goods. Establishing such a position can take many forms—solidifying relationships with favorable customers, differentiating the product either substantively or psychologically through marketing, integrating forward or backward, establishing technological leadership.

DISCUSSION QUESTIONS

1. How do managers actually analyze the nature and scope of the competitive forces in an industry? What resources and methods should be used to perform such an analysis?
2. How often should a general manager assess her company's position in its industry and the competitive forces in that industry? Every 2–3 years? Annually? Monthly? Explain the reasons for the interval you've chosen.
3. Are there disadvantages to constantly repositioning your company and responding to shifts in industry forces? Should a company set a strategic course and follow it through thoroughly in order to better gain long-term results?
4. Choose a firm with which you are familiar, identify the significant industry forces, and describe the company's response to them.
5. Can you identify other forces that govern competition in an industry besides the ones that Porter describes?

From Competitive Advantage to Corporate Strategy

7

MICHAEL E. PORTER

General managers at the head of diversified firms face the challenge of planning corporate strategy. Corporate strategy concerns decisions about what businesses the corporation should be in and how it should manage its business units. In this reading, Michael Porter describes some common diversification mistakes, based on his study of 33 large U.S. corporations. He identifies four concepts of corporate strategy—portfolio management, restructuring, transferring skills, and sharing activities—that can guide a firm's diversification efforts. Familiarity with these concepts will help general managers craft a coherent corporate strategy.

Corporate strategy, the overall plan for a diversified company, is both the darling and the stepchild of contemporary management practice—the darling because CEOs have been obsessed with diversification since the early 1960s, the stepchild because almost no consensus exists about what corporate strategy is, much less about how a company should formulate it.

A diversified company has two levels of strategy: business unit (or competitive) strategy and corporate (or companywide) strategy. Competitive strategy concerns how to create competitive advantage in each of the businesses in which a company competes. Corporate strategy concerns two different questions: what businesses the corporation should be in and how the corporate office should manage the array of business units.

Corporate strategy is what makes the corporate whole add up to more than the sum of its business unit parts. The track record of corporate strategies has been dismal. I studied the diversification records of 33 large, prestigious U.S. companies between 1950 and 1986 and found that most of them had divested many more acquisitions than they had kept. The corporate strategies of most companies have dissipated instead of created shareholder value.

The need to rethink corporate strategy could hardly be more urgent. By taking over companies and breaking them up, corporate raiders thrive on failed corporate strategy. Fueled by junk bond financing and growing acceptability, raiders can expose any company to takeover, no matter how large or blue chip.

Recognizing past diversification mistakes, some companies have initiated large-scale restructuring programs. Others have done nothing at all. Whatever the response, the strategic questions persist. Those who have restructured must decide what to do next to avoid repeating the past; those who have done nothing must awake to their vulnerability. To survive, companies must understand what good corporate strategy is.

A SOBER PICTURE

While there is disquiet about the success of corporate strategies, none of the available evidence satisfactorily indicates the success or failure of corporate strategy. Most studies have approached the question by measuring the stock market valuation of mergers, captured in the movement of the stock prices of acquiring companies immediately before and after mergers are announced. These studies show that the market values mergers as neutral or slightly negative, hardly cause for serious concern.[1] Yet the short-term market reaction is a highly imperfect measure of the long-term success of diversification, and no self-respecting executive would judge a corporate strategy this way.

Studying the diversification programs of a company over a long period of time is a much more telling way to determine whether a corporate strategy has succeeded or failed. Each company entered an average of 80 new industries and 27 new fields. Just over 70% of the new entries were acquisitions, 22% were start-ups, and 8% were joint ventures. IBM, Exxon, Du Pont, and 3M, for example, focused on start-ups, while ALCO Standard, Beatrice, and Sara Lee diversified almost solely through acquisitions (see *Exhibit 1*).

The data paint a sobering picture of the success ratio of these moves (see *Exhibit 2*). I found that on average corporations divested more than half their acquisitions in new industries and more than 60% of their acquisitions in entirely new fields. Fourteen companies left more than 70% of all the acquisitions they had made in new fields. The track record in unrelated acquisitions is even worse—the average divestment rate is a startling 74% (see *Exhibit 3*). Even a highly respected company like General Electric divested a very high percentage of its acquisitions, particularly those in new fields. Companies near the top of the list in *Exhibit 2* achieved a remarkably low rate of divestment. Some bear witness to the success of well-thought-out corporate strategies. Others, however, enjoy a lower rate simply because they have not faced up to their problem units and divested them.

I calculated total shareholder returns (stock price appreciation plus dividends) over the period of the study for each company so that I could compare them with its divestment rate. While companies near the top of the list have above-average shareholder returns, returns are not a reliable measure of diversification success. Shareholder return often depends heavily on the inherent attractiveness of companies' base industries. Companies like CBS and General Mills had extremely profitable base businesses that subsidized poor diversification track records.

---

1. The studies also show that sellers of companies capture a large fraction of the gains from merger. *See* Michael C. Jensen and Richard S. Ruback, "The Market for Corporate Control: The Scientific Evidence," *Journal of Financial Economics* (April 1983): 5, and Michael C. Jensen, "Takeovers: Folklore and Science," *Harvard Business Review* (November–December 1984): 109.

However, linking shareholder value quantitatively to diversification performance only works if you compare the shareholder value that is with the shareholder value that might have been without diversification. Because such a comparison is virtually impossible to make, measuring diversification success by the number of units retained by the company seems as good an indicator as any of the contribution of diversification to corporate performance.

The data give a stark indication of the failure of corporate strategies.[2] Of the 33 companies, 6 had been taken over as my study was being completed (see the note on *Exhibit 2*). Only the lawyers, investment bankers, and original sellers have prospered in most of these acquisitions, not the shareholders.

PREMISES OF CORPORATE STRATEGY

Any successful corporate strategy builds on a number of premises. These are facts of life about diversification. They cannot be altered, and when ignored, they explain in part why so many corporate strategies fail.

Competition Occurs at the Business Unit Level Diversified companies do not compete; only their business units do. Unless a corporate strategy places primary attention on nurturing the success of each unit, the strategy will fail, no matter how elegantly constructed. Successful corporate strategy must grow out of and reinforce competitive strategy.

Diversification Inevitably Adds Costs and Constraints to Business Units Obvious costs such as the corporate overhead allocated to a unit may not be as important or subtle as the hidden costs and constraints. A business unit must explain its decisions to top management, spend time complying with planning and other corporate systems, live with parent company guidelines and personnel policies, and forgo the opportunity to motivate employees with direct equity ownership. These costs and constraints can be reduced but not entirely eliminated.

Shareholders Can Readily Diversify Themselves Shareholders can diversify their own portfolios of stocks by selecting those that best match their preferences and risk profiles.[3] Shareholders can often diversify more cheaply than a

2. Some recent evidence also supports the conclusion that acquired companies often suffer eroding performance after acquisition. See Frederick M. Scherer, "Mergers, Sell-Offs and Managerial Behavior," in *The Economics of Strategic Planning*, ed. Lacy Glenn Thomas (Lexington, Mass.: Lexington Books, 1986), p. 143, and David A. Ravenscraft and Frederick M. Scherer, "Mergers and Managerial Performance," paper presented at the Conference on Takeovers and Contests for Corporate Control, Columbia Law School, 1985.

3. This observation has been made by a number of authors. *See*, for example, Malcolm S. Salter and Wolf A. Weinhold, *Diversification Through Acquisition* (New York: Free Press, 1979).

EXHIBIT 1
Diversification Profiles of 33 Leading U.S. Companies, 1950–1986

Company	*Number Total Entries*	*All Entries into New Industries*	*Percent Acquisitions*	*Percent Joint Ventures*	*Percent Start-ups*	*Entries into New Industries That Represented Entirely New Fields*	*Percent Acquisitions*	*Percent Joint Ventures*	*Percent Start-ups*
ALCO Standard	221	165	99%	0%	1%	56	100%	0%	0%
Allied Corp.	77	49	67	10	22	17	65	6	29
Beatrice	382	204	97	1	2	61	97	0	3
Borden	170	96	77	4	19	32	75	3	22
CBS	148	81	67	16	17	28	65	21	14
Continental Group	75	47	77	6	17	19	79	11	11
Cummins Engine	30	24	54	17	29	13	46	23	31
Du Pont	80	39	33	16	51	19	37	0	63
Exxon	79	56	34	5	61	17	29	6	65
General Electric	160	108	47	20	33	29	48	14	38
General Foods	92	53	91	4	6	22	86	5	9
General Mills	110	102	84	7	9	27	74	7	19
W. R. Grace	275	202	83	7	10	66	74	5	21
Gulf & Western	178	140	91	4	6	48	88	2	10
IBM	46	38	18	18	63	16	19	0	81
IC Industries	67	41	85	3	12	17	88	6	6
ITT	246	178	89	2	9	50	92	0	8
Johnson & Johnson	88	77	77	0	23	18	56	0	44
Mobil	41	32	53	16	31	15	60	7	33
Procter & Gamble	28	23	61	0	39	14	79	0	21
Raytheon	70	58	86	9	5	16	81	19	6

EXHIBIT 1
Diversification Profiles of 33 Leading U.S. Companies, 1950–1986 (Continued)

Company	*Number Total Entries*	*All Entries into New Industries*	*Percent Acquisitions*	*Percent Joint Ventures*	*Percent Start-ups*	*Entries into New Industries That Represented Entirely New Fields*	*Percent Acquisitions*	*Percent Joint Ventures*	*Percent Start-ups*
RCA	53	46	35	15	50	19	37	21	42
Rockwell	101	75	73	24	3	27	74	22	4
Sara Lee	197	141	96	1	4	41	95	2	2
Scovill	52	36	97	0	3	12	92	0	8
Signal	53	45	67	4	29	20	75	0	25
Tenneco	85	62	81	6	13	26	73	8	19
3M	144	125	54	2	45	34	71	3	56
TRW	119	82	77	10	13	28	64	11	25
United Technologies	62	49	57	18	24	17	23	17	39
Westinghouse	129	73	63	11	26	36	61	3	36
Wickes	71	47	83	0	17	22	68	0	32
Xerox	59	50	66	6	28	18	50	11	39
Total	3,788	2,644				906			
Average	114.8	80.1	70.3%	7.9%	21.8%	27.4	67.9%	7.0%	25.9%

Notes: Beatrice, Continental Group, General Foods, RCA, Scovill, and Signal were taken over as the study was being completed. Their data cover the period up through takeover but not subsequent divestments.

The percentage averages may not add up to 100% because of rounding off.

corporation because they can buy shares at the market price and avoid hefty acquisition premiums.

These premises mean that corporate strategy cannot succeed unless it truly adds value—to business units by providing tangible benefits that offset the inherent costs of lost independence and to shareholders by diversifying in a way they could not replicate.

PASSING THE ESSENTIAL TESTS

To understand how to formulate corporate strategy, it is necessary to specify the conditions under which diversification will truly create shareholder value. These conditions can be summarized in three essential tests:

1. ***The attractiveness test.*** The industries chosen for diversification must be structurally attractive or capable of being made attractive.
2. ***The cost-of-entry test.*** The cost of entry must not capitalize all the future profits.
3. ***The better-off test.*** Either the new unit must gain competitive advantage from its link with the corporation or vice versa.

Of course, most companies will make certain that their proposed strategies pass some of these tests. But my study clearly shows that when companies ignored one or two of them, the strategic results were disastrous.

HOW ATTRACTIVE IS THE INDUSTRY?

In the long run, the rate of return available from competing in an industry is a function of its underlying structure, which I have described in another HBR article.[4] An attractive industry with a high average return on investment will be difficult to enter because entry barriers are high, suppliers and buyers have only modest bargaining power, substitute products or services are few, and the rivalry among competitors is stable. An unattractive industry like steel will have structural flaws, including a plethora of substitute materials, powerful and price-sensitive buyers, and excessive rivalry caused by high fixed costs and a large group of competitors, many of whom are state supported.

Diversification cannot create shareholder value unless new industries have favorable structures that support returns exceeding the cost of capital. If the industry doesn't have such returns, the company must be able to restructure the industry or gain a sustainable competitive advantage that leads to returns well above the industry average. An industry need not be attractive before diversifica-

4. *See* Michael E. Porter, "How Competitive Forces Shape Strategy," *Harvard Business Review* (March–April 1979): 86.

tion. In fact, a company might benefit from entering before the industry shows its full potential. The diversification can then transform the industry's structure.

In the course of my research, I often found companies had suspended the attractiveness test because they had a vague belief that the industry "fit" very closely with their own businesses. In the hope that the corporate "comfort" they felt would lead to a happy outcome, the companies ignored fundamentally poor industry structures. Unless the close fit allows substantial competitive advantage, however, such comfort will turn into pain when diversification results in poor returns. Royal Dutch Shell and other leading oil companies have had this unhappy experience in a number of chemicals businesses, where poor industry structures overcame the benefits of vertical integration and skills in process technology.

Another common reason for ignoring the attractiveness test is a low entry cost. Sometimes the buyer has an inside track or the owner is anxious to sell. Even if the price is actually low, however, a one-shot gain will not offset a perpetually poor business. Almost always, the company finds it must reinvest in the newly acquired unit, if only to replace fixed assets and fund working capital.

Diversifying companies are also prone to use rapid growth or other simple indicators as a proxy for a target industry's attractiveness. Many that rushed into fast-growing industries (personal computers, video games, and robotics, for example) were burned because they mistook early growth for long-term profit potential. Industries are profitable not because they are sexy or high tech; they are profitable only if their structures are attractive.

WHAT IS THE COST OF ENTRY?

Diversification cannot build shareholder value if the cost of entry into a new business eats up its expected returns. Strong market forces, however, are working to do just that. A company can enter new industries by acquisition or start-up. Acquisitions expose it to an increasingly efficient merger market. An acquirer beats the market if it pays a price not fully reflecting the prospects of the new unit. Yet multiple bidders are commonplace, information flows rapidly, and investment bankers and other intermediaries work aggressively to make the market as efficient as possible. In recent years, new financial instruments such as junk bonds have brought new buyers into the market and made even large companies vulnerable to takeover. Acquisition premiums are high and reflect the acquired company's future prospects—sometimes too well. Philip Morris paid more than four times book value for Seven-Up Company, for example. Simple arithmetic meant that profits had to more than quadruple to sustain the preacquisition ROI. Since there proved to be little Philip Morris could add in marketing prowess to the sophisticated marketing wars in the soft-drink industry, the result was the unsatisfactory financial performance of Seven-Up and ultimately the decision to divest.

In a start-up, the company must overcome entry barriers. It's a real catch-22 situation, however, since attractive industries are attractive because

EXHIBIT 2
Acquisition Track Records of Leading U.S. Diversifiers Ranked by Percent Divested, 1950–1986

Company	*All Acquisitions in New Industries*	*Percent Made by 1980 and Then Divested*	*Percent Made by 1975 and Then Divested*	*Acquisitions in New Industries That Represented New Fields*	*Percent Made by 1980 and Then Divested*	*Percent Made by 1975 and Then Divested*
Johnson & Johnson	59	17%	12%	10	33%	14%
Procter & Gamble	14	17	17	11	17	17
Raytheon	50	17	26	13	25	33
United Technologies	28	25	13	10	17	0
3M	67	26	27	24	42	45
TRW	63	27	31	18	40	38
IBM	7	33	0*	3	33	0*
Du Pont	13	38	43	7	60	75
Mobil	17	38	57	9	50	50
Borden	74	39	40	24	45	50
IC Industries	35	42	50	15	46	44
Tenneco	50	43	47	19	27	33
Beatrice	198	46	45	59	52	51
ITT	159	52	52	46	61	61
Rockwell	55	56	57	20	71	71
Allied Corp.	33	57	45	11	80	67
Exxon	19	62	20*	5	80	50*
Sara Lee	135	62	65	39	80	76
General Foods	48	63	62	19	93	93
Scovill	35	64	77	11	64	70
Signal	30	65	63	15	70	67
ALCO Standard	164	65	70	56	72	76

EXHIBIT 2
Acquisition Track Records of Leading U.S. Diversifiers Ranked by Percent Divested, 1950–1986 (Continued)

Company	*All Acquisitions in New Industries*	*Percent Made by 1980 and Then Divested*	*Percent Made by 1975 and Then Divested*	*Acquisitions in New Industries That Represented New Fields*	*Percent Made by 1980 and Then Divested*	*Percent Made by 1975 and Then Divested*
W. R. Grace	167	65	70	49	71	70
General Electric	51	65	78	14	100	100
Wickes	38	67	72	15	73	70
Westinghouse	46	68	69	22	61	59
Xerox	33	71	79	9	100	100
Continental Group	36	71	72	15	60	60
General Mills	86	75	73	20	65	60
Gulf & Western	127	79	78	42	75	72
Cummins Engine	13	80	80	6	83	83
RCA	16	80	92	7	86	100
CBS	54	87	89	18	88	88
Total	2,021			661		
Average per company†	61.2	53.4%	56.5%	20.0	61.2%	61.1%

* Companies with three or fewer acquisitions by the cutoff year.

† Companies with three or fewer acquisitions by the cutoff year are excluded from the average to minimize statistical distortions.

Note: Beatrice, Continental Group, General Foods, RCA, Scovill, and Signal were taken over as the study was being completed. Their data cover the period up through takeover but not subsequent divestments.

their entry barriers are high. Bearing the full cost of the entry barriers might well dissipate any potential profits. Otherwise, other entrants to the industry would have already eroded its profitability.

In the excitement of finding an appealing new business, companies sometimes forget to apply the cost-of-entry test. The more attractive a new industry, the more expensive it is to get into.

WILL THE BUSINESS BE BETTER OFF?

A corporation must bring some significant competitive advantage to the new unit, or the new unit must offer potential for significant advantage to the corporation. Sometimes, the benefits to the new unit accrue only once, near the time of entry, when the parent instigates a major overhaul of its strategy or installs a first-rate management team. Other diversification yields ongoing competitive advantage if the new unit can market its product through the well-developed distribution system of its sister units, for instance. This is one of the important underpinnings of the merger of Baxter Travenol and American Hospital Supply.

When the benefit to the new unit comes only once, the parent company has no rationale for holding the new unit in its portfolio over the long term. Once the results of the one-time improvement are clear, the diversified company no longer adds value to offset the inevitable costs imposed on the unit. It is best to sell the unit and free up corporate resources.

The better-off test does not imply that diversifying corporate risk creates shareholder value in and of itself. Doing something for shareholders that they can do themselves is not a basis for corporate strategy. (Only in the case of a privately held company, in which the company's and the shareholder's risk are the same, is diversification to reduce risk valuable for its own sake.) Diversification of risk should only be a by-product of corporate strategy, not a prime motivator.

Executives ignore the better-off test most of all or deal with it through arm waving or trumped-up logic rather than hard strategic analysis. One reason is that they confuse company size with shareholder value. In the drive to run a bigger company, they lose sight of their real job. They may justify the suspension of the better-off test by pointing to the way they manage diversity. By cutting corporate staff to the bone and giving business units nearly complete autonomy, they believe they avoid the pitfalls. Such thinking misses the whole point of diversification, which is to create shareholder value rather than to avoid destroying it.

CONCEPTS OF CORPORATE STRATEGY

The three tests for successful diversification set the standards that any corporate strategy must meet; meeting them is so difficult that most diversification fails. Many companies lack a clear concept of corporate strategy to guide their diversification or pursue a concept that does not address the tests. Others fail because they implement a strategy poorly.

My study has helped me identify four concepts of corporate strategy that have been put into practice—portfolio management, restructuring, transferring skills, and sharing activities. While the concepts are not always mutually exclusive, each rests on a different mechanism by which the corporation creates shareholder value and each requires the diversified company to manage and organize itself in a different way. The first two require no connections among business units; the second two depend on them. (See *Exhibit 4*.) While all four concepts of strategy have succeeded under the right circumstances, today some make more sense than others. Ignoring any of the concepts is perhaps the quickest road to failure.

PORTFOLIO MANAGEMENT

The concept of corporate strategy most in use is portfolio management, which is based primarily on diversification through acquisition. The corporation acquires sound, attractive companies with competent managers who agree to stay on. While acquired units do not have to be in the same industries as existing units, the best portfolio managers generally limit their range of businesses in some way, in part to limit the specific expertise needed by top management.

The acquired units are autonomous, and the teams that run them are compensated according to the unit results. The corporation supplies capital and works with each to infuse it with professional management techniques. At the same time, top management provides objective and dispassionate review of business unit results. Portfolio managers categorize units by potential and regularly transfer resources from units that generate cash to those with high potential and cash needs.

In a portfolio strategy, the corporation seeks to create shareholder value in a number of ways. It uses its expertise and analytical resources to spot attractive acquisition candidates that the individual shareholder could not. The company provides capital on favorable terms that reflect corporatewide fundraising ability. It introduces professional management skills and discipline. Finally, it provides high-quality review and coaching, unencumbered by conventional wisdom or emotional attachments to the business.

The logic of the portfolio management concept rests on a number of vital assumptions. If a company's diversification plan is to meet the attractiveness and cost-of-entry test, it must find good but undervalued companies. Acquired companies must be truly undervalued because the parent does little for the new unit once it is acquired. To meet the better-off test, the benefits the corporation provides must yield a significant competitive advantage to acquired units. The style of operating through highly autonomous business units must both develop sound business strategies and motivate managers.

In most countries, the days when portfolio management was a valid concept of corporate strategy are past. In the face of increasingly well-developed

EXHIBIT 3
Diversification Performance in Joint Ventures, Start-ups, and Unrelated Acquisitions, 1950–1986 (Companies in same order as in Exhibit 2)

Company	*Joint Ventures as a Percent of New Entries*	*Percent Made by 1980 and Then Divested*	*Percent Made by 1975 and Then Divested*	*Start-Ups as a Percent of New Entries*	*Percent Made by 1980 and Then Divested*	*Percent Made by 1975 and Then Divested*	*Acquisitions in Unrelated New Fields as a Percent of Total Acquisitions in New Fields*	*Percent Made by 1980 and Then Divested*	*Percent Made by 1975 and Then Divested*
Johnson & Johnson	0%	†	†	23%	14%	20%	0%	†	†
Procter & Gamble	0	†	†	39	0	0	9	†	†
Raytheon	9	60%	60%	5	50	50	46	40%	40%
United Technologies	18	50	50	24	11	20	40	0*	0*
3M	2	100*	100*	45	2	3	33	75	86
TRW	10	20	25	13	63	71	39	71	71
IBM	18	100*	†	63	20	22	33	100*	100*
Du Pont	16	100*	†	51	61	61	43	0*	0*
Mobil	16	33	33	31	50	56	67	60	100
Borden	4	33	33	19	17	13	21	80	80
IC Industries	3	100*	100*	13	80	30	33	50	50
Tenneco	6	67	67	13	67	80	42	33	40
Beatrice	1	†	†	2	0	0	63	59	53
ITT	2	0*	†	8	38	57	61	67	64
Rockwell	24	38	42	3	0	0	35	100	100
Allied Corp.	10	100	75	22	38	29	45	50	0
Exxon	5	0	0	61	27	19	100	80	50*
Sara Lee	1	†	†	4	75	100*	41	73	73
General Foods	4	†	†	6	67	50	42	86	83
Scovill	0	†	†	3	100	100*	45	80	100
Signal	4	†	†	29	20	11	67	50	50

EXHIBIT 3
Diversification Performance in Joint Ventures, Start-ups, and Unrelated Acquisitions, 1950–1986 (Continued)

Company	*Joint Ventures as a Percent of New Entries*	*Percent Made by 1980 and Then Divested*	*Percent Made by 1975 and Then Divested*	*Start-Ups as a Percent of New Entries*	*Percent Made by 1980 and Then Divested*	*Percent Made by 1975 and Then Divested*	*Acquisitions in Unrelated New Fields as a Percent of Total Acquisitions in New Fields*	*Percent Made by 1980 and Then Divested*	*Percent Made by 1975 and Then Divested*
ALCO Standard	0	†	†	1	†	†	63	79	81
W. R. Grace	7	33	38	10	71	71	39	65	65
General Electric	20	20	33	33	33	44	36	100	100
Wickes	0	†	†	17	63	57	60	80	75
Westinghouse	11	0*	0*	26	44	44	36	57	67
Xerox	6	100*	100*	28	50	56	22	100	100
Continental Group	6	67	67	17	14	0	40	83	100
General Mills	7	71	71	9	89	80	65	77	67
Gulf & Western	4	75	50	6	100	100	74	77	74
Cummins Engine	17	50	50	29	0	0	67	100	100
RCA	15	67	67	50	99	55	36	100	100
CBS	16	71	71	17	86	80	39	100	100
Average per company‡‡	7.9%	50.3%	48.9%	21.8%	44.0%	40.9%	46.1%	74.0%	74.4%

* Companies with two or fewer entries.

† No entries in this category.

‡‡ Average excludes companies with two or fewer entries to minimize statistical distortions.

Note: Beatrice, Continental Group, General Foods, RCA, Scovill, and Signal were taken over as the study was being completed. Their data cover the period up through takeover, but not subsequent divestments.

capital markets, attractive companies with good managements show up on everyone's computer screen and attract top dollar in terms of acquisition premium. Simply contributing capital isn't contributing much. A sound strategy can easily be funded; small to medium-size companies don't need a munificent parent.

Other benefits have also eroded. Large companies no longer corner the market for professional management skills; in fact, more and more observers believe managers cannot necessarily run anything in the absence of industry-specific knowledge and experience. Another supposed advantage of the portfolio management concept—dispassionate review—rests on similarly shaky ground since the added value of review alone is questionable in a portfolio of sound companies.

The benefit of giving business units complete autonomy is also questionable. Increasingly, a company's business units are interrelated, drawn together by new technology, broadening distribution channels, and changing regulations. Setting strategies of units independently may well undermine unit performance. The companies in my sample that have succeeded in diversification have recognized the value of interrelationships and understood that a strong sense of corporate identity is as important as slavish adherence to parochial business unit financial results.

But it is the sheer complexity of the management task that has ultimately defeated even the best portfolio managers. As the size of the company grows, portfolio managers need to find more and more deals just to maintain growth. Supervising dozens or even hundreds of disparate units and under chain-letter pressures to add more, management begins to make mistakes. At the same time, the inevitable costs of being part of a diversified company take their toll and unit performance slides while the whole company's ROI turns downward. Eventually, a new management team is installed that initiates wholesale divestments and pares down the company to its core businesses. The experiences of Gulf & Western, Consolidated Foods (now Sara Lee), and ITT are just a few comparatively recent examples. Reflecting these realities, the U.S. capital markets today reward companies that follow the portfolio management model with a "conglomerate discount"; they value the whole less than the sum of the parts.

In developing countries, where large companies are few, capital markets are undeveloped, and professional management is scarce, portfolio management still works. But it is no longer a valid model for corporate strategy in advanced economies. Nevertheless, the technique is in the limelight today in the United Kingdom, where it is supported so far by a newly energized stock market eager for excitement. But this enthusiasm will wane—as well it should. Portfolio management is no way to conduct corporate strategy.

RESTRUCTURING

Unlike its passive role as a portfolio manager, when it serves as banker and reviewer, a company that bases its strategy on restructuring becomes an active restructurer of business units. The new businesses are not necessarily related to existing units. All that is necessary is unrealized potential.

The restructuring strategy seeks out undeveloped, sick, or threatened organizations or industries on the threshold of significant change. The parent intervenes, frequently changing the unit management team, shifting strategy, or infusing the company with new technology. Then it may make follow-up acquisitions to build a critical mass and sell off unneeded or unconnected parts and thereby reduce the effective acquisition cost. The result is a strengthened company or a transformed industry. As a coda, the parent sells off the stronger unit once results are clear because the parent is no longer adding value and top management decides that its attention should be directed elsewhere.

When well implemented, the restructuring concept is sound, for it passes the three tests of successful diversification. The restructurer meets the cost-of-entry test through the types of company it acquires. It limits acquisition premiums by buying companies with problems and lackluster images or by buying into industries with as yet unforeseen potential. Intervention by the corporation clearly meets the better-off test. Provided that the target industries are structurally attractive, the restructuring model can create enormous shareholder value. Some restructuring companies are Loew's, BTR, and General Cinema. Ironically, many of today's restructurers are profiting from yesterday's portfolio management strategies.

To work, the restructuring strategy requires a corporate management team with the insight to spot undervalued companies or positions in industries ripe for transformation. The same insight is necessary to actually turn the units around even though they are in new and unfamiliar businesses.

These requirements expose the restructurer to considerable risk and usually limit the time in which the company can succeed at the strategy. The most skillful proponents understand this problem, recognize their mistakes, and move decisively to dispose of them. The best companies realize they are not just acquiring companies but restructuring an industry. Unless they can integrate the acquisitions to create a whole new strategic position, they are just portfolio managers in disguise. Another important difficulty surfaces if so many other companies join the action that they deplete the pool of suitable candidates and bid their prices up.

Perhaps the greatest pitfall, however, is that companies find it very hard to dispose of business units once they are restructured and performing well. Human nature fights economic rationale. Size supplants shareholder value as the corporate goal. The company does not sell a unit even though the company no longer adds value to the unit. While the transformed units would be better off in another company that had related businesses, the restructuring company instead retains them. Gradually, it becomes a portfolio manager. The parent company's ROI declines as the need for reinvestment in the units and normal business risks eventually offset restructuring's one-shot gain. The perceived need to keep growing intensifies the pace of acquisition; errors result and standards fall. The restructuring company turns into a conglomerate with returns that only equal the average of all industries at best.

EXHIBIT 4
Concepts of Corporate Strategy

	PORTFOLIO MANAGEMENT	*RESTRUCTURING*	*TRANSFERRING SKILLS*	*SHARING ACTIVITIES*
Strategic Prerequisites	Superior insight into identifying and acquiring undervalued companies Willingness to sell off losers quickly or to opportunistically divest good performers when buyers are willing to pay large premiums Broad guidelines for and constraints on the types of units in the portfolio so that senior maagement can play the review role effectively A private company or undeveloped capital markets Ability to shift away from portfolio management as the capital markets get more efficient or the company gets unwieldy	Superior insight into identifying restructuring opportunities Willingness and capability to intervene to transform acquired units Broad similarities among the units in the portfolio Willingness to cut losses by selling off units where restructuring proves unfeasible Willingness to sell units when restructuring is complete, the results are clear, and market conditions are favorable	Proprietary skills in activities important to competitive advantage in target industries Ability to accomplish the transfer of skills among units on an ongoing basis Acquisitions of beachhead positions in new industries as a base	Activities in existing units that can be shared with new business units to gain competitive advantage Benefits of sharing that outweigh the costs Both start-ups and acquisitions as entry vehicles Ability to overcome organizational resistance to business unit collaboration

EXHIBIT 4
Concepts of Corporate Strategy (Continued)

	PORTFOLIO MANAGEMENT	*RESTRUCTURING*	*TRANSFERRING SKILLS*	*SHARING ACTIVITIES*
Organizational Prerequisites	Autonomous business units A very small, low-cost, corporate staff Incentives based largely on business unit results	Autonomous business units A corporate organization with the talent and resources to oversee the turnarounds and strategic repositionings of acquired units Incentives based largely on acquired units' results	Largely autonomous but collaborative business units High-level corporate staff members who see their role primarily as integrators Cross-business-unit committees, task forces, and other forms to serve as focal points for capturing and transferring skills Objectives of line managers that include skills transfer Incentives based in part on corporate results	Strategic business units that are encouraged to share activities An active strategic planning role at group, sector, and corporate levels High-level corporate staff members who see their roles primarily as integrators Incentives based heavily on group and corporate results
Common Pitfalls	Pursuing portfolio management in countries with efficient capital marketing and a developed pool of professional management talent Ignoring the fact that industry structure is not attractive	Mistaking rapid growth or a "hot" industry as sufficient evidence of a restructuring opportunity Lacking the resolve or resources to take on troubled situations and to intervene in management Ignoring the fact that industry structure is not attractive Paying lip service to restructuring but actually practicing passive portfolio management	Mistaking similarity or comfort with new businesses as sufficient basis for diversification Providing no practical way for skills transfer to occur Ignoring the fact that industry structure is not attractive	Sharing for its own sake rather than because it leads to competitive advantage Assuming sharing will occur naturally without senior management playing an active role Ignoring the fact that industry structure is not attractive

TRANSFERRING SKILLS

The purpose of the first two concepts of corporate strategy is to create value through a company's relationship with each autonomous unit. The corporation's role is to be a selector, a banker, and an intervenor.

The last two concepts exploit the interrelationships between businesses. In articulating them, however, one comes face-to-face with the often ill-defined concept of synergy. If you believe the text of the countless corporate annual reports, just about anything is related to just about anything else! But imagined synergy is much more common than real synergy. GM's purchase of Hughes Aircraft simply because cars were going electronic and Hughes was an electronics concern demonstrates the folly of paper synergy. Such corporate relatedness is an ex post facto rationalization of a diversification undertaken for other reasons.

Even synergy that is clearly defined often fails to materialize. Instead of cooperating, business units often compete. A company that can define the synergies it is pursuing still faces significant organizational impediments in achieving them.

But the need to capture the benefits of relationships between businesses has never been more important. Technological and competitive developments already link many businesses and are creating new possibilities for competitive advantage. In such sectors as financial services, computing, office equipment, entertainment, and health care, interrelationships among previously distinct businesses are perhaps the central concern of strategy.

To understand the role of relatedness in corporate strategy, we must give new meaning to this ill-defined idea. The value chain is a good way to start.[5] Every business unit is a collection of discrete value activities ranging from sales to accounting that allow it to compete. It is at this level, not in the company as a whole, that the unit achieves competitive advantage. These activities may be grouped into nine categories. *Primary* activities create the product or service, deliver and market it, and provide after-sale support. The categories of primary activities include inbound logistics, operations, outbound logistics, marketing and sales, and service. *Support* activities provide the inputs and infrastructure that allow the primary activities to take place. They include company infrastructure, human resource management, technology development, and procurement.

The value chain defines the two types of interrelationships that may create synergy. The first is a company's ability to transfer skills or expertise among similar value chains. The second is the ability to share activities. Two business units, for example, can share the same sales force or logistics network.

The value chain helps expose the last two (and most important) concepts of corporate strategy. The transfer of skills among business units in the diversified company is the basis for one concept. While each business unit has a separate value chain, knowledge about how to perform activities is transferred

---

5. *See* Michael E. Porter, *Competitive Advantage* (New York: Free Press, 1985).

among the units. For example, a toiletries business unit, expert in the marketing of convenience products, transmits ideas on new positioning concepts, promotional techniques, and packaging possibilities to a newly acquired unit that sells cough syrup. Newly entered industries can benefit from the expertise of existing units and vice versa.

These opportunities arise when business units have similar buyers or channels, similar value activities like government relations or procurement, similarities in the broad configuration of the value chain (for example, managing a multisite service organization), or the same strategic concept (for example, low cost). Even though the units operate separately, such similarities allow the sharing of knowledge.

Of course, some similarities are common; one can imagine them at some level between almost any pair of businesses. Countless companies have fallen into the trap of diversifying too readily because of similarities; mere similarity is not enough.

Transferring skills leads to competitive advantage only if the similarities among businesses meet three conditions:

1. The activities involved in the businesses are similar enough that sharing expertise is meaningful. Broad similarities (marketing intensiveness, for example, or a common core process technology such as bending metal) are not a sufficient basis for diversification. The resulting ability to transfer skills is likely to have little impact on competitive advantage.
2. The transfer of skills involves activities important to competitive advantage. Transferring skills in peripheral activities such as government relations or real estate in consumer goods units may be beneficial but is not a basis for diversification.
3. The skills transferred represent a significant source of competitive advantage for the receiving unit. The expertise or skills to be transferred are both advanced and proprietary enough to be beyond the capabilities of competitors.

The transfer of skills is an active process that significantly changes the strategy or operations of the receiving unit. The prospect for change must be specific and identifiable. Almost guaranteeing that no shareholder value will be created, too many companies are satisfied with vague prospects or faint hopes that skills will transfer. The transfer of skills does not happen by accident or by osmosis. The company will have to reassign critical personnel, even on a permanent basis, and the participation and support of high-level management in skills transfer is essential. Many companies have been defeated at skills transfer because they have not provided their business units with any incentives to participate.

Transferring skills meets the tests of diversification if the company truly mobilizes proprietary expertise across units. This makes certain the company can offset the acquisition premium or lower the cost of overcoming entry barriers.

The industries the company chooses for diversification must pass the attractiveness test. Even a close fit that reflects opportunities to transfer skills may not overcome poor industry structure. Opportunities to transfer skills, however, may help the company transform the structures of newly entered industries and send them in favorable directions.

The transfer of skills can be one-time or ongoing. If the company exhausts opportunities to infuse new expertise into a unit after the initial postacquisition period, the unit should ultimately be sold. The corporation is no longer creating shareholder value. Few companies have grasped this point, however, and many gradually suffer mediocre returns. Yet a company diversified into well-chosen businesses can transfer skills eventually in many directions. If corporate management conceives of its role in this way and creates appropriate organizational mechanisms to facilitate cross-unit interchange, the opportunities to share expertise will be meaningful.

By using both acquisitions and internal development, companies can build a transfer-of-skills strategy. The presence of a strong base of skills sometimes creates the possibility for internal entry instead of the acquisition of a going concern. Successful diversifiers that employ the concept of skills transfer may, however, often acquire a company in the target industry as a beachhead and then build on it with their internal expertise. By doing so, they can reduce some of the risks of internal entry and speed up the process. Two companies that have diversified using the transfer-of-skills concept are 3M and Pepsico.

SHARING ACTIVITIES

The fourth concept of corporate strategy is based on sharing activities in the value chains among business units. Procter & Gamble, for example, employs a common physical distribution system and sales force in both paper towels and disposable diapers. McKesson, a leading distribution company, will handle such diverse lines as pharmaceuticals and liquor through superwarehouses.

The ability to share activities is a potent basis for corporate strategy because sharing often enhances competitive advantage by lowering cost or raising differentiation. But not all sharing leads to competitive advantage, and companies can encounter deep organizational resistance to even beneficial sharing possibilities. These hard truths have led many companies to reject synergy prematurely and retreat to the false simplicity of portfolio management.

A cost-benefit analysis of prospective sharing opportunities can determine whether synergy is possible. Sharing can lower costs if it achieves economies of scale, boosts the efficiency of utilization, or helps a company move more rapidly down the learning curve. The costs of General Electric's advertising, sales, and after-sales service activities in major appliances are low because they are spread over a wide range of appliance products. Sharing can also enhance the potential for differentiation. A shared order-processing system, for instance, may allow new features and services that a buyer will value. Sharing can also reduce the cost of differentiation. A shared service network, for example, may make more advanced, remote servicing technology economically feasible. Often, sharing will allow an activity to be wholly reconfigured in ways that can dramatically raise competitive advantage.

Sharing must involve activities that are significant to competitive advantage, not just any activity. P&G's distribution system is such an instance in the diaper and paper towel business, where products are bulky and costly to ship. Conversely, diversification based on the opportunities to share only corporate overhead is rarely, if ever, appropriate.

Sharing activities inevitably involves costs that the benefits must outweigh. One cost is the greater coordination required to manage a shared activity. More important is the need to compromise the design or performance of an activity so that it can be shared. A salesperson handling the products of two business units, for example, must operate in a way that is usually not what either unit would choose were it independent. And if compromise greatly erodes the unit's effectiveness, then sharing may reduce rather than enhance competitive advantage.

Many companies have only superficially identified their potential for sharing. Companies also merge activities without consideration of whether they are sensitive to economies of scale. When they are not, the coordination costs kill the benefits. Companies compound such errors by not identifying costs of sharing in advance, when steps can be taken to minimize them. Costs of compromise can frequently be mitigated by redesigning the activity for sharing. The shared salesperson, for example, can be provided with a remote computer terminal to boost productivity and provide more customer information. Jamming business units together without such thinking exacerbates the costs of sharing.

Despite such pitfalls, opportunities to gain advantage from sharing activities have proliferated because of momentous developments in technology, deregulation, and competition. The infusion of electronics and information systems into many industries creates new opportunities to link businesses. The corporate strategy of sharing can involve both acquisition and internal development. Internal development is often possible because the corporation can bring to bear clear resources in launching a new unit. Start-ups are less difficult to integrate than acquisitions. Companies using the shared-activities concept can also make acquisitions as beachhead landings into a new industry and then integrate the units through sharing with other units. Prime examples of companies that have diversified via using shared activities include P&G, Du Pont, and IBM. The fields into which each has diversified are a cluster of tightly related units. Marriott illustrates both successes and failures in sharing activities over time.

Following the shared-activities model requires an organizational context in which business unit collaboration is encouraged and reinforced. Highly autonomous business units are inimical to such collaboration. The company must put into place a variety of what I call horizontal mechanisms—a strong sense of corporate identity, a clear corporate mission statement that emphasizes the importance of integrating business unit strategies, an incentive system that rewards more than just business unit results, cross-business-unit task forces, and other methods of integrating.

A corporate strategy based on shared activities clearly meets the better-off test because business units gain ongoing tangible advantages from others within the corporation. It also meets the cost-of-entry test by reducing the expense of surmounting the barriers to internal entry. Other bids for acquisitions that do not share opportunities will have lower reservation prices. Even widespread opportunities for sharing activities do not allow a company to suspend the attractiveness test, however. Many diversifiers have made the critical mistake of equating the close fit of a target industry with attractive diversification. Target industries must pass the strict requirement test of having an attractive structure as well as a close fit in opportunities if diversification is to ultimately succeed.

CHOOSING A CORPORATE STRATEGY

Each concept of corporate strategy allows the diversified company to create shareholder value in a different way. Companies can succeed with any of the concepts if they clearly define the corporation's role and objectives, have the skills necessary for meeting the concept's prerequisites, organize themselves to manage diversity in a way that fits the strategy, and find themselves in an appropriate capital market environment. The caveat is that portfolio management is only sensible in limited circumstances.

A company's choice of corporate strategy is partly a legacy of its past. If its business units are in unattractive industries, the company must start from scratch. If the company has few truly proprietary skills or activities it can share in related diversification, then its initial diversification must rely on other concepts. Yet corporate strategy should not be a once-and-for-all choice but a vision that can evolve. A company should choose its long-term preferred concept and then proceed pragmatically toward it from its initial starting point.

Both the strategic logic and the experience of the companies studied over the last decade suggest that a company will create shareholder value through diversification to a greater and greater extent as its strategy moves from portfolio management toward sharing activities. Because they do not rely on superior insight or other questionable assumptions about the company's capabilities, sharing activities and transferring skills offer the best avenues for value creation.

Each concept of corporate strategy is not mutually exclusive of those that come before, a potent advantage of the third and fourth concepts. A company can employ a restructuring strategy at the same time it transfers skills or shares activities. A strategy based on shared activities becomes more powerful if business units can also exchange skills. As the Marriott case illustrates, a company can often pursue the two strategies together and even incorporate some of the principles of restructuring with them. When it chooses industries in which to transfer skills or share activities, the company can also investigate the possibility of transforming the industry structure. When a company bases its strategy on interrelationships, it has a broader basis on which to create shareholder value than if it rests its entire strategy on transforming companies in unfamiliar industries.

This study supports the soundness of basing a corporate strategy on the transfer of skills or shared activities. The data on the sample companies' diversification programs illustrate some important characteristics of successful diversifiers. They have made a disproportionately low percentage of unrelated acquisitions, unrelated being defined as having no clear opportunity to transfer skills or share important activities (see *Exhibit 3*). Even successful diversifiers such as 3M, IBM, and TRW have terrible records when they have strayed into unrelated acquisitions. Successful acquirers diversify into fields, each of which is related to many others. Procter & Gamble and IBM, for example, operate in 18 and 19 interrelated fields respectively and so enjoy numerous opportunities to transfer skills and share activities.

Companies with the best acquisition records tend to make heavier-than-average use of start-ups and joint ventures. Most companies shy away from modes of entry besides acquisition. *Exhibit 3* demonstrates that while joint ventures are about as risky as acquisitions, start-ups are not. Moreover, successful companies often have very good records with start-up units, as 3M, P&G, Johnson & Johnson, IBM, and United Technologies illustrate. When a company has the internal strength to start up a unit, it can be safer and less costly to launch a company than to rely solely on an acquisition and then have to deal with the problem of integration. Japanese diversification histories support the soundness of start-up as an entry alternative.

The data also illustrate that no concept of corporate strategy works when industry structure is poor or implementation is bad, no matter how related the industries are. Xerox acquired companies in related industries, but the businesses had poor structures and its skills were insufficient to provide enough competitive advantage to offset implementation problems.

AN ACTION PROGRAM

To translate the principles of corporate strategy into successful diversification, a company must first take an objective look at its existing businesses and the value added by the corporation. Only through such an assessment can an understanding of good corporate strategy grow. That understanding should guide future diversification as well as the development of skills and activities with which to select further new businesses. The following action program provides a concrete approach to conducting such a review. A company can choose a corporate strategy by:

1. ***Identifying the interrelationships among already existing business units.*** A company should begin to develop a corporate strategy by identifying all the opportunities it has to share activities or transfer skills in its existing portfolio of business units. The company will not only find ways to enhance the competitive

advantage of existing units but also come upon several possible diversification avenues. The lack of meaningful interrelationships in the portfolio is an equally important finding, suggesting the need to justify the value added by the corporation or, alternately, a fundamental restructuring.

2. ***Selecting the core businesses that will be the foundation of the corporate strategy.*** Successful diversification starts with an understanding of the core businesses that will serve as the basis for corporate strategy. Core businesses are those that are in an attractive industry, have the potential to achieve sustainable competitive advantage, have important interrelationships with other business units, and provide skills or activities that represent a base from which to diversify.

   The company must first make certain its core businesses are on sound footing by upgrading management, internationalizing strategy, or improving technology. The study shows that geographic extensions of existing units, whether by acquisition, joint venture, or start-up, had a substantially lower divestment rate than diversification.

   The company must then patiently dispose of the units that are not core businesses. Selling them will free resources that could be better deployed elsewhere. In some cases disposal implies immediate liquidation, while in others the company should dress up the units and wait for a propitious market or a particularly eager buyer.

3. ***Creating horizontal organizational mechanisms to facilitate interrelationships among the core businesses and lay the groundwork for future related diversification.*** Top management can facilitate interrelationships by emphasizing cross-unit collaboration, grouping units organizationally and modifying incentives, and taking steps to build a strong sense of corporate identity.

4. ***Pursuing diversification opportunities that allow shared activities.*** This concept of corporate strategy is the most compelling, provided a company's strategy passes all three tests. A company should inventory activities in existing business units that represent the strongest foundation for sharing, such as strong distribution channels or world-class technical facilities. These will in turn lead to potential new business areas. A company can use acquisitions as a beachhead or employ start-ups to exploit internal capabilities and minimize integrating problems.

5. ***Pursuing diversification through the transfer of skills if opportunities for sharing activities are limited or exhausted.*** Companies can pursue this strategy through acquisition, although they may be able to use start-ups if their existing units have important skills they can readily transfer.

   Such diversification is often riskier because of the tough conditions necessary for it to work. Given the uncertainties, a company should avoid diversifying on the basis of skills transfer alone. Rather it should also be viewed as a stepping-stone to subsequent diversification using shared activities. New industries should be chosen that will lead naturally to other businesses. The goal is to build a cluster of related and mutually reinforcing business units. The strategy's logic implies that the company should not set the rate of return standards for the initial foray into a new sector too high.

6. ***Pursuing a strategy of restructuring if this fits the skills of management or no good opportunities exist for forging corporate interrelationships.*** When a company uncovers undermanaged companies and can deploy adequate management talent and resources to the acquired units, then it can use a restructuring strategy. The more developed the capital markets and the more active the market for companies, the more restructuring will require a patient search for that special opportunity rather than a headlong race to acquire as many bad apples as possible. Restructuring can be a permanent strategy, as it is with Loew's, or a way to build a group of businesses that supports a shift to another corporate strategy.
7. ***Paying dividends so that the shareholders can be the portfolio managers.*** Paying dividends is better than destroying shareholder value through diversification based on shaky underpinnings. Tax considerations, which some companies cite to avoid dividends, are hardly legitimate reasons to diversify if a company cannot demonstrate the capacity to do it profitably.

CREATING A CORPORATE THEME

Defining a corporate theme is a good way to ensure that the corporation will create shareholder value. Having the right theme helps unite the efforts of business units and reinforces the ways they interrelate as well as guides the choice of new businesses to enter. NEC Corporation, with its "C&C" theme, provides a good example. NEC integrates its computer, semiconductor, telecommunications, and consumer electronics businesses by merging computers and communication.

It is all too easy to create a shallow corporate theme. CBS wanted to be an "entertainment company," for example, and built a group of businesses related to leisure time. It entered such industries as toys, crafts, musical instruments, sports teams, and hi-fi retailing. While this corporate theme sounded good, close listening revealed its hollow ring. None of these businesses had any significant opportunity to share activities or transfer skills among themselves or with CBS's traditional broadcasting and record businesses. They were all sold, often at significant losses, except for a few of CBS's publishing-related units. Saddled with the worst acquisition record in my study, CBS has eroded the shareholder value created through its strong performance in broadcasting and records.

Moving from competitive strategy to corporate strategy is the business equivalent of passing through the Bermuda Triangle. The failure of corporate strategy reflects the fact that most diversified companies have failed to think in terms of how they really add value. A corporate strategy that truly enhances the competitive advantage of each business unit is the best defense against the corporate raider. With a sharper focus on the tests of diversification and the explicit choice of a clear concept of corporate strategy, companies' diversification track records from now on can look a lot different.

DISCUSSION QUESTIONS

1. Choose a diversified firm with which you are familiar and identify the concepts of corporate strategy that it employs, as described in the reading.
2. Is diversification an ongoing process in the life of a corporation? Should potential candidates for acquisition continually be monitored?
3. How does a senior GM set corporate strategy?

8 Competing Through Manufacturing

STEVEN C. WHEELWRIGHT AND ROBERT H. HAYES

U.S. manufacturers have become increasingly aware of the central importance of superior production to competitive success. Boosting productivity, product quality, and new product innovation is at the top of many corporate agendas. In this reading, Wheelwright and Hayes provide general managers with a descriptive framework for understanding how their manufacturing organizations are contributing to overall strategic goals. Drawing on extensive field research, they describe four stages that, taken together, identify the different roles that manufacturing can play in a company's efforts to formulate and achieve its strategic objectives; they also make clear the key choices and challenges at each of these stages.

Manufacturing companies, particularly those in the United States, are today facing intensified competition. For many, it is a case of simple survival. What makes this challenge so difficult is that the "secret weapon" of their fiercest competitors is based not so much on better product design, marketing ingenuity, or financial strength as on something much harder to duplicate: superior overall manufacturing capability. For a long time, however, many of these companies have systematically neglected their manufacturing organizations. Now, as the cost of that neglect grows ever clearer, they are not finding it easy to rebuild their lost excellence in production.

In most of these companies, the bulk of their labor force and assets are tied to the manufacturing function. The attitudes, expectations, and traditions that have developed over time in and around that function will be difficult to change. Companies cannot atone for years of neglect simply by throwing large chunks of investment dollars at the problem. Indeed, it normally takes several years of disciplined effort to transform manufacturing weakness into strength. In fact, it can take several years for a company to break the habit of "working around" the limitations of a manufacturing operation and to look on it as a source of competitive advantage.

In practice, of course, the challenge for managers is far more complex than is suggested by the simple dichotomy between "weakness" and "strength." There is no single end that every manufacturing function must serve—and serve well. There are, instead, several generic kinds of roles that the function can play in a company and—as *Exhibit 1* suggests—these roles can be viewed as stages

EXHIBIT 1
Stages in Manufacturing's Strategic Role

STAGE 1	*Minimize Manufacturing's Negative Potential: "Internally Neutral"*	Outside experts are called in to make decisions about strategic manufacturing issues Internal, detailed management control systems are the primary means for monitoring manufacturing performance Manufacturing is kept flexible and reactive
STAGE 2	*Achieve Parity with Competitors: "Externally Neutral"*	"Industry practice" is followed The planning horizon for manufacturing investment decisions is extended to incorporate a single-business cycle Capital investment is the primary means for catching up with competition or achieving a competitive edge
STAGE 3	*Provide Credible Support to the Business Strategy: "Internally Supportive"*	Manufacturing investments are screened for consistency with the business strategy A manufacturing strategy is formulated and pursued Longer-term manufacturing developments and trends are addressed systematically
STAGE 4	*Pursue a Manufacturing-Base Competitive Advantage: "Externally Supportive"*	Efforts are made to anticipate the potential of new manufacturing practices and technologies Manufacturing is involved "up front" in major marketing and engineering decisions (and vice versa) Long-range programs are pursued in order to acquire capabilities in advance of needs.

of development along a continuum. At one extreme, production can offer little contribution to a company's market success; at the other, it provides a major source of competitive advantage.

Understanding the possibilities along this continuum can help managers identify both their company's current position and the transformations in attitude and approach that will be necessary if it is to advance to a higher stage of competitive effectiveness. Such understanding is also useful in judging how quickly a company may reasonably be expected to progress from stage to stage. It is useful, too, in pointing out the changes that must be made in other parts of the company in order to sustain each higher level of manufacturing's contribution.

STAGES OF MANUFACTURING EFFECTIVENESS

Before describing each of these generic roles (or stages) in detail and outlining the problems that can arise when trying to move from one to the next, we must say a few things about the kind of framework we are proposing. First, the stages are not mutually exclusive. Every manufacturing operation embodies a set of important choices about such factors as capacity, vertical integration, human resource policies, and the like. (See *Exhibit 2* for a listing of these.) A given operation may be—and often is—composed of factors that are themselves at different levels of development. What determines the overall level of the operation is where the balance among these factors falls—that is, where in the developmental scheme the operation's center of gravity rests.

Second, it is difficult, if not impossible, for a company to skip a stage. A new business can, of course, attempt to begin operations at any level it chooses, but a manufacturing function that is already up and running has far less freedom of choice. Attitudes and established modes of doing things are well entrenched, and it take a tremendous effort just to move things along from one level to the next. Hence, the organizational strain imposed by an effort to leap-frog a stage makes the probability of failure uncomfortably high. In addition, it is the mastery of activities at one stage that usually provides the underpinnings for a successful transition to the next.

It is possible, however, for a given operation to contain factors of the sort already mentioned that are well separated on the developmental continuum. But here, too, the forces of organizational gravity are remorselessly at work. Over time, the less advanced part of the operation will tend to draw the more advanced part back to its own level.

Third, although it is appealing in theory for companies to move as a single entity through these stages, the real work of development occurs at the business unit level. Certainly, it is nice to have backing from a central corporate office so that several business units can evolve together and help each other, but it is at the business unit, not corporate, level that the critical nuts-and-bolts coordination among factors and across functions takes place.

With these three points in mind, we now turn to a consideration of the stages themselves. We will give special attention to the shift from Stage 3 to Stage 4 because this transition is the most difficult of all and because reaching Stage 4 has the largest pay-off in terms of competitive success. In fact, Stage 4 operations characterize all companies that have achieved the status of world class manufacturers.

STAGE 1

This lowest stage represents an "internally neutral" orientation toward manufacturing: top managers regard the function as neutral—incapable of

EXHIBIT 2
Major Types of Manufacturing Choices

Capacity	Amount, timing, type
Facilities	Size, location, specialization
Equipment and Process Technologies	Scale, flexibility, interconnectedness
Vertical Integration	Direction, extent, balance
Vendors	Number, structure, relationship
New Products	Hand-off, start-up, modification
Human Resources	Selection and training, compensation, security
Quality	Definition, role, responsibility
Systems	Organization, schedules, control

influencing competitive success. Consequently, they seek only to minimize any negative impact it may have. They do not expect manufacturing (indeed, they tend to discourage it from trying) to make a positive contribution.

Stage 1 organizations typically view manufacturing capability as the direct result of a few structural decisions about capacity, facilities, technology, and vertical integration. Managers attach little or no strategic importance to such infrastructure issues as work force policies, planning and measurement systems, and incremental process improvements. When strategic issues involving manufacturing do arise, management usually calls in outside experts in the belief that their own production organization lacks the necessary expertise (a self-fulfilling prophecy).

When they need to change facilities, location, or process technology, their production managers run into top-level insistence to remain flexible and reactive so as not to get locked into the wrong decisions. Similarly, they are expected to source all manufacturing equipment from outside suppliers and to rely on these suppliers for most of their information about manufacturing technology and new technological developments.

On balance, Stage 1 organizations think of production as a low-tech operation that can be staffed with low-skilled workers and managers. They employ detailed measurements and controls of operating performance, oriented to near-term performance, to ensure that manufacturing does not get too far off-track before corrective action can be taken. The aim is not to maximize the function's competitive value but to guard against competitively damaging problems.

Not surprisingly, the top managers of such companies try to minimize their involvement with, and thus their perceived dependence on, manufacturing. They concern themselves primarily with major investment decisions, as viewed through the prism of their capital budgeting process. As a result, they tend to regard their company's production facilities and processes as the embodiment of a series of once-and-for-all decisions. They are uneasy with the notion that manufacturing is a *learning* process that can create and expand its own capabilities—and may therefore not be totally controllable. Hence, they will agree to add capacity only when the need becomes obvious and, when they do, prefer to build large general-purpose facilities employing known—that is, "safe"—technologies purchased from outside vendors. Eager to keep the manufacturing function as simple as possible, they feel justified in thinking that "anybody ought to be able to manage manufacturing," an attitude reflected in their assignment of people to that department.

This Stage 1 view occurs both in companies whose managers see the manufacturing process as simple and straightforward and in those whose managers do not think it likely to have much impact on overall competitive position. Many consumer products and service companies fall into this category. So, too, do a number of sophisticated high-technology companies, which regard *product* technology as the key to competitive success and *process* technology as, at best, neutral.

Experience shows, however, that the competitive difficulties encountered by many U.S. consumer electronics and electrical equipment manufacturers have their roots in the attitude that manufacturing's role is simply to assemble and test products built from purchased components. Even in these high-tech companies, the manufacturing operation can appear clumsy and unprepared when confronted with such straightforward tasks as providing adequate production capacity, helping suppliers solve problems, and keeping equipment and systems up-to-date. With a self-limiting view of what manufacturing can do, managers find it difficult to upgrade their labor-intensive, low-technology processes when products involving a new generation of technology appear. Nor can their unfocused, general-purpose facilities compete effectively with the highly focused, specialized plants of world-class competitors.

STAGE 2

The second stage in our progression also represents a form of manufacturing "neutrality," but Stage 2 companies seek a competitive or "external" neutrality (parity with major competitors) on the manufacturing dimension rather than the internal ("don't upset the apple cart") neutrality of Stage 1. Typified by—but not restricted to—companies in traditional, manufacturing-intensive industries like steel, autos, and heavy equipment, Stage 2 organizations seek competitive neutrality by:

- Following industry practice in matters regarding the work force (industrywide bargaining agreements with national unions, for example), equipment purchases, and the timing and scale of capacity additions.
- Avoiding, where possible, the introduction of major, discontinuous changes in product or process. In fact, such changes tend to come—if at all—from competitors well outside the mainstream of an industry.

- Treating capital investments in new equipment and facilities as the most effective means for gaining a temporary competitive advantage.
- Viewing economies of scale related to the production rate as the most important source of manufacturing efficiency.

As noted, this approach to manufacturing is quite common in America's smokestack industries, most of which have an oligopolistic market structure and a well-defined set of competitors who share a vested interest in maintaining the status quo. It is also common in many companies engaged in electronic instrument assembly and pharmaceutical production, which consider manufacturing to be largely standardized and unsophisticated and which assume product development people can be entrusted with designing process changes whenever they are needed. Like those in Stage 1, Stage 2 companies—when they make an improvement in their process technology—rely on sources outside of manufacturing; unlike companies in Stage 1, however, they often turn to their own (largely product-oriented) R&D labs as well as to outside suppliers.

Top managers of Stage 2 companies regard resource allocation decisions as the most effective means of addressing the major strategic issues in manufacturing. Offensive investments to gain competitive advantage are usually linked to new products; manufacturing investments (other than those for additional capacity to match increases in the demand for existing products) are primarily defensive and cost-cutting in nature. They are usually undertaken only when manufacturing's shortcomings have become obvious.

STAGE 3

Stage 3 organizations expect manufacturing actively to support and strengthen the company's competitive position. As noted in *Exhibit 1*, these organizations view manufacturing as "internally supportive" in that its contribution derives from and is dictated by overall business strategy. That contribution includes:

- Screening decisions to be sure that they are consistent with the organization's competitive strategy.
- Translating that strategy into terms meaningful to manufacturing personnel.
- Seeking consistency within manufacturing through a carefully thought-out sequence of investments and systems changes over time.
- Being on the lookout for longer term developments and trends that may have a significant effect on manufacturing's ability to respond to the needs of other parts of the organization.
- Formulating a manufacturing strategy, complete with plant charters and mission statements, to guide manufacturing activities over an extended period of time.

Companies often arrive at Stage 3 as a natural consequence of both their success in developing an effective business strategy, based on formal planning processes, and their wish to support that strategy in all functional areas. They want manufacturing to be creative and to take a long-term view in managing itself. When push comes to shove, however, the majority of them act as if such creativity is best expressed by making one or two bold moves—the introduction of robots, just-in-time, or CAD/CAM, for example—while they continue to run most of the function as a Stage 2 activity.

While Stage 2 companies at times also pursue advances in manufacturing practice, they tend to regard these in strictly defensive terms: as a means of keeping up with their industry. Stage 3 companies, however, view technological progress as a natural response to changes in business strategy and competitive position.

Another characteristic of Stage 3 organizations is that their manufacturing managers take a broad view of their role by seeking to understand their company's business strategy and the kind of competitive advantage it is pursuing. Some of these managers even follow career paths that lead to general management. Notwithstanding the potential for advancement or the greater equality of titles and pay across all functions in Stage 3 companies, manufacturing managers are expected only to support the company's business strategy, not to become actively involved in helping to formulate it.

STAGE 4

The fourth and most progressive stage of manufacturing development arises when competitive strategy rests to a significant degree on a company's manufacturing capability. By this we do not mean that manufacturing dictates strategy to the rest of the company but only that strategy derives from a coordinated effort among functional peers—manufacturing very much among them.

As noted in *Exhibit 1*, the role of manufacturing in Stage 4 companies is "externally supportive," in that it is expected to make an important contribution to the competitive success of the organization. The leading companies in process-intensive industries, for example, usually give manufacturing a Stage 4 role, for here the evolution of product and process technologies is so intertwined that a company virtually must be in Stage 4 to gain a sustainable product advantage.

What then is special about Stage 4 companies?

- They anticipate the potential of new manufacturing practices and technologies and seek to acquire expertise in them long before their implications are fully apparent.
- They give sufficient credibility and influence to manufacturing for it to extract the full potential from production-based opportunities.

- They place equal emphasis on structural (building and equipment) and infrastructural (management policies) activities as potential sources of continual improvement and competitive advantage.
- They develop long-range business plans in which manufacturing capabilities are expected to play a meaningful role in securing the company's strategic objectives. By treating the manufacturing function as a strategic resource—that is, as a source of strength by itself as well as a means for enhancing the contribution of other functions—they encourage the interactive development of business, manufacturing, and other functional strategies.

Stage 4 organizations are generally of two types. The first includes companies like Emerson Electric, Texas Instruments, Mars (candy), and Blue Bell, whose business strategies place primary emphasis on a manufacturing-based competitive advantage such as low cost. In fact, these companies sometimes regard their manufacturing functions as so important a source of competitive advantage that they relegate other functions to a secondary or derivative role—an action which can be just as dysfunctional as relegating manufacturing to a reactive role. The other type of Stage 4 company seeks a balance of excellence in all its functions and pursues "externally supportive" Stage 4 roles for each of its integrated functions. We describe in detail two such organizations in a later section of this article.

In both types of organization, manufacturing complements its traditional involvement in the capital budgeting process with a considerable amount of qualitative analysis to compensate for the blind spots and biases inherent in financial data. In addition, there are extensive formal and informal horizontal interactions between manufacturing and other functions that greatly facilitate such activities as product design, field service, and sales training. Manufacturing's direct participation in formulating overall business strategy further enhances this functional interaction. Finally, equally with the other functions, manufacturing is a valued source of general management talent for the entire organization.

MANAGING THE TRANSITION

Because the four stages just outlined fall along a continuum, they suggest the path that a company might follow as it seeks to enhance the contribution of its manufacturing function. They suggest, too, the speed with which a company might follow that path. The inertia of most large organizations—their entrenched attitudes and practices—favors a gradual, systematic, and cumulative movement from one developmental stage to the next, not an effort to skip a stage by throwing more resources at problems. Getting from here to there is not simply a question of applying endless resources. Indeed, managing the transition between stages represents a significant and often dramatic challenge for most organizations.

At the least, successfully negotiating such a transition requires leadership from within the manufacturing function. Managing change in an established

EXHIBIT 3
Alternative Views of Work Force Management

STAGES 1, 2, AND 3: TRADITIONAL, STATIC	*STAGE 4: BROAD POTENTIAL, DYNAMIC*
Command and control	Learning
Management of effort	Management of attention
Coordinating information	Problem-solving information
Direct (supervisory) control	Indirect (systems and values) control
Process stability / worker independence	Process evolution / worker dependence

Note: Courtesy of Professor Earl Sasser, Harvard Business School

operation is always difficult, but here that difficulty is compounded by the need to bring all manufacturing personnel to a new view of things long familiar. Consider, for example, the kinds of production choices mentioned in *Exhibit 2*.

As a company or business unit moves along the continuum, dealing with vendors or making facilities choices requires many changes: cost-minimization goals give way to a concern for enlisting vendors' critical capabilities, and planning for general-purpose facilities gives way to an appreciation of focused factories. Said another way, managing these transitions requires a special kind of leadership because the task at hand is to change how people think, not merely how they can be instructed to act.

Nowhere is this deep shift in viewpoint more important than in attitudes toward a company's human resources. As *Exhibit 3* suggests, Stages 1, 2, and 3 adhere fairly closely to the traditional "command and control" style of human resource management. Now, to be sure, moving from Stage 1 to Stage 2 and then on to Stage 3 requires an ever more polished execution of that style, with enhanced management development efforts and more thoughtful analysis of underlying commands. But there is no radical shift within these stages in the way managers think of the work force's contribution to overall competitive performance. In Stage 4, however, the dominant approach to the work force must be in terms of teamwork and problem solving, not command-and-control. In the earlier stages the key leadership task is the management of controlled effort, but getting to Stage 4—and prospering there—demands instead the management of creative experimentation and organizational learning.

WHY MOVE AT ALL?

Most young companies assign either Stage 1 or Stage 2 roles to manufacturing, to some extent because these roles require little attention and specific knowledge on the part of senior managers. In the United States, companies tend to start out with a unique product or with the identification of an unexploited niche in a market. As a result, they place primary emphasis on marketing, product design, or other nonmanufacturing functions. Top management does not see the need to become smart about—or give close attention to—the work of production.

Companies are likely to remain at their initial stage until external pressures force a move. As long as no direct competitor successfully develops Stage 3 or Stage 4 manufacturing capabilities, they will find Stages 1 and 2 comfortable, secure, and apparently effective. The post-World War II experience of many U.S. industries convinced a generation of managers that a policy of stability can remain satisfactory for decades, a view reinforced by the stable economic growth associated with the 1960s. What they first saw as common practice they came to see as *good* practice.

In general, the transition from Stage 1 to Stage 2 comes when problems arise in the manufacturing function that can be solved by the "safe" application of an already proven practice. It can also occur if managers decide that the leading companies in their industry owe at least part of their success to their manufacturing process. The transition to Stage 3, however, usually begins when managers come to doubt the effectiveness of their traditional approaches or to wonder about the implications of new manufacturing technologies. A direct threat from a major competitor that has moved to a higher stage or a recognition of the competitive advantages of moving to Stage 3 (or the potential perils of not doing so) may also trigger action.

During the early 1980s all these factors came together to encourage literally hundreds of companies to shift toward Stage 3. In many industries, long dominated by a few large companies following stable competitive ground rules, the sudden appearance of foreign competition and globalized markets jolted laggards into action. With no end to such competitive pressures in sight, many more companies are likely to attempt transitions to Stage 3 over the next several years.

Unfortunately many, if not most, of these companies are unlikely to achieve a full, lasting move to Stage 3 before they revert to Stage 2. The reasons for such a retreat are subtle, yet powerful. Moving from Stage 2 to Stage 3 often occurs in a crisis atmosphere when—as with U.S. producers of steel, autos, and machine tools—managers and workers alike see their real objective as regaining competitive parity with their attackers. The changes that are required to adapt fully to Stage 3 require such sustained effort and broad-based support, however, that these companies may not be able to cement them in place before improved business conditions relieve some of the competitive pressure. The natural tendency, of course, is to return to a "business as usual" Stage 2 mentality as soon as the crisis appears to have passed.

The great irony here is that too quick success often spells doom for permanent change. If, as often happens, the managers responsible for building manufacturing to Stage 3 levels are quickly promoted into other responsibilities and other, lesser managers are left to be the caretakers of recent changes, the necessary follow-up activities may not occur.

THE BIG JUMP TO STAGE 4

However difficult it is to get from Stage 2 to Stage 3, experience suggests that the shift from Stage 3 to Stage 4 demands an effort substantially greater both in kind and in degree. Earlier transitions, which take place largely within the manufacturing function, are a form of "manufacturing fixing itself." Moving to Stage 4, however, involves changing the way the *rest* of the organization thinks about manufacturing and interacts with it. Because coordination among functions is crucial, manufacturing must first have its own house in order. Entering Stage 4 is not something an organization simply chooses to do. It must first pay its dues by having done all the appropriate groundwork.

The differences between Stages 3 and 4 should not be underestimated. In Stage 3, manufacturing considerations feed into business strategy, but the function itself is still seen as reactive (in that its role is a derived one), not as a source of potential competitive advantage. Stage 4 implies a deep shift in manufacturing's role, in its self-image, and in the view of it held by managers in other functions. It is, at last, regarded as an equal partner and is therefore expected to play a major role in strengthening a company's market position. Equally important, it helps the rest of the organization see the world in a new way. Stage 3 companies will, for example, treat automation as essentially a cost-cutting and labor-saving activity. A Stage 4 manufacturing operation will bring automation into focus as a means of boosting process precision and product quality.

There is an expectation in Stage 4 that all levels of management will possess a high degree of technical competence and will be aware of how their actions may affect manufacturing activities. Further, they are expected to have a general understanding of the way products, markets, and processes interact and to manage actively these interactions across functions. Traditional approaches to improving performance—providing flexibility through excess capacity, for example, or raising delivery dependability through holding finished-goods inventory, or reducing costs through improvements in labor productivity—no longer are considered as the only way to proceed. Tighter integration of product design and process capabilities can also lead to increased flexibility, as well as to faster deliveries (through shorter production cycle times) and to lower costs (through improved product quality and reliability).

Most American top managers, in our experience, regard the transition from Stage 1 to Stage 2, and then on to Stage 3, as a desirable course to pursue. Yet few view achieving Stage 4 capabilities as an obvious goal or strengthen their companies' manufacturing functions with the clear intent of moving there.

In fact, most companies that reach Stage 3 do not perceive a move to Stage 4 as either essential or natural. Their managers, believing that Stage 3 provides 90% of the benefits attainable, resist spending the extra effort to advance further. Many prefer to play it safe by remaining in Stage 3 for a sustained period before deciding how and whether to move on. A sizable number doubt the value of Stage 4—some because they think it extremely risky in organizational terms;

others because they feel threatened by the kind of initiatives manufacturing might take when unleashed. One company, in fact, ruled out a move to Stage 4 as being potentially destabilizing to its R&D group, which historically had played the key role in establishing the company's competitive advantage.

Although the benefits of operating in Stage 4 will vary from company to company and will often be invisible to managers until they are just on the edge of Stage 4 operations, four variables can serve as a sort of litmus test for a company's real attitude toward the competitive role its manufacturing organization can—and should—play and thus indicate its placement in Stage 3 or Stage 4.

The Amount of Ongoing In-House Innovation Stage 4 organizations continually invest in process improvements, not only because they benefit existing products but also because they will benefit future products. This is not to say these companies are uninterested in big-step improvements, but that they place great importance on the cumulative value of continual enhancements in process technology.

The Extent to Which a Company Develops Its Own Manufacturing Equipment The typical Stage 3 operation continues to rely on outside suppliers for equipment development. A Stage 4 company wants to know more than its suppliers about everything that is critical to its business. It may continue to buy much of its equipment, but it will also produce enough internally to ensure that it is close to the state-of-the-art in equipment technology.

Our experience with Stage 4 German and Japanese manufacturers is that they follow this practice much more than most of their American counterparts. Yet even in Germany, where leading companies develop their own equipment, suppliers such as those making machine tools remain strong and innovative. Reducing their market does not cripple their competitive viability. Instead, the increased competition and the greater technical sophistication among equipment users have made the interactions between manufacturers and suppliers more innovative for both.

The Attention Paid to Manufacturing Infrastructure Stage 4 managers take care to integrate measurement systems, manufacturing planning and control procedures, and work force policies in their structural decisions on capacity, vertical integration, and the like. They do not necessarily give infrastructure and structural elements equal weight, but they look on both as important and complementary, sources of competitive strength.

The Link Between Product Design and Manufacturing Process Design Stage 3 companies focus on improving the hand-offs from product design to manufacturing; in Stage 4 the emphasis is on the parallel and interactive development of both products and processes.

If managers choose not to attempt the transition to Stage 4, that choice should be made intentionally, not by default or through a failure to understand the kinds of benefits that new stage could offer. Rather, it should reflect a reasoned judgment that the risks were too great or the rewards insufficient.

GETTING THERE FROM HERE

Two examples of organizations that, in the early 1980s, chose to attempt the transition to Stage 4 are General Electric's dishwasher operation (at the business unit level) and IBM (at the corporate level). Taking a closer look at these two experiences may help bring into focus the benefits of, and the obstacles to, a successfully managed transition.

GENERAL ELECTRIC DISHWASHER

Dishwashers are one of several major consumer appliances that GE has produced for decades. In the late 1970s GE's dishwasher strategic business unit (SBU) did a careful self-analysis and concluded that it had dated and aging resources: a 20-year-old product design, a 10- to 20-year-old manufacturing process, and an aging work force (average seniority of 15 to 16 years) represented by a strong, traditional union. Its manufacturing operations were primarily located, together with five other major appliance plants, at GE's Appliance Park in Louisville, Kentucky. A single labor relations group dealt with all of the site's 14,000 hourly workers, whose relations with management were neutral at best.

Nevertheless, it was a very successful business, holding the leading position in the U.S. dishwasher market and turning out about one-third of the units sold. In late 1977, as part of its normal planning for product redesign, the SBU proposed to corporate management that it invest $18 million in the incremental improvement of the product and its manufacturing process. With dishwasher manufacturing more or less at Stage 2 (it was essentially following "GE Appliance Park manufacturing practice"), those involved saw the request as a proposed foray into Stage 3, and expected the unit to return to Stage 2 once the improvements in products and processes began to age.

GE's senior managers normally would have approved such an investment and allowed the SBU to carry on with its traditional approach. In this case, however, they asked a number of tough questions about the long-term prospects for the business and encouraged SBU managers to think about pursuing a more innovative and aggressive course. The idea of making a fundamental change in the SBU's strategy gained rapid support from some key middle managers, who saw major opportunities if GE could break out of its traditional thinking. They began laying the groundwork for a solid move to Stage 3.

Over the next several months, as this reformulated proposal to upgrade product design and manufacturing processes began to take shape, the nature of the dishwasher business suggested possible benefits from moving on through Stage 3 to Stage 4:

- GE product designers had developed a top-of-the-line product with a plastic tub and plastic door liner. Although currently more expensive than the standard steel model, it offered significantly improved operating performance and used proprietary GE materials.
- More disciplined product design could increase component standardization because little of the product was visible after installation.
- Since only 55% of U.S. households owned dishwashers, there was considerable growth potential in the primary market as well as a sizable replacement market.

In combination with GE's strong competitive position, these factors led management to conclude that if the "right" product were introduced at the "right" price and with the "right" quality, GE could greatly expand both industry demand and its own market share, particularly in the private label business.

Accordingly, SBU managers decided not just to fix current problems but to do it right. They jettisoned their modest proposal for incremental product and process improvement and developed much bolder proposals requiring an investment of more than $38 million.

This revised plan rested on a major commitment to improve the factory's working environment through better communication with the work force as well as to encourage its involvement in redesigning the manufacturing process. Laying the groundwork for this new relationship took almost two years, but the time was well spent. Once established, this relationship markedly enhanced the contribution manufacturing could make to the overall business of the SBU.

The new plan also called for a complete redesign of the product around a central core consisting of a single-piece plastic tub and a single-piece plastic door. To ensure that the product would meet quality standards, management established stringent specifications for GE and for its vendors and demanded that both internal and external suppliers reduce their incidence of defects to one-twentieth of the levels formerly allowed. To meet the new specifications and the new cost targets, managers now had to carry out process and product development in tandem, not separate them as they had done in the past.

The revised proposal addressed, as well, the design of the production process. Automation was essential—not just to reduce costs but also to improve quality. Thus, modifications in product design had to reflect the capabilities and constraints of the new process. In addition, that process had to accommodate more worker control and shorter manufacturing cycle times, along with other nontraditional approaches to improve flexibility, quality, delivery dependability, and the integration of product testing with manufacturing.

By late 1980, there was general agreement on the major building blocks of this new strategy. Each of the functions—product design, marketing, and manufacturing—was to move aggressively toward defining its contribution in Stage 4 terms. To manufacturing management also fell the task of helping to

EXHIBIT 4
General Electric Dishwasher SBU Redesign

PERFORMANCE MEASURE	*1980–1981*	*1983*	*1984 GOAL*
Service call rate (index)*	100	70	55
Unit cost (index)	100	90	88
Number of times tub or door is handled	27+27	1 + 3	1 + 3
Inventory turns	13	25	28
Reject rates (mechanical/electrical test)	10%	3%	2.5%
Output per employee (index)	100	133	142

* Lower is better.

develop performance measures that, if tracked over subsequent years, would indicate how well the function was carrying out its responsibilities.

As *Exhibit 4* shows, by the end of 1983 there was pronounced improvement in such important areas as service call rates, unit costs, materials handling, inventory turns, reject rates, and productivity—with a promise of still further improvements in 1984. Nor was this all. Other benefits included a 70% reduction in the number of parts, the elimination of 20 pounds of weight in the finished product (and thus reduced freight costs), and much more positive worker attitudes. Perhaps most important of all was the large jump in market share that GE won in the 12 months following the new product's introduction. Indeed, during the summer of 1983, *Consumer Reports* rated it as offering the best value among U.S. dishwashers.

Although these results were impressive, SBU managers also gained a much better understanding of the effort needed to secure fully a Stage 4 position for manufacturing. Their experience underlined the need to treat product and process design in a more iterative and interactive fashion and the importance of involving the work force in solving problems.

Of late, a rebounding economy with increased consumer demand has turned up pressure on the SBU to revert to its traditional view that output is paramount, no matter the compromises. Hence, even though the SBU's manufacturing function is now in Stage 4, it must doggedly fight to stay there and to help the rest of the organization complete the transition rather than allow itself to drift back toward Stage 3.

IBM CORPORATION

In the early 1980s, IBM viewed its worldwide activities as comprising 13 major businesses including, for example, typewriters and large computer systems. Like its competitors in each of these product markets, IBM faced rapidly changing environments and so had to be especially careful in designing and coordinating strategies. Hence, in each, the manufacturing organization was expected to play a role equal to that of the other major functions in developing and executing overall business strategy. Unlike its competitors, most of whom still assigned Stage 2 or Stage 3 roles to manufacturing, IBM recognized that production—responsible for 49% of IBM's assets, 110,000 of its employees, and 40% of its final product costs—had much to contribute to the competitive advantage of each business

IBM's worldwide strategy for moving the manufacturing operations of each business into Stage 4 required those businesses to address seven areas of concern in a manner consistent with a Stage 4 approach to production. These areas were:

Low Cost IBM firmly believed that to be successful it must be the low-cost producer in each of its businesses, success being defined as having the best product quality, growing as fast or faster than the market, and being profitable. Reaching this low-cost position required stabilizing the manufacturing environment (reducing uncertainty wherever possible) and linking manufacturing more effectively to marketing and distribution. To this end, marketing had "ownership" of finished-goods inventory, and factory production rates were to be smoothed out by the adoption of a 90-day shipping horizon. In addition, IBM decided to design products around certain standard modules and, although it produced different configurations of these standard modules to customer order, it would not manufacture customized modules.

Inventories IBM's goal was to reduce inventories significantly, first by measuring stock carefully and frequently and then by reducing "order churn" (the fluctuation in mix and volume that occurs before an order actually gets into the final production schedule). Lower in-process inventories, derived in part from the adoption of a just-in-time philosophy and from the standardization of components, helped IBM cut its inventory costs by hundreds of millions of dollars within 18 months while supporting ever-increasing sales.

Quality IBM estimated that 30% of its products' manufacturing cost—the *total* cost of quality prevention, detection, and appraisal—arose directly from not doing it right the first time. Significant improvements in the quality and manufacturability of design, the pursuit of zero defects, and the systematic stress testing of pro- ducts during design and manufacturing all contributed to the lowering of these costs.

Automation Automation in a Stage 4 orientation is of value in that it leads to higher product quality, encourages interaction between product design and process design, and cuts overhead. This, in turn, means managing the evolution of the manufacturing process according to a long-term plan, just as with product evolution.

Organization To provide the product design and marketing functions with a better linkage with manufacturing, IBM defined an additional level of line manufacturing management, a "production management center," which was responsible for all plants manufacturing a product line. For example, the three large system plants (located in France, Japan, and the United States) were all under a single production management center that served as the primary linkage with marketing for that product line, as well as with R&D's efforts to design new products. Such centers were intended not only to create effective functional interfaces but also to be responsible for planning manufacturing processes, defining plant charters, measuring plant performance, and ensuring that the processes and systems employed by different facilities were uniformly excellent.

Manufacturing Systems The purpose here was to develop integrated systems that provided information, linked directly to strategic business variables, for both general and functional managers. Such systems had to be compatible with each other yet flexible enough for each business to be able to select the modules it needed. As part of this systems effort, IBM rethought its entire manufacturing measurement system with the intent of reducing its historical focus on direct labor and giving more emphasis to materials, overhead, energy, and indirect labor. IBM believed that its manufacturing systems, like its product lines, should be made up of standard modules based on a common architecture. Each business could then assemble its own customized configuration yet still communicate effectively with other IBM businesses.

Affordability By making external competitiveness, not internal rules of thumb, the basis for evaluating manufacturing performance, IBM no longer evaluated manufacturing against its own history but rather against its competitors. As part of this concern with affordability, IBM also sought to reduce its overhead, which exceeded 25% of total manufacturing costs.

Out of these seven areas of concern emerged a set of three management principles fully in harmony with the move to a Stage 4 appreciation of the competitive contribution that manufacturing can make. The first—emphasizing activities that facilitate, encourage, and reward effective interaction between manufacturing and both marketing and engineering—requires people able to regard each other as equals and to make significant contributions to areas other than their own. Information, influence, and support should—and must—flow in both directions.

The second principle recognizes that product and process technologies must interact. Process evolution (including automation) and product evolution must proceed in tandem. Indeed, IBM uses the terms "process windows" and "product windows" to describe these parallel paths and the opportunities they offer to exploit state-of-the-art processes in meeting customer needs and competitive realities.

The third principle is a focus of attention and resources on only those factors—manufacturing, quality, and overhead reduction, for example—that are essential to the long-term success of the business.

GETTING THINGS MOVING IN YOUR COMPANY

Our experience suggests that building manufacturing excellence requires that managers do more than simply understand the nature of the current role that manufacturing plays in their organizations and develop a plan for enhancing its competitive contribution. They must also communicate their vision to their organizations and prepare the ground for the changes that have to be made.

In virtually all the Stage 4 companies we have seen, at least one senior manager has been a key catalyst for the transition. Such leaders spring from all functional backgrounds and are concerned not to elevate manufacturing at the expense of other functions but to see their companies "firing on all cylinders." Seeking ways to integrate all functions into an effective whole, they must be strong enough, persuasive enough, and tough enough to push beyond conventional management thinking and to force their organizations to grapple with the deeper challenges prevailing in the increasingly competitive world of industry.

Today, there is considerable pessimism in some quarters about the long-term prospects for U.S. manufacturing. We are neither pessimistic nor optimistic; the answer "lies not in our stars but in ourselves." We have seen many organizations focus their efforts on achieving Stage 4 and make incredible improvements in short periods of time. Unfortunately, we have also seen many of them subsequently lose that commitment. After making tremendous strides, they begin to get comfortable and fall behind again.

Manufacturing can contribute significantly to the competitive success of any business. But it takes managers with determination, vision, and the ability to sustain focused effort over a long period of time and often in the face of stiff organizational resistance. The industrial race is no longer decided (if it ever was) by a fast and furious last-minute cavalry charge. It is a long, patient, persistent process of working together to clear the land, cultivate the fields, and continually extend the frontiers of an organization's capabilities.

DISCUSSION QUESTIONS

1. Discuss specific ways in which general managers may communicate a vision of manufacturing's role in an organization's competitiveness.
2. Is the model presented in this reading appropriate for all manufacturers? Can certain types of manufacturers attain competitive advantage without functioning at Stage 4?
3. As a general manager, would you agree with the author's claim that manufacturing informs and is essential to a firm's strategic goals? Would such an outlook create needless complexity when setting strategy?

9 Making Planning Strategic

RICHARD G. HAMERMESH

When portfolio planning was first introduced, its advocates believed it was the key to most strategic planning problems. Now, case studies and interviews with CEOs reveal something different: portfolio planning can improve business strategy, but only when it is used with other techniques for analyzing industries and competitors. This reading explores the strengths and weaknesses of portfolio planning, using examples to show when it is most useful and when different or additional approaches are more worthwhile. The reading concludes with a series of guidelines for general managers that can help make planning truly strategic.

Portfolio planning has come a long way since it became fashionable in the late 1960s. Listen to these executives describe their experiences:

> Portfolio planning became relevant to me as soon as I became CEO. I was finding it very difficult to manage and understand so many different products and markets. I just grabbed at portfolio planning because it provided me with a way to organize my thinking about our businesses and the resource allocation issues facing the total company. I became, and still am, very enthusiastic.
>
> – Robert Cushman, CEO, Norton Company, 1971–1980

> After two years of doing portfolio planning, I started to get concerned that the process of planning had become too onerous and in a sense had captured us. We were concentrating too much on analysis and not enough on specific decisions and implementation.
>
> – Joseph P. Flannery, CEO, Uniroyal

> Concepts such as the portfolio grid and the product life cycle are very good in theory, but we found that they can get you into a lot of trouble if you really believe that what is theorized will actually happen. What I found was that it was more important for me to challenge our managers to make sure that the theory did *not* come to pass.
>
> – James L. Ferguson, CEO, General Foods

These comments reflect both the praise and the criticism often expressed today about portfolio planning. Yet while many continue to debate the merits of the method, no one has claimed that companies can succeed without coherent strategies and few companies are willing to abandon their planning systems altogether. Indeed, roughly three-fourths of the *Fortune* "500" and many smaller companies with multiple product lines or services practice some form of portfolio planning.[1] Thus rather than debating whether to plan at all, we need to understand how successful companies actually use (and modify) portfolio planning to their advantage.

For three years, I have studied how companies practice portfolio planning and have interviewed many chief executives, staff planners, and division line managers. I have concluded that the companies that plan most effectively have learned these lessons:

- Strategy exists at several different levels, and planning affects the whole system—but no one planning technique or approach is sufficient to address all levels.
- Planning affects the whole organization, and the effects must be anticipated and managed.
- Top managers need to clarify their objectives and adjust their expectations. Effective companies do not rely exclusively on portfolio planning.
- A planning approach may have to change frequently to fit changing situations and circumstances.

THREE LEVELS OF STRATEGY

The portfolio approach to strategic planning became popular in the late 1960s as a result of work done independently by the Boston Consulting Group, McKinsey & Company, and the Strategic Planning Institute. Common to this work—as well as to subsequent studies—is the notion that a diversified company can best understand the performance and prospects of its different businesses by comparing them on several key dimensions. Armed with this information, the company can develop a classification scheme for its businesses that will aid it in making resource allocation decisions, formulating competitive strategies, and identifying sources and use of cash.

Although portfolio planning was designed to aid the overall strategy of an enterprise, in fact, strategy exists on three levels. *Business strategy* refers to the competitive strategy of a particular business unit. *Corporate strategy* refers to decisions affecting what businesses the company will compete in and how it will allocate resources among those businesses. *Institutional strategy* refers to how a company defines and shapes its basic character and vision—what builds a sense of purpose among employees and creates commitment to the goals and mission of the enterprise. Portfolio planning has a different impact at each of these levels.

The Business Unit A widely diversified company has many different business strategies, and portfolio planning has a mixed effect on these. The

1. The 75% figure is based on a questionnaire administered by Philippe Haspeslagh and my own assessment. *See* Philippe Haspeslagh, "Portfolio Planning: Uses and Limits," *Harvard Business Review* (January–February 1982): 58.

approach can help the units recognize and understand the realities of their competitive and market situations. Yet if strategy is set solely on the basis of a business's position on a portfolio matrix, problems may result. For example, portfolio planning typically recommends managing business units in weak markets for maximum cash flow. Yet often these units have opportunities to grow or build share and require investment.[2] As Donald R. Melville, CEO of the Norton Company, said, "One of the biggest dangers of the portfolio concept is paying attention only to a business's position on the matrix. If that is all you pay attention to, portfolio planning can be very dangerous."

It can also be misleading to equate market share and growth objectives with a business unit's strategy. Having such objectives does not preclude the need to develop detailed strategies to achieve long-term competitive advantage in terms of lower costs or higher quality or to focus on a particular market niche. In short, portfolio planning can improve business strategy, but only when it is used cautiously and with other techniques for analyzing industries and competitors.

The Corporation Portfolio planning has had its greatest impact at the corporate level, particularly in helping companies make divestiture decisions. The process of categorizing and ranking business units often throws light on likely disposal candidates—those units whose poor performance is rooted in weak market and competitive conditions. Equally important, portfolio analysis enables top managers to make divestiture decisions in a detached and calculated manner. Such analysis can be a useful antidote to the emotional appeals from the affected divisions that nearly always accompany divestiture decisions.[3]

The divestiture of weak divisions can have a dramatic effect on a company's performance. Portfolio planning techniques highlight not only the low returns of poorly performing divisions but also their competitive standing and the prospects of their industries. Assuming that these are also weak, portfolio planning may then lead management to divest those divisions, with the result that the total company returns would rise dramatically.

Within three years after the introduction of portfolio planning, return on equity in the companies studied rose from three to six percentage points, largely due to divestiture of weak businesses. By helping make divestiture decisions easier, portfolio planning has strengthened the corporate strategies of many large, diversified companies.

Although portfolio planning is extremely helpful in deciding what businesses to sell, it is less useful in guiding management of companies' internal growth and business development. Virtually every CEO interviewed mentioned this problem. These executives indicated that, after several years of using

---

2. *See* William K. Hall, "Survival Strategies in a Hostile Environment," *Harvard Business Review* (September–October 1990): 75; and Richard G. Hamermesh and Steven B. Silk, "How to Compete in Stagnant Industries," *Harvard Business Review* (September–October 1979): 161.

3. *See* S. Clark Gilmour, "The Divestment Decision Process," unpublished doctoral dissertation, Harvard Business School, 1973.

portfolio planning, their companies were having problems generating enough growth and new business development opportunities.

The Institution A company's institutional strategy involves its basic character and purpose. For example, IBM has a particularly well-developed institutional strategy. Even before the coming of the computer, Thomas A. Watson, Sr. believed the company had a "manifest destiny" to become a major worldwide enterprise. His vision lives on in IBM publications, which stress such goals as respect for the individual, customer service, and excellence.

Portfolio planning does little to add to such institutional goals. As a result, companies that already have clear institutional strategies must take care to adapt their planning efforts to reinforce their basic goals and missions. Companies lacking such strategies should not confuse planning with the institution-building activities that create great enterprise. Simply put, planning is not a substitute for top management leadership and vision.

POTENTIAL DRAWBACKS

Portfolio planning can have some serious, unintended effects on the organization. The most important involve the mismanagement of mature businesses, the planning staff's role, and the generation of growth opportunities.

The most common problem with portfolio planning involves mature business units. When these units are labeled cash cows, receive no new investment, and are tightly controlled, employee morale and performance may deteriorate. This, in turn, can lead to divestiture of a previously healthy (albeit mature) business unit.

Many of the managers interviewed cited decisions to harvest businesses that inadvertently led, or nearly led, to the abandonment of those businesses. James L. Ferguson, the CEO of General Foods, said, "We had major problems in trying to run our mature businesses for cash flow. My managers would ask me, 'Don't you want us to think about growth opportunities for our business?' My response would be 'Yes, *but*.' In other words, I would agree with them, but my underlying message would be that their real objective was to produce cash for the corporation. In retrospect, the concept of cash cow and mature business got in the way of both growth and innovation.

"Coffee is a good case in point. Naturally, our coffee business had been classified as a cash cow, or maintenance product. In point of fact, however, this is a very volatile and dynamic business. For example, in recent years, with the advent of automatic coffee makers in the home, there has been a lot of activity in the ground-coffee market to develop new varieties of ground coffees. We didn't miss these opportunities, but I believe we were a little late and not as aggressive in pursuing them because of the cash-cow concept."

No element of the portfolio approach has caused more heated debate than the role played by the planning staff. Many managers are disturbed by the size of staff units and by the extent of their reliance on staff input. Jack Welch, CEO of General Electric, described the problem this way: "Our planning system was dynamite when we first put it in. The thinking was fresh, the form mattered little—the format got no points. It was idea-oriented. We then hired a head of planning and he hired two vice presidents and then he hired a planner, and the books got thicker and the printing got more sophisticated, and the covers got harder and the drawings got better. The meetings kept getting larger. Nobody can say anything with 16 or 18 people there."

The last unintended effect of portfolio planning is that it often limits the thinking of managers in large companies and leads to conservative strategies. As one CEO observed, "I certainly didn't intend for it to be this way, but we are now getting a lot fewer proposals to enter new businesses than when we started using the portfolio concept."

There are several reasons why this problem occurs. First, portfolio planning conditions management to analyze a company's existing businesses rather than new areas of opportunity. The technique thus offers few insights into how to expand the scope of these businesses. Second, portfolio planning's emphasis on market share often leads managers to define their markets as narrowly as possible to maximize their shares. While this approach can benefit business units that should concentrate on market niches, its use throughout a company can lead to a constant narrowing of the company's business base.

Finally, by placing undue emphasis on total costs and the odds against achieving high market share, portfolio planning can discourage managers and hinder growth. In contrast, new business development is usually accomplished through incremental development of many capabilities.[4]

OVERCOMING THE PROBLEMS

Despite these potential drawbacks, most companies that adopted portfolio planning continue to use it. The most successful have overcome the drawbacks by modifying and adding to their portfolio analysis. These companies have taken care to address all three levels of strategy, found ways to control the organizational effects of planning, clarified their objectives in planning, and changed their approach as needed.

Addressing the Levels Successful planners take care to include all three levels of strategy in their portfolio analysis. Since, for example, business strategy cannot be set solely on the basis of the position of a strategic business unit (SBU) on a portfolio grid, shrewd planners also look at market trends, industry conditions, technological changes, competition, and their own strengths and

4. *See* Howard H. Stevenson and David E. Gumpert, "The Heart of Enterpreneurship," *Harvard Business Review* (March–April 1985): 85; and James Brian Quinn, "Managing Innovation: Controlled Chaos," *Harvard Business Review* (May–June 1985): 73.

weaknesses. These planners insist that each SBU's plans deal realistically with its market and competitive situation and identify sources of future competitive advantages. Most important, these companies recognize the value of good business-level strategies. As one CEO said, "We can articulate all sorts of values from the top of our company and make all sorts of plans to acquire and dispose of businesses, but if we can't figure out how to compete successfully in our remaining businesses, those other things won't matter much."

In plotting corporate strategy, the accomplished planners look beyond divestitures and acquisitions to defining and redefining SBUs, shifting priorities as conditions change, and establishing mechanisms and norms to encourage growth. The definition of business units is important to establish because it affects how managers of a unit perceive themselves and their competition. For example, an SBU whose scope is defined as X-ray machines is likely to compete more narrowly and thus miss more opportunities than an SBU whose scope is defined as diagnostic imaging equipment.

At companies where planning is most effective, top executives continually review the scopes of their SBUs. In some cases, market conditions and technological changes may encourage the collapse of several SBUs into one, while in others, a single SBU may be divided into several new units. In either case, corporate management aims to have the structure of its business units correspond to market realities rather than to internal factors alone.

Just as successful planners are willing to change SBU definitions, they are also willing to shift their priorities in response to changing market conditions. For example, throughout the 1970s, one company I studied gave the highest investment priority to SBUs that competed in oil field services. Yet when conditions in that business changed in the early 1980s, corporate management promptly initiated discussions that eventually gave low investment priority to these SBUs. Reginald H. Jones, General Electric's retired CEO, emphasized the importance of such flexibility when he said, "If all of your SBUs are in the same position on the portfolio grid year after year, then you're not doing a very good job of strategic planning. The objective of strategic planning should not be to take your categorization as a given, but to have your efforts aimed at moving the SBUs from one category to another."

Finally, excellent planners distinguish themselves by generating internal growth as well as growth from acquisitions. As noted earlier, most strategic planning techniques—and portfolio planning in particular—help ensure the efficient management of existing resources but fail to generate enough new business opportunities. To overcome this problem, corporate managers must broaden the scope of their SBUs' activities, identify and pursue opportunities in existing businesses, and see that even small new business opportunities are not overlooked. The companies that have planned most successfully for internal growth have required SBUs to identify new opportunities in their business plans and have penalized managers who missed opportunities.

Formal planning systems are most deficient at the level of institutional strategy. Simply put, most planning requires neither spelling out basic values, goals, and principles nor shaping a vision of where the company is headed. Jack Welch highlighted the difference between "corporate culture" and an institutional strategy. "For GE to have one culture makes no sense. We have a lot of different cultures. But we try desperately to have one company with one set of values."

An institutional strategy rests on the willingness of the CEO to articulate his or her vision of the company's future. Without their leadership, institutional strategy simply will not develop. With it, companies can set long-term goals and select and educate employees to help achieve them. At one company studied, for example, the development of institutional goals was followed by a four-year program of employee education.

Managing the Effects The best planners are well aware that they are engaged in more than simple analysis. In addition, they understand the need to manage the organizational effects of their planning systems. Recognizing planning's bias against mature business units, for example, they stress the untapped potential of these units. As a group vice president of a large industrial company explained, "One of the businesses reporting to me is in a very sluggish industry. My job is to show managers there that they have room to innovate and lead. As a result, they have been able to develop some original strategies, have their employees all fired up, and are making a good return." Worth Loomis, president of the Dexter Corporation, expressed a similar view: "The secret of dealing with so-called harvest businesses is never to really harvest them but in a sense to put them in idle. That way, you are ready to put the business back in gear whenever an opportunity arises." Of course, concrete actions, including new investment, must back up the assertion that mature businesses have opportunities.

Successful companies have also worked hard to ensure that line managers, not staff planners, are responsible for strategy and planning. For example, Norton Company has no corporate planner or corporate planning staff. Nonetheless, the company's line managers make extensive and sophisticated use of portfolio planning techniques. While this example is unusual, most companies try to confine the staff's role to providing background analyses for formulating strategies rather than developing strategies themselves.

While the size of planning staffs is an important concern, a more central question is how the different levels of management interact in the planning process. Categorizing SBUs, for example, can be accomplished by corporate-level directive, by the SBUs themselves, or by negotiation. Many of the companies studied have changed their approach. At first, these companies used a process that rested heavily on the input of corporate staff planners, with corporate management assigning labels and categories to each SBU. Today, at most of these companies, staff planners prepare background research, line managers develop SBU strategies, and corporate and business unit managers negotiate categories and basic objectives.

Clarifying Objectives Perhaps the biggest reason for companies' disappointment with strategic planning, and portfolio planning in particular, involves either failing to clarify objectives or setting unreasonably high expectations. Planning can be used for several different purposes, but it seldom provides a quick fix and is not a cure-all. Successful planners are realistic in their expectations and precise in their objectives.

One objective of planning is to improve the quality of resource allocation. By placing emphasis on the competitive performance of each business rather than on individual capital projects, portfolio planning can help ensure that resources flow to the most promising businesses and are not squandered on hopeless causes. But even when allocating resources, companies must set their expectations realistically. Portfolio planning will lead to a rapid shift in a company's business mix only if that company sells important units and makes large acquisitions. Of course, portfolio planning can lead to a shift in a company's business mix without a major restructuring; for this to happen, however, top management must recognize that it will involve shifting resources among its businesses over several years.

These different approaches to allocating resources appear vividly in the contrasting uses of portfolio planning at Allied Corporation under Edward L. Hennessy and at General Electric under Jones. At Allied, Hennessy used portfolio planning to justify a seemingly endless series of divestitures and acquisitions. At GE, while Jones made some acquisitions and many divestitures, his main objective was to use the cash from the company's traditional power systems and industrial businesses to fuel the growth of new efforts in engineered materials, financial services, information services, and medical systems. Thus with the help of portfolio planning, both Jones and Hennessy dramatically shifted their companies' mix of businesses, but Jones's approach was much more gradual than Hennessy's.

Still another objective of planning is to improve the quality of business unit plans. Here the point is not to shift the mix of businesses via resource allocation but to ensure that each SBU develops a sound strategy. Melville described the result at Norton this way: "Our line organization has learned to think strategically. This has taken time to accomplish, but now that we have achieved it, it gives us a tremendous advantage in the marketplace." Worth Loomis of Dexter argued that "the notion that you can allocate resources or restructure corporations from the top is a 'home run' mentality, and I have always tried to avoid that mentality. Instead, I work very hard to get all of our businesses to do things a little bit better each year. If you can do this over time, you usually end up earning superior returns and beating your competitors as they make mistakes."

A third objective of planning is to ensure that key corporatewide issues, such as major technological, regulatory, or market changes, are addressed. Because these issues usually fall between businesses or span more than one SBU, companies may overlook them if they do not make an explicit effort to address them.

These different uses of strategic planning underscore the importance of clarifying expectations, since it is virtually impossible for planning to meet all these needs at once. In successful companies, top management typically uses planning for one purpose at a time, shifting to a different purpose as conditions change and new issues arise. Realistic expectations and a willingness to change are the hallmarks of the most successful planning systems.

MAKING PLANNING WORK

Despite its drawbacks, portfolio planning remains an important tool in most large, diversified companies. Effective planning can improve both strategies and performance.[5] The challenge, then, is for top managers to address strategic issues in planning and to attend to their leadership role. In my research, I have observed eight practices that can help make planning truly strategic:

1. Do not confuse resource allocation with strategy. Top management's role must go beyond the buying and selling of businesses to building integrity in the company's operations and commitment among employees.
2. Pay close attention to business-level strategies. A company won't succeed unless it attains competitive advantages in each market in which it competes. Unfortunately, portfolio planning's emphasis on corporate strategy can undermine the importance of detailed industry and competitive analysis and thorough business strategies. Developing such strategies can help avoid some of the self-fulfilling prophecies (for example, that mature businesses will inevitably decline) that too often accompany portfolio planning efforts.
3. Avoid a home-run mentality. Too often, top managers expect an immediate and big payoff from planning. In reality, the payoff usually comes gradually as a result of avoiding serious blunders, developing consistent strategies, and clearly communicating the corporate strategy throughout the organization. It is the exception when planning produces revolutionary insights and results.
4. Involve line managers in planning. Obviously, staff can contribute immensely by providing detailed and time-consuming analyses that otherwise would be difficult to undertake. But line managers, not the staff, should make strategy.
5. Add approaches that encourage growth. Too often, portfolio planning results in significantly higher ROI but only moderately rising sales. Rather than acquiring businesses only to achieve growth, companies should make generating new opportunities a major corporate objective. To do this, top managers need to define their

5. Richard B. Robinson, Jr. and John A. Pearce II, "The Structure of Generic Strategies and Their Impact on Business-Unit Performance," *Proceedings of the Academy of Management* (San Diego, Calif.: 1985), p. 35.

business units broadly so that new opportunities fall within their purview and to prod SBU managers to respond to technical and economic changes. In addition, top managers must develop evaluation systems that penalize managers who miss growth opportunities and must establish the principle that achieving high returns without growth is not enough.

6. Tailor planning to the situation. There is no single right way to plan. A company facing tight financial constraints will want to use planning to identify divestiture opportunities and to maintain tight control of resource allocation. In contrast, when a company is most concerned about improving business unit performance or corporate understanding of the businesses, planning and resource allocation can be decentralized. In short, planning should serve the purposes of the CEO, address big strategic issues, and be consistent with the company's financial and organizational capabilities.
7. Articulate a vision and formulate an institutional strategy. No amount of planning can substitute for leadership. Top managers must define institutional goals, values, and beliefs and make sure that these are embodied in their organizations. While such tasks may lack the glamour and excitement of wheeling and dealing via acquisitions and divestitures, they are the foundation on which great companies are built.
8. Don't confuse strategic thinking with strategic planning. The purpose of planning is to create winning strategies, not thick planning books. In companies where strategic thinking is prevalent, SBU strategies deal with the realities of market and competitive conditions, new opportunities are pursued aggressively, strategies adapt to external events in a timely and coherent fashion, and planning focuses on substance, not form. Strategic planning can play a key role in making strategic thinking a way of life. Once this happens, companies can reduce emphasis on formal planning requirements. Until it does, however, the discipline of formal strategic planning is the best way to develop strategic thinking.

DISCUSSION QUESTIONS

1. Choose a diversified firm with which you are familiar and compare the strategic positioning of its business units.
2. When there are sharp conflicts between corporate and business unit strategy, should corporate strategy prevail so as to further the interests of the whole firm? Why or why not?
3. What is the difference between strategic thinking and strategic planning?

10 Strategic Intent

GARY HAMEL AND C. K. PRAHALAD

According to this reading, companies that have risen to global leadership invariably began with ambitions out of proportion to their resources and capabilities. These companies succeeded through strategic intent: they set their sights on goals that exceeded their grasp and marshalled both the will and the resources to achieve those goals. Senior managers who compete through strategic intent know that strategy is not simply a matter of properly using strategic planning methods. These GMs focus the organization on the strategic target, motivate people by clearly communicating the strategic intent, encourage individual and team contributions, and use intent consistently to guide resource allocations.

Today managers in many industries are working hard to match the competitive advantages of their new global rivals. They are moving manufacturing offshore in search of lower labor costs, rationalizing product lines to capture global scale economies, instituting quality circles and just-in-time production, and adopting Japanese human resource practices. When competitiveness still seems out of reach, they form strategic alliances—often with the very companies that upset the competitive balance in the first place.

Important as these initiatives are, few of them go beyond mere imitation. Too many companies are expending enormous energy simply to reproduce the cost and quality advantages their global competitors already enjoy. Imitation may be the sincerest form of flattery, but it will not lead to competitive revitalization. Strategies based on imitation are transparent to competitors who have already mastered them. Moreover, successful competitors rarely stand still. So it is not surprising that many executives feel trapped in a seemingly endless game of catch-up—regularly surprised by the new accomplishments of their rivals.

For these executives and their companies, regaining competitiveness will mean rethinking many of the basic concepts of strategy.[1] As "strategy" has blossomed, the competitiveness of Western companies has withered. This may be coincidence, but we think not. We believe that the application of concepts such as "strategic fit" (between resources and opportunities), "generic strategies" (low cost vs. differentiation vs. focus), and the "strategy hierarchy" (goals,

---

1. Among the first to apply the concept of strategy to management were H. Igor Ansoff in *Corporate Strategy: An Analytic Approach to Business Policy for Growth and Expansion* (New York: McGraw-Hill, 1965) and Kenneth R. Andrews in *The Concept of Corporate Strategy* (Homewood, Ill.: Dow Jones-Irwin, 1971).

strategies, and tactics) have often abetted the process of competitive decline. The new global competitors approach strategy from a perspective that is fundamentally different from that which underpins Western management thought. Against such competitors, marginal adjustments to current orthodoxies are no more likely to produce competitive revitalization than are marginal improvements in operating efficiency.

Few Western companies have an enviable track record anticipating the moves of new global competitors. Why? The explanation begins with the way most companies have approached competitor analysis. Typically, competitor analysis focuses on the existing resources (human, technical, and financial) of present competitors. The only companies seen as a threat are those with the resources to erode margins and market share in the next planning period. Resourcefulness, the pace at which new competitive advantages are being built, rarely enters in.

In this respect, traditional competitor analysis is like a snapshot of a moving car. By itself, the photograph yields little information about the car's speed or direction—whether the driver is out for a quiet Sunday drive or warming up for the Grand Prix. Yet many managers have learned through painful experience that a business's initial resource endowment (whether bountiful or meager) is an unreliable predictor of future global success.

Think back. In 1970, few Japanese companies possessed the resource base, manufacturing volume, or technical prowess of U.S. and European industry leaders. Komatsu was less than 35% as large as Caterpillar (measured by sales), was scarcely represented outside Japan, and relied on just one product line—small bulldozers—for most of its revenue. Honda was smaller than American Motors and had not yet begun to export cars to the United States. Canon's first halting steps in the reprographics business looked pitifully small compared with the $4 billion Xerox powerhouse.

If Western managers had extended their competitor analysis to include these companies, it would merely have underlined how dramatic the resource discrepancies between them were. Yet by 1985, Komatsu was a $2.8 billion company with a product scope encompassing a broad range of earth-moving equipment, industrial robots, and semiconductors. Honda manufactured almost as many cars worldwide in 1987 as Chrysler. Canon had matched Xerox's global unit market share.

The lesson is clear: assessing the current tactical advantages of known competitors will not help you understand the resolution, stamina, and inventiveness of potential competitors. Sun-tzu, a Chinese military strategist, made the point 3,000 years ago: "All men can see the tactics whereby I conquer," he wrote, "but what none can see is the strategy out of which great victory is evolved."

Companies that have risen to global leadership over the past 20 years invariably began with ambitions that were out of all proportion to their resources and capabilities. But they created an obsession with winning at all levels of the organization and then sustained that obsession over the 10- to 20-year quest for global leadership. We term this obsession "strategic intent."

On the one hand, strategic intent envisions a desired leadership position and establishes the criterion the organization will use to chart its progress. Komatsu set out to "Encircle Caterpillar." Canon sought to "Beat Xerox." Honda strove to become a second Ford—an automotive pioneer. All are expressions of strategic intent.

At the same time, strategic intent is more than simply unfettered ambition. (Many companies possess an ambitious strategic intent yet fall short of their goals.) The concept also encompasses an active management process that includes: focusing the organization's attention on the essence of winning; motivating people by communicating the value of the target; leaving room for individual and team contributions; sustaining enthusiasm by providing new operational definitions as circumstances change; and using intent consistently to guide resource allocations.

Strategic Intent Captures the Essence of Winning The Apollo program—landing a man on the moon ahead of the Soviets—was as competitively focused as Komatsu's drive against Caterpillar. The space program became the scorecard for America's technology race with the USSR. In the turbulent information technology industry, it was hard to pick a single competitor as a target, so NEC's strategic intent, set in the early 1970s, was to acquire the technologies that would put it in the best position to exploit the convergence of computing and telecommunications. Other industry observers foresaw their convergence, but only NEC made convergence the guiding theme for subsequent strategic decisions by adopting "computing and communications" as its intent. For Coca-Cola, strategic intent has been to put a Coke within "arm's reach" of every consumer in the world.

Strategic Intent Is Stable Over Time In battles for global leadership, one of the most critical tasks is to lengthen the organization's attention span. Strategic intent provides consistency to short-term action, while leaving room for reinterpretation as new opportunities emerge. At Komatsu, encircling Caterpillar encompassed a succession of medium-term programs aimed at exploiting specific weaknesses in Caterpillar or building particular competitive advantages. When Caterpillar threatened Komatsu in Japan, for example, Komatsu responded by first improving quality, then driving down costs, then cultivating export markets, and then underwriting new product development.

Strategic Intent Sets a Target That Deserves Personal Effort and Commitment Ask the CEOs of many American corporations how they measure their contributions to their companies' success and you're likely to get an answer expressed in terms of shareholder wealth. In a company that possesses a strategic intent, top management is more likely to talk in terms of global market leadership. Market share leadership typically yields shareholder wealth, to be sure. But the two goals do not have the same motivational impact. It is hard to imagine middle managers, let alone blue-collar employees, waking up each day with the sole thought of creating more shareholder wealth. But mightn't they feel different given the challenge to "Beat Benz"—the rallying cry at one Japanese auto producer? Strategic intent gives employees the only goal that is worthy of commitment: to unseat the best or remain the best, worldwide.

Many companies are more familiar with strategic planning than they are with strategic intent. The planning process typically acts as a "feasibility sieve." Strategies are accepted or rejected on the basis of whether managers can be precise about the "how" as well as the "what" of their plans. Are the milestones clear? Do we have the necessary skills and resources? How will competitors react? Has the market been thoroughly researched? In one form or another, the admonition "Be realistic!" is given to line managers at almost every turn.

But can you plan for global leadership? Did Komatsu, Canon, and Honda have detailed, 20-year "strategies" for attacking Western markets? Are Japanese and Korean managers better planners than their Western counterparts? No. As valuable as strategic planning is, global leadership is an objective that lies outside the range of planning. We know of few companies with highly developed planning systems that have managed to set a strategic intent. As tests of strategic fit become more stringent, goals that cannot be planned for fall by the wayside. Yet companies that are afraid to commit to goals that lie outside the range of planning are unlikely to become global leaders.

Although strategic planning is billed as a way of becoming more future oriented, most managers, when pressed, will admit that their strategic plans reveal more about today's problems than tomorrow's opportunities. With a fresh set of problems confronting managers at the beginning of every planning cycle, focus often shifts dramatically from year to year. And with the pace of change accelerating in most industries, the predictive horizon is becoming shorter and shorter. So plans do little more than project the present forward incrementally. The goal of strategic intent is to fold the future back into the present. The important question is not "How will next year be different from this year?" but "What must we do differently next year to get closer to our strategic intent?" Only with a carefully articulated and adhered to strategic intent will a succession of year-on-year plans sum up to global leadership.

Just as you cannot plan a 10- to 20-year quest for global leadership, the chance of falling into a leadership position by accident is also remote. We don't believe that global leadership comes from an undirected process of intrapreneurship. Nor is it the product of a skunkworks or other techniques for internal venturing. Behind such programs lies a nihilistic assumption: the organization is so hidebound, so orthodox ridden that the only way to innovate is to put a few bright people in a dark room, pour in some money, and hope that something wonderful will happen. In this "Silicon Valley" approach to innovation, the only role for top managers is to retrofit their corporate strategy to the entrepreneurial successes that emerge from below. Here the value added of top management is low indeed.

Sadly, this view of innovation may be consistent with reality in many large companies.[2] On the one hand, top management lacks any particular point of view about desirable ends beyond satisfying shareholders and keeping

2. Robert A. Burgelman, "A Process Model of Internal Corporate Venturing in the Diversified Major Firm," *Administrative Science Quarterly*, June 1983.

raiders at bay. On the other, the planning format, reward criteria, definition of served market, and belief in accepted industry practice all work together to tightly constrain the range of available means. As a result, innovation is necessarily an isolated activity. Growth depends more on the inventive capacity of individuals and small teams than on the ability of top management to aggregate the efforts of multiple teams towards an ambitious strategic intent.

In companies that overcame resource constraints to build leadership positions, we see a different relationship between means and ends. While strategic intent is clear about ends, it is flexible as to means—it leaves room for improvisation. Achieving strategic intent requires enormous creativity with respect to means. But this creativity comes in the service of a clearly prescribed end. Creativity is unbridled, but not uncorralled, because top management establishes the criterion against which employees can pretest the logic of their initiatives. Middle managers must do more than deliver on promised financial targets; they must also deliver on the broad direction implicit in their organization's strategic intent.

Strategic intent implies a sizable stretch for an organization. Current capabilities and resources will not suffice. This forces the organization to be more inventive, to make the most of limited resources. Whereas the traditional view of strategy focuses on the degree of fit between existing resources and current opportunities, strategic intent creates an extreme misfit between resources and ambitions. Top management then challenges the organization to close the gap by systematically building new advantages.

In this respect, strategic intent is like a marathon run in 400-meter sprints. No one knows what the terrain will look like at mile 26, so the role of top management is to focus the organization's attention on the ground to be covered in the next 400 meters. In several companies, management did this by presenting the organization with a series of corporate challenges, each specifying the next hill in the race to achieve strategic intent. One year the challenge might be quality, the next total customer care, the next entry into new markets, the next a rejuvenated product line. As this example indicates, corporate challenges are a way to stage the acquisition of new competitive advantages, a way to identify the focal point for employees' efforts in the near to medium term. As with strategic intent, top management is specific about the ends (reducing product development times by 75%, for example) but less prescriptive about the means.

Like strategic intent, challenges stretch the organization. To preempt Xerox in the personal copier business, Canon set its engineers a target price of $1,000 for a home copier. At the time, Canon's least expensive copier sold for several thousand dollars. Trying to reduce the cost of existing models would not have given Canon the radical price-performance improvement it needed to delay or deter Xerox's entry into personal copiers. Instead, Canon engineers were challenged to reinvent the copier—a challenge they met by substituting a disposable cartridge for the complex image-transfer mechanism used in other copiers.

Corporate challenges come from analyzing competitors as well as from the foreseeable pattern of industry evolution. Together these reveal potential competitive openings and identify the new skills the organization will need to take the initiative away from better positioned players. The exhibit, "Building Competitive Advantage at Komatsu," illustrates the way challenges helped that company achieve its intent.

For a challenge to be effective, individuals and teams throughout the organization must understand it and see its implications for their own jobs. Companies that set corporate challenges to create new competitive advantages (as Ford and IBM did with quality improvement) quickly discover that engaging the entire organization requires top management to do the following:

- *Create a sense of urgency,* or quasi crisis, by amplifying weak signals in the environment that point up the need to improve, instead of allowing inaction to precipitate a real crisis. (Komatsu, for example, budgeted on the basis of worst-case exchange rates that overvalued the yen.)
- ***Develop a competitor focus at every level through widespread use of competitive intelligence.*** Every employee should be able to benchmark his or her efforts against best-in-class competitors so that the challenge becomes personal. (For example, Ford showed production-line workers videotapes of operations at Mazda's most efficient plant.)
- ***Provide employees with the skills they need to work effectively***—training in statistical tools, problem solving, value engineering, and team building, for example.
- ***Give the organization time to digest one challenge before launching another.*** When competing initiatives overload the organization, middle managers often try to protect their people from the whipsaw of shifting priorities. But this "wait and see if they're serious this time" attitude ultimately destroys the credibility of corporate challenges.
- ***Establish clear milestones and review mechanisms*** to track progress and ensure that internal recognition and rewards reinforce desired behavior. The goal is to make the challenge inescapable for everyone in the company.

It is important to distinguish between the process of managing corporate challenges and the advantages that the process creates. Whatever the actual challenge may be—quality, cost, value engineering, or something else—there is the same need to engage employees intellectually and emotionally in the development of new skills. In each case, the challenge will take root only if senior executives and lower level employees feel a reciprocal responsibility for competitiveness. We believe workers in many companies have been asked to take a disproportionate share of the blame for competitive failure. In one U.S. company, for example, management had sought a 40% wage-package concession from hourly employees to bring labor costs into line with Far Eastern competitors. The result was a long strike and, ultimately, a 10% wage concession from employees on the line. However, direct labor costs in manufacturing accounted for less than 15% of total value added. The company thus succeeded in demoralizing its entire blue-collar work force for the sake of a 1.5% reduction in total

EXHIBIT
Building Competitive Advantage at Komatsu

Corporate Challenge		*Protect Komatsu's Home Market Against Caterpillar*		*Reduce Costs While Maintaining Quality*		*Make Komatsu an International Enterprise and Build Export Markets*		*Respond to External Shocks That Threaten Markets*		*Create New Products and Markets*
Programs	**early 1960s**	Licensing deals with Cummins Engine, International Harvester, and Bucyrus-Erie to acquire technology and establish benchmarks	**1965**	C D (Cost Down) program	**early 1960s**	Develop Eastern bloc countries	**1975**	V-10 program to reduce costs by 10% while maintaining quality; reduce parts by 20%; rationalize manufacturing system	**late 1970s**	Accelerate product development to expand line
	1961	Project A (for Ace) to advance the product quality of Komatsu's small and medium-sized bulldozers above Caterpillar's	**1966**	Total C D program	**1967**	Komatsu Europe marketing subsidiary established	**1977**	Y-180 program to budget companywide for 180 yen to the dollar when exchange rate was 240	**1979**	Future and Frontiers program to identify new businesses based on society's needs and company's know-how
	1962	Quality Circles companywide to provide training for all employees			**1970**	Komatsu America established	**1979**	Project E to establish teams to redouble cost and quality efforts in response to oil crisis	**1981**	EPOCHS program to reconcile greater product variety with improved production efficiencies
					1972	Project B to improve the durability and reliability and to reduce costs of large bulldozers				
					1972	Project C to improve payloaders				
					1972	Project D to improve hydraulic excavators				
					1974	Establish presales and service departments to assist newly industrializing countries in contruction projects				

costs. Ironically, further analysis showed that their competitors' most significant costs savings came not from lower hourly wages but from better work methods invented by employees. You can imagine how eager the U.S. workers were to make similar contributions after the strike and concessions. Contrast this situation with what happened at Nissan when the yen strengthened: Top management took a big pay cut and then asked middle managers and line employees to sacrifice relatively less.

Reciprocal responsibility means shared gain and shared pain. In too many companies, the pain of revitalization falls almost exclusively on the employees least responsible for the enterprise's decline. Too often, workers are asked to commit to corporate goals without any matching commitment from top management—be it employment security, gain sharing, or an ability to influence the direction of the business. This one-sided approach to regaining competitiveness keeps many companies from harnessing the intellectual horsepower of their employees.

Creating a sense of reciprocal responsibility is crucial because competitiveness ultimately depends on the pace at which a company embeds new advantages deep within its organization, not on its stock of advantages at any given time. Thus we need to expand the concept of competitive advantage beyond the scorecard many managers now use: Are my costs lower? Will my product command a price premium?

Few competitive advantages are long lasting. Uncovering a new competitive advantage is a bit like getting a hot tip on a stock: the first person to act on the insight makes more money than the last. When the experience curve was young, a company that built capacity ahead of competitors, dropped prices to fill plants, and reduced costs as volume rose went to the bank. The first mover traded on the fact that competitors undervalued market share—they didn't price to capture additional share because they didn't understand how market share leadership could be translated into lower costs and better margins. But there is no more undervalued market share when each of 20 semiconductor companies builds enough capacity to serve 10% of the world market.

Keeping score of existing advantages is not the same as building new advantages. The essence of strategy lies in creating tomorrow's competitive advantages faster than competitors mimic the ones you possess today. In the 1960s, Japanese producers relied on labor and capital cost advantages. As Western manufacturers began to move production offshore, Japanese companies accelerated their investment in process technology and created scale and quality advantages. Then as their U.S. and European competitors rationalized manufacturing, they added another string to their bow by accelerating the rate of product development. Then they built global brands. Then they deskilled competitors through alliances and outsourcing deals. The moral? An organization's capacity to improve existing skills and learn new ones is the most defensible competitive advantage of all.

To achieve a strategic intent, a company must usually take on larger, better financed competitors. That means carefully managing competitive engagements so that scarce resources are conserved. Managers cannot do that simply by playing the same game better—making marginal improvements to competitors' technology and business practices. Instead, they must fundamentally change the game in ways that disadvantage incumbents—devising novel approaches to market entry, advantage building, and competitive warfare. For smart competitors, the goal is not competitive imitation but competitive innovation, the art of containing competitive risks within manageable proportions.

Four approaches to competitive innovation are evident in the global expansion of Japanese companies. These are: building layers of advantage, searching for loose bricks, changing the terms of engagement, and competing through collaboration.

The wider a company's portfolio of advantages, the less risk it faces in competitive battles. New global competitors have built such portfolios by steadily expanding their arsenals of competitive weapons. They have moved inexorably from less defensible advantages such as low wage costs to more defensible advantages like global brands. The Japanese color television industry illustrates this layering process.

By 1967, Japan had become the largest producer of black-and-white television sets. By 1970, it was closing the gap in color televisions. Japanese manufacturers used their competitive advantage—at that time, primarily, low labor costs—to build a base in the private-label business, then moved quickly to establish world-scale plants. This investment gave them additional layers of advantage—quality and reliability—as well as further cost reductions from process improvements. At the same time, they recognized that these cost-based advantages were vulnerable to changes in labor costs, process and product technology, exchange rates, and trade policy. So throughout the 1970s, they also invested heavily in building channels and brands, thus creating another layer of advantage, a global franchise. In the late 1970s, they enlarged the scope of their products and businesses to amortize these grand investments, and by 1980 all the major players—Matsushita, Sharp, Toshiba, Hitachi, Sanyo—had established related sets of businesses that could support global marketing investments. More recently, they have been investing in regional manufacturing and design centers to tailor their products more closely to national markets.

These manufacturers thought of the various sources of competitive advantage as mutually desirable layers, not mutually exclusive choices. What some call competitive suicide—pursuing both cost and differentiation—is exactly what many competitors strive for.[3] Using flexible manufacturing technologies and better marketing intelligence, they are moving away from standardized "world products" to products like Mazda's mini-van, developed in California expressly for the U.S. market.

Another approach to competitive innovations—searching for loose bricks—exploits the benefits of surprise, which is just as useful in business battles as it

3. For example, *see* Michael E. Porter, *Competitive Strategy* (New York: Free Press, 1980).

is in war. Particularly in the early stages of a war for global markets, successful new competitors work to stay below the response threshold of their larger, more powerful rivals. Staking out underdefended territory is one way to do this.

To find loose bricks, managers must have few orthodoxies about how to break into a market or challenge a competitor. For example, in one large U.S. multinational, we asked several country managers to describe what a Japanese competitor was doing in the local market. The first executive said, "They're coming at us in the low end. Japanese companies always come in at the bottom." The second speaker found the comment interesting but disagreed: "They don't offer any low-end products in my market, but they have some exciting stuff at the top end. We really should reverse engineer that thing." Another colleague told still another story. "They haven't taken any business away from me," he said, "but they've just made me a great offer to supply components." In each country, their Japanese competitor had found a different loose brick.

The search for loose bricks begins with a careful analysis of the competitor's conventional wisdom: How does the company define its "served market"? What activities are most profitable? Which geographic markets are too troublesome to enter? The objective is not to find a corner of the industry (or niche) where larger competitors seldom tread but to build a base of attack just outside the market territory that industry leaders currently occupy. The goal is an uncontested profit sanctuary, which could be a particular product segment (the "low end" in motorcycles), a slice of the value chain (components in the computer industry), or a particular geographic market (Eastern Europe).

When Honda took on leaders in the motorcycle industry, for example, it began with products that were just outside the conventional definition of the leaders' product-market domains. As a result, it could build a base of operations in underdefended territory and then use that base to launch an expanded attack. What many competitors failed to see was Honda's strategic intent and its growing competence in engines and power trains. Yet even as Honda was selling 50cc motorcycles in the United States, it was already racing larger bikes in Europe—assembling the design skills and technology it would need for a systematic expansion across the entire spectrum of motor-related businesses.

Honda's progress in creating a core competence in engines should have warned competitors that it might enter a series of seemingly unrelated industries—automobiles, lawn mowers, marine engines, generators. But with each company fixated on its own market, the threat of Honda's horizontal diversification went unnoticed. Today companies like Matsushita and Toshiba are similarly poised to move in unexpected ways across industry boundaries. In protecting loose bricks, companies must extend their peripheral vision by tracking and anticipating the migration of global competitors across product segments, businesses, national markets, value-added stages, and distribution channels.

Changing the terms of engagement—refusing to accept the front runner's definition of industry and segment boundaries—represents still another form of competitive innovation. Canon's entry into the copier business illustrates this approach.

During the 1970s, both Kodak and IBM tried to match Xerox's business system in terms of segmentation, products, distribution, service, and pricing. As a result, Xerox had no trouble decoding the new entrants' intentions and developing countermoves. IBM eventually withdrew from the copier business, while Kodak remains a distant second in the large copier market that Xerox still dominates.

Canon, on the other hand, changed the terms of competitive engagement. While Xerox built a wide range of copiers, Canon standardized machines and components to reduce costs. Canon chose to distribute through office-product dealers rather than try to match Xerox's huge direct sales force. It also avoided the need to create a national service network by designing reliability and serviceability into its product and then delegating service responsibility to the dealers. Canon copiers were sold rather than leased, freeing Canon from the burden of financing the lease base. Finally, instead of selling to the heads of corporate duplicating departments, Canon appealed to secretaries and department managers who wanted distributed copying. At each stage, Canon neatly sidestepped a potential barrier to entry.

Canon's experience suggests that there is an important distinction between barriers to entry and barriers to imitation. Competitors that tried to match Xerox's business system had to pay the same entry costs—the barriers to imitation were high. But Canon dramatically reduced the barriers to entry by changing the rules of the game.

Changing the rules also short-circuited Xerox's ability to retaliate quickly against its new rival. Confronted with the need to rethink its business strategy and organization, Xerox was paralyzed for a time. Xerox managers realized that the faster they downsized the product line, developed new channels, and improved reliability, the faster they would erode the company's traditional profit base. What might have been seen as critical success factors—Xerox's national sales force and service network, its large installed base of leased machines, and its reliance on service revenues—instead became barriers to retaliation. In this sense, competitive innovation is like judo: the goal is to use a larger competitor's weight against it. And that happens not by matching the leader's capabilities but by developing contrasting capabilities of one's own.

Competitive innovation works on the premise that a successful competitor is likely to be wedded to a "recipe" for success. That's why the most effective weapon new competitors possess is probably a clean sheet of paper. And why an incumbent's greatest vulnerability is its belief in accepted practice.

Through licensing, outsourcing agreements, and joint ventures, it is sometimes possible to win without fighting. For example, Fujitsu's alliances in Europe with Siemens and STC (Britain's largest computer maker) and in the United States with Amdahl yield manufacturing volume and access to Western markets. In the early 1980s, Matsushita established a joint venture with Thorn (in the United Kingdom), Telefunken (in Germany), and Thomson (in France), which allowed it to quickly multiply the forces arrayed against Philips in the battle for leadership in the European VCR business. In fighting larger global rivals by proxy, Japanese companies have adopted a maxim as old as human conflict itself: my enemy's enemy is my friend.

Hijacking the development efforts of potential rivals is another goal of competitive collaboration. In the consumer electronics war, Japanese competitors attacked traditional businesses like TVs and hi-fis while volunteering to manufacture "next generation" products like VCRs, camcorders, and compact disc players for Western rivals. They hoped their rivals would ratchet down development spending, and in most cases that is precisely what happened. But companies that abandoned their own development efforts seldom reemerged as serious competitors in subsequent new product battles.

Collaboration can also be used to calibrate competitors' strengths and weaknesses. Toyota's joint venture with GM, and Mazda's with Ford, give these automakers an invaluable vantage point for assessing the progress their U.S. rivals have made in cost reduction, quality, and technology. They can also learn how GM and Ford compete—when they will fight and when they won't. Of course, the reverse is also true: Ford and GM have an equal opportunity to learn from their partner-competitors.

The route to competitive revitalization we have been mapping implies a new view of strategy. Strategic intent assures consistency in resource allocation over the long term. Clearly articulated corporate challenges focus the efforts of individuals in the medium term. Finally, competitive innovation helps reduce competitive risk in the short term. This consistency in the long term, focus in the medium term, and inventiveness and involvement in the short term provide the key to leveraging limited resources in pursuit of ambitious goals. But just as there is a process of winning, so there is a process of surrender. Revitalization requires understanding that process too.

Given their technological leadership and access to large regional markets, how did U.S. and European countries lose their apparent birthright to dominate global industries? There is no simple answer. Few companies recognize the value of documenting failure. Fewer still search their own managerial orthodoxies for the seeds for competitive surrender. But we believe there is a pathology of surrender that gives some important clues.

It is not very comforting to think that the essence of Western strategic thought can be reduced to eight rules for excellence, seven S's, five competitive forces, four product life-cycle stages, three generic strategies, and innumerable two-by-two matrices.[4] Yet for the past 20 years, "advances" in strategy have taken the form of ever more typologies, heuristics, and laundry lists, often with dubious empirical bases. Moreover, even reasonable concepts like the product life cycle, experience curve, product portfolios, and generic strategies often have toxic side effects: They reduce the number of strategic options management is

---

4. Strategic frameworks for resource allocation in diversified companies are summarized in Charles W. Hofer and Dan E. Schendel, *Strategy Formulation: Analytical Concepts* (St. Paul, Minn.: West Publishing, 1978).

willing to consider. They create a preference for selling businesses rather than defending them. They yield predictable strategies that rivals easily decode.

Strategy "recipes" limit opportunities for competitive innovation. A company may have 40 businesses and only four strategies—invest, hold, harvest, or divest. Too often strategy is seen as a positioning exercise in which options are tested by how they fit the existing industry structure. But current industry structure reflects the strengths of the industry leader; and playing by the leader's rules is usually competitive suicide.

Armed with concepts like segmentation, the value chain, competitor benchmarking, strategic groups, and mobility barriers, many managers have become better and better at drawing industry maps. But while they have been busy mapmaking, their competitors have been moving entire continents. The strategist's goal is not to find a niche within the existing industry space but to create new space that is uniquely suited to the company's own strengths, space that is off the map.

This is particularly true now that industry boundaries are becoming more and more unstable. In industries such as financial services and communications, rapidly changing technology, deregulation, and globalization have undermined the value of traditional industry analysis. Mapmaking skills are worth little in the epicenter of an earthquake. But an industry in upheaval presents opportunities for ambitious companies to redraw the map in their favor, so long as they can think outside traditional industry boundaries.

Concepts like "mature" and "declining" are largely definitional. What most executives mean when they label a business mature is that sales growth has stagnated in their current geographic markets for existing products sold through existing channels. In such cases, it's not the industry that is mature, but the executives' conception of the industry. Asked if the piano business was mature, a senior executive in Yamaha replied, "Only if we can't take any market share from anybody anywhere in the world and still make money. And anyway, we're not in the 'piano' business, we're in the 'keyboard' business." Year after year, Sony has revitalized its radio and tape recorder businesses, despite the fact that other manufacturers long ago abandoned these businesses as mature.

A narrow concept of maturity can foreclose a company from a broad stream of future opportunities. In the 1970s, several U.S. companies thought that consumer electronics had become a mature industry. What could possibly top the color TV? they asked themselves. RCA and GE, distracted by opportunities in more "attractive" industries like mainframe computers, left Japanese producers with a virtual monopoly in VCRs, camcorders, and compact disc players. Ironically, the TV business, once thought mature, is on the verge of a dramatic renaissance. A $20 billion-a-year business will be created when high-definition television is launched in the United States. But the pioneers of television may capture only a small part of this bonanza.

Most of the tools of strategic analysis are focused domestically. Few force managers to consider global opportunities and threats. For example, portfolio planning portrays top management's investment options as an array of businesses rather than as an array of geographic markets. The result is predictable: As businesses come under attack from foreign competitors, the company attempts to abandon them and enter others in which the forces of global competition are not yet so strong. In the short term, this may be an appropriate response to waning competitiveness, but there are fewer and fewer businesses in which a domestic-oriented company can find refuge. We seldom hear such companies asking: Can we move into emerging markets overseas ahead of our global rivals and prolong the profitability of this business? Can we counterattack in our global competitors' home market and slow the pace of their expansion? A senior executive in one successful global company made a telling comment: "We're glad to find a competitor managing by the portfolio concept—we can almost predict how much share we'll have to take away to put the business on the CEO's 'sell list.'"

Companies can also be overcommitted to organizational recipes, such as strategic business units and the decentralization an SBU structure implies. Decentralization is seductive because it places the responsibility for success or failure squarely on the shoulders of line managers. Each business is assumed to have all the resources it needs to execute its strategies successfully, and in this no-excuses environment, it is hard for top management to fail. But desirable as clear lines of responsibility and accountability are, competitive revitalization requires positive value added from top management.

Few companies with a strong SBU orientation have built successful global distribution and brand positions. Investments in a global brand franchise typically transcend the resources and risk propensity of a single business. However, in the recent past, Japanese companies have created a score or more—NEC, Fujitsu, Panasonic (Matsushita), Toshiba, Sony, Seiko, Epson, Canon, Minolta, and Honda, among them.

General Electric's situation is typical. In many of its businesses, this American giant has been almost unknown in Europe and Asia. GE made no coordinated effort to build a global corporate franchise. Any GE business with international ambitions had to bear the burden of establishing its credibility and credentials in the new market alone. Not surprisingly, some once-strong GE businesses opted out of the difficult task of building a global brand position. In contrast, smaller Korean companies like Samsung, Daewoo, and Lucky Gold Star are busy building global-brand umbrellas that will ease market entry for a whole range of businesses. The underlying principle is simple: Economies of scope may be as important as economies of scale in entering global markets. But capturing economies of scope demands interbusiness coordination that only top management can provide.

We believe that inflexible SBU-type organizations have also contributed to the deskilling of some companies. For a single SBU, incapable of sustaining investment in a core competence such as semiconductors, optical media, or combustion engines, the only way to remain competitive is to purchase key components from potential (often Japanese or Korean) competitors. For an SBU defined in product-market terms, competitiveness means offering an end product that is competitive in price and performance. But that gives an SBU manager little incentive to distinguish between external sourcing that achieves "product embodied" competitiveness and internal development that yields deeply embedded organizational competences that can be exploited across multiple businesses. Where upstream component manufacturing activities are seen as cost centers with cost-plus transfer pricing, additional investment in the core activity may seem a less profitable use of capital than investment in downstream activities. To make matters worse, internal accounting data may not reflect the competitive value of retaining control over core competence.

Together a shared global corporate brand franchise and shared core competence act as mortar in many Japanese companies. Lacking this mortar, a company's businesses are truly loose bricks—easily knocked out by global competitors that steadily invest in core competences. Such competitors can co-opt domestically oriented companies into long-term sourcing dependence and capture the economies of scope of global brand investment through interbusiness coordination.

Last in decentralization's list of dangers is the standard of managerial performance typically used in SBU organizations. In many companies, business unit managers are rewarded solely on the basis of their performance against return on investment targets. Unfortunately, that often leads to denominator management because executives soon discover that reductions in investment and head count—the denominator—"improve" the financial ratios by which they are measured more easily than growth in the numerator—revenues. It also fosters a hair-trigger sensitivity to industry downturns that can be very costly. Managers who are quick to reduce investment and dismiss workers find it takes much longer to regain lost skills and catch up on investment when the industry turns upward again. As a result, they lose market share in every business cycle. Particularly in industries where there is fierce competition for the best people and where competitors invest relentlessly, denominator management creates a retrenchment ratchet.

The concept of the general manager as a movable peg reinforces the problem of denominator management. Business schools are guilty here because they have perpetuated the notion that a manager with net present value calculations in one hand and portfolio planning in the other can manage any business anywhere.

In many diversified companies, top management evaluates line managers on numbers alone because no other basis for dialogue exists. Managers move so many times as part of their "career development" that they often do not understand the nuances of the businesses they are managing. At GE, for example, one fast-track manager heading an important new venture had moved across five businesses in five years. His series of quick successes finally came to an end when he confronted a Japanese competitor whose managers had been plodding along in the same business for more than a decade.

Regardless of ability and effort, fast-track managers are unlikely to develop the deep business knowledge they need to discuss technology options, competitors' strategies, and global opportunities substantively. Invariably, therefore, discussions gravitate to "the numbers," while the value added of managers is limited to the financial and planning savvy they carry from job to job. Knowledge of the company's internal planning and accounting systems substitutes for substantive knowledge of the business, making competitive innovation unlikely.

When managers know that their assignments have a two- to three-year time frame, they feel great pressure to create a good track record fast. This pressure often takes one of two forms. Either the manager does not commit to goals whose time line extends beyond his or her expected tenure. Or ambitious goals are adopted and squeezed into an unrealistically short time frame. Aiming to be number one in a business is the essence of strategic intent; but imposing a three- to four-year horizon on the effort simply invites disaster. Acquisitions are made with little attention to the problems of integration. The organization becomes overloaded with initiatives. Collaborative ventures are formed without adequate attention to competitive consequences.

Almost every strategic management theory and nearly every corporate planning system is premised on a strategy hierarchy in which corporate goals guide business unit strategies and business unit strategies guide functional tactics.[5] In this hierarchy, senior management makes strategy and lower levels execute it. The dichotomy between formulation and implementation is familiar and widely accepted. But the strategy hierarchy undermines competitiveness by fostering an elitist view of management that tends to disenfranchise most of the organization. Employees fail to identify with corporate goals or involve themselves deeply in the work of becoming more competitive.

The strategy hierarchy isn't the only explanation for an elitist view of management, of course. The myths that grow up around successful top managers—"Lee Iacocca saved Chrysler," "De Benedetti rescued Olivetti," "John Sculley turned Apple around"—perpetuate it. So does the turbulent business environment. Middle managers buffeted by circumstances that seem to be beyond their control desperately want to believe that top management has all the answers. And top management, in turn, hesitates to admit it does not for fear of demoralizing lower-level employees.

The result of all this is often a code of silence in which the full extent of a company's competitiveness problem is not widely shared. We interviewed business unit managers in one company, for example, who were extremely anxious because top management wasn't talking openly about the competitive challenges the company faced. They assumed the lack of communication indicated a lack of awareness on their senior managers' part. But when asked whether they were open with their own employees, these same managers replied that while they could face up to the problems, the people below them could not. Indeed, the only time the work force heard about the company's competitiveness problems was during wage negotiations when problems were used to extract concessions.

---

5. For example, *see* Peter Lorange and Richard F. Vancil, *Strategic Planning Systems* (Englewood Cliffs, N.J.: Prentice-Hall, 1977).

Unfortunately, a threat that everyone perceives but no one talks about creates more anxiety than a threat that has been clearly identified and made the focal point for the problem-solving efforts of the entire company. That is one reason honesty and humility on the part of top management may be the first prerequisite of revitalization. Another reason is the need to make participation more than a buzzword.

Programs such as quality circles and total customer service often fall short of expectations because management does not recognize that successful implementation requires more than administrative structures. Difficulties in embedding new capabilities are typically put down to "communication" problems, with the unstated assumption that if only downward communication were more effective—"if only middle management would get the message straight"—the new program would quickly take root. The need for upward communication is often ignored, or assumed to mean nothing more than feedback. In contrast, Japanese companies win, not because they have smarter managers, but because they have developed ways to harness the "wisdom of the anthill." They realize that top managers are a bit like the astronauts who circle the earth in the space shuttle. It may be the astronauts who get all the glory, but everyone knows that the real intelligence behind the mission is located firmly on the ground.

Where strategy formulation is an elitist activity it is also difficult to produce truly creative strategies. For one thing, there are not enough heads and points of view in divisional or corporate planning departments to challenge conventional wisdom. For another, creative strategies seldom emerge from the annual planning ritual. The starting point for next year's strategy is almost always this year's strategy. Improvements are incremental. The company sticks to the segments and territories it knows, even though the real opportunities may be elsewhere. The impetus for Canon's pioneering entry into the personal copier business came from an overseas sales subsidiary—not from planners in Japan.

The goal of the strategy hierarchy remains valid—to ensure consistency up and down the organization. But this consistency is better derived from a clearly articulated strategic intent than from inflexibly applied top-down plans. In the 1990s, the challenge will be to enfranchise employees to invent the means to accomplish ambitious ends.

We seldom found cautious administrators among the top managements of companies that came from behind to challenge incumbents for global leadership. But in studying organizations that had surrendered, we invariably found senior managers who, for whatever reason, lacked the courage to commit their companies to heroic goals—goals that lay beyond the reach of planning and existing resources. The conservative goals they set failed to generate pressure and enthusiasm for competitive innovation or give the organization much useful guidance. Financial targets and vague mission statements just cannot provide the consistent direction that is a prerequisite for winning a global competitive war.

This kind of conservatism is usually blamed on the financial markets. But we believe that in most cases investors' so-called short-term orientation simply reflects their lack of confidence in the ability of senior managers to conceive and deliver stretch goals. The chairman of one company complained bitterly that even after improving return on capital employed to over 40% (by ruthlessly divesting lackluster businesses and downsizing others), the stock market held the company to an 8:1 price/earnings ratio. Of course the market's message was clear: "We don't trust you. You've shown no ability to achieve profitable growth. Just cut out the slack, manage the denominators, and perhaps you'll be taken over by a company that can use your resources more creatively." Very little in the track record of most large Western companies warrants the confidence of the stock market. Investors aren't hopelessly short-term, they're justifiably skeptical.

We believe that top management's caution reflects a lack of confidence in its own ability to involve the entire organization in revitalization—as opposed to simply raising financial targets. Developing faith in the organization's ability to deliver on tough goals, motivating it to do so, focusing its attention long enough to internalize new capabilities—this is the real challenge for top management. Only by rising to this challenge will senior managers gain the courage they need to commit themselves and their companies to global leadership.

DISCUSSION QUESTIONS

1. Does the business environment change too rapidly for most firms to realize their strategic intent?
2. What is the relationship between strategic planning and strategic intent?
3. Is the concept of strategic intent equally applicable to all firms, or are some companies too small or too narrowly focused to benefit from it?

PART THREE

BUILDING THE ORGANIZATION

Muscle-Build the Organization 11

ANDRALL E. PEARSON

One of the most difficult challenges facing a general manager is the responsibility for recruiting and developing outstanding people. Solid performers are key to an organization's success. Yet many GMs are reluctant to take the aggressive measures required to achieve this. Andrall Pearson, the former president of PepsiCo, offers some tough-minded suggestions for strengthening an organization's managerial quality. The general manager must be willing to hire only the best people, to develop them, and to create a nucleus of talented people from which to draw on. The GM must also set high standards, constantly measure people by them, and replace those who fail to meet these standards. In short, the GM has to be willing to risk an organizational shakeup. In the long run, says Pearson, such a shakeup can help turn a good company into a great one.

Most top managers know they should be doing a better job of building the superior organization they want. They may not, however, know what more successful managers are doing—or how to do it themselves. And while most would agree that their business's success hinges on the quality of its people, very few executives are willing to adopt the tough, aggressive approach to managing people that's required to produce a dynamic organization.

The hard truth is, only an aggressive approach can make a big difference, quickly. But it has its costs: at least initially, managers have to be willing to sacrifice continuity for a thorough shake-up. Nevertheless, most top-notch companies have been through the experience; it's what transformed the company into an outstanding organization. And once the transformation has taken place, things can settle down without a loss of momentum.

In my 15 years with PepsiCo and 20 years of consulting for other corporations, I have seen that "winners"—IBM, Hewlett-Packard, Marriott, Avery International, among others—emphasize "people development" as the way to "muscle-build" their organizations. By stressing the identifying and grooming of talent at every level, these companies eventually create a huge gulf between themselves and their competitors. They also hold on to most of their best managers even though other companies may recruit them aggressively.

If you think you do a good job of managing people, try stepping back and asking yourself the following questions. They're a solid indication of whether people development is your company's number one daily priority.

Do you maintain consistent, demanding standards for everyone in your company—or are you willing to tolerate a mediocre division manager, an uneven sales force, a weak functional department head?

What are your hiring standards? Are you bringing in people who can upgrade the quality of your company significantly, or are you just filling holes? Are you willing to leave a vacancy open until you find an outstanding candidate—for months, if necessary?

Are you hiring *enough* people? Does your organization have sufficient depth—a bank of talent to draw on—or do you sometimes promote people you know will never really produce outstanding results?

How effective is each area of your company at identifying high-potential managers and developing them quickly? Are promising people rotated carefully to expose them to different problems and functions?

Do you know specifically where your organization's biggest performance problems are? Are you taking steps to solve them, or are you looking the other way?

Do you make measurable progress each year in the quality of your senior management group and in the people heading each functional area? Are you generating clearly better quality executives and backups—not just people whose bosses assert are better managers?

As the above questions suggest, traditional approaches to people development—like promotion from within based chiefly on job tenure—are no longer good enough. A company that uses experience as its primary criterion for advancement is encouraging organizational hardening of the arteries—especially if that experience came in an undemanding environment. Businesses today need better, brighter managers with a broader repertoire of skills—a repertoire people cannot master by working their way up the steps of a one-dimensional career ladder. Mergers and acquisitions, new technology, price pressures, and the information explosion all require a stronger and more savvy management team, people who can innovate and win in an uncertain future.

Ironically, as the need for more capable managers has heightened, the talent pool has shrunk. More and more of the most promising future business leaders are choosing the service industries—Wall Street, consulting, and smaller entrepreneurial companies—rather than moving into the big manufacturing enterprises.

These trends all call for upgrading the organization: strengthening your company's entire management group from top to bottom and attracting and preparing future leaders through new approaches—in effect, muscle building. For most companies, I believe that this aggressive approach is the only way to make a business live up to its potential.

Muscle building an organization requires five separate but interrelated steps:

1. Set higher performance standards for everyone—*and keep raising the standards*. Recognize that performance can always be improved, and cultivate a spirit of constructive dissatisfaction with current performance among all executives and managers.
2. Develop managers through fresh assignments and job rotation; keep everyone learning. Don't let high-potential people stay in the same position or the same functional area too long.
3. Adjust every facet of the work environment—corporate culture, organizational structure, policies—to facilitate and reward managers' development, rather than thwart the upgrading effort (as many formal systems do).
4. Infuse each level of the company with new talent. Bring in seasoned managers to solve organizational problems, to serve as backups for management succession, and to lead by example.
5. Use the personnel department as an active agent for change. Make personnel executives partners in the upgrading process. Expect as much from them as from other top managers.

Let's look at each step in more detail.

KEEP RAISING STANDARDS

The heart of any management upgrading process is the establishment of higher performance standards across the board. This responsibility rests with the top manager—the CEO or division general manager, depending on the company. If you're a senior manager and you delegate this task, you will convey the message that managerial development is not really that important, and every manager will set different standards.

Raising performance goals entails analyzing the company's current situation (where you are today versus where you want to be), establishing higher expectations (ways of bridging the gap), selling the entire management team on the upgrading process, and developing an action plan.

Step one is the situation analysis—looking at every important position in the company and asking, "What do we expect of this job? How should this position be moving our business forward? How close does the incumbent come to meeting the ideal?" In other words, you will be judging people against the company's mission and priorities. This questioning will indicate where the organization's weak links are and will give you a good sense of which executives already have high standards and which are most skillful at developing other people.

The way to get started is to sit down with your top executives—division managers and key staff leaders—and ask these reviewers to assess everyone who reports to them. You should also ask them how they could enhance their *own* performance.

Here are some of the questions you should explore:

> Who are our best performers, and how are we going to make them even better? How can we stretch them and accelerate their professional growth?
>
> Which senior managers and department heads tolerate marginal performance? Which do not emphasize enough their people's development?
>
> Where are our biggest performance problems, and what are we going to do about them? (You cannot build muscle in your organization unless you are willing to replace marginal performers.)
>
> Which groups of managers (e.g., marketing managers, operations managers) have the necessary mix of talents and skills to achieve more ambitious goals? Who in each group is promotable, and who is not?

For example, I'd be interested to find out specifically what each manager did this year to change the results of his or her unit. I'd look for measurable things like formulating or implementing a new competitive strategy, successfully launching a new product, or quickly cutting costs in a downturn. I'd be less interested in plans a manager has for the future, or a laundry list of routine programs he or she implemented, or personal characteristics like how smart someone is—all of which are difficult to relate to better performance.

I'd also be interested in how each manager compares with people the reviewer regards as future stars. Usually, people are better at comparing and ranking subordinates than at measuring someone's performance in a vacuum. By comparing people with star performers, you start to set higher standards and expectations. And if a unit has no stars (or only a few), you can also start to enrich the mix of talent there.

With a fix on each manager's current performance and development needs, you can then take a look at each executive's potential. A single question asking how far each person can advance (measured by the number of job layers) will usually start a lively and productive discussion, especially when a manager is ranked as high-potential yet has remained in the same job for four or five years.

You should repeat your questioning with all important department heads. Ideally, you should gather in-depth information on at least two or three levels of people under you. Your personal involvement is the best way to galvanize top managers into action—into recognizing your commitment to big changes in the way the organization operates. In implementing a management upgrading process at PepsiCo, I developed firsthand knowledge of the strengths and weaknesses of well over 100 executives. Going through this process, unit by unit and manager by manager, is obviously hard work, but there is no easy way to establish and enforce tougher performance standards and focus everyone's attention on management development.

I should add that the work is not only time-consuming but also emotionally charged. It leads to heated discussions, especially early on, when standards are likely to differ widely. Using elaborate performance-appraisal forms and systems, as most companies do, is easier, but these systems are usually a triumph of form over substance—an annual exercise to be gotten over with quickly. A simple, informal, face-to-face approach is what's needed to boost performance. You must be willing to engage in frank, tough-minded discussions of each manager's weaknesses—and you must convince each person to use equal candor with subordinates.

You are likely to find that many executives are initially either unwilling or unable to give you useful staff evaluations. For example, a division manager might say that everyone in the division is doing a pretty good job. If this happens, you will have to bear down and force the manager to draw distinctions—say, to identify who the single best performer is. It is also helpful to ask the executive to categorize the managers into four groups, from poor to superior, and then ask for a specific plan for the people in each group. Always focus first on the bottom group. The manager should specify who should be replaced, who should be reassigned, and when these decisions will be implemented.

Rooting out the poorest performers will foster a climate of continual improvement. If everyone in the bottom quartile is replaced, the third quartile becomes the new bottom group and the focus of subsequent improvement efforts.

The human tendency to avoid confrontation allows companies to fall into the trap of complacency and subpar performance. Upgrading the organization, by contrast, requires managers to make tough decisions: to fire some people, demote or bypass others, and tell poor performers where they stand. No one enjoys delivering bad news, but good managers will understand how critical it is to the company's long-term success—particularly if the CEO personally sets the example.

Some managers might object that this relentless scrutiny—and the inevitable firings—will demoralize employees. My experience suggests precisely the opposite. Top performers relish the challenge of meeting ever higher goals. What does demoralize them is a climate that tolerates mediocrity; under such circumstances, they may slow down their work to the tempo of the organization—or they may leave the company.

After you have completed your preliminary situation analysis, you are ready to formulate the specific actions you will take over the next 9 to 12 months to muscle-build your organization. What are your goals for each key manager and each department? What are the implications of those plans for recruiting and job assignments? This action plan sets the stage for a more demanding and results-oriented environment, one in which measurable progress will occur.

In my experience, focusing on a limited number of high-impact results, conducting comparative evaluations, and separating current performance from potential will produce far better effects than focusing on personal traits, making exhaustive MBO lists, or using rigorous forms.

The analysis, of course, does not stop here but should become an ongoing process, a day-to-day questioning. What's working well? Where can we improve? Over time, you may wish to supplement your face-to-face interviews with surveys to gather this kind of information.

WORSHIP SUCCESS AND POTENTIAL

The situation analysis is the cornerstone of your upgrading effort. Having identified how well your managers and divisions are performing, you are now in a position to determine how best to deploy your people. If you want to grow fast and improve fast, you have to develop people fast. And the secret to that is to produce challenging, fresh, *taxing* assignments.

It goes without saying that you want to put the best qualified person into each important job (and to move marginal performers aside so they don't block new talent). What may be less obvious is that you want to keep every high-potential manager constantly challenged and learning. Make sure that talented people don't stay in one job too long. Most people need about a year to master a new assignment; after four years, they're usually just repeating what they've already done, and they may go to sleep on the job. In most companies, people work in a single area for years, moving slowly and ponderously up the career ladder. By the time they reach senior positions, many have run out of steam—they've become "deadwood."

Just reassigning a top performer isn't enough. You don't want a talented person simply to repeat the same experience in a different region or at a somewhat higher level. You need to round out executives' experience through challenging new assignments that will give them a broader business viewpoint. Entirely different positions can accomplish this—for example, moving someone from domestic operations to international, putting a manager in a new functional area, or letting a high achiever engineer a turnaround.

At PepsiCo, we thought nothing of making the CFO of Frito-Lay a general manager of Pepsi-Cola in Canada, or promoting the North American Van Lines CEO to head up corporate planning, or putting a good, hands-on Pepsi marketing vice president into restaurant operations. We tried to make sure that every division president served in at least two operating divisions and in at least one staff assignment (not just in line jobs). We also moved promising mangers into our best-run divisions to minimize business disruptions and expose them to better work environments.

Large companies should rotate their managers through different divisions both to keep them challenged and to help the organization prepare future leaders who understand its many facets. Companies that have a number of smaller divisions or a significant international business can easily move people around like this. Managers in these enterprises have many opportunities to be tested and to learn in freestanding situations at lower risk.

Decisions about reassignments are best made once a year as part of the annual performance review, not on a piecemeal basis throughout the year. Making a series of moves at one time allows you to consider the needs of the whole organization and to deploy your entire pool of talent most productively. Also, when assignments are shuffled all at once, the company has time to settle down and assimilate the changes. In the real world, of course, you will also be faced with a few piecemeal decisions, but that doesn't negate the approach.

The aim of rearranging things is to make the best corporate use of all your managers, instead of asking each business unit to do the best it can with existing resources. To be sure, you take some chances when you bypass traditional channels of promotion. Moving someone to an entirely new division is not without risks: the new unit may resent your interference, or—worse—a person may fail in the new job.

To prevent resentment and resistance, don't just foist your selections on your operating people. Take particular care when implementing this portion of the upgrading process, and choose candidates whose odds of succeeding in a new division are high. Operating managers must realize that these people are top performers and not someone another area wanted to get rid of. You should also give your operating managers veto power over candidates, or give them a slate to choose from. Eventually, they will accept and support "corporate musical chairs" as they realize they're getting better qualified people for their openings.

If you promote on the basis of potential and not just on experience, you're bound to make some mistakes. The safest route is to promote someone already in the department rather than an outsider with less experience in the function. But you'll never shake up the organization enough if you stick to safe choices. If you see one of your assignments not working out, face it quickly, and try to find another slot for the person. Over time you'll learn which jobs require pertinent experience (there are some) and which ones don't (there are many of these).

There is one other risk in rotating people throughout a company. You are running a business, after all, not a finishing school for executives. Continuity and experience are important in building relationships and relevant skills. The priorities shouldn't be one-sided in either direction. The company needs a balance. Avoid moving people so much that you destroy continuity and nobody really gets developed, but also be as careful as you can to keep people from getting stale.

UNCLOG THE ORGANIZATION

The way a corporation is organized and runs can either facilitate or thwart the upgrading process. Unfortunately, organizations often become so complicated over time that some of the things I've recommended here simply won't work. If companies have tightly drawn "empires," for example, they'll have difficulty transferring executives across divisions. For that reason, a new emphasis on people development often calls for a complete transformation of the work environment.

Consider the ways in which a multilayered organizational structure can impede performance. With broken-up jobs, no one has clear-cut responsibility or a feeling of ownership and as a result, people may sit back and wait for the group to solve problems. It's difficult to assess individual performance. Decision-making mechanisms can be so complicated that people dissipate all their energy simply trying to get a question answered.

For reasons like these, a slow-moving, bureaucratic environment usually flushes talented people out the door faster than it brings them in. Innovators can't thrive in a highly centralized organization. If you want more original thinking, you have to decentralize responsibility throughout the company and get rid of red tape. Give people the freedom to stick their necks out and to take independent action.

Here are four suggestions for creating a climate conducive to executive development:

1. Keep your organizational structure as simple as possible. With fewer layers, there can be more individual responsibility, less second-guessing, clearer decision making, and greater accountability for results.
2. Break down organizational barriers. Emphasize that managers are corporate assets rather than the property of a single division or function.
3. By the same token, formally encourage cross-fertilization. Expose your best managerial prospects to top functional leaders. Some companies conduct reviews where all the senior marketing vice presidents, for example, evaluate prospects for marketing posts. In other corporations, the executives attend personnel reviews in other divisions.
4. Finally, make sure that every unit is rewarding its best achievers appropriately. This may sound obvious, but most businesses do a poor job of relating pay to performance. Sometimes better performers receive larger raises than less promising people (personnel policies or other factors don't always encourage this), but the differences may be so slight that they're demotivating. Nothing frustrates high-potential people more than hearing a lot of praise at their reviews and then learning that their efforts won't be rewarded accordingly. In the more demanding work environment you're creating by muscle building, it's especially important to peg pay to performance.

CREATE A NUCLEUS OF LEADERS

If you want to make sweeping improvements in your organization, you'll have to bring in fresh talent. The upgrading steps I've described are all crucial, but they take time to implement and bear fruit. An essential ingredient in the process is to bring in several high performers *quickly*—to fill important posts and to develop a talent pool you can draw on for promotions later.

Simply deciding to look outside the company for the next two or three openings isn't the answer. That's like trying to empty the ocean with a thimble; you'll never get anywhere. You may also be tempted to bring in new talent only at the entry level, especially if your employees tend to make their careers in your company. But are your present managers capable of supervising top performers? I recommend that you introduce new people at the highest levels of your organization and let the upgrading trickle down.

In a large, decentralized enterprise, the best way to start this talent infusion is to hire a group of proven managers without having any particular jobs in mind for them. (In football, this is called drafting for talent, not for position.) Ultimately, these people will be fed into the system as openings occur, but initially they can work directly for you or another senior person on special projects—assuming the role of in-house consultants. They can be assigned to divisions or functions that are in particular need of help, or to new endeavors. The important point is that proficient managers will be in place (setting an example for others) and learning about your company (preparing for more specific assignments).

This approach worked well at PepsiCo, where we brought in seven "floaters" over a three-year period. Within nine months, they were all working in key jobs, and five of them eventually ended up running big divisions. As another example, we felt we had too few promotable individuals in our food-service division, so we wanted to build a broader bank of talent. We considered 200 food-service executives, interviewed 50 of them, and brought in the best two we could find. Within two years, one was running a division and the other held an important operating position. Ernie Breech had similar success at Ford when he brought in the "whiz kids" (including Robert McNamara and Tex Thornton).

As these examples show, you can bring in people with assorted backgrounds or you can concentrate on a single area, like corporate finance. Your goal may be to get the best financial people you can find and give them a group of divisions to follow. They will not only make important contributions as in-house consultants but usually an operating unit will snap them up quickly, and they'll end up serving as a division CFO or even running a unit or company themselves.

Hiring people to serve as general resources may sound like an expensive proposition. But the cost is almost certainly less than you would pay for a consultant to handle the same special projects, and this method promises a significant impact on the upgrading process. Also, a cost-conscious CEO can usually eliminate enough low-impact current jobs or managers to pay for the floaters.

Eventually, you'll be able to focus your recruiting at the lower levels of management. Here as elsewhere, you must make the commitment to work consistently and effectively to develop the best staff possible. This goal usually means emphasizing campus recruiting—year after year, at the best schools—rather than just hiring people from other companies. It means that recruiting must be a top-management priority.

MAKE PERSONNEL A PARTNER

You can't improve an entire organization by yourself. As you would expect, you certainly need the support of all your executives and managers. As you might not expect, your other partner in the process is the personnel department. I'll talk about each of these in turn.

Muscle-building an organization is impossible without the active involvement of your line managers. But how do you convince a busy general manager to shoulder a new set of responsibilities? You need to do more than express your own commitment to the upgrading process: you have to be unrelenting in your emphasis on people development.

Make it clear that you are asking executives to do more than just preside over annual reviews. (And if you feel someone isn't emphasizing even this part of the process enough, try attending a couple of review sessions with subordinates.) Every time you see or call a manager, you should stress your interest in the key people and their individual performance. Ask specific questions. What has been done about the marginal production manager? What progress has there been in the Cleveland office? What projects is the new recruit working on? After a few run-throughs, the answers will be ready before you ask the questions.

You can deepen your executives' involvement in other ways, for instance, by asking them to showcase their "comers" at periodic business reviews or to nominate people to serve on special task forces. You should also make time for observing the best people in action during your field visits.

Commitment from line managers often doesn't come easily; you have to create it, nurture it, even push it. You're asking them to rethink their job priorities and make more difficult decisions. The personnel department can be a valuable ally in this effort and serve as a burr under the saddle of resistant managers.

Personnel people are often seen as peripheral to the real action in a company—a group of paper shufflers who develop benefits packages, collect evaluation forms, and process paychecks. But these activities are not their most important reason for being. Outstanding personnel people can be a force for positive change in the organization. They can help ensure that line managers handle their people responsibilities properly, and they can help the whole company make the best possible use of its assets.

Unfortunately, business leaders rarely recognize the potential of the personnel function, so they often fail to staff the department with high-caliber people. Their low expectations then become a self-fulfilling prophecy.

Personnel executives can facilitate organizational muscle building in several ways:

- They can push executives to make consistent, demanding evaluations of their subordinates. This might include, for example, pointing out differences between a criticism-shy manager's performance appraisals and other managers' evaluations of their people, and giving advice on how to deliver bad news in an appropriate way.
- They can force managers to take action on marginal performers (reassignment, coaching, allowing time for improvement) and insist that poor performers be replaced.

- They can help search out the best people in the company and the best slot for each person. They can encourage executives to take risks on high-potential prospects. (Superior personnel executives, plugged into every part of the company, are especially valuable here.) One of the most offbeat successful deployment decisions we made at PepsiCo, for example, was to shift our trucking company president to head up the corporate staff. Another success involved appointing an international division area vice president as chief of restaurant operations and marketing. Our corporate personnel vice president spearheaded both moves; if he hadn't prodded neither would have happened.
- They can encourage executives to focus on results and heap rewards on the best performers. (Some personnel systems set rigid limits on compensation, so pay increases average out, and no one is motivated.)

If you want valuable assistance from your personnel department, you will probably need brighter, more highly skilled personnel executives than you may have now. The good news is that if you give personnel more responsibility and integrate it with other executive functions, you should attract better people.

THE FULL-COURT PRESS

The five-step upgrading process I advocate is undeniably a huge undertaking. It requires time, energy, money, and possibly the restructuring of the entire company—in short, a full-court press.

You can't achieve the results I'm talking about by implementing just one part of the process or by working to improve your organization gradually. Nor can you hire a few MBAs or a new marketing vice president and expect the organization to change to its roots. A piecemeal or incremental approach won't foster the broad-based involvement, ownership, and conviction that make real progress; you'll move one step forward, one step back, and you'll never get off dead center. Your goal is to advance.

Some CEOs may feel that management muscle building is not worth the effort it takes. As is true with other improvement programs, the companies most in need of upgrading will probably be the ones least likely to attempt it. Many company chiefs who have implemented a systematic people-development program, however, have told me that it became the most rewarding part of their jobs. Muscle building makes a difference on the bottom line, in the company's strategic success, and in the way people feel when they come to work in the morning—including the CEOs.

DISCUSSION QUESTIONS

1. Pearson urges general managers to continually raise performance standards for all managers. Does this approach penalize managers whose results are unavoidably affected by economic forces, competitor moves, etc.? Or should no mitigating circumstances be allowed when evaluating a manager's performance?
2. The author suggests that managers constantly be rotated through positions in order to develop their experience. Can a company absorb these continual reassignments without adversely affecting morale or losing a sense of continuity?
3. "A cost-conscious CEO can usually eliminate enough low-impact current jobs or managers to pay for the floaters," those persons the author suggests hiring to round out the talent in a firm. Should GMs focus instead on strengthening these "low-impact jobs," rather than eliminating them to pay for people who will not fill particular jobs when hired?
4. Pearson argues that "muscle-building the organization" can't be done incrementally; in order to be effective, it must cause a shakeup, if not restructuring, of the firm. Do you agree? What are the advantages of incremental change?

12 Organization Design: Fashion or Fit?

HENRY MINTZBERG

A general manager is responsible for the overall design of his or her organization—for structuring the company so that all its parts fit into a coherent whole. This task, which is essential to the health and productivity of the organization, is highly complex. Organizational configurations are, in part, abstract ideals, simplifications of reality. And each of the parts affects the whole—the organization does not function effectively when one or more of the parts is out of place. In this reading, Henry Mintzberg identifies five natural configurations of organizations, each a combination of structure and situation. These five configurations serve as an effective tool in diagnosing problems in an organization's design. General managers who are familiar with these patterns can better achieve harmony and coherence in their firms.

- A conglomerate takes over a small manufacturer and tries to impose budgets, plans, organizational charts, and untold systems on it. The result: declining sales and product innovation—and near bankruptcy—until the division managers buy back the company and promptly turn it around.
- Consultants make constant offers to introduce the latest management techniques. Years ago LRP and OD were in style, later, QWL and ZBB.
- A government sends in its analysts to rationalize, standardize, and formalize citywide school systems, hospitals, and welfare agencies. The results are devastating.

These incidents suggest that a great many problems in organizational design stem from the assumption that organizations are all alike: more collections of component parts to which elements of structure can be added and deleted at will, a sort of organizational bazaar.

The opposite assumption is that effective organizations achieve a coherence among their component parts, that they do not change one element without considering the consequences to all of the others. Spans of control, degrees of job enlargement, forms of decentralization, planning systems, and matrix structure should not be picked and chosen at random. Rather, they should be selected according to internally consistent groupings. And these groupings should be consistent with the situation of the organization—its age and size, the conditions of the industry in which it operates, and its production technology. In essence, like all phenomena from atoms to stars, the characteristics of organizations fall into natural clusters, or *configurations.* When these characteristics are mismatched—when the wrong ones are put together—the organization does not function effectively, does not achieve a natural harmony. If managers are to design effective organizations, they need to pay attention to the fit.

If we look at the enormous amount of research on organizational structuring in light of this idea, a lot of the confusion falls away and a striking convergence is revealed. Specifically, five clear configurations emerge that are distinct in their structures, in the situations in which they are found, and even in the periods of history in which they first developed. They are the simple structure, machine bureaucracy, professional bureaucracy, divisionalized form, and adhocracy.

DERIVING THE CONFIGURATIONS

An adaptable picture of five component parts (see part A, *Exhibit 1*) describes the five configurations. An organization begins with a person who has an idea. This person forms the strategic apex or top management. He or she hires people to do the basic work of the organization, in what can be called the operating core. As the organization grows, it acquires intermediate managers between the chief executive and the workers. These managers form the middle line. The organization may also find that it needs two kinds of staff personnel. First are the analysts who design systems concerned with the formal planning and control of the work; they form the technostructure. Second is the support staff, providing indirect services to the rest of the organization—everything from the cafeteria and the mail room to the public relations department and the legal counsel.

These five parts together make the whole organization (see part B, *Exhibit 1*). Not all organizations need all of these parts. Some use few and are simple, others combine all in rather complex ways. The central purpose of structure is to coordinate the work divided in a variety of ways; how that coordination is achieved—by whom and with what—dictates what the organization will look like (see *Exhibit 2*):

- In the simplest case, coordination is achieved at the strategic apex by direct supervision—the chief executive officer gives the orders. The configuration called *simple structure* emerges, with a minimum of staff and middle line.
- When coordination depends on the *standardization of work,* an organization's entire administrative structure—especially its technostructure, which designs the standards—needs to be elaborated. This gives rise to the configuration called *machine bureaucracy.*

EXHIBIT 1
The Five Basic Parts of the Organizaion

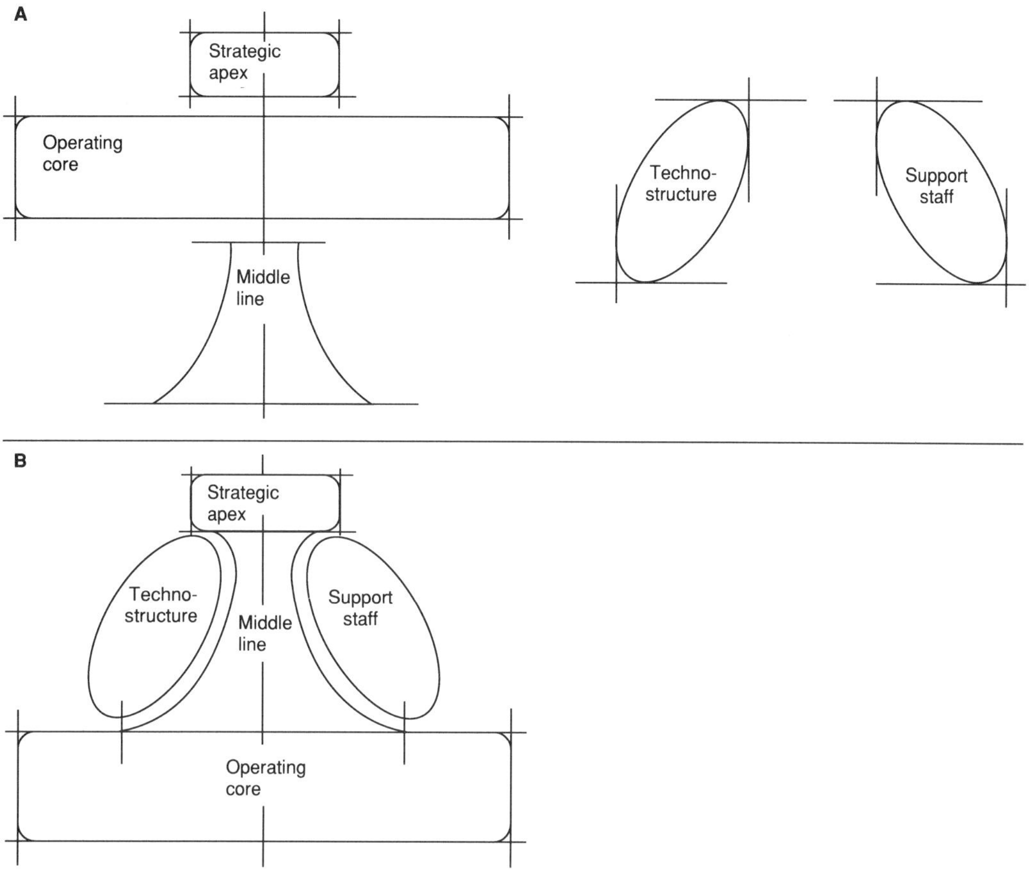

- When, instead, coordination is through the standardization of skills of its employees, the organization needs highly trained professionals in its operating core and considerable support staff to back them up. Neither its technostructure nor its middle line is very elaborate. The resulting configuration is called *professional bureaucracy.*
- Organizations will sometimes be divided into parallel operating units, allowing autonomy to the middle-line managers of each, with coordination achieved through the standardization of outputs (including performance) of these units. The configuration called the *divisionalized form* emerges.
- Finally, the most complex organizations engage sophisticated specialists, especially in their support staffs, and require them to combine their efforts in project teams coordinated by mutual adjustment. This results in the *adhocracy* configuration, in which line and staff as well as a number of other distinctions tend to break down.

The elements of structure include the following:

- Specialization of tasks
- Formalization of procedures (job descriptions, rules, and so forth)
- Formal training and indoctrination required for the job
- Grouping of units (notably by function performed or market served)
- Size of each of the units (that is, the span of control of its manager)
- Action planning and performance control systems
- Liaison devices, such as task forces, integrating managers, and matrix structure
- Delegation of power down the chain of authority (called *vertical decentralization*)
- Delegation of power out from that chain of authority to non-managers (called *horizontal decentralization*)

The sections that follow describe how all of these elements cluster into the five configurations. These descriptions are summarized in *Exhibit 3*, where all the elements are displayed in relation to the configurations. In each configuration, all the elements of structure and situation form themselves into a tightly knit, highly cohesive package. No one element determines the others; rather, all are locked together to form an integrated system.

SIMPLE STRUCTURE

The name tells all, and *Exhibit 2* shows all. The structure is simple—not much more than one large unit consisting of one or a few top managers and a group of operators who do the basic work. The most common simple structure is, of course, the classic entrepreneurial company.

What characterizes this configuration above all is what is missing. Little of its behavior is standardized or formalized, and minimal use is made of planning, training, or the liaison devices. The absence of standardization means that the organization has little need for staff analysts. Few middle-line managers are hired because so much of the coordination is achieved at the strategic apex by direct supervision. That is where the real power in this configuration lies. Even the support staff is minimized to keep the structure lean and flexible—simple structures would rather buy than make.

The organization must be flexible because it operates in a dynamic environment, often by choice because that is the one place it can outmaneuver the bureaucracies. And that environment must be simple, as must the organization's system of production, so that the chief executive can retain highly centralized control. In turn, centralized control makes the simple structure ideal for rapid, flexible innovation, at least of the simple kind. With the right chief executive, the organization can turn on a dime and run circles around the slower-moving bureaucracies. That is why so much innovation comes not from the giant mass producers but from small entrepreneurial companies. But where complex forms of innovation are required, the simple structure falters because of its centralization. As we shall

EXHIBIT 2
The Five Configurations

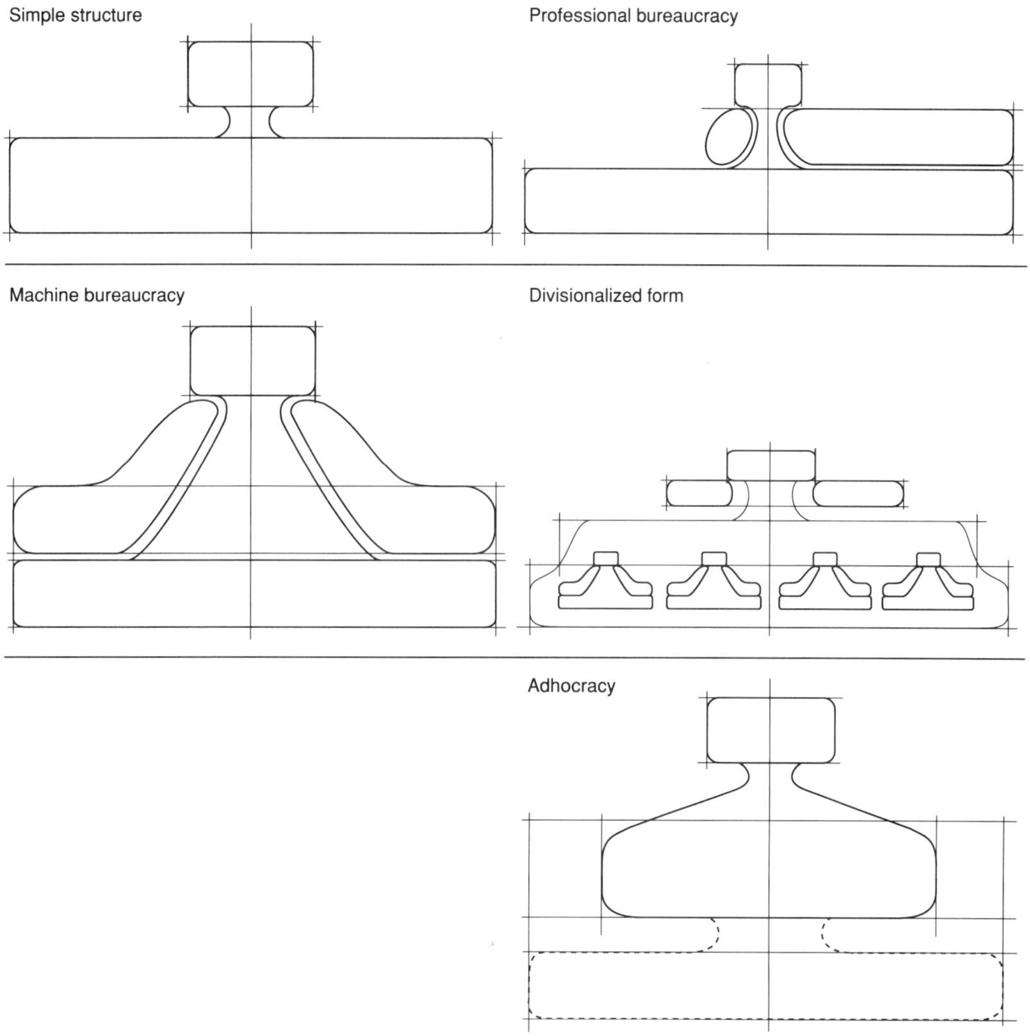

see, that kind of innovation requires another configuration, one that engages highly trained specialists and gives them considerable power.

Simple structures are often young and small, in part because aging and growth encourage them to bureaucratize but also because their vulnerability causes many of them to fail. They never get a chance to grow old and large. One heart attack can wipe them out—as can a chief executive so obsessed with innovation that he or she forgets about the operations, or vice versa. The corporate landscape is littered with the wrecks of entrepreneurial companies whose leaders encouraged growth and mass production yet could never accept the transition to bureaucratic forms of structure that these changes required.

EXHIBIT 3
Dimensions of the Five Configurations

	SIMPLE STRUCTURE	*MACHINE BUREAUCRACY*	*PROFESSIONAL BUREAUCRACY*	*DIVISIONAL-IZED FORM*	*ADHOCRACY*
Key Means of Coordination	Direct supervision	Standardization of work	Standardization of skills	Standardization of outputs	Mutual adjustment
Key Part of Organization	Strategic apex	Technostructure	Operating core	Middle line	Support staff (with operating core in operating adhocracy)
STRUCTURAL ELEMENTS					
Specialization of Jobs	Little specialization	*Much horizontal and vertical specialization*	*Much horizontal specialization*	Some horizontal and vertical specialization (between divisions and headquarters)	*Much horizontal specialization*
Training and Indoctrination	Little training and indoctrination	Little training and indoctrination	*Much training and indoctrination*	Some training and indoctrination (of division managers)	Much training
Formalization of Behavior—Bureaucratic/Organic	*Little formalization—organic*	*Much formalization—bureaucratic*	*Little formalization—bureaucratic*	Much formalization (within divisions)—bureaucratic	*Little formalization—organic*
Grouping	Usually functional	*Usually functional*	Functional and market	*Market*	Functional and market
Unit Size	Wide	Wide at bottom, narrow elsewhere	Wide at bottom, narrow elsewhere	Wide at top	Narrow throughout
Planning and Control Systems	Little planning and control	Action planning	Little planning and control	*Much performance control*	Limited action planning (esp. in administrative adhocracy)
Liaison Devices	Few liaison devices	Few liaison devices	Liaison devices in administration	Few liaison devices	*Many liaison devices throughout*
Decentralization	*Centralization*	*Limited horizontal decentralization*	*Horizontal and vertical decentralization*	*Limited vertical decentralization*	*Selective decentralization*

EXHIBIT 3
Dimensions of the Five Configurations (Continued)

	SIMPLE STRUCTURE	*MACHINE BUREAUCRACY*	*PROFESSIONAL BUREAUCRACY*	*DIVISIONAL-IZED FORM*	*ADHOCRACY*
SITUATIONAL ELEMENTS					
Age and Size	Typically young and small	Typically old and large	Varies	Typically old and very large	Typically young (operating adhocracy
Technical System	Simple, not regulating	Regulating but not automated, not very complex	Not regulating or complex	Divisible, otherwise like machine bureaucracy	Very complex, often automated (in administrative adhocracy), not regulating or complex (in operating adhocracy)
Environment	Simple and dynamic; sometimes hostile	Simple and stable	Complex and stable	Relatively simple and stable; diversified markets (esp. products and services)	Complex and dynamic; sometimes disparate (in administrative adhocracy)
Power	Chief executive control; often owner managed; not fashionable	Technocratic and external control; not fashionable	Professional operator control; fashionable	Middle-line control; fashionable (esp. in industry)	Expert control; very fashionable

Note: Italic type in columns 2–6 indicates key design parameters.

Yet some simple structures have managed to grow very large under the tight control of clever, autocratic leaders, the most famous example being the Ford Motor Co. in the later years of its founder.

Almost all organizations begin their lives as simple structures, granting their founding chief executives considerable latitude to set them up. And most revert to simple structure—no matter how large or what other configuration normally fits their needs—when they face extreme pressure or hostility in their environment. In other words, systems and procedures are suspended as power reverts to the chief executive to give him or her a chance to set things right.

The heyday of the simple structure probably occurred during the period of the great American trusts, late in the nineteenth century. Although today less in fashion and to many a relic of more autocratic times, the simple structure remains a widespread and necessary configuration—for building up most new organizations and for operating those in simple, dynamic environments and those facing extreme, hostile pressures.

MACHINE BUREAUCRACY

Just as the simple structure is prevalent in pre-Industrial Revolution industries such as agriculture, the machine bureaucracy is the offspring of industrialization, with its emphasis on the standardization of work for coordination and its resulting low-skilled, highly specialized jobs. *Exhibit 2* shows that, in contrast to simple structure, the machine bureaucracy elaborates its administration. First, it requires many analysts to design and maintain its systems of standardization—notably those that formalize its behaviors and plan its actions. And by virtue of the organization's dependence on these systems, these analysts gain a degree of informal power, which results in a certain amount of horizontal decentralization.

A large hierarchy emerges in the middle line to oversee the specialized work of the operating core and to keep the lid on conflicts that inevitably result from the rigid departmentalization, as well as from the alienation that often goes with routine, circumscribed jobs. That middle-line hierarchy is usually structured on a functional basis all the way up to the top, where the real power of coordination lies. In other words, machine bureaucracy tends to be centralized in the vertical sense—formal power is concentrated at the top.

And why the large support staff shown in *Exhibit 2*? Because machine bureaucracies depend on stability to function (change interrupts the smooth functioning of the system), they tend not only to seek out stable environments in which to function but also to stabilize the environments they find themselves in. One way they do this is to envelop within their structures all of the support services possible, ones that simple structures prefer to buy. For the same reason they also tend to integrate vertically—to become their own suppliers and customers. And that of course causes many machine bureaucracies to grow very large. So we see the two-sided effect of size here: size drives the organization to bureaucratize ("We do that every day; let's standardize it!"), but bureaucracy also encourages the organization to grow larger. Aging also encourages this configuration; the organization standardizes its work because "we've done that before."

To enable the top managers to maintain centralized control, both the environment and the production system of the machine bureaucracy must be fairly simple. In fact, machine bureaucracies fit most naturally with mass production, where the products, processes, and distribution systems are usually rationalized and thus easy to comprehend. And so machine bureaucracy is most common among large, mature mass-production companies, such as automobile manufacturers, as well as the largest of the established providers of mass services, such as insurance companies and railroads. Thus McDonald's is a classic example of this configuration—achieving enormous success in its simple industry through meticulous standardization.

Because external controls encourage bureaucratization and centralization, this configuration is often assumed by organizations that are tightly controlled from the outside. That is why government agencies, which are subject to many such controls, tend to be driven toward the machine bureaucracy structure regardless of their other conditions.

The problems of the machine bureaucracy are legendary—dull and repetitive work, alienated employees, obsession with control (of markets as well as workers), massive size, and inadaptability. These are machines suited to specific purposes, not to adapting to new ones. For all of these reasons, the machine bureaucracy is no longer fashionable. Bureaucracy has become a dirty word. Yet this is the configuration that gets the products out cheaply and efficiently. And here too there can be a sense of harmony, as in the Swiss railroad system whose trains depart as the second hand sweeps past the twelve.

In a society consumed by its appetite for mass-produced goods, dependent on consistency in so many spheres (how else to deliver millions of pieces of mail every day?) and unable to automate a great many of its routine jobs, machine bureaucracy remains indispensable—and probably the most prevalent of the five configurations today.

PROFESSIONAL BUREAUCRACY

This bureaucratic configuration relies on the standardization of skills rather than work processes or outputs for its coordination and so emerges as dramatically different from the machine bureaucracy. It is the structure hospitals, universities, and accounting firms tend most often to favor. Most important, because it relies for its operating tasks on trained professionals—skilled people who must be given considerable control over their own work—the organization surrenders a good deal of its power not only to the professionals themselves but also to the associations and institutions that select and train them in the first place. As a result, the structure emerges as very decentralized; power over many decisions, both operating and strategic, flows all the way down the hierarchy to the professionals of the operating core. For them this is the most democratic structure of all.

Because the operating procedures, although complex, are rather standardized—taking out appendixes in a hospital, teaching the American Motors case in a business school, doing an audit in an accounting firm—each professional can work independently of his or her colleagues, with the assurance that much of the necessary coordination will be effected automatically through standardization of skills. Thus a colleague of mine observed a five-hour open heart operation in which the surgeon and anesthesiologist never exchanged a single word!

As can be seen in *Exhibit 2*, above the operating core we find a unique structure. Since the main standardization occurs as a result of training that takes place outside the professional bureaucracy, a technostructure is hardly needed. And because the professionals work independently, the size of operating units can be very large, and so few first-line managers are needed. (I work in a business school where 55 professors report directly to one dean.) Yet even those few managers, and those above them, do little direct supervision; much of their time is spent linking their units to the broader environment, notably to ensure adequate financing. Thus to become a top manager in a consulting firm is to become a salesperson.

On the other hand, the support staff is typically very large in order to back up the high-priced professionals. But that staff does a very different kind of work—much of it the simple and routine jobs that the professionals shed. As a result, parallel hierarchies emerge in the professional bureaucracy—one democratic with bottom-up power for the professionals, a second autocratic with top-down control for the support staff.

Professional bureaucracy is most effective for organizations that find themselves in stable yet complex environments. Complexity requires that decision-making power be decentralized to highly trained individuals, and stability enables these individuals to apply standardized skills and so to work with a good deal of autonomy. To further ensure that autonomy, the production system must be neither highly regulating, complex, nor automated. Surgeons use their scalpels and editors their pencils; both must be sharp but are otherwise simple instruments that allow their users considerable freedom in performing their complex work.

Standardization is the great strength as well as the great weakness of professional bureaucracy. That is what enables the professionals to perfect their skills and so achieve great efficiency and effectiveness. But that same standardization raises problems of adaptability. This is not a structure to innovate but one to perfect what is already known. Thus, so long as the environment is stable, the professional bureaucracy does its job well. It identifies the needs of its clients and offers a set of standardized programs to serve them. In other words, pigeonholing is its great forte; change messes up the pigeonholes. New needs arise that fall between or across the slots, and the standard programs no longer apply. Another configuration is required.

Professional bureaucracy, a product of the middle years of this century, is a highly fashionable structure today for two reasons. First, it is very democratic, at least for its professional workers. And second, it offers them considerable autonomy, freeing the professionals even from the need to coordinate closely with each other. To release themselves from the close control of administrators and analysts, not to mention their own colleagues, many people today seek to have themselves declared "professional"—and thereby turn their organizations into professional bureaucracies.

DIVISIONALIZED FORM

Like the professional bureaucracy, the divisionalized form is not so much an integrated organization as a set of rather independent entities joined together by a loose administrative overlay. But whereas those entities of the professional bureaucracy are individuals—professionals in the operating core—in the divisionalized form they are units in the middle line, called divisions.

The divisionalized form differs from the other four configurations in one central respect: it is not a complete but a partial structure, superimposed on others. Those others are in the divisions, each of which is driven toward machine bureaucracy.

An organization divisionalizes for one reason above all—because its product lines are diversified. (And that tends to happen most often in the largest and most mature organizations, those that have run out of opportunities or become stalled in their traditional markets.) Such diversification encourages the organization to create a market-based unit, or division, for each distinct product line (as indicated in *Exhibit* 2) and to grant considerable autonomy to each division to run its own business.

That autonomy notwithstanding, divisionalization does *not* amount to decentralization, although the terms are often equated with each other. Decentralization is an expression of the dispersal of decision-making power in an organization. Divisionalization refers to a structure of semiautonomous market-based units. A divisionalized structure in which the managers at the heads of these units retain the lion's share of the power is far more centralized than many functional structures where large numbers of specialists get involved in the making of important decisions.

In fact, the most famous example of divisionalization involved centralization. Alfred Sloan adopted the divisionalized form at General Motors to reduce the power of the different units, to integrate the holding company William Durant had put together. That kind of centralization appears to have continued to the point where the automotive units in some ways seem closer to functional marketing departments than true divisions.[1]

But how does top management maintain a semblance of control over the divisions? Some direct supervision is used—headquarters managers visit the divisions periodically and authorize some of their more important decisions. But too much of that interferes with the necessary autonomy of the divisions. So headquarters relies on performance control systems or, in other words, on the standardization of outputs. It leaves the operating details to the divisions and exercises control by measuring their performance periodically. And to design these control systems, headquarters creates a small technostructure. It also establishes a small central support staff to provide certain services common to the divisions (such as legal counsel and external relations).

This performance control system has an interesting effect on the internal structure of the division. First, the division is treated as a single integrated entity with one consistent, standardized, and quantifiable set of goals. Those goals tend to get translated down the line into more and more specific subgoals and, eventually, work standards. In other words, they encourage the bureaucratiza-

---

1. *See* Leonard Wrigley, "Diversification and Divisional Autonomy," DBA thesis, Harvard Business School, 1970.

tion of structure. And second, headquarters tends to impose its standards through the managers of the divisions, whom it holds responsible for divisional performance. That tends to result in centralization within the divisions. And centralization coupled with bureaucratization gives machine bureaucracy. That is the structure that works best in the divisions.

Simple structures and adhocracies make poor divisions because they abhor standards—they operate in dynamic environments where standards of any kind are difficult to establish. And professional bureaucracies are not logically treated as integrated entities, nor can their goals be easily quantified. (How does one measure cure in a psychiatric ward or knowledge generated in a university?)

This conclusion is, of course, consistent with the earlier argument that external control (in this case, from headquarters) pushes an organization toward machine bureaucracy. The point is invariably illustrated when a conglomerate takes over an entrepreneurial company and imposes a lot of bureaucratic systems and standards on its simple structure.

The divisionalized form was created to solve the problem of adaptability in machine bureaucracy. By overlaying another level of administration that could add and subtract divisions, the organization found a way to adapt itself to new conditions and to spread its risk. But there is another side to these arguments. Some evidence suggests that the control systems of these structures discourage risk taking and innovation, that the division head who must justify his or her performance every month is not free to experiment the way the independent entrepreneur is.[2]

Moreover, to spread risk is to spread the consequences of that risk; a disaster in one division can pull down the entire organization. Indeed, the fear of this is what elicits the direct control of major new investments, which is what often discourages ambitious innovation. Finally, the divisionalized form does not solve the problem of adaptability of machine bureaucracy, it merely deflects it. When a division goes sour, all that headquarters seems able to do is change the management (as an independent board of directors would do) or divest it. From society's point of view, the problem remains.

Finally, from a social perspective, the divisionalized form raises a number of serious issues. By enabling organizations to grow very large, it leads to the concentration of a great deal of economic power in a few hands. And there is some evidence that it sometimes encourages that power to be used irresponsibly. By emphasizing the measurement of performance as its means of control, a bias arises in favor of those divisional goals that can be operationalized, which usually means the economic ones, not the social ones. That the division is driven by such measures to be socially unresponsive would not seem inappropriate—for the business of the corporation is, after all, economic.

---

2. *See* Wrigley, "Diversification and Divisional Autonomy."

The problem is that in big businesses (where the divisionalized form is prevalent) every strategic decision has social as well as economic consequences. When the screws of the performance control system are turned tight, the division managers, in order to achieve the results expected of them, are driven to ignore the social consequences of their decisions. At that point, *un*responsive behavior becomes *ir*responsible.[3]

The divisionalized structure has become very fashionable in the past few decades, having spread in pure or modified form through most of the *Fortune* "500" in a series of waves and then into European companies. It has also become fashionable in the nonbusiness sector in the guise of "multiversities," large hospital systems, unions, and government itself. And yet it seems fundamentally ill suited to these sectors for two reasons.

First, the success of the divisionalized form depends on goals that can be measured. But outside the business sector, goals are often social in nature and nonquantifiable. The result of performance control, then, is an inappropriate displacement of social goals by economic ones.

Second, the divisions often require structures other than machine bureaucracy. The professionals in the multiversities, for example, often balk at the technocratic controls and the top-down decision making that tends to accompany external control of their campuses. In other words, the divisionalized form can be a misfit just as can any of the other configurations.

ADHOCRACY

None of the structures discussed so far suits the industries of our age—industries such as aerospace, petrochemicals, think-tank consulting, and filmmaking. These organizations need above all to innovate in complex ways. The bureaucratic structures are too inflexible, and the simple structure is too centralized. These industries require "project structures" that fuse experts drawn from different specialties into smoothly functioning creative teams. Hence they tend to favor our fifth configuration, adhocracy, a structure of interacting project teams.

Adhocracy is the most difficult of the five configurations to describe because it is both complex and nonstandardized. Indeed, adhocracy contradicts much of what we accept on faith in organizations—consistency in output, control by administrators, unity of command, strategy emanating from the top. It is a tremendously fluid structure, in which power is constantly shifting and coordination and control are by mutual adjustment through the informal communication and interaction of competent experts. Moreover, adhocracy is the newest of the five configurations, the one researchers have had the least chance

3. For a full discussion of the problems of implementing social goals in the divisionalized form, *see* Robert W. Ackerman, *The Social Challenge to Business* (Cambridge: Harvard University Press, 1975).

to study. Yet it is emerging as a key structural configuration, one that deserves a good deal of consideration.

These comments notwithstanding, adhocracy is a no less coherent configuration than any of the others. Like the professional bureaucracy, adhocracy relies on trained and specialized experts to get the bulk of its work done. But in its case, the experts must work together to create new things instead of working apart to perfect established skills. Hence, for coordination adhocracy must rely extensively on mutual adjustment, which it encourages by the use of the liaison devices—integrating managers, task forces, and matrix structure.

In professional bureaucracy, the experts are concentrated in the operating core, where much of the power lies. But in adhocracy, they tend to be dispersed throughout the structure according to the decisions they make—in the operating core, middle line, technostructure, strategic apex, and especially support staff. Thus, whereas in each of the other configurations power is more or less concentrated, in adhocracy it is distributed unevenly. It flows, not according to authority or status but to wherever the experts needed for a particular decision happen to be found.

Managers abound in the adhocracy—functional managers, project managers, integrating managers. This results in narrow "spans of control" by conventional measures. That is not a reflection of control but of the small size of the project teams. The managers of adhocracy do not control in the conventional sense of direct supervision; typically they are experts too who take their place alongside the others in the teams, concerned especially with linking the different teams together.

As can be seen in *Exhibit 2*, many of the distinctions of conventional structure disappear in the adhocracy. With power based on expertise instead of authority, the line/staff distinction evaporates. And with power distributed throughout the structure, the distinction between the strategic apex and the rest of the structure also blurs. In a project structure, strategy is not formulated from above and then implemented lower down; rather, it evolves by virtue of the multitude of decisions made for the projects themselves. In other words, the adhocracy is continually developing its strategy as it accepts and works out new projects, the creative results of which can never be predicted. And so everyone who gets involved in the project work—and in the adhocracy that can mean virtually everyone—becomes a strategy maker.

There are two basic types of adhocracy, operating and administrative. The *operating* adhocracy carries out innovative projects directly on behalf of its clients, usually under contract, as in a creative advertising agency, a think-tank consulting firm, a manufacturer of engineering prototypes. Professional bureaucracies work in some of these industries too, but with a different orientation. The operating adhocracy treats each client problem as a unique one to be solved in creative fashion; the professional bureaucracy pigeonholes it so that it can provide a standard skill.

For example, there are some consulting firms that tailor their solutions to the client's order and others that sell standard packages off the rack. When the latter fits, it proves much cheaper. When it does not, the money is wasted. In one case, the experts must cooperate with each other in organic structures to innovate; in the other, they can apply their standard skills autonomously in bureaucratic structures.

In the operating adhocracy, the operating and administrative work blend into a single effort. That is, the organization cannot easily separate the planning and design of the operating work—in other words, the project—from its actual execution. So another classic distinction disappears. As shown above the dotted lines in *Exhibit 2*, the organization emerges as an organic mass in which line managers, staff, and operating experts all work together on project teams in ever-shifting relationships.

The *administrative* adhocracy undertakes projects on its own behalf, as in a space agency—NASA, for example, during the Apollo era—or a producer of electronic components. In this type of adhocracy, in contrast to the other, we find a sharp separation of the administrative from the operating work—the latter shown by the dotted lines in *Exhibit 2*. This results in a two-part structure. The administrative component carries out the innovative design work, combining line managers and staff experts in project teams. And the operating component, which puts the results into production, is separated or "truncated" so that its need for standardization will not interfere with the project work.

Sometimes the operations are contracted out altogether. Other times, they are set up in independent structures, as in the printing function in newspapers. And when the operations of an organization are highly automated, the same effect takes place naturally. The operations essentially run themselves, while the administrative component tends to adopt a project orientation concerned with change and innovation, with bringing new facilities on line. Note also the effects of automation—a reduction in the need for rules, since these are built right into the machinery, and a blurring of the line/staff distinction, since control becomes a question more of expertise than authority. What does it mean to supervise a machine? Thus the effect of automation is to reduce the degree of machine bureaucracy in the administration and to drive it toward administrative adhocracy.

Both kinds of adhocracy are commonly found in environments that are complex as well as dynamic. These are the two conditions that call for sophisticated innovation, which requires the cooperative efforts of many different kinds of experts. In the case of administrative adhocracy, the production system is also typically complex and, as noted, often automated. These production systems create the need for highly skilled support staffers, who must be given a good deal of power over technical decisions.

For its part, the operating adhocracy is often associated with young organizations. For one thing, with no standard products or services, organizations that use it tend to be highly vulnerable, and many of them disappear at an early age. For another, age drives these organizations toward bureaucracy, as the employees themselves age and tend to seek an escape from the instability of the structure and its environment. The innovative consulting firm converges on a few of its most successful projects, packages them into standard skills, and settles down to life as a professional bureaucracy; the manufacturer of prototypes hits on a hot product and becomes a machine bureaucracy to mass-produce it.

But not all adhocracies make such a transition. Some endure as they are, continuing to innovate over long periods of time. We see this, for example, in studies of the National Film Board of Canada, famous since the 1940s for its creativity in both films and the techniques of filmmaking.

Finally, fashion is a factor associated with adhocracy. This is clearly the structure of our age, prevalent in almost every industry that has grown up since World War II (and none I can think of established before that time). Every characteristic of adhocracy is very much in vogue today—expertise, organic structure, project teams and task forces, diffused power, matrix structure, sophisticated and often automated production systems, youth, and dynamic, complex environments. Adhocracy is the only one of the five configurations that combines some sense of democracy with an absence of bureaucracy.

Yet, like all the others, this configuration too has its limitations. Adhocracy in some sense achieves its effectiveness through inefficiency. It is inundated with managers and costly liaison devices for communication; nothing ever seems to get done without everyone talking to everyone else. Ambiguity abounds, giving rise to all sorts of conflicts and political pressures. Adhocracy can do no ordinary thing well. But it is extraordinary at innovation.

CONFIGURATIONS AS A DIAGNOSTIC TOOL

What in fact are these configurations? Are they (1) abstract ideals, (2) real-life structures, one of which an organization had better use if it is to survive, or (3) building blocks for more complex structures? In some sense, the answer is a qualified yes in all three cases. These are certainly abstract ideals, simplifications of the complex world of structure. Yet the abstract ideal can come to life too. Every organization experiences the five pulls that underlie these configurations: the pull to centralize by the top management, the pull to formalize by the technostructure, the pull to professionalize by the operators, the pull to balkanize by the managers of the middle line, and the pull to collaborate by the support staff.

Where one pull dominates—where the conditions favor it above all—then the organization will tend to organize itself close to one of the configurations. I have cited examples of this throughout my discussion—the entrepreneurial company, the hamburger chain, the university, the conglomerate, the space agency.

But one pull does not always dominate; two may have to exist in balance. Symphony orchestras engage highly trained specialists who perfect their skills, as do the operators in professional bureaucracy. But their efforts must be tightly coordinated hence, the reliance on the direct supervision of a leader—a conductor—as in simple structure. Thus a hybrid of the two configurations emerges that is eminently sensible for the symphony orchestra (even if it does generate a good deal of conflict between leader and operators).

Likewise, we have companies that are diversified around a central theme that creates linkages among their different product lines. As a result, they continually experience the pull to separate, as in the divisionalized form, and also integrate, as in machine bureaucracy or perhaps adhocracy. And what configuration should we impute to an IBM? Clearly, there is too much going on in many giant organizations to describe them as one configuration or another. But the framework of the five configurations can still help us to understand how their different parts are organized and fit together—or refuse to.

The point is that managers can improve their organizational designs by considering the different pulls their organizations experience and the configurations toward which they are drawn. In other words, this set of five configurations can serve as an effective tool in diagnosing the problems of organizational design, especially those of the *fit* among component parts. Let us consider four basic forms of misfit to show how managers can use the set of configurations as a diagnostic tool.

ARE THE INTERNAL ELEMENTS CONSISTENT?

Management that grabs at every structural innovation that comes along may be doing its organization great harm. It risks going off in all directions: yesterday long-range planning to pin managers down, today Outward Bound to open them up. Quality of working life programs as well as all those fashionable features of adhocracy—integrating managers, matrix structure, and the like—have exemplary aims: to create more satisfying work conditions and to increase the flexibility of the organization. But are they appropriate for a machine bureaucracy? Do enlarged jobs really fit with the requirements of the mass production of automobiles? Can the jobs ever be made large enough to really satisfy the workers—and the cost-conscious customers?

I believe that in the fashionable world of organizational design, fit remains an important characteristic. The *hautes structurières* of New York—the consulting firms that seek to bring the latest in structural fashion to their clients—would do well to pay a great deal more attention to that fit. Machine bureaucracy functions best when its reporting relationships are sharply defined and its operating core staffed with workers who prefer routine and stability. The nature of the work in this configuration—managerial as well as operating—is rooted in the reality of mass production, in the costs of manual labor compared with those of automated machines, and in the size and age of the organization.

Until we are prepared to change our whole way of living—for example, to pay more for handcrafted instead of mass-produced products and so to consume less—we would do better to spend our time trying not to convert our machine bureaucracies into something else but to ensure that they work effectively as the bureaucracies they are meant to be. Organizations, like individuals, can avoid identity crises by deciding what it is they wish to be and then pursuing it with a healthy obsession.

ARE THE EXTERNAL CONTROLS FUNCTIONAL?

An organization may achieve its own internal consistency and then have it destroyed by the imposition of external controls. The typical effect of those controls is to drive the organization toward machine bureaucracy. In other words, it is the simple structures, professional bureaucracies, and adhocracies that suffer most from such controls. Two cases of this seem rampant in our society: one is the takeover of small, private companies by larger divisionalized ones, making bureaucracies of entrepreneurial ventures; the other is the tendency for governments to assume increasingly direct control of what used to be more independent organizations—public school systems, hospitals, universities, and social welfare agencies.

As organizations are taken over in these ways—brought into the hierarchies of other organizations—two things happen. They become centralized and formalized. In other words, they are driven toward machine bureaucracy. Government administrators assume that just a little more formal control will bring this callous hospital or that weak school in line. Yet the cure—even when the symptoms are understood—is worse than the disease. The worst way to correct deficiencies in professional work is through control by technocratic standards. Professional bureaucracies cannot be managed like machines.

In the school system, such standards imposed from outside the classroom serve only to discourage the competent teachers, not to improve the weak ones. The performance of teachers—as that of all other professionals—depends primarily on their skills and training. Retraining or, more likely, replacing them is the basic means to improvement.

For almost a century now, the management literature—from time study through operations research to long-range planning—has promoted machine bureaucracy as the "one best way." That assumption is false; it is one way among a number suited to only certain conditions.

IS THERE A PART THAT DOES NOT FIT?

Sometimes an organization's management, recognizing the need for internal consistency, hives off a part in need of special treatment—establishes it in a pocket off in a corner to be left alone. But the problem all too often is that it is not left alone. The research laboratory may be built out in the country, far from the managers and analysts who run the machine bureaucracy back home. But the distance is only physical.

Standards have a long administrative reach: it is difficult to corner off a small component and pretend that it will not be influenced by the rest. Each organization, not to mention each configuration, develops its own norms, traditions, beliefs—in other words, its own ideology. And that permeates every part of it. Unless there is a rough balance among opposing forces—as in the symphony orchestra—the prevailing ideology will tend to dominate. That is why adhocracies need especially tolerant controllers, just as machine bureaucracies must usually scale down their expectations for their research laboratories.

IS THE RIGHT STRUCTURE IN THE WRONG SITUATION?

Some organizations do indeed achieve and maintain an internal consistency. But then they find that it is designed for an environment the organization is no longer in. To have a nice, neat machine bureaucracy in a dynamic industry calling for constant innovation or, alternately, a flexible adhocracy in a stable industry calling for minimum cost makes no sense. Remember that these are configurations of situation as well as structure. Indeed, the very notion of configuration is that all the elements interact in a system. One element does not cause another; instead, all influence each other interactively. Structure is no more designed to fit the situation than situation is selected to fit the structure.

The way to deal with the right structure in the wrong environment may be to change the environment, not the structure. Often, in fact, it is far easier to shift industries or retreat to a suitable niche in an industry than to undo a cohesive structure. Thus the entrepreneur goes after a new, dynamic environment when the old one stabilizes and the bureaucracies begin to move in. When a situation changes suddenly—as it did for oil companies some years ago—a rapid change in situation or structure would seem to be mandatory. But what of a gradual change in situation? How should the organization adapt, for example, when its long-stable markets slowly become dynamic?

Essentially, the organization has two choices. It can adapt continuously to the environment at the expense of internal consistency—that is steadily redesign its structure to maintain external fit. Or it can maintain internal consistency at the expense of a gradually worsening fit with its environment, at least until the fit becomes so bad that it must undergo sudden structural redesign to achieve a new internally consistent configuration. In other words, the choice is between evolution and revolution, between perpetual mild adaptation, which favors external fit over time, and infrequent major realignment, which favors internal consistency over time.

In his research on configuration, Danny Miller found that effective companies usually opt for revolution. Forced to decide whether to spend most of their time with a good external fit or with an established internal consistency, they choose consistency and put up with brief periods of severe disruption to realign the fit occasionally. It is better, apparently, to maintain at least partial configuration than none at all. Miller called this process, appropriately enough, a "quantum" theory of structural change.[4]

---

4. Danny Miller, *Revolution and Evolution: A Quantum View of Organizational Adaptation*, working paper, McGill University, 1980.

FIT OVER FASHION

To conclude, consistency, coherence, and fit—harmony—are critical factors in organization design, but they come at a price. An organization cannot be all things to all people. It should do what it does well and suffer the consequences. Be an efficient machine bureaucracy where that is appropriate and do not pretend to be highly adaptive. Or be an adaptive adhocracy and do not pretend to be highly efficient. Or create some new configuration to suit internal needs. The point is not really *which* configuration is chosen; it is *that* configuration is achieved.

DISCUSSION QUESTIONS

1. Are there other organizational configurations besides the five described in this piece? If so, are they specific to an industry or a particular type of work?
2. What is the relationship between a firm's configuration and its strategy?
3. Choose a company that you know well and identify its configuration, according to Mintzberg's types. Does the configuration seem coherent? If not, how would you modify it to achieve "fit"?
4. The author refers to "the pull to centralize by . . . top management." What are the advantages of centralization? As a senior general manager, how would you balance this tendency in order to achieve a harmonious configuration?

From Control to Commitment in the Workplace

13

RICHARD E. WALTON

A general manager must have a clear sense of how best to manage the company's work force and motivate employees. This reading describes two radically different strategies for doing so, one based on imposing control and the other based on eliciting commitment. The control strategy seeks to impose order on the work force. This strategy assumes that employees will perform only up to the minimum and that their skills and motivation are, in general, just average. Therefore, jobs are narrowly defined and minimum productivity goals are the norm. A commitment strategy expects superior performance from employees. Jobs are broadly defined, and workers are expected to manage themselves as much as possible. Frequent training allows employees to upgrade their skills. Not surprisingly, according to Richard Walton, a commitment strategy often leads to outstanding corporate results. General managers are beginning to recognize that employees are best motivated by having much expected of them and by being responsible for their own performance.

The larger shape of institutional change is always difficult to recognize when one stands right in the middle of it. Today, throughout American industry, a significant change is under way in long-established approaches to the organization and management of work. Although this shift in attitude and practice takes a wide variety of company-specific forms, its larger shape—its overall pattern—is already visible if one knows where and how to look.

Consider, for example, the marked differences between two plants in the chemical products division of a major U.S. corporation. Both make similar products and employ similar technologies, but that is virtually all they have in common.

The first, organized by businesses with an identifiable product or product line, divides its employees into self-supervising 10- to 15-person work teams that are collectively responsible for a set of related tasks. Each team member has the training to perform many or all of the tasks for which the team is accountable, and pay reflects the level of mastery of required skills. These teams have received assurances that management will go to extra lengths to provide continued employment in any economic downturn. The teams have also been thoroughly briefed on such issues as market share, product costs, and their implications for the business.

Not surprisingly, this plant is a top performer economically and rates well on all measures of employee satisfaction, absenteeism, turnover, and safety. With its employees actively engaged in identifying and solving problems, it operates with fewer levels of management and fewer specialized departments than do its sister plants. It is also one of the principal suppliers of management talent for these other plants and for the division manufacturing staff.

In the second plant, each employee is responsible for a fixed job and is required to perform up to the minimum standard defined for that job. Peer pressure keeps new employees from exceeding the minimum standards and from taking other initiatives that go beyond basic job requirements. Supervisors, who manage daily assignments and monitor performance, have long since given up hope for anything more than compliance with standards, finding sufficient difficulty in getting their people to perform adequately most of the time. In fact, they and their workers try to prevent the industrial engineering department, which is under pressure from top plant management to improve operations, from using changes in methods to "jack up" standards.

A management campaign to document an "airtight case" against employees who have excessive absenteeism or sub-par performance mirrors employees' low morale and high distrust of management. A constant stream of formal grievances, violations of plant rules, harassment of supervisors, wildcat walkouts, and even sabotage have prevented the plant from reaching its productivity and quality goals and has absorbed a disproportionate amount of division staff time. Dealings with the union are characterized by contract negotiations on economic matters and skirmishes over issues of management control.

No responsible manager, of course, would ever wish to encourage the kind of situation at this second plant, yet the determination to understand its deeper causes and to attack them at their root does not come easily. Established modes of doing things have an inertia all their own. Such an effort is, however, in process all across the industrial landscape. And with that effort comes the possibility of a revolution in industrial relations every bit as great as that occasioned by the rise of mass production the better part of a century ago. The challenge is clear to those managers willing to see it—and the potential benefits, enormous.

APPROACHES TO WORK-FORCE MANAGEMENT

What explains the extraordinary differences between the plants just described? Is it that the first is newer and the other old? Yes and no. Not all new plants enjoy so fruitful an approach to work organization; not all older plants have such intractable problems. Is it that one plant is not unionized and the other is? Again, yes and no. The presence of a union may institutionalize conflict and lackluster performance, but it seldom causes them.

At issue here is not so much age or unionization but two radically different strategies for managing a company's or a factory's work force, two incompatible views of what managers can reasonably expect of workers and of the kind of partnership they can share with them. For simplicity, I will speak of these profound differences as reflecting the choice between a strategy based on imposing *control* and a strategy based on eliciting *commitment*.

THE 'CONTROL' STRATEGY

The traditional—or control-oriented—approach to work-force management took shape during the early part of this century in response to the division of work into small, fixed jobs for which individuals could be held accountable. The actual definition of jobs, as of acceptable standards of performance, rested on "lowest common denominator" assumptions about workers' skill and motivation. To monitor and control effort of this assumed caliber, management organized its own responsibilities into a hierarchy of specialized roles buttressed by a top-down allocation of authority and by status symbols attached to positions in the hierarchy.

For workers, compensation followed the rubric of "a fair day's pay for a fair day's work" because precise evaluations were possible when individual job requirements were so carefully prescribed. Most managers had little doubt that labor was best thought of as a variable cost, although some exceptional companies guaranteed job security to head off unionization attempts.

In the traditional approach, there was generally little policy definition with regard to employee voice unless the work force was unionized, in which case damage-control strategies predominated. With no union, management relied on an open-door policy, attitude surveys, and similar devices to learn about employees' concerns. If the work force was unionized, then management bargained terms of employment and established an appeal mechanism. These activities fell to labor relations specialists, who operated independently from line management and whose very existence assumed the inevitability and even the appropriateness of an adversarial relationship between workers and managers. Indeed, to those who saw management's exclusive obligation to be to a company's shareowners and the ownership of property to be the ultimate source of both obligation and prerogative, the claims of employees were constraints, nothing more.

At the heart of this traditional model is the wish to establish order, exercise control, and achieve efficiency in the application of the work force. Although it has distant antecedents in the bureaucracies of both church and military, the model's real father is Frederick W. Taylor, the turn-of-the-century "father of scientific management," whose views about the proper organization of work have long influenced management practice as well as the reactive policies of the U.S. labor movement.

Recently, however, changing expectations among workers have prompted a growing disillusionment with the apparatus of control. At the same time, of course, an intensified challenge from abroad has made the competitive obsolescence of this strategy clear. A model that assumes low employee commitment and that is designed to produce reliable if not outstanding performance simply cannot match the standards of excellence set by world-class competitors. Especially in a high-wage country like the United States, market success depends on a superior level of performance, a level that, in turn, requires the deep commitment, not merely the obedience—if you could obtain it—of workers. And as painful experience shows, this commitment cannot flourish in a workplace dominated by the familiar model of control.

THE 'COMMITMENT' STRATEGY

Over the past 20 years, companies have experimented at the plant level with a radically different work-force strategy. The more visible pioneers—among them, General Foods at Topeka, Kansas; General Motors at Brookhaven, Mississippi; Cummins Engine at Jamestown, New York; and Procter & Gamble at Lima, Ohio—have shown how great and productive the contribution of a truly committed work force can be. For a time, all new plants of this sort were nonunion, but by 1980 the success of efforts undertaken jointly with unions—GM's cooperation with the UAW at the Cadillac plant in Livonia, Michigan, for example—was impressive enough to encourage managers of both new and existing facilities to rethink their approach to the work force.

Local managers and union officials increasingly talk about common interests, working to develop mutual trust, and agreeing to sponsor quality-of-work-life (QWL) or employee involvement (EI) activities. Although most of these ventures have been initiated at the local level, there have been major exceptions.

More recently, a growing number of manufacturing companies have begun to remove levels of plant hierarchy, increase managers' spans of control, integrate quality and production activities at lower organizational levels, combine production and maintenance operations, and open up new career possibilities for workers. Some corporations have even begun to chart organizational renewal for the entire company. Cummins Engine, for example, has ambitiously committed itself to inform employees about the business, to encourage participation by everyone, and to create jobs that involve greater responsibility and more flexibility.

In this commitment-based approach to the work force, jobs are designed to be broader than before, to combine planning and implementation, and to include efforts to upgrade operations, not just maintain them. Individual responsibilities are expected to change as conditions change, and teams, not individuals, often are the organizational units accountable for performance. With management hierarchies relatively flat and differences in status minimized, control and lateral coordination depend on shared goals, and expertise rather than formal position determines influence.

Under the commitment strategy, performance expectations are high and serve not to define minimum standards but to provide "stretch objectives," emphasize continuous improvement, and reflect the requirements of the marketplace. Accordingly, compensation policies reflect less the old formulas of job evaluation than the heightened importance of group achievement, the expanded scope of individual contribution, and the growing concern for such questions of "equity" as gain sharing, stock ownership, and profit sharing.

Equally important to the commitment strategy is the challenge of giving employees some assurance of security, perhaps by offering them priority in training and retraining as old jobs are eliminated and new ones are created. Guaranteeing employees access to due process and providing them the means to be heard on such issues as production methods, problem solving, and human resources policies and practices is also a challenge. In unionized settings, the additional tasks include making relations less adversarial, broadening the agenda for joint problem solving and planning, and facilitating employee consultation.

Underlying all these policies is a management philosophy, often embodied in a published statement, that acknowledges the legitimate claims of a company's multiple stakeholders—owners, employees, customers, and the public. At the center of this philosophy is a belief that eliciting employee commitment will lead to enhanced performance. The evidence shows this belief to be well-grounded. In the absence of genuine commitment, however, new management policies designed for a committed work force may well leave a company distinctly more vulnerable than would older policies based on the control approach. The advantages—and risks—are considerable.

THE COSTS OF COMMITMENT

Because the potential leverage of a commitment-oriented strategy on performance is so great, the natural temptation is to assume the universal applicability of that strategy. Some environments, however, especially those requiring intricate teamwork, problem solving, organizational learning, and self-monitoring, are better suited than others to the commitment model. Indeed, the pioneers of the deep commitment strategy—a fertilizer plant in Norway, a refinery in the United Kingdom, a paper mill in Pennsylvania, a pet-food processing plant in Kansas—were all based on continuous process technologies and were all capital- and raw-material intensive. All provided high economic leverage to improvements in workers' skills and attitudes, and all could offer considerable job challenge.

Is the converse true? Is the control strategy appropriate whenever—as with convicts breaking rocks with sledgehammers in a prison yard—work can be completely prescribed, remains static, and calls for individual, not group, effort? In practice, managers have long answered yes. Mass production, epitomized by the assembly line, has for years been thought suitable for old-fashioned control.

But not any longer. Many mass producers, not least the automakers, have recently been trying to reconceive the structure of work and to give employees a significant role in solving problems and improving methods. Why? For many reasons, including to boost in-plant quality, lower warranty costs, cut waste, raise machine utilization and total capacity with the same plant and equipment, reduce operating and support personnel, reduce turnover and absenteeism, and speed up implementation of change. In addition, some managers place direct value on the fact that the commitment policies promote the development of human skills and individual self-esteem.

The benefits, economic and human, of worker commitment extend not only to continuous process industries but to traditional manufacturing industries as well. What, though, are the costs? To achieve these gains, managers have had to invest extra effort, develop new skills and relationships, cope with higher levels of ambiguity and uncertainty, and experience the pain and discomfort associated with changing habits and attitudes. Some of their skills have become obsolete, and some of their careers have been casualties of change. Union officials, too, have had to face the dislocation and discomfort that inevitably follow any upheaval in attitudes and skills. For their part, workers have inherited more responsibility and, along with it, greater uncertainty and a more open-ended possibility of failure.

Part of the difficulty in assessing these costs is the fact that so many of the following problems inherent to the commitment strategy remain to be solved.

EMPLOYMENT ASSURANCES

As managers in heavy industry confront economic realities that make such assurances less feasible and as their counterparts in fiercely competitive high-technology areas are forced to rethink early guarantees of employment security, pointed questions await.

Will managers give lifetime assurances to the few, those who reach, say, 15 years' seniority, or will they adopt a general no-layoff policy? Will they demonstrate by policies and practices that employment security, though by no means absolute, is a higher priority item than it was under the control approach? Will they accept greater responsibility for outplacement?

COMPENSATION

In one sense, the more productive employees under the commitment approach deserve to receive better pay for their better efforts, but how can managers balance this claim on resources with the harsh reality that domestic pay rates have risen to levels that render many of our industries uncompetitive internationally? Already, in such industries as trucking and airlines, new domestic competitors have placed companies that maintain prevailing wage rates at a significant disadvantage. Experience shows, however, that wage freezes and concession bargaining create obstacles to commitment, and new approaches to compensation are difficult to develop at a time when management cannot raise the overall level of pay.

Which approach is really suitable to the commitment model is unclear. Traditional job classifications place limits on the discretion of supervisors and encourage workers' sense of job ownership. Can pay systems based on employees' skill levels, which have long been used in engineering and skilled crafts, prove widely effective? Can these systems make up in greater mastery, positive motivation, and work-force flexibility what they give away in higher average wages?

In capital-intensive businesses, where total payroll accounts for a small percentage of costs, economics favors the move toward pay progression based on deeper and broader mastery. Still, conceptual problems remain with measuring skills, achieving consistency in pay decisions, allocating opportunities for learning new skills, trading off breadth and flexibility against depth, and handling the effects of "topping out" in a system that rewards and encourages personal growth.

There are also practical difficulties. Existing plants cannot, for example, convert to a skill-based structure overnight because of the vested interests of employees in the higher classifications. Similarly, formal profit- or gain-sharing plans like the Scanlon Plan (which shares gains in productivity as measured by improvements in the ratio of payroll to the sales value of production) cannot always operate. At the plant level, formulas that are responsive to what employees can influence, that are not unduly influenced by factors beyond their control, and that are readily understood, are not easy to devise. Small stand-alone businesses with a mature technology and stable markets tend to find the task least troublesome, but they are not the only ones trying to implement the commitment approach.

TECHNOLOGY

Computer-based technology can reinforce the control model or facilitate movement to the commitment model. Applications can narrow the scope of jobs or broaden them, emphasize the individual nature of tasks or promote the work of groups, centralize or decentralize the making of decisions, and create performance measures that emphasize learning or hierarchical control.

To date, the effects of this technology on control and commitment have been largely unintentional and unexpected. Even in organizations otherwise pursuing a commitment strategy, managers have rarely appreciated that the side effects of technology are not somehow "given" in the nature of things or that they can be actively managed. In fact, computer-based technology may be the least deterministic, most flexible technology to enter the workplace since the industrial revolution. As it becomes less hardware-dependent and more software-intensive and as the cost of computer power declines, the variety of ways to meet business requirements expands, each with a different set of human implications. Management has yet to identify the potential role of technology policy in the commitment strategy, and it has yet to invent concepts and methods to realize the potential.

SUPERVISORS

The commitment model requires first-line supervisors to facilitate rather than direct the work force, to impart rather than merely practice their technical and administrative expertise, and to help workers develop the ability to manage

EXHIBIT
Work-Force Strategies

	CONTROL	*TRANSITIONAL*	*COMMITMENT*
Job Design Principles	Individual attention limited to performing individual job.	Scope of individual responsibility extended to upgrading system performance.	Individual responsibility extended to upgrading system performance.
	Job design deskills and fragments work and separates doing and thinking.	No change in traditional job design or accountability.	Job design enhances content of work, emphasizes whole task, and combines doing and thinking.
	Accountability focused on individual.		Frequent use of teams as basic accountable unit.
	Fixed job definition.		Flexible definition of duties, contingent on changing conditions.
Performance Expectations	Measured standards define minimum performance. Stability seen as desirable.		Emphasis placed on higher, "stretch objectives," which tend to be dynamic and oriented to the marketplace.
Management Organization: Structure, Systems, and Style	Structure tends to be layered, with top-down controls.	No basic changes in approaches to structure, control, or authority.	Flat organization structure with mutual influence systems.
	Coordination and control rely on rules and procedures.		Coordination and control based more on shared goals, values, and traditions.
	More emphasis on prerogatives and positional authority.		Management emphasis on problem solving and relevant information and expertise.
	Status symbols distributed to reinforce hierarchy.	A few visible symbols change.	Minimum status differentials to de-emphasize inherent hierarchy.

EXHIBIT
Work-Force Strategies (Continued)

	CONTROL	*TRANSITIONAL*	*COMMITMENT*
Compensation Policies	Variable pay where feasible to provide individual incentive.	Typically no basic changes in compensation concepts.	Variable rewards to create equity and to reinforce group achievements, e.g., gain sharing.
	Individual pay geared to job evaluation.		Individual pay linked to skills and mastery.
	In downturn, cuts concentrated on hourly payroll.	Equality of sacrifice among employee groups.	Equality of sacrifice.
Employment Assurances	Employees regarded as variable costs.	Assurances that participation will not result in loss of job.	Assurances that participation will not result in loss of job.
		Extra effort to avoid layoffs.	High commitment to avoid or assist in reemployment.
			Priority for training and retaining existing work force.
Employee Voice Policies	Employee input allowed on relatively narrow agenda. Attendant risks emphasized. Methods include open-door policy, attitude surveys, grievance procedures, and collective bargaining in some organizations.	Addition of limited, ad hoc consultation mechanisms. No change in corporate governance.	Employee participation encouraged on wide range of issues. Attendant benefits emphasized. New concepts of corporate governance.
	Business information distributed on strictly defined "need to know" basis.	Additional sharing of information.	Business data shared widely.
Labor-Management Relations	Adversarial labor relations; emphasis on interest conflict.	Thawing of adversarial attitudes; joint sponsorship of QWL or EI; emphasis on common fate.	Mutuality in labor relations; joint planning and problem solving on expanded agenda.
			Unions, management, and workers redefine their respective roles.

themselves. In practice, supervisors are to delegate away most of their traditional functions—often without having received adequate training and support for their new team-building tasks or having their own needs for voice, dignity, and fulfillment recognized.

These dilemmas are even visible in the new titles many supervisors carry—"team advisers" or "team consultants," for example—most of which imply that supervisors are not in the chain of command, although they are expected to be directive if necessary and assume functions delegated to the work force if they are not being performed. Part of the confusion here is the failure to distinguish the behavioral style required of supervisors from the basic responsibilities assigned them. Their ideal style may be advisory, but their responsibilities are to achieve certain human and economic outcomes. With experience, however, as first-line managers become more comfortable with the notion of delegating what subordinates are ready and able to perform, the problem will diminish.

Other difficulties are less tractable. The new breed of supervisors must have a level of interpersonal skill and conceptual ability often lacking in the present supervisory work force. Some companies have tried to address this lack by using the position as an entry point to management for college graduates. This approach may succeed where the work force has already acquired the necessary technical expertise, but it blocks a route of advancement for workers and sharpens the dividing line between management and other employees. Moreover, unless the company intends to open up higher level positions for these college-educated supervisors, they may well grow impatient with the shift work of first-line supervision.

Even when new supervisory roles are filled—and filled successfully—from the ranks, dilemmas remain. With teams developed and functions delegated, to what new challenges do they turn to utilize fully their own capacities? Do these capabilities match the demands of the other managerial work they might take on? If fewer and fewer supervisors are required as their individual span of control extends to a second and third work team, what promotional opportunities exist for the rest? Where do they go?

UNION-MANAGEMENT RELATIONS

Some companies, as they move from control to commitment, seek to decertify their unions and, at the same time, strengthen their employees' bond to the company. Others pursue cooperation with their unions, believing that they need their active support.

These developments open up new questions. Where companies are trying to preserve the non-union status of some plants and yet promote collaborative union relations in others, will unions increasingly force the company to choose? After General Motors saw the potential of its joint QWL program with the UAW, it signed a neutrality clause and then an understanding about automatic recognition in new plants. If forced to choose, what will other managements do? Further, where union and management have collaborated in promoting QWL, how can the union prevent management from using the program to appeal directly to the workers about issues, such as wage concessions, that are subject to collective bargaining?

And if, in the spirit of mutuality, both sides agree to expand their joint agenda, what new risks will they face? Do union officials have the expertise to deal effectively with new agenda items like investment, pricing, and technology? To support QWL activities, they already have had to expand their skills and commit substantial resources at a time when shrinking employment has reduced their membership and thus their finances.

THE TRANSITIONAL STAGE

Although some organizations have adopted a comprehensive version of the commitment approach, most initially take on a more limited set of changes, a "transitional" stage or approach. The challenge here is to modify expectations, to make credible the leaders' stated intentions for further movement, and to support the initial changes in behavior. These transitional efforts can achieve a temporary equilibrium, provided they are viewed as part of a movement toward a comprehensive commitment strategy.

The cornerstone of the transitional stage is the voluntary participation of employees in problem-solving groups like quality circles. In unionized organizations, union-management dialogue leading to a jointly sponsored program is a condition for this type of employee involvement, which must then be supported by additional training and communication and by a shift in management style. Managers must also seek ways to consult employees about changes that affect them and to assure them that management will make every effort to avoid, defer, or minimize layoffs from higher productivity. When volume-related layoffs or concessions on pay are unavoidable, the principle of "equality of sacrifice" must apply to all employee groups, not just the hourly work force.

As a rule, during the early stages of transformation, few immediate changes can occur in the management system itself. It is easy, of course, to attempt to change too much too soon. A more common error, especially in established organizations, is to make only "token" changes that never reach a critical mass. All too often managers try a succession of technique-oriented changes one by one: job enrichment, sensitivity training, management by objectives, group brainstorming, quality circles, and so on. Whatever the benefits of these techniques, their value to the organization will rapidly decay if the management philosophy—and practice—does not shift accordingly.

A different type of error—"overreaching"—may occur in newly established organizations based on commitment principles. In one new plant, managers allowed too much peer influence in pay decisions; in another, they underplayed the role of first-line supervisors as a link in the chain of command; in a third, they overemphasized learning of new skills and flexibility at the expense of mastery in critical operations. These design errors by themselves are not fatal, but the organization must be able to make mid-course corrections.

RATE OF TRANSFORMATION

How rapidly is the transformation in work-force strategy occurring? (See the *Exhibit* on pages 204–5 for a summary of work-force strategies.) Early change focused on the blue-collar work force and on those clerical operations that most closely resemble the factory. Although clerical change has lagged somewhat—because the control model has not produced such overt employee disaffection, and because management has been slow to recognize the importance of quality and productivity improvement—there are signs of a quickened pace of change in clerical operations.

Only a small fraction of U.S. workplaces today can boast of a comprehensive commitment strategy, but the rate of transformation continues to accelerate, and the move toward commitment via some explicit transitional stage extends to a still larger number of plants and offices. This transformation may be fueled by economic necessity, but other factors are shaping and pacing it—individual leadership in management and labor, philosophical choices, organizational competence in managing change, and cumulative learning from change itself.

DISCUSSION QUESTIONS

1. Is a commitment strategy economically feasible for most firms? What are the hidden costs of implementing such a strategy?
2. Are some elements of the traditional control strategy still essential to competitiveness? Would a mix of the two strategies better serve some companies, or should all firms seek to move from control to commitment?
3. With a commitment strategy, "compensation policies reflect less the old formulas of job evaluation than the heightened importance of group achievement. . . ." Does a commitment strategy remove individual incentive to perform well?
4. Should a commitment strategy change the way general managers approach their work? Would it affect their perceived status?

Reward Systems and the Role of Compensation 14

MICHAEL BEER AND RICHARD E. WALTON

A company's reward system is a key component of general management's efforts to attract, motivate, and satisfy employees. Workers who feel adequately compensated are more likely to be productive. Yet what a reward system is designed to do and what it actually does are often contradictory. General managers must be aware of the balance between extrinsic and intrinsic rewards, must take employee perceptions of fair compensation into consideration, and must determine the appropriate level of employee involvement in the design and administration of reward systems. Perhaps most important, the general manager must be able to inspire trust and confidence in the compensation system.

The design and management of reward systems present the general manager with one of the most difficult HRM (human-resource-management) tasks. This HRM policy area contains the greatest contradictions between the promise of theory and the reality of implementation. Consequently, organizations sometimes go through cycles of innovation and hope as reward systems are developed, followed by disillusionment as these reward systems fail to deliver.[1]

REWARDS AND EMPLOYEE SATISFACTION

Gaining an employee's satisfaction with the rewards given is not a simple matter. Rather, employee satisfaction is a function of several factors that organizations must learn to manage.

- ***The individual's satisfaction with rewards is, in part, related to what is expected and how much is received.*** Feelings of satisfaction or dissatisfaction arise when individuals compare their input—job skills, education, effort, and performance—with output—the mix of extrinsic and intrinsic rewards they receive.

1. This reading consists of material adapted from *Managing Human Assets* by Michael Beer, Bert Spector, Paul Lawrence, D. Quinn Mills, and Richard Walton (New York: The Free Press, 1984).

- ***Employee satisfaction is also affected by comparisons with other people in similar jobs and organizations.*** In effect, employees compare their own input/output ratio with that of others. People vary considerably in how they weigh various inputs in that comparison. They tend to weigh their strong points more heavily, such as certain skills or a recent incident of effective performance. Individuals also tend to give their own performance a higher rating than the one they receive from their supervisors. The problem of unrealistic self-ratings exists partly because supervisors in most organizations do not communicate a candid evaluation of their subordinates' performances to them. Such candid communication to subordinates, unless done skillfully, seriously risks damaging self-esteem. The bigger dilemma is that failure by managers to communicate a candid appraisal of performance makes it difficult for employees to develop a realistic view of their own performance, thus increasing the possibility of dissatisfaction with the pay they are receiving.
- ***Employees often misperceive the rewards of others.*** Evidence shows that individuals tend to overestimate the pay of fellow workers doing similar jobs and to underestimate their performance (a defense or self-esteem-building mechanism). Misperceptions of the performance and rewards of others also occur because organizations do not generally make available accurate information about the salary or performance of others.
- ***Overall satisfaction results from a mix of rewards rather than from any single reward.*** The evidence suggests that both intrinsic rewards and extrinsic rewards are important and cannot be directly substituted for each other. Employees who are paid well for repetitious, boring work will be dissatisfied with the lack of intrinsic rewards, just as employees who are paid poorly for interesting, challenging work may be dissatisfied with extrinsic rewards.

REWARDS AND MOTIVATION

From the organization's point of view, rewards are intended to motivate certain behaviors. But under what conditions will rewards actually motivate employees? To be useful, rewards must be seen as timely and tied to effective performance.

One theory suggests that the following conditions are necessary for employee motivation:[2]

- Employees must believe effective performance (or certain specified behavior) will lead to certain rewards. For example, attaining certain results will lead to a bonus or approval from others.

---

2. Edward E. Lawler, *Pay and Organizational Effectiveness: A Psychological View* (New York: McGraw-Hill, 1971), pp. 267–272.

- Employees must feel that the rewards offered are attractive. Although some employees may desire promotions because they seek power, others may want a fringe benefit, such as a pension, because they are older and want retirement security.
- Employees must believe a certain level of individual effort will lead to achieving the corporation's standards of performance.

As indicated, motivation to exert effort is triggered by the prospect of desired rewards: money, recognition, promotion, and so forth. If effort leads to performance and performance leads to desired rewards, the employee is satisfied and motivated to perform again.

As previously mentioned, rewards fall into two categories: extrinsic and intrinsic. *Extrinsic rewards* come from the organization as money, perquisites, or promotions or from supervisors and co-workers as recognition. *Intrinsic rewards* accrue from performing the task itself and may include the satisfaction of accomplishment or a sense of influence. The process of work and the individual's response to it provide the intrinsic reward. But the organization seeking to increase intrinsic rewards must provide a work environment that allows these satisfactions to occur; therefore, more organizations are redesigning work and delegating responsibility to enhance employee involvement.

EQUITY AND PARTICIPATION

The ability of a reward system to both motivate and satisfy depends on who influences and/or controls the system's design and implementation. Even though considerable evidence suggests that participation in decision making can lead to greater acceptance of decisions, participation in both the design and administration of reward systems is rare. Such participation is time-consuming.

Perhaps a greater roadblock is that pay has been one of the last strongholds of managerial prerogatives. Concerned about employee self-interest and compensation costs, corporations do not typically allow employees to participate in pay-system design or decisions. Thus, it is not possible to test thoroughly the effects of widespread participation on acceptance of and trust in reward systems.

COMPENSATION SYSTEMS: THE DILEMMAS OF PRACTICE

A body of experience, research, and theory has been developed about how money satisfies and motivates employees. Virtually every study on the importance of pay compared with other potential rewards has shown that pay is important. It consistently ranks among the top five rewards. Many factors, however, affect the importance of pay and other rewards. Money, for example, is likely to be viewed differently at various points in one's career, because the need for money versus other rewards (status, growth, security, and so forth) changes at each stage. National culture is another important factor. U.S. managers and employees emphasize pay for individual performance more than do their European or Japanese counterparts. European and Japanese companies, however, rely more on slow promotions and seniority as well as some degree of employment security. Even within a single culture, shifting national forces may alter people's needs for money versus other rewards.

Companies have developed various compensation systems and practices to achieve pay satisfaction and motivation. In manufacturing firms, payroll costs can run as high as 40% of sales revenues, whereas in service organizations payroll costs can top 70%. General managers, therefore, take an understandable interest in payroll costs and how these dollars are spent.

The traditional view of managers and compensation specialists is that the right system would solve most problems. This assumption is not plausible because there is no one right answer or objective solution to what or how someone should be paid. What people will accept, be motivated by, or perceive as fair is highly subjective. Pay is a matter of perceptions and values that often generate conflict.

MANAGEMENT'S INFLUENCE ON ATTITUDES TOWARD MONEY

Many organizations are caught in a vicious cycle that they partly create. In their recruitment and internal communications, firms often emphasize compensation levels and a belief in individual pay for performance. This is likely to attract people with high needs for money as well as to heighten that need in those already employed. Thus, the meaning employees attach to money is partly shaped by management's views. If merit increases, bonuses, stock options, and perquisites are held out as valued symbols of recognition and success, employees will come to see them in this light even more than they might have at first. Having heightened money's importance as a reward, management must then respond to employees who may demand more money or better pay-for-performance systems.

Firms must establish a philosophy about rewards and the role of pay in the mix of rewards. Without such a philosophy, the compensation practices that happen to be in place will continue to shape employees' expectations, and those expectations will sustain the existing practices. If money has been emphasized as an important symbol of success, that emphasis will continue even though a compensation system with a slightly different emphasis might have equal motivational value with fewer administrative problems and perhaps even lower cost. Money is important, but its degree of importance is influenced by the type of compensation system and philosophy that management adopts.

PAYROLL STRATIFICATION: A ONE- OR TWO-CLASS SOCIETY?

An organization with different compensation systems for different levels of the organization that offer different fringe benefits, pay-for-performance rewards, and administrative procedures is sending employees a message about more than just the specific behavior the compensation system is intended to reward. That message is that there are differences in the company's expectations of the commitment and role of employees at different levels and the degree to which they are full and responsible members of the organization.

Several understandable reasons exist for these differences. To circumvent the intended effects of progressive tax laws, corporations pay managers in a form different from that of lower-level employees. Deferred compensation, stock options, and various perquisites protect executives from taxation that reduces the value of their rewards.

In the United States, all organizations must distinguish between *exempt employees* (those who, according to the wage-and-hour laws, have significant decision-making responsibility—typically, managers and professional employees) and *nonexempt employees* (all other regular members of the organization—typically clerical white-collar and hourly blue-collar employees). Federal law requires nonexempt employees to receive overtime pay for a workweek that exceeds 40 hours; exempt employees are, as the name implies, exempt from such legislative protection. Because of this legal requirement, organizations must maintain records of time worked by nonexempt employees, which often results in the use of time clocks. These groups are also given different payroll labels: salaried payroll for exempt employees and hourly payroll for production employees. Thus, a two-class language is created.

Federal law governing overtime pay for nonexempt employees was created in the 1930s to protect employees from exploitation by management. It can, and often does, have the unintended result of creating or reinforcing certain assumptions made by managers about their employees' commitment to the organization. It might also affect employees' perceptions of their roles in the organization and thereby alter their commitment. A two-class society is subtly reinforced within the organization.

All-Salaried System Some organizations have attempted to overcome this legislated division of the work force through an all-salaried compensation system. Workers traditionally paid by the hour join management in receiving a weekly or monthly salary (nonexempt employees are still paid on an hourly basis for overtime work).

Although an all-salaried system cannot eliminate the legislated distinction between exempt and nonexempt employees, it can at least remove one symbolic, but nonetheless important, difference: Workers join managers in having more flexibility, because time can be taken off from work with no loss in pay. Thus, workers can be given more responsibility for their hours. Such treatment, in turn, could increase their commitment and loyalty to the organization.

Some managers fear that adopting a salaried system across the board will lead to greater absenteeism, but this does not appear to have happened. However, such a system by itself will not increase commitment. Nevertheless, as part of an overall shift in corporate philosophy and style, it can play an important supporting role. Companies such as Hewlett-Packard and IBM as well as participative nontraditional plants at Procter & Gamble, Dana, TRW, and Cummins Engine have successfully used the all-salaried payroll in this way.

SYSTEMS FOR MAINTAINING EQUITY

To maintain employee satisfaction with pay, corporations have developed systems to maintain pay equity with comparable internal and external persons and groups.

The consequences of inequity in employee pay regarding the external labor markets are potentially severe for a corporation, which would be unable to attract and keep the talent required. The costs of maintaining that equity, however, are also high. Meeting all competitive wage offers obtainable by employees—the extreme form of maintaining external equity—can encourage employees to search for the highest job offers to convince management to increase their pay. This results in a market system for determining compensation much like the free-agent system in sports—a time-consuming and expensive proposition for employers that can lead to internal inequities. It can also lead an employee to a self-centered orientation toward career and pay.

Some companies, such as IBM, intentionally position their total compensation package at the high end of the market range. High total compensation does not, however, ensure that the best employees are retained. To keep them, a company must also pay its better performers more than it pays poorer performers, and the difference must be significant in the judgment of individual employees.

The potential consequences of internal pay inequity are employee dissatisfaction, witholding of effort, and lack of trust in the system. Internal inequity can result in conflict within the organization, which consumes the time and energy of managers and personnel. Maintaining high internal equity, however, can result in overpaying some people compared to the market, while underpaying others—thus destroying external equity.

There is continual tension in an organization between concerns for external and internal equity. Line personnel may be willing to sacrifice corporate internal equity to attract and keep the talent they want for their departments. Because they perceive efforts to pay whatever is needed to attract a candidate as a threat to internal equity, human-resource personnel, with their corporate perspectives, often oppose such efforts by line managers. Human-resource personnel insist on the integrity of the job-evaluation and wage-survey systems to avoid the costly conflicts that they fear will result from numerous exceptions to the job-evaluation system. This dilemma remains insoluble; no new system will eliminate it. The balance must be continually managed to reduce problems and maintain a pay system that yields equity and cost effectiveness.

Job Evaluation In the United States, most firms determine pay levels by evaluating the worth of a job to the organization through a job-evaluation system.

Job evaluations begin by describing the various jobs within an organization. Then jobs are evaluated by considering several job factors: working conditions, necessary technical knowledge, required managerial skills, and importance to the organization. A rating for each factor is made on a standard scale, and the total rating points are used to rank jobs. Next, a salary survey identifies comparable jobs in other organizations and learns what those organizations are paying for similarly rated jobs.

The salary survey and other considerations—such as legislation, job-market conditions, and the organization's willingness to pay—establish pay ranges for jobs. (The tighter the labor market, the more closely wages will be tied to the going rate. In a loose labor market, the other factors will tend to dominate.) Jobs may then be grouped into a smaller number of classifications and assigned a salary range. The level of the individual employee within his or her particular range is determined by a combination of job performance, seniority, and experience or any other combination of factors selected by the organization.

Job-evaluation plans, along with wage surveys, have been used in wage-and-salary administration for over 50 years. They have proved useful for maintaining internal and external equity.

Even if these steps are taken, however, no job-evaluation system can solve the problem of salary compression or inequities that inevitably occur when new employees are hired. To recruit successfully in the labor market, firms must offer competitive wages, and these competitive wages sometimes create inequities with the salaries of employees who have been with the firm for some time. These inequities occur because corporations usually do not raise the salaries of incumbents when salary surveys result in an upward movement of the salary range. To do so would be costly; not doing so also allows the firms to keep the pay of poorer performers behind the market by denying merit increases.

Some analysts argue that companies should solve inequities due to compression by regularly raising wages for everyone when salary surveys so indicate and by managing poor performers through other means. Some companies ask managers to position their subordinates within the appropriate pay range according to performance, providing larger increases for good performers over several years so they will be near the top of their range and giving poor performers lower increases or no increases to keep them at the bottom of the range.

The conflicting objectives—keeping costs down and rewarding good performers—not the job-evaluation system itself cause inequity and dissatisfaction. Of these objectives, cost effectiveness is the critical factor, because good performance can be rewarded and poor performance discouraged in other monetary and nonmonetary ways. General managers must decide if the cost of across-the-board increases is worth the benefits of greater internal and external equity. To solve the equity problems, they must clarify their philosophy and make choices between objectives of cost and equity, a process determined more by values and financial constraints than by systems.

Pay systems structured by job evaluation have special problems. Salary ranges associated with jobs limit the pay increases an individual can obtain. Thus, significant advancements in status and pay can come only through promotions. This need for promotion can cause technical people to seek promotions to management positions, even though their real skills and interests might be in technical work. If no promotions are available, individuals' needs for advancement and progress are frustrated.

Additionally, job-evaluation systems cause a certain loss of flexibility in transferring people within an organization. If that transfer is to a job with a lower pay grade, fear of lower pay and status will reduce the individual's willingness to transfer. Although companies usually make an exception and maintain the individual's salary above the range of the new job, the perception of loss and the reality of an actual loss of pay over time makes such a transfer difficult.

To solve problems of job-evaluation systems, some companies have come up with an alternative: a person- or skill-based evaluation system. This system promises to solve the flexibility and limited growth problem of job evaluation, but it does not solve all the equity problems already discussed.

Person/Skill Evaluation Person- or skill-based evaluation systems base salary on the person's abilities. Pay ranges are arranged in steps, from least skilled to most skilled. Employees come into the organization at an entry-level pay grade and after demonstrating competence at that level, begin to move up the skill-based ladder. Such a system should lead to higher pay for the most-skilled individuals and encourage the acquisition of new skills.

Skill-based systems generally allow flexibility in moving people from one job to another and in introducing new technology. A skill-based compensation system can also change management's orientation. Rather than limiting assignments to be consistent with job level, managers must try to utilize the available skills of people, since employees are being paid for those skills. Moreover, a skill-based evaluation system's greatest benefit is that it communicates to employees a concern for their development. This concern leads management to develop competence and utilize it, resulting in greater employee well-being and organizational effectiveness.

Person-based evaluation systems that have been applied to technical personnel in R&D organizations are often called *technical ladders*. Technical ladders could be applied to other technical specialists, such as lawyers, sales personnel, and accountants. Their use might encourage good specialists to stay in these roles rather than seek management jobs that pay more but for which they may not have talent. The organizations would avoid losing good technical specialists and gaining poor managers.

Skill-based pay systems have also been applied to production-level employees in the past decade. In some of their more progressive plants, companies such as Procter & Gamble, General Motors, and Cummins Engine have introduced plans that pay workers for the skills they possess rather than for the jobs they hold. The benefits of flexibility and employee growth and satisfaction, mentioned earlier, have been experienced in these plants.

Some problems exist in a person- or skill-based approach, however. For example, many individual employees may, after several years, reach the top skill level and find themselves with no place to go. At this point, the organization might consider some type of profit-sharing scheme to encourage these employees to continue to seek ways of improving organizational effectiveness. Another problem is that a skills-evaluation program calls for a large investment in training, because pay increases depend upon the learning of new skills. Furthermore, external equity is more difficult to manage. Because each organization has its own unique configurations of jobs and skills, it is unlikely that individuals with similar skills can be found elsewhere, particularly in the same community, which is where production workers typically look for comparisons. This is less of a problem for professional employees whose jobs are more similar across companies. Because skill-based systems emphasize learning new tasks, employees may come to feel that their higher skills call for higher pay than the system provides, particularly when they compare their wages with those of workers in traditional jobs. Without effective comparisons expectations could rise, unchecked by a good reality test.

The most difficult problem facing a skills-evaluation plan is its administration. To make the system work properly, attention must be paid to the skill level of every employee. Some method must be devised, first, to determine how many and what new skills must be learned to receive a pay boost and, second, to determine whether or not the individual employee has, in fact, mastered those new skills. The ease with which the first point is achieved depends on how measurable or quantifiable the necessary skills are. Identification of particular skills is more easily accomplished for lower-level positions than for top management or professional positions.

Skill-based pay systems hold out some promise of improving competence in a cost-effective way and enhancing both organizational effectiveness and employee well-being. They are not solutions for all situations and depend heavily on solving the problem of measuring and assessing skills or competencies. Only an organization with a climate of trust is likely to use the system successfully. Moreover, skill-based compensation systems work only in those organizations where skilled workers are essential and where flexibility is required. They are also hard to introduce in organizations where a traditional job-evaluation system exists.

SENIORITY

Seniority has been accepted as a valid criterion for pay in some countries. Japanese companies, for instance, use seniority-based pay along with other factors, such as slow-but-steady promotion, to help achieve a desired organizational culture. In the United States, proponents of a seniority-based pay system tend to be trade unions. Distrustful of management, unions often feel that any pay-for-performance system will end up increasing paternalism, unfairness, and inequities. Thus, unions often prefer a strict seniority system. Many U.S. managers, however, feel that seniority runs contrary to the country's individualistic ethos, which maintains that individual effort and merit should be rewarded above all else.

PAY FOR PERFORMANCE

Some reasons organization pay their employees for performance are as follows:

- Under the right conditions, a pay-for-performance system can motivate desired behavior.
- A pay-for-performance system can help attract and keep achievement-oriented individuals.
- A pay-for-performance system can help to retain good performers while discouraging the poor performers.
- In the United States, at least, many employees, both managers and workers, prefer a pay-for-performance system, although white-collar workers are significantly more supportive of the notion than are blue-collar workers.

However, there is a wide gap between the desire to devise a pay-for-performance system and the ability to make such a system work.

The most important distinction among various pay-for-performance systems is the level of aggregation at which performance is defined—individual, group, and organizationwide.[3] The *exhibit* summarizes several pay-for-performance systems.

Historically, pay for performance has meant pay for individual performance. Piece-rate incentive systems for production employees and merit salary increases or bonus plans for salaried employees have been the dominant means of paying for performance. In the past, piece-rate incentive systems have dramatically declined because managers have discovered that such systems result in dysfunctional behavior, such as low cooperation, artificial limits on production, and resistance to changing standards. Similarly, more questions are being asked about individual bonus plans for executives as top managers discover their negative effects.

Meanwhile, organizationwide incentive systems are becoming more popular, particularly because managers are finding that these systems foster

---

3. Edward E. Lawler, *Pay and Organization Development* (Reading, Mass.: Addison-Wesley, 1981), pp. 82–85.

EXHIBIT
Pay-for-Performance Systems

INDIVIDUAL PERFORMANCE	*GROUP PERFORMANCE*	*ORGANIZATIONWIDE PERFORMANCE*
Merit system	Productivity incentive	Profit sharing
Piece rate	Cost effectiveness	Productivity sharing (Scanlon Plan)
Executive bonus		

cooperation, which leads to productivity and innovation. To succeed, however, these plans require certain conditions. A review of the key considerations for designing a pay-for-performance plan and a discussion of the problems that arise when these considerations are not observed follow.

Individual Pay For Performance The design of an individual pay-for-performance system requires an analysis of the task. Does the individual have control over the performance (result) that is to be measured? Is there a significant effort-to-performance relationship? For motivational reasons already discussed, such a relationship must exist. Unfortunately, many individual bonus, commission, or piece-rate incentive plans fall short in meeting this requirement. An individual may not have control over a performance result, such as sales or profit, because economic cycles or competitive forces beyond his or her control affect that result. Indeed, few outcomes in complex organizations are not dependent on other functions or individuals, and fewer still are not subject to external factors.

Choosing an appropriate measure of performance on which to base pay is a related problem incurred by individual bonus plans. For reasons discussed earlier, effectiveness on a job can include many facets not captured by cost, units produced, or sales revenues. Failure to include all activities that are important for effectiveness can lead to negative consequences. For example, sales personnel who receive a bonus for sales volume may push unneeded products, thus damaging long-term customer relations, or they may push an unprofitable mix of products just to increase volume. These same salespeople may also take orders and make commitments that cannot be met by manufacturing. Instead of rewarding salespeople for volume, why not reward them for profits, a more inclusive measure of performance? The obvious problem with this measure is that sales personnel do not have control over profits.

These dilemmas are constantly encountered and have led to the use of more subjective but inclusive behavioral measures of performance. Why not observe if the salesperson or executive is performing all aspects of the job well? Most merit salary increases are based on subjective judgments and so are some individual bonus plans. Subjective evaluation systems, though they can be all-inclusive if based on a thorough analysis of the job, require deep trust in management, good manager-subordinate relations, and effective interpersonal skills. Unfortunately, these conditions are not fully met in many situations, though they can be developed if judged to be sufficiently important.

Group and Organizationwide Pay Plans Organizational effectiveness depends on employee cooperation in most instances. An organization may elect to tie pay, or at least some portion of pay, indirectly to individual performance. Seeking to foster teamwork, a company may tie an incentive to some measure of group performance, or it may offer some type of profit- or productivity-sharing plan for the whole plant or company.

Gain-sharing plans have been used for years and in many varieties. The real power of a gain-sharing plan comes when it is supported by a climate of participation.[4] Various structures, systems, and processes involve employees in decisions that improve the organization's performance and result in a bonus throughout the organization. The Scanlon Plan is one such example. When the plan is installed in cooperation with workers and unions, a management-labor committee is created. Then committees seek and review suggestions for reducing costs. Payout is based on improvements in the sales-to-cost ratio of the plant compared to some agreed-upon base period before the adoption of the plan.

Organizationwide incentive plans that are part of a philosophy of participation require strong labor-management cooperation in design and administration. For example, the Scanlon Plan requires a direct employee vote with 75% approval before implementation. Without joint participation, commitment to any organizationwide incentive plan system will be low, and its symbolic and motivational value will be minimal.

Several critical decisions influence the effectiveness of a gain-sharing plan:

- Who should participate in the plan's design and administration, and how much participation will be allowed by management and union?
- What will be the size of the unit covered? Small units obviously offer easier identification with the organization's performance and the bonuses that result.
- What standard will be used to judge performance? Employees, the union (if involved), and management must agree on this for strong commitment. There are inevitable disagreements.
- How will the gains be divided? Who shares in the gains? What percentage of the gain goes to the company and what percentage to the employees?

When management and employees have gone through a process of discussion and negotiation, allowing a consensus to emerge on these questions, a real change in management-employee and union relations can occur. A top-down process would not yield the same benefits. Gain-sharing approached

---

4. Christopher S. Miller and Michael H. Schuster, "Gain-sharing Plan: A Comparative Analysis," *Organizational Dynamics* (Summer 1987), pp. 44–67.

participatively can create a fundamental change in the psychological and economic ownership of the firm. Therein lies its primary motivational and satisfactional value; however, only a management that embraces values consistent with participation can make it work.

DISCUSSION QUESTIONS

1. Shouldn't everyone be paid solely on the basis of his or her performance?
2. Are you motivated more by extrinsic or intrinsic rewards? Why? How have your motivational criteria been matched by the reward systems in the organizations where you've been employed?
3. Should general managers encourage employee involvement in the design and implementation of reward systems? How much control should employees have over their compensation?
4. Do some reward systems actually serve to make employees less productive?
5. "Firms must establish a philosophy about rewards and the role of pay in the mix of rewards." As a general manager, what would be your philosophy about rewards and compensation, and how would you communicate it?

15 Managing Resource Allocation

JOSEPH L. BOWER

Allocating scarce resources can be among the most rewarding aspects of a general manager's job and also one of the most difficult. The task is especially challenging at the corporate level because companies or divisions often make conflicting demands for resources. In this reading, Joseph Bower offers general managers a strategy-based model of resource allocation, arguing that decisions made in the context of a clear corporate strategy are more likely to gain broad organizational support as well as to further the objectives of the organization.

INTRODUCTION

For a general manager, corporate strategy is how to use scarce resources—money, people, time—whatever is key. In turn, freeing up those resources, considering how best to use them, and then executing those plans depends upon the quality of specialists and general management, the design of the organization and information systems, and the incentives that direct the attention and energy of managers. Because access to resources that support plans is critical to the success of a manager or an organization, competition for access can be intense.

For strategy to succeed, the ability to focus is very important. When managers try to select among rival businesses and projects, they face dramatic economic uncertainty. Because all the critical proposals involve judgment, the problem of selection is compounded because the choices are inherently social and political as well as economic. When a GM bets on certain projects, he or she is implicitly betting on the success of these judgments. The allocation of resources determines which groups rise and fall and which careers are made or broken.

To perceive resource allocation as more than just a political competition, it must be viewed as serving corporate ends. This means it has to be strategy driven. But achieving legitimacy is not enough. The executive team has to be dealt with as a human equation, which may involve short-term compromises in strategy or in the composition of the team.

A SIMPLE VIEW OF RESOURCE ALLOCATION

The CEO's challenge is to understand what opportunities are available, to select the most promising, and then to use whatever resources are available effectively and efficiently. This process is complicated, because in large organizations the authors and evaluators of annual budgets and project plans do not share the same information, perspectives, or objectives.

Projects are developed by business unit managers and their staffs, who are responsible for operating and growing specific business activities. In the Home Appliance Group of GE, someone is "responsible" for refrigerators. In Dow Chemical, someone is "responsible" for polyethylene. These lower-level general managers propose budgets and projects according to their notions of what is right for their business. The future of their business as well as their own career prospects depend on the quality of their plans and their access to resources to support them.

Projects are planned in concrete terms. At GE, a new refrigerator design, for example, might incorporate features proposed by the marketing group, a newly conceptualized compressor recommended by the engineering group, and new plastics offered by the plastics division. The proposed manufacturing facility can be built on an existing site or at a new location.

The market success of the eventual refrigerator will depend on competitors' moves, which includes any foreign companies entering the American market. And achieving financial returns that meet corporate objectives will depend on the health of the housing industry, which in turn depends on interest rates and employment levels.

Assessing the project's viability is further complicated because the refrigerator business is part of an appliance group consisting of dishwashers, ranges, clothes washers, and driers. A strategic move in refrigerators will need to be coordinated with the managers of the other appliance businesses.

CHOOSING ACCORDING TO THEORY

In the end, how should GE's corporate management evaluate and act on the proposal? According to finance theory, the projected financial returns on the project are compared with all the other proposals that management receives from its 14 other "core businesses," including chemicals, defense, medical instruments, electrical power equipment, and financial services. The estimated returns in the proposals, however, are summaries of judgments about very uncertain future developments extending over five to ten years. These judgments are based on the experience and knowledge of engineers, designers, salespeople, marketers, consultants, and managers.

Some sense of the reliability of such forecasts can be grasped from *Exhibit 1*, which is drawn from one corporation's experience with 50 capital budget proposals. The exhibit compares actual discounted results to the forecasts in the proposals.

This kind of comparison was described wryly by a manager in another company as, "We're making 5% on all those 35% projects." He might have

EXHIBIT 1
Discounted Actual Results Compared With the Discounted Forecast

TYPE OF PROJECT	*RATIO OF PRESENT VALUE OF ACTUAL RESULTS TO PRESENT VALUE OF FORECASTED RESULTS*
Cost Reduction	1.1
Sales Expansion	0.6
New Products	0.1

added, "We're losing market share in 20% ROI businesses because we didn't use that money to invest in cost reduction."

Planning theory provides a different approach to the same problem. In one version, top management or its planners assess the environment and establish corporate goals, which are then broken down into specific missions for the individual businesses. In turn, the managements of these businesses set their plans and budgets in accordance with the objectives they have been given. The operating and capital budgets that result are then "scrubbed" for validity and summed to see if they meet corporate objectives and resources. Since often they do not, they are cycled back for further scrubbing and modification until they are approved.

The process of producing acceptable budgets highlights one of the toughest aspects of the corporate leader's job in a diversified business. If the company is to be more than the sum of its parts, and in particular if it is to justify the economic and administrative costs of the corporate office, top management has to be more than a bank. The process of gathering in and doling out resources has to be closely tied to the communication of corporate strategy to the divisions, and it has to enrich the development of strategy by the divisions.

A MODEL OF THE RESOURCE ALLOCATION PROCESS

Corporate management can leverage business-unit strength by understanding how to allocate resources. Resource allocation can be conceived of in terms of the three following questions:

1. How are the strategic *contents* of plans shaped and developed?
2. How are particular projects and plans selected for *commitment* of corporate resources?
3. How does the organizational *context* influence the definition of the content and the commitment of the resources?

In a big company, different groups are involved in each task.

The content of business unit plans is usually defined by specialists—engineers, production managers, product managers, and sales managers—in terms of current needs and opportunities they perceive will improve their operations. The responsible managers define business needs and opportunities according to their information on current performance, customers, and competitors. They formulate plans according to *their* understanding of corporate strategy.

The work environment and operating systems are powerful, if implicit, communicators of the real corporate strategy. If the cost system allocates overhead according to direct labor, for example, then the "right way" to cut overhead is to cut direct labor. And if a corporation says it wants entrepreneurs, but it pays and promotes and gives new resources only to those who "make their quarterly budget," then managers quickly understand that the company seeks current earnings.

Specialists in the business units are constantly defining the need for new resources. Engineering or the controllers say costs can be cut. Sales argues that quality must be improved, and Research knows how to do it. Market studies are designed, advertising programs are proposed, and training programs are planned. Looking ahead, some see the need for new capacity. Not all these proposals make sense, nor can all be funded. The manager in charge of a unit must prepare an annual plan and initiate at least the first steps of a capital proposal as the credibility of the longer-term proposal rests substantially on the manager's reputation for fulfilling his or her annual plans. Beyond this fundamental test, the request must clearly support the strategic plan. General managers must learn to argue effectively for both operating and capital resources.

At the same time that business units deal with the physical, human, and financial specifics of their needs, the managers of the corporation are seeking to define their goals and objectives for the short and long term. Where operating units may see business as usual, top managers may see financial crisis in the form of rising interest rates, a falling yen, or an aggressive raider. A shifting advantage in labor productivity or in centers of research excellence may be on the corporate mind at a time when the business units believe themselves to be undisputed leaders. And the reverse can also be true. Top management may believe all is well even though the troops in the trenches know that new competitive conditions threaten survival of the business unit. The need to link the two views is obvious, but resources are frequently committed without any integration of top management and business views.

Who decides which of the many projects initiated by the business units deserves funding? Which operating plans should be cut back and which supported? Usually it is the middle levels of general management, the division and group managers, who oversee clusters of business units, thereby reducing the span of corporate control to something feasible. These middle managers broker the many claims on the corporate purse. Their backing is critical to any corporate commitment.

How do they decide what projects are worth backing, where corporate resources should be committed? Generally they commit themselves on the basis of their sense of corporate strategy, their understanding of how the potential

EXHIBIT 2
The Role of Different Kinds of General Managers in Resource Allocation

ROLES/LEVELS	*STRATEGIC CONTENT*	*RESOURCE COMMITMENT*	*ORGANIZATIONAL CONTEXT*
Corporate	Set Broad Goals	Decide/Commit	Determine systems/structure/culture/people
Integrating (e.g., Group VP)	Translate	Screen/Support	Adapt/apply context to units
Business Unit	Respond/Initiate	Propose	Use context to win resources

contributions of a particular business will play out over the long and short term, and the way in which they will be personally measured and rewarded. In theory, the judgment of the middle-level general managers about the prospects of different businesses for the corporate portfolio will be key. In fact, while they may be the highest-ranking officers in the corporation with enough substantive understanding of a business to make an informed assessment of it vis-à-vis corporate objectives, how they use that skill will be strongly influenced by the way the corporate game is structured.

While observing the work of a group vice president of a major corporation, I listened to the following conversation.

Boss: (the group VP): Should we make this new product investment?
VP: There's a lot of uncertainty.
Boss: What are the odds?
VP: 50-50 that the research pans out.
Boss: What would you do?
VP: Go ahead.
Boss: OK.

Six months later, I met the vice president. He had been fired. The project didn't work out. He recalled: "When I reminded 'Jim' that I had told him 50-50, he said, 'But you told me to do it.' " Other VPs learned that their company was uninterested in risk and since then the company has lost much of its technological edge.

No matter how powerful the research culture of a company, it can be changed—destroyed—by top executives who want to manage a portfolio of opportunities, but who want the managers in the middle to risk their jobs on the outcome of 50-50 projects. Nothing has more influence on the way information about business unit prospects and performance moves up and down the corporation than the way failure is managed. Kill a few messengers and the information dries up. Substitute fancy control systems for top management risk taking, and the ability of a corporation to manage long-term projects with major uncertainties dies.

Consider how a top manager deals with a major proposal. The executive's eye scans the page almost instinctively, looking for the signature. The chairman of one corporation put the point this way: "Some groups in the corporation are such that you know their numbers are optimistic. In others you know that if 'Morris' says that something is going to be so good, then it's probably going to be a good deal better."

Division and group managers understand this. Said one, "What it really comes down to is your batting average. Obviously anything cooked up, I have to sell and approve. My contribution is more in the area of deciding how much confidence we have in things. The whole thing—the size, the sales estimate, the return—is based on judgment. The key question is 'How much confidence has the management built up over the years in my judgment?' I can lose management's confidence by being too aggressive or too pessimistic. I can lose the confidence of the people below me as well if they think that I can't get them the ammunition they need."

Top management's perspective on the same issue is revealed in a story told about GM's legendary chairman Alfred Sloan, Jr. He was asked by an HBS researcher to explain what he had liked about a $10 million plant expansion just approved. "I didn't like it. It won't work out." "Then why did you approve it?" "Young man, you have no idea how expensive it is to train good general managers."

In short, the information available to the mid-level managers, the ways in which their businesses are measured and given resources, and the ways in which they are rewarded or punished are all powerful determinants of how the managers will invest their reputation in backing projects. In other words, the organizational context of a company—what we have been calling the work environment and organization of a company, as well as its approach to operations—has a great deal to do with how opportunities are defined and resources are allocated. *Exhibit 2* provides a way of mapping the different activities that have been discussed.

The implications of this model of resource allocation are clear.

1. Communication between specialists who initiate, mid-level generalists who translate, and corporate executives who provide overall direction is both vital and difficult.
2. If top management does not provide strategic direction, specialists will drive the use of resources. Aggressive, entrepreneurial specialists will inevitably fight hard for their business needs as they perceive them. Thus, tremendous effort is needed to implement strategies that call for cross-unit cooperation and coordination, and do so without discouraging promising people or smoothing over conflicts of strategic objectives.
3. If the specialists do not do their job well, no allocation process can make up for poor-quality plans. Top management and the mid-level integrators must understand enough business to calibrate the quality of business plans as well as the capability of the initiators.

4. When specialists seek help in developing plans, they may want to turn to the control or planning staff. Indeed, top management often gives these staffs some sort of consulting role. But if these staffs are also used to measure performance, the business unit managers are seldom candid. Their short-term personal stakes are too high.
5. Sequencing is key. When commitments are made before plans are fully developed, it can be very difficult to shut down a project that begins to develop flaws. The middle managers who backed the project see their credibility eroded and move to "make things work out right."
6. Making sure that organizational context—work environment, organization structure, and people-development systems—fit corporate and business needs is critical to effective use of resources.

Thus, top management must address three basic problems:

1. ***Organization context.*** Keep the organization, measures, and rewards up to date. Too many companies are organized around past objectives and use financial accounting to measure performance. Jobs are defined mechanically, and managers do not know their true costs or their market share. Strategy suffers.
2. ***Strategic context.*** Be involved in communicating the substance of corporate strategy and do not just rely on indirect messages of bonus formulas or personnel assignments; listen for business-unit strategic problems. Explicit financial goals, especially ratios, are too aggregate for business units, and they often drive out substance. Short-term measures of operating performance can warp the learning and risk-taking necessary to pursue an ambitious strategy.
3. ***Resource commitment.*** Be sure that in marshalling resources aggressively to focus on the main corporate ventures, other business units are not starved of funds for keeping valuable projects alive. Good general managers like to have a gamble or two hidden away.

It is clear why many managers prefer small single-business companies: They are much less complex. Certainly translating corporate objectives into terms meaningful to business units is not hard, for they are one and the same. Multibusiness corporations and multinationals, however, are usually very difficult to run because the problems that specialists face are likely to be fundamentally different in the different businesses and countries. Managers of separate parts of the process may literally not speak the same language.

But context, which has such enormous importance, can be directly influenced by top management, and that's the "good news." For some companies, this is a powerful revelation. They conclude that if they can just get the organizational structure right, strategy takes care of itself in some sort of "bottom-up" process. This conclusion overlooks corporate strategy. If a company has no strategy, it is possible to invest in all kinds of projects and businesses without any focus. Without a corporate strategy or vision of where the company is heading and in which arenas it will compete, resource allocation becomes a mere political contest for corporate resources, and the company a candidate for a break-up.

DISCUSSION QUESTIONS

1. Why doesn't a strict top-down approach to resource allocation always work?
2. Should projected financial returns be the most important criterion when distributing funds? What other factors should be considered?
3. How should top GMs communicate corporate strategy in order to facilitate the resource allocation process?
4. Does the structure of a multibusiness firm preclude an efficient distribution of resources?
5. Discuss the roles of different levels of general managers in allocating resources. Where are possible areas of overlap, or when might these roles be confused?

16 Fast-Cycle Capability for Competitive Power

JOSEPH L. BOWER AND THOMAS M. HOUT

Today, time is a source of competitive advantage, and the speed of an organization's operations are critical parts of a general manager's responsibility. This reading describes practices that companies can use to save time in their operations and provide customers with better products and services and lower costs. Based on analysis of successful time-based competitors, it shows general managers how to develop fast-cycle capabilities—how to "get the clock started"—and how to motivate employees to be active partners in this process.

All managers appreciate, at least intuitively, that time is money, and most will invest to save time—and the money it represents—if they see a clear opportunity. The travel agent computerizes to be able to confirm customers' reservations instantly. The apparel manufacturer develops a just-in-time production process to make what's wanted and avoid the inevitable discounts caused by overproduction.

But actions like these don't create much competitive advantage, because competitors will soon see the same opportunity and most will do the very same thing. Taking time out of a business gets interesting, however, when it represents a systematic change in the way a company accomplishes its work and serves its customers. Then saving time can provide sustainable competitive advantage.

Fast cycle time is not a new operating concept in business strategy. It has long been a key factor in the success of businesses ranging from Hong Kong's custom tailors to McDonald's. But today, executives in more and more large, complex businesses are achieving sustained competitive advantage by making radical changes in how they manage time within their companies. These companies make decisions faster, develop new products earlier, and convert customer orders into deliveries sooner than their competitors. As a result, they provide unique value in the markets they service, value that can translate into faster growth and higher profits.

In these top-performing companies, fast cycle time plays two important roles. First, it is an organizational capability, a level of performance that management shapes and builds into the company's operating systems and the attitudes of its employees. The basic idea is to design an organization that performs without the bottlenecks, errors, and inventories most companies live with. The faster information, decisions, and materials can flow through a large organization, the faster it can respond to customer orders or adjust to changes in market demand and competitive conditions. Less time is spent fighting fires and coordinating. More time is available for planning, for initiating competitive activity.

Second, fast cycle time is a management paradigm, a way of thinking about how to organize and lead a company and how to gain real advantage over competitors. It is a powerful organizing message because its basic premise is so simple. It is also extremely effective since compressing time reinforces and supports what capable managers are already trying to do.

Analysis of competitive developments in a wide range of industries indicates that fast-cycle capability contributes to better performance across the board. Costs drop because production materials and information collect less overhead and do not accumulate as work-in-process inventory. Customer service improves because the lead time from receipt of order to shipment diminishes. Quality is higher because you cannot speed up the production cycle overall unless everything is done right the first time. Innovation becomes a characteristic behavior pattern because rapid new-product development cycles keep the company in close touch with customers and their needs.

Developing fast-cycle capability isn't easy nor can it be done overnight. It requires fundamental rethinking of how a company's goods or services are delivered to customers, and it means that various parts of the organization will have to work together in new and different ways. But these days, the penalty for standing still is far higher than the cost of change.

EVERY COMPANY IS A SYSTEM

People in fast-cycle companies think of themselves as part of an integrated system, a linked chain of operations and decision-making points that continuously delivers value to the company's customers. In such organizations, individuals understand how their own activities relate to the rest of the company. They know how work is supposed to flow, how time is supposed to be used.

In small companies, this way of thinking is usually second nature. People find it easy to stay focused on creating value because almost everyone works directly on the product or with a customer. Policies, procedures, practices, or people that interfere with getting the product out the door are easy to see and can be dealt with quickly.

As companies grow, however, the system like nature of the organization often gets hidden. Distances increase as functions focus on their own needs, support activities multiply, specialists are hired, reports replace face-to-face conversations. Before long the clear visibility of the product and the essential elements of the delivery process are lost. Instead of operating as a smoothly linked system, the company becomes a tangle of conflicting constituencies whose own demands and disagreements frustrate the customer. "I don't care what your job is," the overwhelmed customer finally complains. "When can I get my order?"

Fast-cycle companies—especially the big ones—recognize this danger and work hard to avoid it by heightening everyone's awareness of how and where time is spent. They make the main flow of operations from start to finish visible and comprehensible to all employees, and they invest in this understanding with training. They highlight the main interfaces between functions and show how they affect the flow of work. They are aware of the way policies and procedures in one part of the company influence work in others. They compensate on the basis of group success. And, most important, they reinforce the systemic nature of the organization in their operations architecture.

To illustrate, let's look at Toyota, a classic fast-cycle company. The heart of the auto business consists of four interrelated cycles: product development, ordering, plant scheduling, and production. Over the years, Toyota has designed its organization to speed information, decisions, and materials through each of these critical operating cycles, individually and as parts of the whole. The result is better organizational performance on the dimensions that matter to customers—cost, quality, responsiveness, innovation.

Self-organizing, multifunctional teams take charge of product development, focusing on a particular model series. In rapid response to demand patterns, they develop products and manufacturing processes simultaneously to collapse time and ensure better manufacturability. The teams are responsible for managing ongoing styling, performance, and cost decisions, and they control their own schedules and reviews. They also select and manage suppliers, who are brought into the design process early on. The result is an ever-faster development cycle—three years, on average, as compared with four or five years in Detroit—frequent new product introductions, and a constant flow of major and minor innovations on existing models.

The production cycle begins as soon as a customer orders a car from a dealer. Dealers in Japan are connected on-line to the factory scheduling system, so that an order, complete with specifications and the customer's option package, can be entered and slotted into the factory schedule right away. Toyota schedules its plants to minimize sharp fluctuations in daily volume and to turn out a full mix of models every day. Customers get on-the-spot confirmation of their expected delivery date. Suppliers are automatically notified of the new order and given a stable production schedule so that they won't deliver the wrong components on the day of final assembly.

Actual production is executed in small lots by flexible manufacturing cells that can accommodate a mixed flow of units with little changeover time. Plants are managed to maintain high uptime (all the steps in the production sequence are functioning) and high yield (all the production processes are under control and turning out quality products). The result is a fast-paced production cycle, which squeezes out all the overhead except what's needed to get work done right the first time through, and a reliable, continuous manufacturing process.

Much of Toyota's competitive success is directly attributable to the fast-cycle capability it has built into its product development, ordering, scheduling, and production processes. By coming up with new products faster than competitors do, it puts other manufacturers on the marketing defensive. By translating a customer's order into a finished product delivered faster, it captures large numbers of time-sensitive buyers and puts cost and inventory pressure on other manufacturers. By continuously bringing out a variety of fresh products and observing what consumers buy or don't buy, it stays current with their changing needs and gives product development an edge market research cannot match. The faster Toyota can develop and deliver automobiles, the more it can control the competitive game.

In their ability to preempt new sources of value and force other companies to respond to their initiatives, Toyota and other fast-cycle companies resemble the World War II fighter pilots who consistently won dogfights, even when flying in technologically inferior planes. The U.S. Air Force found that the winning pilots completed the so-called OODA loop—Observation, Orientation, Decision, Action—faster than their opponents. Winning pilots sized up the dynamics in each new encounter, read its opportunities, decided what to do, and acted before their opponents could. As a result, they could take control of the dogfight, preempt the opposition moves, and throw the enemy plane into a confused reactive spiral.

Companies in many industries are operating in much the same way today. Responding to a challenge from Yamaha, Honda nearly doubled its range of motorcycle models in less than two years—destroying Yamaha's short-lived edge. Liz Claiborne has introduced two additional apparel seasons to match consumer buying patterns more closely. Seiko has strengthened its hold on the watch market with a highly automated factory capable of producing new models each day. In semiconductors, the battle for global share is being fought largely on the basis of the speed with which new technology can be applied to larger chips.

Other manufacturing companies go beyond their own boundaries to include customers and suppliers in one integrated delivery system. Milliken, the large U.S. textile manufacturer, collaborates with General Motors on auto interiors, with Sears on upholstery fabrics, and with Wal-Mart on apparel. Because they see one another as partners in delivering a product, not separate operations, Milliken and its customers have been able to share upstream order input and scheduling information, coordinate production cycles to minimize imbalances, and eliminate duplicate inspections and buffer inventories. The results are dramatic. Costs have fallen. Inventory turns have typically doubled. Sales have risen. Stock shortages and markdowns occur less often. The time it takes the Milliken-customer system to fill an order has been cut in half.

Finally, competing through fast-cycle capability is as powerful a strategy in services as it is in manufacturing. By automating its analysis and trading functions, Batterymarch, the Boston-based equity fund manager, collapsed the time it takes to decide on a portfolio change for a customer and put it through. The customer gets into rising stocks and out of falling ones faster than before. Batterymarch has lower costs and higher profits: revenues per employee triple the industry average.

WHAT MAKES FAST-CYCLE COMPANIES RUN

Fast-cycle companies differ from traditional organizations in how they structure work, how they measure performance, and how they view organizational learning. They favor teams over functions and departments. They use time as a critical performance measure. They insist that *everyone* learn about customers, competitors, and the company's own operations, not just top management.

Each of these characteristics is a logical outgrowth of the management mind-set Toyota exemplifies, the mind-set that sees a company as an integrated system for delivering value to customers. Conversely, practices and policies that compartmentalize the company—a strong functional organization, for example, or buffer inventories, or measurement and control systems that focus exclusively on the numbers—have to be modified or done away with. In a fast-cycle company they're counterproductive, however useful they've been in the past and however reassuring they are to employees.

Organize Work in Multifunctional Teams To compress time and gain the benefits, a company has to work in and manage through relatively small, self-managing teams made up of people from different parts of the organization. The teams must be small because large groups create communication problems of their own and almost always include members whose areas of responsibility are peripheral to the team's task. The teams must be self-managing and empowered to act because referring decisions back up the line wastes time and often leads to poorer decisions. The teams must be multifunctional because that's the best—if not the only—way to keep the actual product and its essential delivery system clearly visible and foremost in everyone's mind.

AT&T and Ford have used teams staffed with members from different disciplines to develop new telephones and new cars. By bringing people from product engineering, manufacturing, marketing, and purchasing together throughout the development process and giving them the authority to make the real business decisions, these companies have cut enormous time and expense out of their new product efforts. In the telephone business, for example, it takes laggards three to four times as long to bring their products and services to market.

Fast-cycle companies use multifunctional teams for everyday work at all levels, not just for special projects. One bank we're familiar with successfully reorganized its personal lending practices and collapsed the time it takes for a customer to get a decision from several days to 30 minutes. Formerly loan applications were handled by a series of supervisors, with clerks as intermediaries to do the processing work. Now an application comes to a single group made up of a credit analyst, an experienced collateral appraiser, and a bank procedures expert who can draw on their collective knowledge and experience to respond to the customer almost at once.

As this example suggests, putting together a successful team often means broadening the scope of individual jobs, organizing the team around market-oriented purposes rather than departmentally defined tasks, and placing business responsibility as far down in the organization as possible.

In effect, it redefines what is commonly meant by multifunctional work. In our experience, many large companies like to think that they work multifunctionally because they form special task forces that cross organizational lines or encourage managers to wander around informally and share their observations. And devices like these can make employees more aware of a company's working mechanisms and opportunities to improve them incrementally, to be sure. But they cannot create well-designed, day-in and day-out, cross-functional relationships down in the organization, where the work gets done and the opportunities to learn are greatest.

Similarly, skunk works that bypass the organization's regular review mechanisms won't develop fast-cycle capability or help managers root out quality and time problems in their operation. Fast-cycle managers know that routine work determines a company's effectiveness, not special projects. So rather than circumvent a slow-moving core by creating outlying units that are smaller, quicker, and more responsive, these executives work to build those qualities into the company as a whole—even if that means taking themselves out of some critical decision loops.

Senior managers typically have lots of good ideas to contribute. But their interventions also carry great weight and often come at awkward times in a project's life. Moreover, their calendars are so crowded that the more they get involved in a project, the harder it becomes to schedule important meetings and keep decisions on track. Senior executives in fast-cycle companies understand this problem and appreciate the way the bottlenecks they create can demotivate junior people. They concentrate on improving the system, therefore, and delegate routine operating decisions to others.

Because of all these differences, the organization charts of fast-cycle companies bear little resemblance to the traditional pyramid of hierarchical boxes. Neither responsibility nor authority is so neatly decentralized and isolated. Instead, the organization chart is more likely to be a set of interlocked circles or a systems flow chart with arrows and feedback loops indicating the actual path of decisions and work. The organization chart for the Taurus-Sable product development effort at Ford, for example, was a circle with the core project management team in the center and working groups branching out in all directions.

Track Cycle Times Throughout the Organization To assure that information and materials will move through the entire organization with little or no delay, fast-cycle companies manage both the cycle time of individual activities and the cycle time of the whole delivery system—the number of days it takes to ship a customer's order, for instance, or develop a new product. Managers in these companies track each stage's output to see that it is flowing easily into the next and meeting that user's specifications. They make continuing efforts to reduce each activity's characteristic cycle time and therefore the time of the entire sequence. And they are alert to opportunities to compress time by eliminating stages, for example, combining once-separate data preparation and processing activities.

Most organizations manage the cycle time of the longest or most visible part of their operation, but neglect others that are less obvious like order processing or engineering tests. They also allow information in process and decisions to pile up between stages. In-company studies indicate that often less than 10% of the time between receipt of an order and shipment of the product is spent adding value. Material and information spend the rest of the time waiting to be acted on. In factories, for instance, processing in large batches slows down total plant throughput because each workstation has to wait for a large batch to accumulate before it can begin to work. And the same thing happens in white-collar work such as scheduling shipments and pricing orders. Often the only measures used to control these buildups are limits on working capital and overhead expense. Those costs are merely a crude approximation of the lost value to customers.

In contrast, Toyota appears to manage all the cycle times in its operation chain. As we have seen, for example, its management recognized that applying just-in-time principles in production would not greatly change the time a customer had to wait for a new car if retail orders spent weeks moving through the company's regional sales and scheduling departments. So Toyota's order-entry and scheduling procedures are designed to couple without intermediate steps or queues. Toyota's near-term goal is to produce and deliver a new car within a few days of the customer's order.

Benetton, the well-known Italian sportswear producer and retailer, is another company that owes much of its explosive growth and success to across-the-board cycle time reduction. Time compression starts in new product development, where a CAD system automatically explodes the new design into a full range of sizes, then transmits these patterns to computer numerically controlled fabric-cutting machines to await orders for the new product. Fabric is inventoried in neutral greige and then cut and dyed to order. This allows the company to minimize rolled-goods inventory and still respond quickly to the full range of customer demand. Orders are sent to a chain of pull-scheduled, just-in-time factories that allow Benetton to replenish its U.S. retail shelves in 15 days, a response time previously unimaginable in fashion retailing. That not only satisfies customers but lets the company avoid under- and over-production as well.

Finally, fast-cycle companies know just where in the system compressing time will add the most value for customers. Not surprisingly, those are the activities they attack first and upgrade regularly. For example, consider Freightliner, which has more than doubled its share of the U.S. heavy-duty, on-highway truck market over the last decade. Unlike many companies in this customized business, Freightliner didn't invest heavily in speeding up its in-plant production process. Instead, its management invested in pre-engineering hundreds of possible truck combinations, so that customers can order the drive trains, cabs, and other optional features they need from a pretested menu. The company avoids the on-line errors that plague some competitors and make hasty redesign and rework necessary. And it can deliver a truck weeks ahead of most of the industry at a lower price.

A key factor in achieving end-to-end, fast cycle time is a disciplined approach to schedules. Time-based competitors avoid the seemingly inevitable delays of organizational life by creating calendars for important events and insisting that *everyone* meet their commitments, so review and decision activities stay on track.

Build Learning Loops into the Organization Markets, products, and competitors move so quickly today that organizations with centralized intelligence functions simply cannot keep up. This is why fast-cycle managers want active sensors and interpreters of data at every level of the company. And why they emphasize on-line learning, which is the catalyst for continuous process innovation.

Designing rapid feedback loops into routine operations is a standard practice in fast-cycle companies. Benetton, for example, collects data daily at the retail level so it knows what is selling and what is not. Because what sells changes from month to month and from neighborhood to neighborhood, these data help the company decide what to produce currently, what new styles and colors to develop, and what merchandise to stock in particular outlets. Fast-cycle companies like Benetton don't waste time building inventory that won't be used immediately to satisfy customer needs.

Companies with fast-cycle capability also emphasize informal, ad hoc communication. Current information goes straight to where it can be most useful. It doesn't get lost in the chain of command. At Marks & Spencer, the great U.K. retailer, for example, managers at all levels are taught to bring important market information to senior management's attention at once. Thus the manager of a key store would be expected to call a vice chairman immediately if deliveries of basic products suggested the possibility of a systemwide shortage. From retail sales assistants, who are expected to reject defective merchandise and provide feedback on customer satisfaction, to a hands-on top management, everyone works to speed goods through the stores and information to the managers who can use it.

Companies with fast-cycle capability don't stay that way automatically. Their managers frequently renew and redesign the delivery system, continually gathering information about what makes it effective and what is getting in the way. They study competitors and superior performers in other industries for helpful ideas. They use new technologies like artificial intelligence to cut time out of routine activities. They encourage an unusual degree of mobility and initiative among their employees. At Du Pont, for example, production workers now visit customers just as salespeople and product engineers do to learn their needs firsthand.

GETTING THE CLOCK STARTED

Delivery dates, lead times, upcoming production dates—managers deal with time every day in an episodic manner. But they rarely stand back and consider time systematically or as a key to competitive position. Two facts of organizational life explain why time is so easily overlooked and undermanaged.

First, decision options are rarely presented to managers in terms of the effect they would have on time. A proposal for a new production process may highlight cost and labor savings but neglect to mention that the larger economic batch size will slow the whole organization down. Proponents of a new headquarters building will talk about more space and amenities but fail to point out that the floor plan separates marketing from engineering and thus will lengthen the new product development process. In short, it takes a special effort for executives to focus routinely on elapsed system time as something to be managed.

Second, and more problematic, most people in organizations like to have stability in their working procedures and social patterns. Serious efforts at cycle time reduction disrupt both. Multifunctional teams break up existing departments and routines. Compressing cycle time sweeps away long-standing crutches such as quality inspection and redundant data entry that existed only because work wasn't designed or done right the first time through. Some valued specialists are exposed as the cause of bottlenecks, while others become completely unnecessary. You don't need sophisticated short-term market forecasts if you can respond immediately to any change in the level of demand.

Strong as these internal forces are, however, today's executives have an even stronger incentive to manage their company's cycle time—the competitive world outside. Fast, smooth, skillful operations and an ability to learn in real time are potent sources of competitive advantage. Based on our observations in successful companies, here are some suggestions that can help management get started.

Examine Cycle Times and Raise Standards First, calibrate your performance against that of your toughest competitors, not only on response time but also on cost, quality, and rate of innovation because all these are causally related. Then use these performance benchmarks as *minimum* targets in your strategic plan: Improvements of 5% per year won't challenge the status quo. When Toyota set out to achieve a one-minute die change on a 50-ton press to make a cheap custom car possible, that wasn't incremental; it was inconceivable! But it became a foundation of Toyota's new level of competitiveness.

Map and model your company's decision making and operations flows so you can identify major interfaces, bottlenecks, and behavior patterns. Find out exactly where and how time is wasted and where quality problems arise, and share this intelligence with all of your employees. The organization has to learn how it actually works before it can usefully talk about changes.

Describe and highlight past successes in making changes, even modest ones, in how the company works. Build a belief that the company's circuitry is not fixed, that people can design and implement better ways to operate. Keep raising performance standards.

Set Up Unusual Organization Mechanisms to Focus on Cycle Time Form temporary teams to study what's slowing down a few key cross-functional activities in the company. Staff these teams with energetic, well-respected middle managers who must make the eventual solutions work. Ask them to articulate and evaluate a few options, especially radical ones. Crudely remap how the company would work under each proposal, then test it and determine what changes in policies and behavior would be needed to make it work. Keep discussing the best proposals until people begin to accept their feasibility.

Pursue conflict in meetings as a way to uncover and explore how the organization's working mechanisms slow down and where people's assumptions and beliefs diverge. After identifying the core of the conflict, develop a way to resolve it with data, not more opinion.

Treat bottlenecks, downtime problems, and other breakdowns as opportunities to learn. Don't just ascribe them to "life in a large organization" and assume they have to be lived with.

Keep asking "why" until you get to the root of a problem. Companies vary greatly in how they attack operating problems. Many fix today's problem: they adjust the machine that's turning out bad parts. Some go further and find the immediate cause of the problem: they adjust the machine and replace the worn tool that's throwing it off. Superior companies don't stop until they find the root cause—the poorly designed process or defective part that made the tool wear down in the first place.

Develop Information Systems to Track Value-Adding Activities Distinguish the main operating sequence—the organization's central, value-adding activities—from time-consuming support and preparatory steps. Move the latter off-line. Give decision authority and responsibility for results to employees involved in the main sequence.

Organize working units around the flow of decisions, information, and material, not to accommodate departmental neuroses that have deformed the process over the years. Use training to give these groups the skills and support they need.

Connect stages in the operations chain as directly as possible. Design away gaps and queues. Develop target cycle times for specific stages, and schedule decisions and work flows so that people can meet them routinely.

Make Time Count in Managing Employees Evaluate individuals on the basis of their contribution to the working team of which they are part. Be explicit about the group's cycle time and quality objectives and the individual's role in meeting them.

Avoid creating specialists unless they're absolutely essential. Specialists tend to be cut off from other perspectives and often have difficulty understanding new contexts. They also tend to push issues higher up in the organization where valuable management time gets taken up resolving them. Multifunctional teams can usually settle these issues at a working level.

Ask each individual to have at least an informal plan for the positive changes he or she intends to make. Get people accustomed to challenging and rethinking their activities continuously in the working-team context.

Position Your People to Accelerate Their Learning Vary interactions among key managers, especially senior executives. Have them spend more time with peers on work substance and less time on policy problems. Imagine what would happen if you moved your senior managers' desks into a single room for three months, as Honda sometimes does, so that they could get to know the day-to-day business from their colleagues' point of view.

Devote meeting time to the effect of cycle time on the company's competitive position. Make sure everyone knows where the bottlenecks are, especially those they contribute to themselves.

Maximize key managers' exposure to operations downstream that depend on them. Sometimes an exchange of jobs between adjacent department heads is useful. With good people, a tour of duty that brings the vice president of marketing and sales to manufacturing—and vice versa—can be positive all around.

Ask each senior manager to prepare a flow chart that maps out how key reports make decisions and relate to one another operationally. Then compare the map with what the organization chart says. Explore the contrast and how it affects cycle time.

Implementation—A Delicate Balance Managers who begin to move their organizations toward time compression face an inescapable dilemma: how to achieve faster cycles in the long term without being badly damaged by work interruptions in the short term. Most organizations cover their delays and errors with slack resources and loosely fitting interfaces. But when a company begins to compress its cycles, the delays and errors can rarely be fixed as quickly as the slack is taken away. Temporary breakdowns occur, and fast response to customers—the whole objective—is undermined.

Every management must find its own pace and mechanisms to walk this tightrope. A pilot project—walking before running—often helps. So does a simulation of new procedures before they are fully implemented. Temporary buffers of material or information may also help as long as they are deliberately reduced during the transition period. What's critical is that managers keep pushing the change process and don't suspend their efforts when the inevitable problems arise. As fast-cycle competitors everywhere remind us, operating crises are opportunities to learn and improve.

Many of these suggestions run counter to traditional ideas about good management. Efficiency was often thought to follow from fixed objectives, clear lines of organization, measures reduced to profit, and as few changes in basic arrangements as possible. But that was the logic of the mass-production machine. It has been superseded by the logic of innovation. And that logic, in turn, demands new organization and management practices.

DISCUSSION QUESTIONS

1. Do you think the authors are realistic about the ease with which fast-cycle methods and attitudes can be achieved in a large, complex firm?
2. Must a fast-cycle organization be flat? How does fast-cycle time affect a company's hierarchy?
3. The authors allude to the disruption that moving to a fast-cycle approach can cause. Discuss the potential disruption and confusion that such a shift might produce, and how GMs should manage it.

PART FOUR

MANAGING COMPLEXITY

A Framework for Analyzing Government Involvement in Business

17

J. RONALD FOX

When surveying the marketplace, general managers must take into account not only their competitors but also the government. In this reading, J. Ronald Fox, an expert in business-government relations, provides general managers with a systematic approach for analyzing government involvement in business. He discusses why government often intervenes in the business world, how to assess the interaction between the two, and how to identify the best response business can make. General managers need to understand the benefits and pitfalls of government intervention in business on issues such as product safety, pollution, and equal employment opportunity. General managers who can forge a productive relationship with government while protecting their own business interests will gain competitive advantage in the marketplace

Problems involving the interaction of business and government can arise in areas as diverse as environmental pollution, equal employment opportunity, product safety, workplace safety, use of limited resources, and foreign or domestic competition, to name but a few. In order for managers in business and government to deal effectively with these problems, they must understand the causes of the actual or potential government involvement, the alternatives available for dealing with these needs or interests, and the relative impact of each alternative on the short-term and long-term interests of corporations as well as on the rest of society.

What follows is a systematic framework of steps for managers to use in analyzing actual and potential government involvement and for selecting appropriate courses of action in business-government relations.

INTRODUCTION: GOVERNMENT INVOLVEMENT IN BUSINESS

Throughout U.S. history, the primary economic control of business activities has been competition in the marketplace to satisfy consumer desire. In the process of responding to competition, most, if not all, individuals responsible for business firms seek to gain an advantage over their competition, with or without the aid of government. When a legislature or government agency is persuaded to act to the benefit or detriment of one interest group (including any segment of business) relative to another, government personnel normally justify their actions on the basis of correcting perceived deficiencies in the marketplace. These actions usually include steps to strengthen competition (e.g., by divestiture), or to impose government regulations, taxes or subsidies, or government ownership to achieve public policy objectives.

The deficiencies in the marketplace most frequently cited as justifying goverment involvement in business activities include:

1. Imperfect information available to the buyer
   - Information that is too costly in absolute terms
   - Information that is too costly relative to price/risk
   - Information that is only available after major purchase;

2. Natural monopolies (e.g., distribution of natural gas, electricity, telephone service)
   - Economies of scale restraining entry of competitors
   - Immense capital requirements restraining entry of competitors;

3. External factors (e.g., papermill polluting a stream)
   - Situations where the full costs of economic activity are borne not by the producer of goods or services, but by the other members of society;

4. Goals other than economic efficiency
   - Maintaining health or safety
   - Preserving a domestic industry
   - Stimulating innovation (patents)
   - Other: alcoholic beverages, sports, medicine;

5. Gross inequality in power of participants
   - Labor (i.e., the individual worker)
   - Agriculture;

6. Products or services considered a necessity or right
   - Housing
   - Water
   - Energy
   - Defense.

STEP I: ANALYZE THE INTERACTION OF GOVERNMENT AND BUSINESS

1. ANALYZE THE CAUSES OF PERCEIVED DEFICIENCIES IN THE MARKETPLACE

a. Are the perceived deficiencies in the marketplace real, or do they result from a failure in perception?

In order to understand the causes of government involvement in business, a manager must examine the situation to determine whether there are actual deficiencies in the marketplace or whether the deficiencies lie in the ability of a corporation to communicate how it operates and whether the trade-off decisions it makes are reasonable. If unreasonable deficiencies in the marketplace actually exist, then a business manager who wishes to influence the actions imposed by a legislature or government agency must diagnose the deficiencies as the government perceives them, and propose corrective actions, as well as persuasive arguments for accepting them. If, on the other hand, a business manager determines that government representatives misperceive the situation, then the manager needs to determine the causes of this perceptual error, gather facts and arguments in support of his or her case, and present them, along with the opinions of credible experts and constituents, to the concerned government representatives.

2. IDENTIFY PROBLEMS AND OPPORTUNITIES POSED BY PERCEIVED DEFICIENCIES IN THE MARKETPLACE

a. What problems and opportunities does the corporation or industry pose for the government?

b. What problems and opportunities does the government pose for the corporation or industry?

Government actions often constrain corporations in the pursuit of their business activities. However, government actions frequently provide competitive benefits or ameliorate the operating problems of some companies relative to others. For example, government-mandated entitlements to domestic oil supplies for small oil refineries lowered the costs of operation for these refineries relative to large refineries. On the other hand, costly testing and pollution control investments imposed on many industries are usually borne more easily by large corporations, which have the advantage of large volume production, than by small companies, which must spread the costs over fewer products.

3. ANALYZE THE PROCESS BY WHICH GOVERNMENT BECOMES INVOLVED IN BUSINESS

a. What are the key steps by which government becomes involved in business activities in this situation? (Legislative? Executive? Judicial?)

b. What is the legitimate and accepted role for business and other interest groups in these steps?

c. What are the key inputs required for the process to operate? (e.g., information, votes, other resources)

A review of the process by which government becomes involved with business is the basis for identifying the opportunities for business and other interest groups to influence the process. Typically, the process requires inputs in the form of information, analyses, meetings of key participants, well-supported arguments, written statements, and organized support from constituents. Representatives of business and other interest groups are often the only source of these inputs.

4. IDENTIFY KEY PARTICIPANTS IN THE PROCESS

a. Who are the key individuals and groups in the process by which government becomes involved in business?

b. What are their values and objectives? What rewards and penalties apply to them?

c. What are their political and technical strengths and weaknesses?

d. What are their perceptions and assumptions about the causes of and alternatives to the perceived deficiencies in the marketplace?

Because of the political nature of the government process, identifying the key individuals and groups is important. Government involvement in business often arises from conflicting views of the relative importance of various community needs, and the manner in which trade-offs should be made among these needs. Hence, an important part of problem diagnosis is understanding the values and objectives held by key parties, their strengths and weaknesses as participants in the process, and the assumptions they hold about alternatives for dealing with the perceived deficiencies in the marketplace.

5. EVALUATE THE COSTS AND BENEFITS RESULTING FROM PERCEIVED DEFICIENCIES IN THE MARKETPLACE

a. Which groups incur costs from perceived deficiencies in the marketplace? Are the costs concentrated or diffused?

b. Which groups gain benefits from perceived deficiencies in the marketplace? Are the benefits concentrated or diffused?

Identifying individuals and groups that experience costs and benefits from perceived deficiencies in the marketplace will serve as an important part of diagnosing a problem by locating those who are likely to support or oppose changes from the status quo. Determining whether the costs and benefits of the status quo are concentrated or diffused will also help in anticipating the degree of difficulty in organizing groups to support or oppose a change.

STEP II: SELECT A SATISFACTORY RESPONSE TO GOVERNMENT INVOLVEMENT IN BUSINESS

1. IDENTIFY ALTERNATIVE COURSES OF ACTION

a. What are the alternatives available for dealing with government involvement?

b. What are the steps that must occur for each alternative to achieve the desired results?

In order to deal effectively with the government, business managers need to identify reasonable responses to perceived deficiencies in the marketplace and to analyze the feasibility and the results of the steps required to carry out these responses. This analysis is a necessary part of preparing to deal effectively with the perceived deficiencies in the marketplace and with alternatives proposed by government representatives or other interest groups.

2. EVALUATE THE COSTS AND BENEFITS OF EACH ALTERNATIVE

a. Which individuals or groups experience costs and benefits (including political costs and benefits) associated with each alternative in the near term? Long term?

b. Are the costs and benefits concentrated or diffused?

c. Are the costs and benefits acceptable to organized interest groups and government agencies? If not, are there reasonable changes that will make the costs and benefits more acceptable?

In evaluating responses, as in diagnosing problems, an appraisal of the costs and benefits resulting from a proposed response is useful in identifying sympathetic constituents and appraising the potential support and resistance to a particular course of action.

The costs and benefits associated with each alternative include the effects it will have on

1. Government personnel
2. Other interest groups
3. Efficiency
4. Equity
5. Competition
6. Individual motivation
7. Cost of government operations
8. Small vs. large producers
9. Domestic vs. foreign producers
10. The costs, quantity, and quality of products and services.

3. ORGANIZE THE AUTHORITY AND COMPETENCE TO PRODUCE THE DESIRED RESULTS

a. For each step being considered, who has the authority and who has the competence to achieve the desired results?

b. If the competence and authority do not reside in the same individual or group, how can they be brought together?

In order to ascertain the feasibility of each alternative, one must examine the location of the authority and the competence to carry out each of the required steps. If the authority and competence reside in different individuals or groups, find ways to bring the authority and competence together.

4. ORGANIZE AND MOTIVATE CONSTITUENT SUPPORT

a. Which participants (constituents) are needed for a response to be successful?

b. What reasonable steps can be taken to gain the support of the required participants? (Are there contingent benefits that can be provided to the required participants?)

c. How can these participants be supplied with the information, tools, and funds needed to increase the likelihood that an alternative will be successful?

In evaluating responses to government involvement, business managers need to identify the interested (as well as the required) participants as a key element in evaluating alternatives. Solutions to problems involving government usually require coalitions of motivated constituents to perform the steps required for each response. In many cases, constituents need to be supplied with information and other resources to insure their effective support.

5. SELECT A RESPONSE

Considering the feasibility of producing each response, which alternative is most likely to produce the desired benefits within acceptable costs?

DISCUSSION QUESTIONS

1. Is government necessarily involved to some degree in business, or can it remain completely uninvolved? Explain your reasoning.
2. Should general managers actively form alliances with government? Or should they adopt a wait-and-see approach, carefully gauging the extent of government activity before responding?
3. What is the author's stance toward government involvement in business?
4. Suggest ways in which GMs can monitor government activity in the business sector. Are some ways more effective than others?
5. Should general managers devote resources to educating all levels of employees about the implications of government involvement in their business or industry? Or should they limit their educational commitment to top management alone? Explain your reasoning.

18 Managing for Efficiency, Managing for Equity

JOSEPH L. BOWER

Business-government relations can be a problematic part of the complex world that GMs administer. Difficulties arise because business and government operate by two different management systems, one technocratic, the other political. These systems vary in the implicit contract they offer to participants. Their organizational structure, choice of purpose, and reason for allocating resources also differ. In this reading, Joseph Bower charts the consequences of senior managers in industry confronting their opposite numbers in government. He also provides a framework for understanding and ameliorating the tensions that arise between the two management systems.

Why is the relationship between business and government in the United States perceived as unsatisfactory? It does not make sense that so important a class of transactions should regularly frustrate all participants, especially when the competitiveness of the U.S. economy is at stake. Conventional diagnoses of the problem lead nowhere. Attempts to make government more "business-like" regularly fail, and no one wants to make business more like government.

The fundamental problem arises from the use of two very different systems for managing our affairs. The first of these systems rests on the principle that managers should make the most efficient and effective use possible of the resources at their disposal. We measure organizations of this sort by their results. The other system rests on the principle that managers should try to ensure that the system treats fairly most of the people it affects. We measure organizations of this type by the legitimacy of their internal processes and by the public accountability of their officers. These general distinctions have important practical consequences.

Consider, for example, the case of William Ruckelshaus, who was appointed in November 1970 by President Nixon to head up the then newly organized Environmental Protection Agency. Ruckelshaus, a stranger to the agency, was attacked for "doing too little" by Nixon's rival, Senator Edmund Muskie, then chairman of the Senate Subcommittee on Environmental Pollution. Ruckelshaus was threatened by the very conservative Representative Jamie Whitten of Mississippi, who set the EPA's budget in the Agriculture Subcommittee of the House Appropriations Committee, and constantly subjected to scrutiny on TV and in the newspapers. Although he was unsure of the quality of his organization and still needed to fill key staff positions, Ruckelshaus nonetheless had to take positions within 60 days that would affect the U.S. auto industry, the use of DDT by farmers and states, and the nation's standards for clean air and water.

Consider, as well, one of the men who would tangle with Ruckelshaus' agency—Henry Ford II, CEO of the Ford Motor Company—who had been responsible for the company since fighting his late father's cronies for control in 1948. With the budget, personnel, and substantive policies of the company demonstrably in his command, Ford's task was to manage the development of a line of passenger cars and trucks so that the company would remain economically healthy.

Ruckelshaus and Ford were both managers, of course, but the circumstances of their work were so different that no one label can easily cover both. The power of the purse, the power to hire and fire, the ability to operate out of the corrosive glare of the press, the ability to limit objectives so that they can be achieved, the time to study, organize, and act efficiently—these Ford had, but not Ruckelshaus. The right to set policy for the United States, the right to attack cities and companies with speeches and legal actions, the right to ignore potential short-term costs to industry in order to establish the credibility and integrity of the EPA—these Ruckelshaus had, but not Ford. The differences here are not superficial. They separate two quite distinct kinds of management.

TWO DISTINCT MANAGEMENT SYSTEMS

Business people often say that without the power of the purse and the power to hire and fire, you can't manage. They believe that a true system of management requires control over budgets, information, and personnel. But, in fact, not all business managers control these administrative tools. Nor, for that matter, do all managers with such control find themselves in a corporate setting.

Let us, therefore, avoid confusion by using the phrase *technocratic management* to describe those organizational systems—whether private or public—geared to the achievement of efficiency and effectiveness in the production and distribution of goods and services. And let us use the phrase *political management* to describe those organizational systems—again, whether public or private—geared to the equitable (or at least, legitimate) distribution of costs and benefits to which there are common or overlapping claims.

Most people do not distinguish between these two worlds of management and regularly talk of corporate politics and government business as if they were identical. Here, however, by exaggerating their differences a bit, we bring into sharp focus that nature of the line that divides them—and the problems that result when they collide.

To be sure, technocratic and political features can both be found in most systems for controlling large complex organizations, but as the *Exhibit* suggests, the systems vary markedly.

EXHIBIT
Managerial Systems

	TECHNOCRATIC	*POLITICAL*
The Contract	Long term	Revised from issue to issue
	Fosters loyalty to institution	Fosters loyalty to self or country
	Gives money for services in proportion to seniority, rank, and performance	Gives psychic rewards and rank in proportion to power to extract and ability to contribute
	Permits surplus shared or reinvested	Permits surplus spent or returned to the polity
Careers	Professionals	"Tourists"
	Trained members of a cadre	Trained in other professions; members of a party or network
	Rise from technical doer to generalist, planner, cooperator, and then leader	Rise project by project or from state office to federal office
Organization	Contingent on future strategy	Contingent on personality and current issues
	Highly differentiated by function, time horizon, and primary orientation	Largely undifferentiated, based on constituency and region
	Stable culture	
Information	Extensive and systematic; organized by level and phase of activity, e.g., planning vs. control	Fragmented, qualitative, concerned with perceptions; few systems; gossip and informal networks are key
	Generally closed to the public	Often open to the public
Strategy Formulation and Resource Allocation	Goals relatively clear: survival, growth, and surplus	Goals are diffuse or abstract slogans
	Selectivity understood to serve the organization as distinct from its parts	Selectivity not legitimate
	Return on investment to organization a key measure	Organization is "bureaucracy"
	Budget control can be tight by program	Budget control can sometimes be tight by line expenditures

DIFFERENT CONTRACTS FOR PARTICIPANTS

In a technocratic organization, recruitment of new members is taken seriously, for unless the people do not work out, they will be around for a long time. Indeed, in many large corporations, the contract is for "life." From its members the technocratic organization expects complete commitment. Demands on managers may become so great as to threaten family life and personal privacy, and senior executives may find it hard to speak as individuals separate from their organizations.

In return for such loyalty and service, members receive compensation—usually money but also a range of perquisites—in proportion to rank, seniority, and contribution. Moreover, they often share in the surplus generated by successful activity: profits are distributed as bonuses; salespeople are given trips to the Caribbean in recognition of increased productivity. Organizations try to reward group effort equally and individual effort in proportion to contribution.

The contract in political managerial systems works in a very different fashion. In corporate systems, for example, the person who does not measure up can be fired. By contrast, it takes enormous effort to dismiss a political appointee, who can fight dismissal through effective use of Congress and the press. More often what happens is that political managers, frustrated by low pay and limited influence, quit.

There is, moreover, no obvious referent organization in political systems—that is, issues have a life of their own, and ad hoc networks of individuals and organizations join to work at influencing policy and the distribution of resources. To whom the contract in a political system applies depends on the issue at hand without regard to technocratic notions of chain of command.

Consider the situation of Philip Heymann, who, while serving as acting assistant secretary of state for security and consular affairs, tried to liberalize U.S. visa policy. Heymann arrived at the assistant secretary's job in 1964 following the departure of Abba Schwartz, who had been driven out by his subordinate Frances Knight, the bureaucratically and politically powerful head of the passport office.

In reviewing his responsibilities, Heymann concluded that the granting of visas was an unnecessarily tedious process and not really useful to internal security. None of the other interested players—his superiors in the State Department, including the secretary, Dean Rusk; the Justice Department, including the FBI and the Immigration and Naturalization Service; the consular affairs bureaucracy; the White House staff; those congressmen interested in trade, foreign affairs, the communist threat; and, especially, the oversight subcommittee, chaired by Representative Michael A. Feighan, responsible for the budget of the State Department—viewed the visa problem the same way Heymann did. It was an era when J. Edgar Hoover was still powerful at the FBI and anticommunism was a salient agenda issue.

Indeed, most players saw Heymann's efforts as leading to the easier entry of potentially disloyal foreigners, the loss of consular jobs, or a bureaucratic flap with Hoover or Frances Knight. In short, no one had a reason to be positive, and Heymann had limited authority and resources to act.

Nonetheless, Heymann got his new "indefinite visa" policy approved by:

- Getting the proposal studied by his career subordinate and enlisting that subordinate's commitment by naming the proposal after him;
- Using high-level friends in the Justice Department to neutralize the potential objections of Hoover;

- Redefining the issues so the White House could propose it as a pro-tourism step to improve the nation's balance of payments;
- Exploiting the long-standing relationship of his committed career subordinate with the key subcommittee chairman;
- Informing the secretary of state of the action under way with a memo that explained that certain regulatory language would be changed on such and such a date unless the Secretary disapproved.

Under these circumstances, what was the nature of Heymann's contract? To whom or what was Heymann loyal? It was certainly to his concept of what was right for the country. He was also loyal to a school of thought that believed the country was best served by free trade, market-oriented economics, and due process in its politics.

At the same time, Heymann had personal goals. The indefinite visa had the advantage of being compact enough that Heymann had a real chance to accomplish a change in policy within his tenure, despite his relatively low level position. Like most political system managers, Heymann was a quasi-independent entrepreneur, not a technocrat able to rely on organization and superiors for resources and advancement—or, for that matter, on manipulating salary or incentive compensation to implement policy.

In practice, of course, these limitations on managerial control, qualified as they are by the exercise of patronage, often lead to cronyism. Students of the presidency, as of the office of governor and mayor, know well that elected executives need a cadre of trustworthy subordinates—a kitchen cabinet—who are loyal because of family, friendship, or total dependency.

DIFFERENT CAREER PATHS

The contrast between the structured long-term commitment within technocratic systems and the temporary syndicate quality of political systems is especially visible in managerial careers. Increasingly, technocratic managers are professionally educated, carefully recruited, and painstakingly trained or developed as they rise through a sequence of ever more demanding jobs.

In the political sector, however, most top jobs, especially in elective positions, go to inexperienced people. Achieving success, they often set their sights on higher office—and on the requirement to raise money continually for the next campaign. They typically begin their political careers working in campaign organizations and eventually run for office themselves. For example, starting as county commissioner, Paul Tsongas of Massachusetts won six elections in nine years, eventually rising to the U.S. Senate.

High level appointed officials almost always move laterally. Having established themselves as lawyers, academics, or entrepreneurs, they turn to "get some public experience" or return with their party for another round of public service. These "in and outers" or, as one career government official has called them, "tourists," view their movement through high levels of government as part of their nongovernmental careers. Those who are lawyers are trained to work on a project-by-project basis, often in temporary alliances, but always by adopting an adversarial posture. Academics, who focus on substantive issues and verbal debate, not on the mechanics of institutional life, are equally unprepared for management.

And what of career managers in our political system? Except for those older departments managed by essentially technocratic systems (the military, say, or the foreign service), there are almost none.

DIFFERENT ORGANIZATIONAL STRUCTURE

The differences between technocratic and political management are also visible in organizational structure, which in the technocratic world is a critical source of managerial influence. Technocratic executives work hard to devise a structure to suit their organization's strategy; as that strategy shifts, they fine-tune or reshape the structure accordingly.

They aim to strike an appropriate balance between the advantages of specialization and the costs of the administrative effort required to achieve integration. Some well-run corporations attempt to tie their long-term strategic plans to operating and capital budgets and to measure operations against both the short-term and long-term goals set up in those budgets.

The point, of course, is not that all or even most technocratic systems develop so sophisticated an organizational-cum-information system. But it is sensible and legitimate for them to try. For political managers, this sort of complexity makes no sense. Their tenure is too short, and control over structure is almost always shared among executive and legislative bodies.

DIFFERING PURPOSES AND ALLOCATION OF RESOURCES

In technocratic systems, resource allocation serves three clear goals—survival, growth, and surplus—according to a simple rule: resources should be invested where they will do the organization most good. Return on investment is a familiar measure by which managers can compare and rank equally appealing opportunities. Hence, the essential aspect of a technocratic system is not profit but selectivity. Profit is just a marvelously simple tool by which selectivity can be guided. Given a goal, the test of efficiency implies selectivity: Resources should be allocated where they can be most useful.

Because goals in political systems are often diffuse and vaguely specified—for example, "put an end to poverty"—it is usually difficult to rank objectives or to be legitimately selective among them. Although they can give voice to the aspirations and expectations of conflicting interest groups, political systems are notoriously ill equipped to disadvantage one part of their constituency in order to help another. At the national level, the consequence is that often we cannot close obsolete military bases or cut the pension expenditures that overwhelm our budgets. Instead, we print money and let inflation hide the distribution of harm.

WHEN POLITICIAN MEETS TECHNOCRAT

What happens when these two worlds of management collide? Often there is friction and seldom an attractive public policy outcome. Unlike Solomon, we usually cut the baby in half. As long as the nation was strong relative to its industrial competition, this incompatibility did not matter. Today, however, the awkwardness of the relationship between politician and technocrat is both painful and destructive. It is a luxury we can no longer afford.

When a company deals with those parts of the government that use technocratic systems to carry out its objectives, it will face counterparts similar in organizational capability and orientation. The government managers will be career bureaucrats. As in business, some will be competent, some not; but unless the agency is badly run or very new, most of its members will respect competence. It will have continuity in staffing—sometimes less than desirable, sometimes more, but the principle will be understood and valued. The agency's talent and time horizon will permit technical knowledge to be applied where it is relevant. When an issue under consideration lies within the purview of a government technocratic managerial system, a company can do business in relatively normal ways across the public-private boundary.

But where government uses political systems, a company can expect to deal with counterparts almost totally different in capability, orientation, experience, and values. Worse, to business managers, politicians will often appear incompetent (because their skills and knowledge are not those of the technocracy) or even untrustworthy (because the rules and procedures they hold dear are politically oriented).

Managers of technocratic systems believe purpose to be a matter of focus, structure a question of hierarchy, and contract a problem for managed incentives. Managers of political systems believe purpose to be a game of fair division, structure a version of cavalry charge, and incentives a problem for skillful bargaining. The two worlds of management have different perceptions of reality.

When they work together, the awkwardness can be comical. Business executives have a sense of the competent but fallible organizations behind them. They know how much time it takes to get even simple things done and are aware of the web of personal commitments embodied in a particular strategy. They also have a sense of how their organizations can be used constructively to work on problems; systems exist for doing these things.

Political managers see issues in the context of the many other items that require their time and that of their staff. They will know which issues are "hot" and which are "off the screen" for the time being. Indeed, in the busy schedule of political managers, noncrises are almost always distractions. When attention does turn to a specific issue—altering a piece of tax legislation, keeping a plant open, or getting an increased appropriation for an agency's regional office—politicians instinctively measure how any given stance will be viewed by political allies and opponents and, equally important, how it will play in the media. Until there is widespread public awareness of a problem, there may be little political managers can do.

THE DRIFT TOWARD POLITICIZATION

When, for whatever reasons, the world of politics impinges on the relatively well-ordered world of technocratic organizations, a loss of efficiency is the inevitable result. As the management of these organizations shifts attention away from the consistent pursuit of long-term objectives and toward immediate political considerations, the self-sustaining quality of technocratic systems gets lost. Each new political bargain, each new negotiation, produces compromise among demands—not selectivity in the application of resources.

Another cost of the present conflict of systems is best embodied in the remark of the past chairman of General Electric, Reginald Jones, that he spent more than half his time in Washington. In order to deal with the public sector, senior managers of major technocratic organizations have been forced to join the political world. The greatest price we pay for our approach to economic affairs may well be this politicizing of the technocracy. The job of top management shifts from direction setting and organization building to influencing the laws and public institutions that determine whether a company or agency can prosper or even survive.

The point is simple to see if hard to deal with. Once a market-based organization becomes dependent on the intervention of a government agency for its survival, it must deal with the politics of that agency at least as seriously as with its market. Where the politics are negative, companies can get boxed into an uneconomic Catch-22: the steps they take to survive each year lead them to a political never-never land. Where the politics are positive, a potentially unsound business can become a permanent ward of the state.

In such situations, technocratic managers trade the implicit or explicit promise of economic (and political) benefits—usually in the form of increased jobs or low consumer prices—for immediate economic support. The politicians, in turn, offer equity or loans the market will not provide or guaranteed sales at prices the market will not pay or in volumes the market will not accept. For example, at various times the only reason many French or British agencies bought French or British computer products is that they were ordered to.

The consequence of such transactions is that the jobs thus saved or created become an entitlement. The workers who fill them soon recognize that their elected representatives—not the market—have protected them. At that point, workers view the withdrawal of protection as a hostile act, as grounds for voting for someone else. Eventually the point comes when society vigorously supports economically obsolete but politically important activity. This type of growing politicization threatens the ability of public managers to achieve—or even address—long-term national objectives.

RIGHTING THE BALANCE

Why is politicization so troublesome a problem today? Several reasons suggest themselves. Most obviously, when economic growth slows, the losers complain loudly and point to the seeming inability of technocratic management to produce an equitable distribution of costs and benefits.

Today, people hurt by these processes do not react passively. With the passage of amendments to the Civil Rights Act, the one-man-one-vote court decisions, and the sophisticated use by narrow interest groups of the media and the courts, people no longer think they merely deserve an opportunity to succeed; they believe they are entitled to a comfortable living. And when technocratically managed institutions falter, those on whom the burden of failure rests perceive themselves to be treated inequitably. After all, the government did not do its job of protecting their "rights."

Technocratic managements that have proven unequal to market or legislative mandates discover among their employees and political representatives a new source of support. If nothing else, they can "sell" their ability to provide employment. In short, when technocratic systems face serious challenges and cannot deliver to their own constituencies, then one of the few routes to survival is to provide something a legislature will buy—that is, to become politicized.

The basic problem identified here is the creeping politicization of technocratic organizations in both private and public sectors, not the growth of government. Technocratic systems are vulnerable to politicization because their narrow focus tends to blind them to broad shifts in taste and values. When companies or agencies fail to respond to fundamental changes in sentiment, political managers are ready to intervene.

For the most part, our political systems respond reasonably swiftly to such shifts with new policies and laws. The challenge is for technocratic managers to work constructively with political managers by forming nonpoliticizing alliances of effective operating organizations. By this route alone can the United States find its way to a coherent industrial policy. The alternative, a centrally driven or guided policy, would impose a burden on our political apparatus that could only do harm.

The two worlds of management can and must collaborate, but each functions better when there is room between them. This is a simple fact, not an argument for laissez-faire. When values shift and technocratically managed institutions do not respond, as in the case of environmental protection, politicians should intervene. But when political managers do intervene, there are always economic consequences.

The problem comes when politics asks more of technocracy than technocracy can deliver. Politicians must learn that technocratic management is also an art of the possible—that failure to meet legislated objectives is not always evidence of some devious obstruction of the public's will requiring instant remedy. Politicizing the world of management that strives for efficiency will not make it more equitable. It will only make it less efficient. We can no longer afford this cost.

DISCUSSION QUESTIONS

1. Are there advantages to politicizing technocracy? Shouldn't technocratic systems be more equitable in response to their constituents?
2. Are managing for efficiency and managing for equity mutually exclusive goals?
3. Is the author's description of technocratic and political systems fair? Does he favor one system of management over the other?

19 The Challenges, Motivations, and Mentalities of MNC Management

CHRISTOPHER BARTLETT

The multinational corporation presents general managers with an array of challenges and opportunities not found in domestic firms. The management issues are complex; indeed, the task of leading an MNC requires a unique mentality or vision. Christopher Bartlett's reading looks at the shape and scope of multinational corporation management. He defines the multinational company, describes how its management challenges differ from those of domestic companies, outlines the forces that motivate the internationalization of companies, and describes the evolution of strategic approaches to managing worldwide operations. This discussion gives general managers a framework for understanding the multinational mentality.

THE CHALLENGES: NEW MANAGEMENT TASKS

An economic historian could trace the origins of international business back to the seafaring traders operating in ancient Egypt. Through the centuries, the international flow of goods continued, and in medieval Venice, the merchant traders had developed much of the sophistication of modern day international trading companies.

An important chapter in this history was written by the great British and Dutch trading companies that flourished in the seventeenth and eighteenth centuries, establishing outposts from Hudson Bay to the East Indies. By the nineteenth century, the newly emerged capitalists in industrialized Europe began investing in the less developed areas of the world (including the United States), particularly within the vast empires held by Britain, France, Holland, and Germany.

However, few if any of these historical entities could be called true multinational corporations (MNCs). Most of the traders would be excluded by the first criterion of an MNC definition, which requires that MNCs have *substantial direct investment* in foreign countries, not just export business. And most of the companies with international operations in the nineteenth century would be excluded by the second criterion, which requires that they be engaged in the active management of those offshore assets rather than simply hold them in a passive financial portfolio.

Thus, while companies that source raw materials offshore, license technology abroad, export products into foreign markets, or even hold equity positions in overseas ventures may regard themselves as international, by our definition, they are not multinational corporations unless they have substantial direct investment in foreign countries *and* they actively manage those operations and regard them as an integral part of the corporation, strategically and organizationally.

Under this definition, the MNC is a very recent phenomenon, dating back fewer than 100 years. In fact, the vast majority of MNCs developed only in the post-World War II years.

Historically, one of the great limitations to understanding more about the behavior and impact of MNCs has been that much of the analysis has taken place within the discipline of economics. This is not to say that economists' descriptions of the workings of the international environment were not helpful. Indeed, they created very useful models of many of the forces, structures, and institutions that provide the context in which international business operates. Yet there remained some important limitations to their approach.

First, they tended to take a macro approach, in which countries or industries were the unit of analysis. Second, their primary focus tended to be on trade flows, and this often reduced discussion of foreign investment to an analysis of capital flows. Finally, in keeping with the normal practice in their discipline, they often made limiting and sometimes unrealistic assumptions, such as the existence of pure competition, or the immobility of factors of production.

It was during the late 1960s and early 1970s that a helpful new perspective on the nature of international business began attracting considerable attention. In contrast to much of the previous work, the focus of this body of research was on the multinational enterprise and management behavior rather than on global economic forces and international institutions. With the company as the primary unit of analysis, and management decisions as the key variables, many of the critical issues of international business became more clearly understood.

DIFFERENCES BETWEEN MNCs AND DOMESTIC COMPANIES

The following characteristics distinguish the MNC from the purely domestic company:

1. The purely domestic company operates in a single national environment where consumer preferences, government policies and regulations, and union demands tend to be fairly consistent. The MNC faces a diverse and often conflicting pattern of demands and pressures from multiple host country interest groups (and particularly from host country governments). The MNC also faces the political risk of operating in countries with different political

philosophies, legal systems, and social attitudes toward private property, corporate responsibility, and free enterprise.

2. The purely domestic company can respond to competitive challenges only within the context of its single market. The MNC can (and often *must*) play a much more complex competitive game. Global scale or low cost sourcing may be necessary to achieve competitive costs—implying the need for complex logistical coordination. Furthermore, competitive interaction can take place on an international battlefield, and sound global competitive strategy might dictate that response to an attack in one overseas market be taken in a different country—perhaps in the competitor's home market. These are options a purely domestic company does not have.
3. The purely domestic company can measure its performance in a single comparable unit, the local currency. The MNC is required to measure results with a flexible measuring stick, as the values of currencies fluctuate widely against each other. In addition, to the extent that it is moving funds internationally, it is exposed to the economic risks associated with fluctuations and abrupt devaluations in exchange rates.
4. The purely domestic company must manage an organization structure that typically reflects its product and functional diversity. The MNC organization is intrinsically more complex since it must provide for management control over its product, functional *and* geographic diversity. Furthermore, the resolution of this three-way tension must be accomplished in an organization that is divided by barriers of distance and time, and impeded by differences in language and culture that are virtually nonexistent in purely domestic companies.

MOTIVATIONS: THE PUSHES AND PULLS TO INTERNATIONALIZE

Given the additional difficulties, risks, and complexities that face companies as they expand abroad, why would companies choose to become multinational? What were the external forces and internal motivations that led managers to accept the challenges and complexities that were an integral part of multinational operations? How did foreign opportunities fit into strategies in which markets were normally defined by the home country boundaries?

HISTORICAL TRIGGERS AND INVESTMENT PATTERNS

Among the earliest motivations that drove companies to invest abroad was the need to *secure key supplies*, especially minerals, energy, and scarce raw material resources. Aluminum producers needed to assure their supply of bauxite, tire companies went abroad to develop rubber plantations, and oil companies wanted to open up new fields in Canada, the Middle East, and Venezuela. By the early part of the century, Standard Oil, British Petroleum, Anaconda Copper, and International Nickel were among the largest of the emerging MNCs.

Another strong trigger of internationalization could be described as the *market-seeking* behavior. This motivation was strong in companies that had some advantage, typically related to their technology or brand recognition, that gave them access to offshore markets. Although their initial attitude was often opportunistic, many companies eventually realized that these additional sales allowed them to exploit economies of scale and scope, thereby reducing costs and allocating scarce resources more efficiently.[1]

The market-seeking motive induced many of the manufacturing companies to venture abroad, first building a sales and distribution organization, then following with manufacturing plants to consolidate and defend their new market positions. The trend was encouraged by the rising tide of protectionism in the 1920s and 1930s. However, it was in the post-World War II era that international expansion exploded. Between 1950 and 1980, the direct foreign investment (DFI) of U.S. companies increased from $11.8 billion to over $200 billion.

At least among U.S.-based companies, a clear pattern of market-seeking behavior was evident in the early expansion abroad. In the 1950s, there was a strong investment bias towards neighboring countries, particularly Canada but also Latin America. By the early 1960s, attention had shifted to Europe as the EEC opened that market internally. The EEC share of U.S. companies' DFI increased from 16% in 1957 to 32% by 1966. Finally, as EEC markets matured, attention shifted to developing countries, which grew from 18% of U.S. businesses' DFI in 1974 to 25% in 1980.

Another important trigger of internationalization was to *access low cost factors* of production. Particularly as tariff barriers declined in the 1960s, many companies for whom labor represented a major cost found they were at a competitive disadvantage to imports. In response, many firms in the clothing, electronics, watchmaking and other such industries began exploring the possibility of establishing offshore sourcing locations for components and whole product lines.

Soon it became clear that labor was not the only factor cost that could be sourced more efficiently overseas. For example, the availability of lower-cost capital (perhaps through a government investment subsidy) also became a strong force for strategic internationalization.[2]

---

1. The eminent business historian Alfred D. Chandler sees this factor as the key to the long-term success of the modern large industrial corporation and the most important force of internationalization of the early MNCs.

2. These changing historical motivations suggest a pattern that was captured in the "product cycle theory" of international investment developed by Raymond Vernon and others. This theory suggested that companies were drawn offshore by demand for their innovative products. To protect these new export markets from local competition, they established foreign plants. As the product matured, the low-cost foreign plants became the source of the company's continued competitiveness.

Thus, the shift in attention from the maturing European market to developing countries was driven not only by market-seeking behavior but also by competitive forces that focused management attention on cost efficiency. In this quest for low cost sources, Far Eastern countries such as Korea, Singapore, and Hong Kong have been the main beneficiaries of new foreign investment by MNCs from most of the developed nations in which labor costs are comparatively high.

These three motives—(or two, if we ignore the historical differences, and combine "materials seeking" and "low cost factor access" into a single "resource seeking" motive)—were the forces behind the overseas expansion of the vast majority of MNCs. That is not to imply, however, that such motives remained at the core of these companies' international strategies. Often they were simply the initial enabling conditions that allowed management to develop a much richer and thus more complex rationale for their worldwide operations.

EMERGING MOTIVATIONS

An examination of the decisions that triggered a company's early international expansion reveals that few did so with any clearly defined global objectives or well-developed international strategy. Internationalization was typically a gradual and an incremental process, most often linked to the company's basic home market strategic objectives, for example, to secure raw material supplies or lower cost sources.

However, once they had established international sales and production operations, the perceptions and strategic motivations of these companies changed. Initially, the typical attitude was that the foreign operations were strategic and organizational appendages to the domestic business and should be managed opportunistically. Gradually, as managers recognized some of the important advantages of operating internationally, they began to think about their strategy in a more integrated worldwide sense. The forces that originally triggered their expansion overseas often became secondary or tertiary factors in their emerging global strategies.

Although it was seldom the original trigger that induced overseas investment, an important secondary effect that often became a critical factor in a company's international strategy was its global scanning capability. A company drawn offshore to secure supplies of raw materials was more likely to become aware of alternative low-cost production sources around the globe; a company tempted abroad by market opportunities was often exposed to new technologies or market needs that stimulated innovative product development. The very nature of an MNC's worldwide presence gave it a huge informational advantage that could result in locating more efficient sources or more advanced product or process technology. Thus, a company whose international strategy was triggered by a technological or marketing advantage could enhance that leadership position through its global scanning capability.

Another benefit that soon became evident was that being a multinational rather than a national company brought important *competitive advantages*. In addition to the potential benefits that flowed from global scale economies and global scanning capability, MNCs were also able to engage in competitive strategies based on the cross subsidization of markets. For example, a Korean TV producer could challenge a national company in the U.S. market by subsidizing U.S. losses with funds from its profitable Asian or South American operations. If the U.S. company depended entirely on its home market, its competitive response could only be to defend its position—typically by seeking government intervention or by matching or offsetting the competitive price reduction. International investment decisions began to reflect not only market attractiveness or factor cost efficiency choices, but also the leverage such investment provided over competitors.

Although for purposes of analysis, and also to reflect some sense of historical development, the motives behind the expansion of MNCs have been reduced to a few distinct categories, it should be clear that management behavior was rarely driven by a single motivating force. Indeed, as companies became more knowledgeable about the international environment, the diverse and vague motivations became recognized as more concrete potential benefits of operating as worldwide companies.

Soon, the more adaptable managers began to capitalize on all of the potential advantages available to companies with international operations—assuring critical supplies, entering new markets, tapping low cost factors of production, leveraging their global information access, and capitalizing on the competitive advantages of their multiple market positions. As these multiple motivations merged and evolved, so too did management attitudes towards the strategic options available to the MNC.

THE EVOLVING MENTALITY: INTERNATIONAL TO TRANSNATIONAL

Even in this brief and sketchy description of the changing motivations for internationalization, one develops a sense of historical evolution in the strategic role that foreign operations played in the emerging MNC. We will categorize this evolutionary pattern into four stages that may be thought of as a typical evolution of the strategic mentality in an MNC.

Although such classification is necessarily overgeneralized and arbitrary, it allows us to achieve two objectives: It highlights the fact that for most MNCs, the forces that initially induced them to go overseas often evolve into a very different set of motivations that underlie management's thinking and actions. Such a classification also allows us to clarify a confusing array of terms used to describe the strategies adopted by MNCs.

The evolving stages of strategic mentality may be defined as:

- *International*
- *Multinational*
- *Global*
- *Transnational*

INTERNATIONAL MENTALITY

In the earliest stages of MNC development, many managers think of the company's overseas operations as distant outposts whose main role is to support the domestic parent company—for example, by contributing incremental sales of the domestic product line or by supplying raw materials or components to the domestic manufacturing operation.

Companies with an "international" strategic mentality regarded themselves fundamentally as domestic operations with some foreign appendages. Managers assigned to overseas operations were often domestic misfits whose primary qualification was that they spoke a foreign language or had previously lived abroad. Decisions relating to these operations were typically made incrementally, and often opportunistically.

MULTINATIONAL MENTALITY

The exposure of the organization to the overseas environment, and more importantly, the growing importance of sales and profits from these sources often convinced management that a potential opportunity of more than marginal importance existed there. Increasingly, companies realized that they had to do more than ship out old equipment, technology, or product lines that had been developed for the home market. Local competitors and host governments often accelerated the learning of companies that retained an unresponsive "international" strategic mentality too long.

A multinational strategic mentality developed as managers began to recognize and emphasize the differences among national markets and operating environments. Particularly in the late 1950s and early 1960s, when the rate of growth of U.S. overseas investment reached its peak, it became managerially fashionable to understand and adopt a more flexible approach to overseas markets. Companies responded by emphasizing the need to modify their products, their strategies and even their management practices country by country. Typically under the protective umbrella of an international division organization, these companies developed and managed a strategic approach that was literally multinational—the worldwide strategy was the sum of the multiple national subsidiary strategies.

Managers of foreign operations were often young fast-track entrepreneurs. Using their local market knowledge and the parent company's willingness to invest in growing opportunities, these entrepreneurial managers were able to build up their independence from headquarters intervention.

GLOBAL MENTALITY

Although the multinational approach often resulted in very responsive marketing approaches, it also gave rise to an inefficient manufacturing infrastructure within the MNC. Plants were built more to provide local marketing advantages or to improve political relations than to maximize production efficiency. Similarly, the proliferation of products designed to meet local needs usually compromised the efficiencies that had existed when the domestic product was sold into foreign markets.

As lowering trade barriers opened world markets, a new strategic mentality began to dominate world business. Some MNCs, notably of Japanese origin, began to think in terms of creating products for a world market, and manufacturing them on global scale in a few highly efficient plants. This "global" strategic mentality assumed that national tastes and preferences were more similar than different, or that they could be *made to be* more similar. The dream of a unified global shopping center drove many of these strategies.

This strategic approach required considerably more central coordination and central control than before, and was typically associated with an organization structure in which various product or business managers had worldwide responsibility. Many activities were managed centrally (particularly research and manufacturing), and most strategic decisions were also taken at the center.

TRANSNATIONAL MENTALITY

As highly efficient global competitors began claiming victories against local and multinational companies alike, host governments predictably became concerned. In many ways, these global MNCs seemed to be a more powerful and thus more threatening version of the earlier unresponsive MNCs with their unsophisticated "international" strategic mentality. The trend back to more centralized control concerned them, particularly in an era when many countries faced crushing interest burdens and mounting trade deficits. In response, many host governments increased both the restrictions and the demands they placed on those MNCs operating with a global mentality.

Thus, by the late 1970s and early 1980s, many MNCs began to recognize that the pressure to develop global-scale competitive efficiency and the demands to be responsive to local market and political needs were simultaneous. Under these conditions, the either/or attitude reflected in both the multinational and global strategic mentalities seemed inappropriate.

Those MNCs that developed an ability to respond to important host country needs *while retaining* global competitiveness exhibited what we call a "transnational" strategic mentality. The role of national units was increased, as manufacturing and even R&D facilities were shifted from the center to the country subsidiaries. However, the retention of central coordination and control ensured that the MNC did not regress to the old multinational strategic mentality.

This strategic mentality not only recognized the importance of locally responsive country-level operations—as signified by the return of 'national' to the terminology—but also, the importance of linking and coordinating operations to retain competitive effectiveness and economic efficiency (hence, the prefix "trans"). The resulting intensive communication between headquarters and subsidiaries, and the need for shared decision making implied the need for a multidimensional organization structure and a flexible management process.

There is no inevitability in either the direction or the end point of the evolving strategic mentality we have described. Depending on the industry, the individual company's strategic position, the host countries' diverse needs, and a variety of other factors, an MNC might reasonably operate with any one of these strategic mentalities. More likely, bearing in mind that these are arbitrary classifications, it will probably exhibit attributes of all of them.

DISCUSSION QUESTIONS

1. Choose a multinational firm with which you are familiar. What strategic mentality, or combination of mentalities, characterizes its international focus?
2. Imagine that you are a division general manager in a foreign country. Should your loyalties lie solely with corporate headquarters, or should your operations be somewhat responsive to your host government?
3. Do the challenges of multinational management appeal to you? Why or why not? Would you rather assume general management responsibilities in a purely domestic, and therefore less complex, firm?
4. What general management skills are necessary in an MNC that are not required in a strictly domestic firm?
5. What are the means by which a corporate general manager conveys to international divisions what the author calls a transnational mentality?

General Management in Diversified Firms

20

JOSEPH BADARACCO AND RICHARD L. ELLSWORTH

The general manager's role in a diversified firm is often more challenging than in a single-business firm. Strategy, resource allocation, and management are approached differently because of the complexity of a diversified company. According to Joseph Badaracco and Richard Ellsworth, GMs in these firms must manage the context *in which decisions are made at the division or company level. This means fine-tuning organization design, supporting open communication at all levels, and promoting an atmosphere of trust and innovation. This reading shows how senior managers in diversified firms achieve these goals by setting strategy, managing other general managers, allocating corporate resources, and balancing top-down and bottom-up influences on decisions.*

ESTABLISHING STRATEGY

Large, diversified firms dominate the *Fortune* 500 in the United States, accounting for nearly half of all U.S. industrial production, jobs, and corporate profits. Their role in other developed economies is comparable.

For a single-business company, strategy encompasses, among other things, the concept of the business as a part of the task facing the management of the firm. This, in turn, is made up of the following:

1. The business definition—what types of results a company will or won't achieve for customers;
2. The overall mission, in terms of value to be created for various stakeholders;
3. The competitive position to be achieved in relation to customers, suppliers, and competitors;
4. Functional goals and efforts needed to achieve the desired competitive position.

For diversified companies, strategy is more complicated, because these firms consist of several different businesses. Each business is usually called a division, each usually has its own general manager and functional managers, and each has its own business strategy. The strategy of an entire diversified firm is its corporate strategy. It involves the same basic elements as a strategy of a single business, but each element takes a different form.

For a diversified company, for example, the concept of the business describes the range of businesses in which the firm will compete and how these businesses will relate to each other. For many diversified companies, the basic business concept is related diversification—that is, the firm's businesses share manufacturing facilities, channels, brand image, management skills, or some other factor. Related diversifiers often have large corporate offices that pursue "synergy" by coordinating the strategies and operations of the divisions.

The alternative business concept is unrelated or conglomerate diversification. In this case, separate businesses within the firm deal with each other at arm's length and compete for funds in an internal capital market. Such firms are usually managed by small, often tiny, corporate offices.

The corporate strategy of a multi-business company sets economic targets for profit, return, and growth. These firm-wide targets break down into economic objectives that differ among divisions. Some divisions may concentrate on profit while others concentrate on growth. In principle, the economic objectives of all the businesses in the corporate portfolio mesh into the broad economic objectives for the entire company.

In general, the strategy of a multi-business firm does not specify goals or efforts. (These are part of the business strategies of the divisions.) But there are exceptions to this broad statement. Diversified companies do set corporation-wide financial policies for capital structure, dividend payout, and external financing. Many have corporate policies for personnel and legal affairs. And corporate strategies sometimes specify basic themes, such as cost leadership or innovation, that are expected to run through the functional goals and efforts of all the company's separate businesses. Finally, corporate strategy sometimes defines the basic mission and values of the entire company.

MANAGING GENERAL MANAGERS

In small, single-business companies, the general manager usually has direct responsibility for functional managers. This is also true for the general managers of divisions in diversified firms. What distinguishes senior general managers in diversified firms is that they are responsible for managing other general managers rather than functional reports.

For example, CEOs of some diversified firms have group general managers reporting to them. The group general managers, in turn, are responsible for the general managers running the divisions.

Because they are managing one or more layers of general managers, the work of senior executives in diversified firms becomes especially challenging. The senior executives often know less about the businesses, strategies, and industries than the division heads. Unless they worked earlier in their careers for a particular division, they do not have the direct, tangible, hands-on knowledge of the operations of their divisions.

Nevertheless, the senior executives of diversified firms have ultimate responsibility for the performance of these divisions, and they must manage the efforts and careers of the division managers. These tasks are complicated by the fact that senior executives can spend only limited time with each division manager. It often takes years to fully evaluate the effectiveness of a division strategy. But senior executives must make interim judgments on the performance of a division's general manager, despite the handicaps of limited time and familiarity with the business. Making such judgments is further complicated when the divisions and their managers are far from the headquarters and when division managers have substantial autonomy.

ALLOCATING RESOURCES

One of the most demanding tasks of corporate general managers, in both intellectual and practical terms, is allocating funds among divisions.

The corporate manager has the conceptual problem of reconciling four powerful, often conflicting views of how to allocate funds, each with its own internally consistent logic. The first, *corporate financial logic*, is concerned with the aggregate funding available to the entire corporation for the present and the future. Corporate financial logic generally places an overall limit and other restrictions on a firm's spending, regardless of how great the firm's investment opportunities are. Restrictions include targets for capital structure, dividend payout, and equity financing. Corporate financial logic often leads to capital rationing among divisions in order to meet the broad financial targets and ratios.

Corporate strategic planning logic is aimed at allocating funds so that the investments and efforts of the divisions together create a focused, cohesive, balanced corporate strategy. During the 1970s, portfolio planning models that classified a firm's businesses in terms of their competitive positions and the attractiveness of their product markets became widely used tools for corporate strategic planning. Applying the models usually involves designating strategic business units (SBUs) and allocating capital to the SBUs in ways that balance cash flows, product life cycles, risk levels, and other factors across the portfolio. There is no guarantee, however, that the needs of the growing businesses in the portfolio can be met by funds generated by other businesses. Consequently, portfolio logic can collide with the aggregate funding limits set by corporate financial logic.

Business unit logic originates with division managers. They have direct contact with customers and competitors. They naturally focus on what their business needs to be successful. Divisions GMs pay less attention to the corporate concerns of rates of return, company-wide cash flow patterns, and earnings per share. They push corporate executives to provide the resources their businesses need. These insistent requests often conflict with corporate financial logic or corporate strategic planning logic.

The *logic of capital budgeting* is the fourth way of thinking about resource allocation. In its pure form, the theory of capital budgeting suggests that a company allocate resources by ranking all of its potential investments according to their risk-adjusted rates of return and investing in all the projects whose returns exceed the company cost of capital. In essence, a project or a business either increases shareholder wealth or does not. It should be funded only if it does.

Capital budgeting logic can conflict with the other ways of thinking. Some projects with returns below the cost of capital may support the strategic mission of a business. Projects in businesses with poor competitive prospects must sometimes be abandoned even if they offer returns above the costs of capital.

These four logical views of resource allocation do not always conflict. But they may become difficult managerial challenges because, in practice, different individuals and units approach resource allocation decisions from different perspectives. Recommendations often collide, sometimes sharply. In the end, senior general managers must resolve these conflicts when they allocate funds.

RELIANCE ON PROCESS AND SUBSTANCE

In practice, senior executives in diversified corporations must decide how much to rely on process and substance. For example, strategy and resource allocation inevitably depend on information and judgments that are gathered, aggregated, and analyzed by many people throughout the corporation. Different structural components (organization, controls, standards, rewards, policies, and processes) guide these individuals. These structural components determine what sort of information general managers receive and how information flows among managers and among levels of the organization. Managers' behavior is influenced by them. And they describe the roles that various individuals and organizational units (strategic planners, line managers, controllers, finance committees, and so forth) play in allocating resources.

Ultimately, components of structure define the form and substance of the strategic plans and capital spending proposals that emerge from an organization. Consequently, a fundamental issue is balancing the degree to which a manager relies on structural components to shape the process by which others in the company formulate and approve proposals to commit resources and the degree to which a manager becomes directly and personally involved in making the decisions. Managing the process of resource allocation is quite a different activity from actually making the strategic allocation decisions.

In diversified companies, the procedures for planning and allocating capital are generally explicit, detailed, and elaborate. This creates two problems. First, the standard operating procedures take on a life of their own. They grow ever more complex as they are adapted to unforeseen situations, and as more data are gathered to improve the accuracy and fairness of decisions. The elaboration of systems can become an intriguing intellectual challenge for those who design the system. In addition, the staff members who oversee the systems often press to expand them and demand more information in order to do their jobs more effectively and, at times, to expand their personal influence. Systems grow more detailed and elaborate; the number of checks and balances grows;

and the danger of process dominating substance arises. But corporate general managers cannot get directly involved in all the detailed thinking and judgments that produce requests for capital and strategic plans from divisions. Hence, the essence of this dilemma is to balance the need for structural components that direct, monitor, and control the decision making within divisions, with the need for direct, personal involvement by senior executives.

MANAGING THE CONTEXT

In its broadest terms, much of the work of senior executives in diversified firms can be described as managing the context in which division managers and staff personnel interact with each other and make their decisions. Managing context means fine-tuning a company's organization, work environment, and standards in ways that help advance the overall corporate strategy.

Managing context also means reinforcing values that enhance strategic decision making and resource allocation. Among these are open communication and candor, a sense that capital requests and strategic plans must be thought through carefully, an atmosphere that permits or encourages the questioning of conventional wisdom, a tolerance of trial and error, and a widespread belief that career opportunities will be distributed fairly among the managers of growing as well as mature businesses. Without such values, information reaching headquarters will be distorted, elaborate bureaucracies will be needed to suppress politicking for resources, risky but attractive opportunities will languish because managers will be reluctant to champion them, and ultimately, company performance will suffer.

DISCUSSION QUESTIONS

1. What are the means by which general managers can "manage the context" of decisions and interactions in a firm?
2. The author describes four methods that corporate GMs use to allocate resources. In general, which do you think is the most effective method, and why?
3. Should senior GMs in diversified firms ensure that strategy and resource allocation are subject to strictly defined processes and systems? Given the complexity of diversified companies, does this promote the most fair and logical outcomes?

21 Can the Best Corporations Be Made Moral?

KENNETH R. ANDREWS

According to Kenneth Andrews, corporations can, indeed, must be answerable to society's needs. Corporations are powerful institutions, and that power carries implicit social responsibility. Andrews argues that social responsibility ought to be embedded in corporate strategy. A company's obligations should be related to its business or the community in which it is based. But many companies thwart efforts toward public responsibility by imposing narrow measurement and reward-and-penalty systems. Employees striving for strictly quantifiable goals are not motivated to attend to social responsibilities of the company. General managers, therefore, must take action to correct the bias toward short-term results and must clearly communicate a corporate strategic response to societal need. This reading suggests the outlines of a management program of action.

The concept of corporate social responsibility has made steady progress during the past 40 years. The words mean in part voluntary restraint of profit maximization. More positively, they mean sensitivity to the social costs of economic activity and to the opportunity to focus corporate power on objectives that are possible but sometimes less economically attractive than socially desirable. The term includes:

- The determination of a corporation to reduce its profit by voluntary contributions to education and other charities;
- The election of an ethical level of operations higher than the minimum required by law and custom;
- The choice between businesses of varying economic opportunity on grounds of their imputed social worth;
- The investment for reasons other than (but obviously still related to) economic return in the quality of life within the corporation itself.

This doctrine of corporate social responsibility is vigorously opposed, honestly and openly by conservative lawyers and economists, and covertly by the adherents of business as usual. Milton Friedman, the conservative economist, denounces the concern for responsibility as "fundamentally subversive" to a free society. He argues that "there is one and only one social responsibility of business—to use its resources and engage in activities designed to increase its profits so long as it . . . engages in open and free competition without deception or fraud."[1]

Thus, for example, the manager who makes decisions affecting immediate profit by reducing pollution and increasing minority employment more than present law requires is in effect imposing taxes upon his stockholders and acting without authority as a public legislative body.

Other critics of the doctrine like to point out:

- The difficulty of combining profitable and socially responsive corporate action;
- Businesspeoples' lack of experience with social questions;
- The urgency of survival in hard times and against competition;
- Social issues dictated by management are coercive of individual opinion;
- Scarcely anyone has the intelligence, compassion, knowledge of issues, and morality required of the manager presumptuous enough to factor social responsibility into economic decisions.

Given the slow rate at which verbalized good intentions are being converted into action, many critics of the large corporation suspect that for every chief executive announcing pious objectives there are a hundred closet rascals quietly conducting business in the old ways and taking immoral comfort in Friedman's moral support.

The interventionists question the effectiveness of the "invisible hand" of competition as the ethical regulator of great corporations capable of shaping in significant degree their environments. Interventionists think also that regulation by government, while always to some degree essential under imperfect competition, is not sufficiently knowledgeable, subtle, or timely to reconcile the self-interest of corporate entrepreneurship and the needs of the society being sore-tried and well served by economic activity.

The advocates of public responsibility for a so-called private enterprise assert that, in an industrial society, corporate power, vast in potential strength, must be brought to bear on certain social problems if the latter are to be solved at all. They argue that corporate executives of the integrity, intelligence, and humanity required to run companies whose revenues often exceed the gross national product of whole nations cannot be expected to confine themselves to economic activity and ignore its consequences, and that henceforth, able young men and women coming into business will be sensitive to the social worth of corporate activity.

To reassure those uneasy about the dangers of corporate participation in public affairs, the social interventionists say to the economic isolationists that these hazards can be contained through professional education, government control, and self-regulation.

1. Milton Friedman, *Capitalism and Freedom* (Chicago: University of Chicago Press, 1962): 133.

This is not the place to argue further against Friedman's simplistic faith in the powers of the market to purify self-interest. We must observe, however, that the argument for the active participation of corporations in public affairs, for responsible assessment of the impact of economic activity, and for concern with the quality of corporate purposes is gaining ground, even as uneasiness increases about the existence of corporate power in the hands of managers who (except in cases of crisis) are answerable only to themselves or to boards of directors they have themselves selected.

Criticism of corporate activity is manifest currently in consumerism, in the movement to introduce social legislation into stockholder meetings and to reform board memberships, and (more dangerously) in apathy or antipathy among the young. The most practicable response to this criticism by those holding corporate power is to seek to justify limited government by using power responsibly—the ultimate obligation of free persons in any relatively free society.

We need the large corporation, not for its size but for its capacity. On the assumption, then, that corporate social responsibility is not only here to stay, but must increase in scope and complexity as corporate power increases, I suggest that we look forward to the administrative and organizational consequences of the incursion of private corporations into public responsibility.

THE NATURE OF THE PROBLEM

Among the many considerations confronting the executive who would make social responsibility effective, there are some so well known that we can quickly pass them by. Hypocrisy, insincerity, and hollow piety are not really dangerous, for they are easily detected.

In fact, it is much more likely that genuinely good intentions will be thought insincere than that hypocritical protestations of idealism will be mistaken for truth. "Mr. Ford (or Mr. Kaiser or Mr. Rockefeller) doesn't really mean what he says," as an organization refrain is more Mr. Ford's or Mr. Kaiser's or Mr. Rockefeller's problem than what he should say. Cynicism, the by-product of impersonal bureaucracy, remains one of the principal impediments to the communication of corporate social policy.

I would like to set aside also the problem of choice of what social contribution should be attempted—a problem which disparity between the infinite range of social need and the limits of available corporate resources always brings to mind.

SELF-CONSISTENT STRATEGY

The formulation of specific corporate social policy is as much a function of strategic planning as the choice of product and market combinations, the establishment of profit and growth objectives, or the choice of organization structure and systems for accomplishing corporate purposes.

Rather than supporting wholly personal or idiosyncratic contributions (like the museum one's spouse is devoted to) or safe and sound contributions like the standard charities, or faddist entry into fashionable areas, it makes sense to be socially responsive to the economic functions of the company or to the peculiar problems of the community in which it operates.

For a paper company, it would seem a strategic necessity to give first priority to eliminating the poisonous effluents from its mills rather than, for example, to support cultural institutions like traveling art exhibits. Similarly, for an oil company it would seem a strategic necessity to look at its refinery stacks, at spillage, and at automobile exhaust.

The fortunate company that is paying the full social cost of its production function can make contributions to problems it does not cause—like juvenile delinquency, illiteracy, and so on—or to other forms of environmental improvement more appropriate to corporate citizenship than directly related to its production processes.

As leaders of business move beyond conventional philanthropic contributions to strategy-related investments in social betterment, they begin to combine the long-run economic interests of their companies with the public's priorities—(as for pollution)—seeking those points where indeed what is good for the country is good for General Motors.

Once the conscious planning that a fully developed corporate strategy requires is understood, a company's practical alternatives are not impossibly difficult to identify and to rank according to relevance to economic strategy or to organization needs and resources.

The outcome is an integrated self-consistent strategy embodying defined obligations to society relevant to, but not confined to, its economic purposes. The top management of a large company, once it elects to, can be expected to have less difficulty in articulating such a strategy than in dealing with the problems of organization behavior to which I now turn.

ORGANIZATION BEHAVIOR

The advance of the doctrine of corporate social responsibility has been the apparent conversion of more and more chief executive officers. Change toward responsible behavior and the formulation of strategic intentions are obviously not possible without their concern, compassion, and conviction.

So long as the organization remains small enough to be directly influenced by the chief executive, certain results can be traced to his or her leadership—as in centrally decided investments, specific new ventures, cash contributions to charity, and compensation, promotion, and other personnel policies.

But as an organization grows larger and as operations become more decentralized, the power and influence of the chief executive are reinterpreted and diffused. For example:

If a large company is to be sufficiently decentralized to make worldwide operations feasible, power must be distributed throughout a hierarchy inhabited by persons (a) who may not share their chief executive's determination or fervor, (b) who may not believe (more often) the chief executive's words, and (c) who may be impelled to postpone action on problems such as management development, pollution, or employment and advancement of minorities.

At this point, the overriding problem now impeding the further progress of corporate responsibility is the difficulty of making credible and effective, throughout a large organization, the social component of a corporate strategy originating in the values of the chief executive.

Quantifiable Performance The source of the difficulty is the nature and impact of our systematic planning processes, forms of control, systems of measurement, and pattern of incentives, and the impersonal way all these are administered. The planning we know most about is quantitative information furnished to the process, and quantitative measures of results coming out.

Once plans are put into effect, managers are measured, evaluated, promoted, shelved, or discharged according to the relation of their accomplishments against the plan. In the conventions of accounting and the time scale of exact quantification, performance becomes short-run economic or technical results inside the corporation. Evaluation typically gives full marks for current accomplishment, with no estimate of the charges against the future which may have been made in the effort to accomplish the plan.

Since progress in career, dependent on favorable judgments of quantifiable performance, is the central motivation in a large organization, general and functional managers at divisional, regional, district, and local levels are motivated to do well what is best and most measured, to do it now, and to focus their attention on the internal problems that affect immediate results.

In short, the more quantification and the more supervision of variance, the less attention there will be to such intangible topics as the social role of Plant X in Community Y or the quality of corporate life in the office at Sioux City.

The leaner the central staff of a large organization is kept, the more stress there will be on numbers; and, more importantly, the more difficulty there will be in making qualitative evaluation of such long-term processes as individual and management development, the steady augmentation of organizational competence, and the progress of programs for making work meaningful and exciting, and for making more than economic contributions to society.

The small headquarters group supervising the operations of a conglomerate of autonomous organizations hitherto measured by ranking them with respect to return on equity would not expect to have before it proposals from the subsidiaries for important investments in social responsibility. Such investments could only be made by the corporate headquarters, which would not itself be knowledgeable about or much motivated to take action on opportunities existing throughout the subsidiaries.

Corporate Amorality One colleague of mine, Joseph L. Bower, examined the process by which corporate resources are allocated in large organizations.[2] Another, Robert W. Ackerman, has documented through field studies the dilemmas which a financially oriented and present-tense accounting system pose for the forward progress of specific social action, like pollution abatement and provision of minority opportunity.[3] Still a third, Malcolm S. Salter, has studied the impact of compensation systems in multinational corporations.[4]

It appears that the outcome of these and other research studies will establish what we have long suspected—that good works, the results of which are long term and hard to quantify, do not have a chance in an organization using conventional incentives and controls and exerting pressure for ever more impressive results.

It is quite possible then, and indeed quite usual, for a highly moral and humane chief executive to preside over an "amoral organization"—one made so by processes developed before the liberalization of traditional corporate economic objectives. The internal force which stubbornly resists efforts to make the corporation compassionate (and exacting) toward its own people and responsible (as well as economically efficient) in its external relationships is the incentive system forcing attention to short-term quantifiable results.

The sensitivity of upward-oriented career executives at lower and middle levels to what quantitative measures say about them is part of their ambition, their interest in their compensation, and their desire for the recognition and approval of their superiors. When, as they usually do, they learn how to beat the system, the margin of capacity they reserve for a rainy day is hoarded for survival, not expended in strengthening their suborganization's future capability or in part-time participation in corporate good works or responsible citizenship on their own time.

With individuals, as with organizations, survival takes precedence over social concern. All we need do to keep even experienced, capable, and profit-producing managers on the ropes of survival is to focus the spotlight on their day-to-day activities and exhaust their ingenuity in outwitting the system by increasing the level of short-term results they are asked to attain.

The isolationists should be quite content with the amorality of an organization motivated by career-oriented responsiveness to narrowly designed measurement and reward-and-penalty systems. The interventionists are not. They look for solutions in the experience, observation, and research I have been drawing on in describing the set of problems a new breadth of vision reveals to us.

---

2. Joseph L. Bower, *Managing the Resource Allocation Process* (Boston, Division of Research, Harvard Business School, 1969).

3. Robert W. Ackerman, "Managing Corporate Responsibility," *Harvard Business Review* (July–August 1973).

4. Malcom S. Salter, "Tailor Incentive Compensation to Strategy," *Harvard Business Review* (March–April 1973): 94.

Thus the art of using the two-edged sword of contribution to society and of stimulation to creative achievement within the corporation becomes even more sophisticated when that institution must not only relate to the societies of different countries and cultures but also attract and keep the dedication of men and women with values and desires not typically American.

PROGRAM OF ACTION

Inquiry into the nature of the problem suggests the outlines of a program of action. It begins with the incorporation into strategic and operating plans—of subsidiaries, country or area organizations, or profit centers—of specific objectives in areas of social concerns strategically related to the economic activity and community environment of the organization unit.

Since the executive in New York cannot specify the appropriate social strategy for the company in Brazil or the branch in Oregon, or even know what the people there want to work on, intermediate managers who are aware of the social and organization policy of the company must elicit (with staff help, if necessary) proposals for investment of money, energy, time, or concern in these areas.

The review of plans submitted may result in reduction or increase in commitments in all areas; it is essential that the negotiation include attention to social and organization objectives, with as much quantification as reasonable but with qualitative objectives where appropriate.

The development of such strategic and operating plans turns critically on the initiative of responsible corporate individuals, who must be competent enough to accomplish demanding economic and social tasks and have time as well for their families and private affairs.

Financial, production, and sales requirements may be transmitted down rather than drawn upward in an efficient (though often sterilizing) compaction of the planning process. The top-down promulgation of an imaginative and community-centered social and organization strategy, except in terms so general as to be ineffective, is not only similarly unwise in stifling creativity and commitment but also virtually impossible.

QUALITATIVE ATTENTION

Once targets and plans have been defined (in the negotiation between organization levels), the measurement system must incorporate in appropriate proportion quantitative and qualitative measures. The bias to short-term results can be corrected by qualitative attention to social and organization programs. The transfer and promotion of managers successful in achieving short-term results is a gamble until their competence in balancing short- and long-term objectives is demonstrated.

Incidentally, rapid rotation virtually guarantees a low level of interest in the particular city through which the manager is following his or her career; one day it will be seen to be as wasteful as an organization-building and management-development device as it is useful in staffing a growing organization. The alternative—to remain in a given place, to develop fully the company's business in a given city assisted by knowledge and love of the region—needs to become open to executives who do not wish to become president of their companies.

When young middle managers fall short of their targets, inquiry into the reasons and ways to help them achieve assigned goals should precede adverse judgment and penalty. Whenever measurement and control can be directed toward ways to correct problems observed, the shriveling effects of over-emphatic evaluation are postponed. In addition, managers learn that something is important to their superiors other than a single numerical indicator of little significance when detached from the future results to which it relates.

Internal Audit The curse of unquantifiability which hangs over executive action in the areas of corporate responsibility may someday be lifted by the "social audit."[5] In its simplest form, this is a kind of balance sheet and operating statement. On it are listed the dollar values of such corporate investments as training programs, individual development activities, time devoted by individuals to community projects, contributions to pollution abatement, transportation, taxes, and the like. All of these investments call the attention of a company and community to the cumulative dollar worth of corporate functions ancillary to production and sales.

But the further evolvement of the social audit, which one day may develop the conventions that make comparison possible, is not essential to immediate qualitative attention to progress made by managers at all organizational levels toward noneconomic goals. Consider, for example:

- Internal audit groups, necessarily oriented to examining what the public accounting firm must ultimately certify, can be supplemented by permanent or temporary public relations or general management persons who are qualified to examine, comment on, and counsel with managers on their success and difficulties in the areas of social contribution and organization morale.
- It is possible to judge, although not in hard numbers, the role in the community of a local branch office, the morale of the work force, clerical and functional staffs, and the expertise and enthusiasm of the sales staff.
- The public relations and personnel staffs of organizations are all too often assigned to superficial and trivial tasks. The employment of such persons in the internal audit function, especially if they have—

5. Raymond A. Bauer and Dan H. Fenn, Jr., "What Is a Corporate Social Audit?" *Harvard Business Review* (January–February 1973): 37.

without necessarily the qualifications or temperament of high-spirited doers—the experience, perspective, and judgment of long service in the organization, would raise the usefulness, and hence, importance of these functions.

Maturity of Judgment Every large corporation develops (unintentionally) a group of highly experienced but, after a time, uncompulsive managers who are better assigned to jobs requiring maturity of judgment rather than sprinting ability. The internal qualitative audit, combined with a parallel inquiry by a committee of outside directors, to which I shall allude in a moment, could be an internal counseling, review, and support function epitomizing effective staff support of line operations. It could also provide opportunity for the cadre of older managers no longer motivated by primitive incentives.

People with executive responsibility, including accountants and controllers, often exercise judgment only distantly affected by numbers; this is not a new requirement or experience. To the extent that managers in the hierarchy are capable of interpreting numbers intelligently, they must be capable of relating results produced to those in gestation. Furthermore, they must be able to judge the significance of a profit figure (not to be found in the figure itself) at a given point of time.

Incentive Modification If measurement of performance is to be broad and knowledgeable enough to encompass progress under a strategy containing social and organizational objectives, then the incentive system in a company or organization unit must reward and penalize accomplishments other than those related to economic efficiency.

Moreover, it must become well known in such an organization that persons can be demoted or discharged for failure to behave responsibly toward their subordinates, for example, even if they are successful in economic terms. Career-oriented middle managers must learn, from the response that their organization leadership and community activities receive, how to appreciate the intrinsic worth and how to estimate the value to their own future of demonstrated responsibility.

MANAGEMENT DEVELOPMENT

Besides liberating the evaluation process by adding qualitative judgment to numbers, the activity which needs expansion in making an organization socially effective and internally healthy is management development—not so much in terms of formal training programs (although I should be the last person to demean the importance of these)—as in planned careers.

If organizations elect, as interesting organizations will, high standards of profit and social contribution to be achieved simultaneously, then much is required of the character, general education, and professional competence of managers. They must show themselves—whatever their schooling—as liberally educated.

It follows from the argument I am making that, in moderating the amorality of organizations, we must expect executive mid-career education to include exposure to the issues of responsibility raised here and to the invaluable experience of participating in nonprofit community or government organizations. Under short-term pressures, attention to development is easily postponed, either as a cost that should be avoided for now or as a process requiring more attention to persons than is convenient or possible.

The management action so far suggested does not constitute innovation so much as reemphasis: it requires not heroic action but maturity and breadth of perspective. Once the aspiration to reach beyond economic to social and human objectives is seen to require extending conventional incentive and performance measurement systems, it is not difficult to avoid imbalance and the unintended organizational consequences of which I have spoken. Awareness of the problem generates its solution.

AUDIT BY DIRECTORS

But the current move toward revitalization of the board of directors does provide a formal resource to the secure and interested chief executive. Committees of outside directors are now being formed in a number of companies to meet regularly with the internal audit and outside audit staffs to look closely at the thoroughness and adequacy of the procedures used to ensure that the true condition of the company is reflected in its published accounting statements.

If internal audit teams were to extend their counsel, nonpunitive inspection, and recommendations for improvement to social performance and to the quality of organization life as felt by its members, the information they would gather and the problems they would encounter could be summarized for the board committee in the same way as the more conventional subjects of their scrutiny.

In any case, the pervasiveness of the chief executive's posture on social responsibility can be inquired into, and the quality of the management across the organization can be reported on. The board of directors, supposed to provide judgment and experience not available inside the organization, can be—in its proper role of constructive inquiry into the quality of the corporation's management and its support for investment in improving it—a potent force in moderating the management's understandable internal interest in day-to-day achievement.

CONCLUSION

Nothing will happen, either inward or outward, to further advance the doctrine of social responsibility unless those in charge of the corporation want it to happen and unless their associates share their values and put their backs into solving the problem. There must be desire and determination first. It must be embodied in a strategy that makes a consistent whole of private economic opportunity and public social responsibility, planned to be implemented in an organization which will be humanely and challengingly led and developed.

A few good individuals cannot change the course of a large corporation by their personal influence, but they can arrange that the systems of implementation are appropriate in scope to the breadth of corporate economic and social purpose. Now that enlightened chief executives have made this commitment, it would be tragic to have their will subverted, their determination doubted, and their energy dissipated by bureaucratic organization.

The giant corporation, which in small numbers does half the work of our economic system, is here to stay. It is the dominant force of our industrial society. In its multinational forms it has no higher sovereignty to which it reports; in its national forms it is granted wide latitude. Thus it is important to all of us that its affairs be responsibly conducted and that limited knowledge of the art of managing a large organization not be permitted to thwart us.

If organizations cannot be made moral, the future of capitalism will be unattractive—to all of us and especially to those young people whose talents we need. It is not the attack of the muckrakers we should fear but the apathy of our corporate citizenry.

DISCUSSION QUESTIONS

1. Does the author fully support his assertion of the moral responsibility of corporations to participate in public matters?
2. Are quantitative goals the most objective measure of performance? Why or why not?
3. The author urges companies to adopt "a strategy that makes a consistent whole of private economic opportunity and public social responsibility." When setting strategy, should general managers give equal consideration to financial goals and public responsibilities? What if a firm's economic and social goals conflict?
4. Should all employees help define the social responsibilities of a firm? Or is that the prerogative of top management?

The Social Responsibility of Business Is to Increase Its Profits

22

MILTON FRIEDMAN

In this reading, Milton Friedman argues for a strict definition of "the social responsibility of business." According to Friedman, only individuals have social responsibilities, which they may fulfill on their own time and with their own resources. Senior managers must be responsible primarily to their employers—those who own the business. Acting in the firm's best interest as an agent of the company's owners, the general manager must maximize profits, and do so legally and ethically. Spending corporate profits on social objectives is wrong, because this imposes taxes on money that belongs to the company, its employees, and its stockholders. General managers must be clear, in Friedman's view, that their principal objective is to maximize corporate profits; they are not responsible, nor should they be, for spending profits on societal needs.

When I hear businesspeople speak eloquently about the "social responsibilities of business in a free-enterprise system," I am reminded of the wonderful line about the Frenchman who discovered at the age of 70 that he had been speaking prose all his life. The businesspeople believe that they are defending free enterprise when they declaim that business is not concerned "merely" with profit but also with promoting desirable "social" ends; that business has a "social conscience" and takes seriously its responsibilities for providing employment, eliminating discrimination, avoiding pollution, and whatever else may be the catchwords of the contemporary crop of reformers. In fact they are—or would be if they or anyone else took them seriously—preaching pure and unadulterated socialism. Businesspeople who talk this way are unwitting puppets of the intellectual forces that have been undermining the basis of a free society these past decades.

The discussions of the "social responsibilities of business" are notable for their analytical looseness and lack of rigor. What does it mean to say that "business" has responsibilities? Only people can have responsibilities. A corporation is an artificial person and in this sense may have artificial responsibilities, but "business" as a whole cannot be said to have responsibilities, even in this vague sense. The first step toward clarity in examining the doctrine of the social responsibility of business is to ask precisely what it implies for whom.

Presumably, the individuals who are to be responsible are businesspeople, which means individual proprietors or corporate executives. Most of the discussion of social responsibility is directed at corporations, so in what follows I shall mostly neglect the individual proprietor and speak of corporate executives.

In a free-enterprise, private-property system, corporate executives are employees of the owners of the business. They have direct responsibility to their employers. That responsibility is to conduct the business in accordance with the owners' desires, which generally will be to make as much money as possible while conforming to the basic rules of the society, both those embodied in law and those embodied in ethical custom. Of course, in some cases the employers may have a different objective. A group of persons might establish a corporation for an eleemosynary purpose—for example, a hospital or a school. The manager of such a corporation will not have money profit as an objective, but the rendering of certain services.

In either case, the key point is that, in his or her capacity as a corporate executive, the manager is the agent of the individuals who own the corporation or establish the eleemosynary institution, and owes primary responsibility to them.

Needless to say, this does not mean that it is easy to judge how well a manager is performing the task. But at least the criterion of performance is straightforward, and the persons among whom a voluntary contractual arrangement exists are clearly defined.

Of course, the corporate executive is also a person. As a person, he or she may have many other responsibilities recognized or assumed voluntarily—to a family, to conscience, feelings of charity, church, clubs, city, country. Managers may feel impelled by these responsibilities to devote part of their income to causes they regard as worthy, to refuse to work for particular corporations, and even to leave their jobs, for example, to join their country's armed forces. If we wish, we may refer to some of these responsibilities as "social responsibilities." But in these respects the manager is acting as a principal, not an agent; he or she is spending personal money or time or energy, not the employers' money or the time or energy contracted to the employers' purposes. If these are "social responsibilities," they are the social responsibilities of individuals, not of business.

What does it mean to say that corporate executives have a "social responsibility" in their capacity as businesspeople? If this statement is not pure rhetoric, it must mean that they are to act in some way that is not in the interest of their employers. For example, that they are to refrain from increasing the price of the product in order to contribute to the social objective of preventing inflation, even though a price increase would be in the best interest of the corporation. Or that they are to make expenditures on reducing pollution beyond the amount that is in the best interests of the corporation or that is required by law in order to contribute to the social objective of improving the environment. Or that, at the expense of corporate profits, they are to hire hard-core unemployed instead of better-qualified available workers to contribute to the social objective of reducing poverty.

In each of these cases, the corporate executive would be spending someone else's money for a general social interest. Insofar as their actions, in accord with their "social responsibility," reduce returns to stockholders, they are spending stockholders' money. Insofar as their actions raise the price to customers, they are spending the customers' money. Insofar as their actions lower the wages of some employees, they are spending employees' money.

The stockholders or the customers or the employees could separately spend their own money on the particular action if they wished to do so. The executive is exercising a distinct "social responsibility," rather than serving as an agent of the stockholders or the customers or the employees, only if he or she spends the money in a different way than they would have spent it.

But a manager who does this is, in effect, imposing taxes, on the one hand, and deciding how the tax proceeds shall be spent, on the other.

This process raises political questions on two levels: principle and consequences. On the level of political principle, the imposition of taxes and the expenditure of tax proceeds are governmental functions. We have established elaborate constitutional, parliamentary, and judicial provisions to control these functions, to assure that taxes are imposed so far as possible in accordance with the preferences and desires of the public—after all, "taxation without representation" was one of the battle cries of the American Revolution. We have a system of checks and balances to separate the legislative function of imposing taxes and enacting expenditures from the executive function of collecting taxes and administering expenditure programs and from the judicial function of mediating disputes and interpreting the law.

Here the businessperson—self-selected or appointed directly or indirectly by stockholders—is to be simultaneously legislator, executive, and jurist. He or she is to decide whom to tax by how much and for what purpose, and to spend the proceeds—all this guided only by general exhortations from on high to restrain inflation, improve the environment, fight poverty, and so on and on.

The whole justification for permitting corporate executives to be selected by the stockholders is that the executive is an agent serving the interest of his or her principals. This justification disappears when corporate executives impose taxes and spend the proceeds for "social" purposes. They become in effect public employees, civil servants, even though they remain in name employees of a private enterprise. On grounds of political principle, it is intolerable that such civil servants—insofar as their actions in the name of social responsibility are real and not just window dressing—should be selected as they are now. If they are to be civil servants, then they must be selected through a political process. If they are to impose taxes and make expenditures to foster "social" objectives, then political machinery must be set up to guide the assessment of taxes and to determine through a political process the objectives to be served.

This is the basic reason why the doctrine of social responsibility involves the acceptance of the socialist view that political mechanisms, not market mechanisms, are the appropriate way to determine the allocation of scarce resources to alternative uses.

On the grounds of consequences, can corporate executives in fact discharge their alleged social responsibilities? On the one hand, suppose they could get away with spending the stockholders' or customers' or employees' money. How are they to know how to spend it? They are told that they must contribute to fighting inflation. How are they to know what action of theirs will contribute to that end? They are presumably experts in running the company—in producing a product or selling it or financing it. But nothing about their selection makes them experts on inflation. Will their holding down the price of products reduce inflationary pressure? Or, by leaving more spending power in the hands of customers, simply divert it elsewhere? Or, by forcing the company to produce less because of the lower price, will it simply contribute to shortages? Even if corporate executives could answer these questions, how much cost is it justifiable to impose on stockholders, customers, and employees for this social purpose? What is an appropriate share for the executive and what is the appropriate share of others?

And, whether they want to or not, can they get away with spending stockholders', customers', or employees' money? Will not the stockholders fire them? (Either the present ones or those who take over when, in the name of social responsibility, the corporation's profits and the price of its stock have been reduced.) Customers and employees can choose other producers and employers less scrupulous in exercising their social responsibilities.

This facet of "social responsibility" doctrine is brought into sharp relief when the doctrine is used to justify wage restraint by trade unions. The conflict of interest is naked and clear when union officials are asked to subordinate the interest of their members to some more general social purpose. If the union officials try to enforce wage restraint, the consequence is likely to be wildcat strikes, rank-and-file revolts, and the emergence of strong competitors for their jobs. We thus have the ironic phenomenon that union leaders—at least in the U.S.—have objected to government interference with the market far more consistently and courageously than have business leaders.

The difficulty of exercising social responsibility illustrates, of course, the great virtue of private competitive enterprise—it forces people to be responsible for their own actions and makes it difficult for them to "exploit" other people for either selfish or unselfish purposes. They can do good—but only at their own expense.

Many a reader who has followed the argument this far may be tempted to remonstrate that it is all well and good to speak of government's having the responsibility to impose taxes and determine expenditures for such "social" purposes as controlling pollution or training the hard-core unemployed, but that the problems are too urgent to wait on the slow course of political processes, that the exercise of social responsibility by businesspeople is a quicker and surer way to solve pressing current problems.

Aside from the question of fact—I share Adam Smith's skepticism about the benefits that can be expected from "those who affected to trade for the public good"—this argument must be rejected on grounds of principle. What it amounts to is an assertion that those who favor the taxes and expenditures in question have failed to persuade a majority of their fellow citizens to be of like mind and that they are seeking to attain by undemocratic procedures what they cannot attain by democratic procedures. In a free society, it is hard for "good" people to do "good," but that is a small price to pay for making it hard for "evil" people to do "evil," especially since one man's good is another's evil.

I have, for simplicity, concentrated on the special case of the corporate executive, except only for the brief digression on trade unions. But precisely the same argument applies to the new phenomenon of calling upon stockholders to require corporations to exercise social responsibility. In most of these cases, what is in effect involved is some stockholders trying to get other stockholders (or customers or employees) to contribute against their will to "social" causes favored by the activists. Insofar as they succeed, they are again imposing taxes and spending the proceeds.

The situation of the individual proprietor is somewhat different. If an individual owner acts to reduce the returns of the enterprise in order to exercise "social responsibility," he is spending his own money, not someone else's. If he wishes to spend his money on such purposes, that is his right, and I cannot see that there is any objection to his doing so. In the process, an individual proprietor, too, may impose costs of employees and customers. However, because an individual is far less likely than a large corporation or union to have monopolistic power, any such side effects will tend to be minor.

Of course, in practice the doctrine of social responsibility is frequently a cloak for actions that are justified on other grounds rather than a reason for those actions.

To illustrate, it may well be in the long-run interest of a corporation that is a major employer in a small community to devote resources to providing amenities to that community or to improving its government. That may make it easier to attract desirable employees, it may reduce the wage bill or lessen losses from pilferage and sabotage, or have other worthwhile effects. Or it may be that, given the laws about the deductibility of corporate charitable contributions, the stockholders can contribute more to charities they favor by having the corporation make the gift than by doing it themselves, since they can in that way contribute an amount that would otherwise have been paid as corporate taxes.

In each of these—and many similar—cases, there is a strong temptation to rationalize these actions as an exercise of "social responsibility." This is one way for a corporation to generate goodwill as a by-product of expenditures that are entirely justified in its own self-interest.

It would be inconsistent of me to call on corporate executives to refrain from this hypocritical window dressing because it harms the foundations of a free society. That would be to call on them to exercise a "social responsibility"!

If our institutions and the attitudes of the public make it in their self-interest to cloak their actions in this way, I cannot summon much indignation to denounce them. At the same time, I can express admiration for those individual proprietors or owners of closely held corporations or stockholders of more broadly held corporations who disdain such tactics as approaching fraud.

Whether blameworthy or not, the use of the cloak of social responsibility, and the nonsense spoken in its name by influential and prestigious business leaders, does clearly harm the foundations of a free society. I have been impressed time and again by the schizophrenic character of many businesspeople. They are capable of being extremely farsighted and clearheaded in matters that are internal to their businesses. They are incredibly shortsighted and muddleheaded in matters that are outside their businesses but affect the possible survival of business in general. This shortsightedness is strikingly exemplified in the calls from many businesspeople for wage and price guidelines or controls or income policies. There is nothing that could do more in a brief period to destroy a market system and replace it by a centrally controlled system than effective governmental control of prices and wages.

The shortsightedness is also exemplified in speeches on social responsibility. This may gain them kudos in the short run. But it helps to strengthen the already too prevalent view that the pursuit of profits is wicked and immoral and must be curbed and controlled by external forces. Once this view is adopted, the external forces that curb the market will not be the social consciences, however highly developed, of the pontificating executives; it will be the iron fist of government bureaucrats. Here, as with price and wage controls, businesspeople seem to me to reveal a suicidal impulse.

The political principle that underlies the market mechanism is unanimity. In an ideal free market resting on private property, no individual can coerce any other, all cooperation is voluntary, all parties to such cooperation benefit or they need not participate. There are no "social" values, no "social" responsibilities in any sense other than the shared values and responsibilities of individuals. Society is a collection of individuals and of the various groups they voluntarily form.

The political principle that underlies the political mechanism is conformity. The individual must serve a more general social interest—whether that be determined by a church or a dictator or a majority. The individual may have a vote and a say in what is to be done, but if overruled, must conform. It is appropriate for some to require others to contribute to a general social purpose whether they wish to or not.

Unfortunately, unanimity is not always feasible. There are some respects in which conformity appears unavoidable, so I do not see how one can avoid the use of the political mechanism altogether.

But the doctrine of social responsibility taken seriously would extend the scope of the political mechanism to every human activity. It does not differ in philosophy from the most explicitly collectivist doctrine. It differs only by professing to believe that collectivist ends can be attained without collectivist means. That is why, in my book *Capitalism and Freedom,* I have called it a "fundamentally subversive doctrine" in a free society, and have said that in such a society, "there is one and only one social responsibility of business—to use its resources and engage in activities designed to increase its profits so long as it stays within the rules of the game, which is to say, engages in open and free competition without deception or fraud."

DISCUSSION QUESTIONS

1. Do you agree with Friedman's assertion that "'business' as a whole cannot be said to have responsibilities"? Is business amoral?
2. Friedman argues that executives are responsible only to the owners of a business, who he says will generally seek to "make as much money as possible while conforming to the basic rules of society." What if a business owner wanted his or her company to participate in public matters? Would Friedman find that acceptable?
3. What is the social responsibility of business?

PART FIVE

LEADERSHIP

The Effective Decision 23

PETER F. DRUCKER

Although decision making is a crucial component of a general manager's job, it is important to remember that general managers do not make very many decisions. Rather, they need to make a few important decisions effectively. Peter Drucker here outlines the sequence of steps that characterizes effective decision making. This sequence determines whether a problem is generic or unique, defines the issues of the problem, specifies what the decision must accomplish, decides what is right rather than what is acceptable, and builds action into the decision. Taken together, these steps frame the parameters of the decisions that senior managers must make—decisions that affect entire organizations.

Effective executives do not make a great many decisions. They try to make the few important decisions on the highest level of conceptual understanding. They try to find the constants in a situation, to think through what is strategic and generic rather than to "solve problems." They are, therefore, not overly impressed by speed in decision making; rather, they consider virtuosity in manipulating a great many variables a symptom of sloppy thinking. They want to know what the decision is all about and what the underlying realities are which it has to satisfy. They want impact rather than technique. And they want to be sound rather than clever.

Effective executives know when a decision has to be based on principle and when it should be made pragmatically, on the merits of the case. They know the trickiest decision is that between the right and the wrong compromise, and they have learned to tell one from the other. They know that the most time-consuming step in the process is not making the decision but putting it into effect. Unless a decision has degenerated into work, it is not a decision; it is at best a good intention. This means that, while the effective decision itself is based on the highest level of conceptual understanding, the action commitment should be as close as possible to the capacities of the people who have to carry it out. Above all, effective executives know that decision making has its own systematic process and its own clearly defined elements.

SEQUENTIAL STEPS

The elements do not by themselves "make" the decisions. Indeed, every decision is a risk-taking judgment. But unless these elements are the stepping stones of the decision process, the executive will not arrive at a right, and certainly not at an effective, decision. Therefore, I shall describe the sequence of steps involved in the decision-making process:

1. ***Classifying the problem.*** Is it generic? Is it exceptional and unique? Or is it the first manifestation of a new genus for which a rule has yet to be developed?
2. ***Defining the problem.*** What are we dealing with?
3. ***Specifying the answer to the problem.*** What are the "boundary conditions"?
4. ***Deciding what is "right," rather than what is acceptable, in order to meet the boundary conditions.*** What will fully satisfy the specifications before attention is given to the compromises, adaptations, and concessions needed to make the decision acceptable?
5. ***Building into the decision the action to carry it out.*** What does the action commitment have to be? Who has to know about it?
6. ***Testing the validity and effectiveness of the decision against the actual course of events.*** How is the decision being carried out? Are the assumptions on which it is based appropriate or obsolete?

Let us take a look at each of these individual elements.

THE CLASSIFICATION

The effective decision maker asks: Is this a symptom of a fundamental disorder or a stray event? The generic always has to be answered through a rule, a principle. But the truly exceptional event can only be handled as such and as it comes.

Strictly speaking, the executive might distinguish among four, rather than between two, different types of occurrences.

First, there is the truly generic event, of which the individual occurrence is only a symptom. Most of the "problems" that come up in the course of the executive's work are of this nature. Inventory decisions in a business, for instance, are not "decisions." They are adaptations. The problem is generic. This is even more likely to be true of occurrences within manufacturing organizations. For example, a product control and engineering group will typically handle many hundreds of problems in the course of a month. Yet, whenever these are analyzed, the great majority prove to be just symptoms—and manifestations—of underlying basic situations. The individual process control engineer or production engineer who works in one part of the plant might have a few problems each month with the couplings in the pipes that carry steam or hot liquids, but usually cannot see this.

Only when the total workload of the group over several months is analyzed does the generic problem appear. Then it is seen that temperatures or pressures have become too great for the existing equipment and that the couplings holding the various lines together need to be redesigned for greater loads. Until this analysis is done, process control will spend a tremendous amount of time fixing leaks without ever getting control of the situation.

The second type of occurrence is the problem which, while a unique event for the individual institution, is actually generic. Consider the company that receives an offer to merge from another, larger one; it will never receive such an offer again if it accepts. This is a nonrecurrent situation as far as the individual company, its board of directors, and its management are concerned. But it is, of course, a generic situation which occurs all the time. Thinking through whether to accept or to reject the offer requires some general rules. For these, however, the executive has to look to the experience of others.

Next there is the truly exceptional event that the executive must distinguish. To illustrate, the huge power failure that plunged into darkness the whole of Northeastern North America in November 1965 was, according to first explanations, a truly exceptional situation. So was the thalidomide tragedy which led to the birth of so many deformed babies in the early 1960s. The probability of either of these events occurring, we were told, was one in ten million or one in a hundred million, and concatenations of these events were as unlikely ever to recur again as it is unlikely, for instance, for the chair on which I sit to disintegrate into its constituent atoms.

Truly unique events are rare, however. Whenever one appears, the decision maker has to ask: Is this a true exception or only the first manifestation of a new genus? And this—the early manifestation of a new generic problem—is the fourth and last category of events with which the decision process deals. Thus, we know now that both the Northeastern power failure and the thalidomide tragedy were only the first occurrences of what, under conditions of modern power technology or of modern pharmacology, are likely to become fairly frequent occurrences unless generic solutions are found.

All events but the truly unique require a generic solution. They require a rule, a policy, or a principle. Once the right principle has been developed, all manifestations of the same generic situation can be handled pragmatically—that is, by adaptation of the rule to the concrete circumstances of the case. Truly unique events, however, must be treated individually. The executive cannot develop rules for the exceptional.

The effective decision maker spends time determining which of the four different situations is happening. The wrong decision will be made if the situation is classified incorrectly.

By far the most common mistake is to treat a generic situation as if it were a series of unique events—that is, to be pragmatic when lacking the generic understanding and principle.

Equally common is the mistake of treating a new event as if it were just another example of the old problem and to apply the old rules. This was the error that snowballed the local power failure on the New York–Ontario border into the great Northeastern blackout. The power engineers, especially in New York City, applied the right rule for a normal overload. Yet their own instruments had signaled that something quite extraordinary was going on which called for exceptional, rather than standard, countermeasures.

THE DEFINITION

Once a problem has been classified as generic or unique, it is usually fairly easy to define. "What is this all about?" "What is pertinent here?" "What is the key to this situation?" Questions such as these are familiar. But only the truly effective decision makers are aware that the danger in this step is not the wrong definition; it is the plausible but incomplete one.

There is only one safeguard against becoming the prisoner of an incomplete definition: check it again and again against *all* the observable facts, and throw out a definition the moment it fails to encompass any of them.

Effective decision makers always test for signs that something is atypical or something unusual is happening, always asking: Does the definition explain the observed events, and does it explain all of them? They always write out what the definition is expected to make happen—for instance, make automobile accidents disappear—and then test regularly to see if this really happens. Finally, they go back and think the problem through again whenever they see something atypical, when they find unexplained phenomena, or when the course of events deviates, even in details, from expectations.

These are in essence the rules Hippocrates laid down for medical diagnosis well over 2,000 years ago. They are the rules for scientific observation first formulated by Aristotle and then reaffirmed by Galileo 300 years ago. These, in other words, are old, well-known, time-tested rules, which an executive can learn and apply systematically.

THE SPECIFICATIONS

The next major element in the decision process is defining clear specifications as to what the decision has to accomplish. What are the objectives the decision has to reach? What are the minimum goals it has to attain? What are the conditions it has to satisfy? In science these are known as "boundary conditions." A decision, to be effective, needs to satisfy the boundary conditions. Consider:

Can our needs be satisfied, Alfred P. Sloan, Jr. presumably asked himself when he took command of General Motors in 1922, by removing the autonomy of our division heads? His answer was clearly in the negative. The boundary conditions of his problem demanded strength and responsibility in the chief operating positions. This was needed as much as unity and control at the center. Everyone before Sloan had seen the problem as one of personalities—to be solved through a struggle for power from which one man would emerge victorious. The boundary conditions, Sloan realized, demanded a solution to a constitutional problem—to be solved through a new structure: decentralization which balanced local autonomy of operations with central control of direction and policy.

A decision that does not satisfy the boundary conditions is worse than one which wrongly defines the problem. It is all but impossible to salvage the decision that starts with the right premises but stops short of the right conclusions. Furthermore, clear thinking about the boundary conditions is needed to know when a decision has to be abandoned. The most common cause of failure in a decision lies not in its being wrong initially. Rather, it is a subsequent shift in the goals—the specifications—which makes the prior right decision suddenly inappropriate. And unless the decision maker has kept the boundary conditions clear, so as to make possible the immediate replacement of the outflanked decision with a new and appropriate policy, he may not even notice that things have changed. For example, Franklin D. Roosevelt was bitterly attacked for his switch from conservative candidate in 1932 to radical president in 1933. But it wasn't Roosevelt who changed. The sudden economic collapse which occurred between the summer of 1932 and the spring of 1933 changed the specifications. A policy appropriate to the goal of national economic recovery—which a conservative economic policy might have been—was no longer appropriate when, with the bank holiday, the goal had to become political and social cohesion. When the boundary conditions changed, Roosevelt immediately substituted a political objective (reform) for his former economic one (recovery).

Above all, clear thinking about the boundary conditions is needed to identify the most dangerous of all possible decisions: the one in which the specifications that have to be satisfied are essentially incompatible. In other words, this is the decision that might—just might—work if nothing whatever goes wrong.

A classic case is President Kennedy's Bay of Pigs decision, in which one specification was clearly Castro's overthrow. The other was to make it appear that the invasion was a spontaneous uprising of the Cubans. But these two specifications would have been compatible with each other only if an immediate island-wide uprising against Castro would have completely paralyzed the Cuban army. And while this was not impossible, it clearly was not probable in such a tightly controlled police state.

Decisions of this sort are usually called gambles. But actually they arise from something much less rational than a gamble—namely, a hope against hope that two (or more) clearly incompatible specifications can be fulfilled simultaneously. This is hoping for a miracle; and the trouble with miracles is not that they happen so rarely, but that they are, alas, singularly unreliable.

Everyone can make the wrong decision. In fact, everyone will sometimes make a wrong decision. But no executive needs to make a decision which, on the face of it, seems to make sense but, in reality, falls short of satisfying the boundary conditions.

THE DECISION

The effective executive has to start out with what is "right" rather than what is acceptable precisely because a compromise is always necessary in the end. But if what will satisfy the boundary conditions is not known, the decision maker cannot distinguish between the right compromise and the wrong compromise—and may end up by making the wrong compromise.

I was taught this lesson in 1944 when I started on my first big consulting assignment. It was a study of the management structure and policies of General Motors Corporation. Alfred P. Sloan, Jr., who was then chairman and chief executive officer of the company, called me to his office at the start of my assignment and said: "I shall not tell you what to study, what to write, or what conclusions to come to. This is your task. My only instruction to you is to put down what you think is right as you see it. Don't you worry about our reaction. Don't you worry about whether we will like this or dislike that. And don't you, above all, concern yourself with the compromises that might be needed to make your conclusions acceptable. There is not one executive in this company who does not know how to make every single conceivable compromise without any help from you. But he can't make the right compromise unless you first tell him what right is."

The effective executive knows that there are two different kinds of compromise. One is expressed in the old proverb, "Half a loaf is better than no bread." The other, in the story of the judgment of Solomon, is clearly based on the realization that "half a baby is worse than no baby at all." In the first instance, the boundary conditions are still being satisfied. The purpose of bread is to provide food, and half a loaf is still food. Half a baby, however, does not satisfy the boundary conditions. For half a baby is not half of a living and growing child.

It is a waste of time to worry about what will be acceptable and what the decision maker should or should not say so as not to evoke resistance. (The things one worries about seldom happen, while objections and difficulties no one thought about may suddenly turn out to be almost insurmountable obstacles.) In other words, the decision maker gains nothing by starting out with the question, "What is acceptable?" For in the process of answering it, he or she usually gives away the important things and loses any chance to come up with an effective—let alone the right—answer.

THE ACTION

Converting the decision into action is the fifth major element in the decision process. While thinking through the boundary conditions is the most difficult step in decision making, converting the decision into effective action is usually the most time-consuming one. Yet a decision will not become effective unless the action commitments have been built into it from the start. In fact, no decision has been made unless carrying it out in specific steps has become someone's work assignment and responsibility. Until then, it is only a good intention.

The flaw in so many policy statements, especially those of business, is that they contain no action commitment—to carry them out is no one's specific work and responsibility. Small wonder then that the people in the organization tend to view such statements cynically, if not as declarations of what top management is really not going to do.

Converting a decision into action requires answering several distinct questions: Who has to know of this decision? What action has to be taken? Who is to take it? What does the action have to be so that the people who have to do it *can* do it? The first and the last of these questions are too often overlooked—with dire results. A story that has become a legend among operations researchers illustrates the importance of the question, "Who has to know?"

A major manufacturer of industrial equipment decided several years ago to discontinue one of its models that had for years been standard equipment on a line of machine tools, many of which were still in use. It was, therefore, decided to sell the model to present owners of the old equipment for another three years as a replacement, and then to stop making and selling it. Orders for this particular model had been going down for a good many years. But they shot up immediately as customers reordered against the day when the model would no longer be available. No one had, however, asked, "Who needs to know of this decision?"

Consequently, nobody informed the purchasing clerk who was in charge of buying the parts from which the model itself was being assembled. His instructions were to buy parts in a given ratio to current sales—and the instructions remained unchanged.

Thus, when the time came to discontinue further production of the model, the company had in its warehouse enough parts for another 8 to 10 years of production, parts that had to be written off at a considerable loss.

The action must also be appropriate to the capacities of the people who have to carry it out. Thus, a large U.S. chemical company found itself, in recent years, with fairly large amounts of blocked currency in two West African countries. To protect this money, top management decided to invest it locally in businesses which would: (1) contribute to the local economy, (2) not require imports from abroad, and (3) if successful, be the kind that could be sold to local investors if and when currency remittances became possible again. To establish these businesses, the company developed a simple chemical process to preserve a tropical fruit—a staple crop in both countries—which, up until then, had suffered serious spoilage in transit to its Western markets.

The business was a success in both countries. But in one country the local manager set the business up in such a manner that it required highly skilled and technically trained management of a kind not easily available in West Africa. In the other country, the local manager thought through the capacities of the people who would eventually have to run the business. Consequently, he worked hard at making both the process and the business simple, and at staffing his operation from the start with local nationals right up to the top management level.

A few years later it became possible again to transfer currency from these two countries. But, though the business flourished, no buyer could be found for it in the first country. No one available locally had the necessary managerial and technical skills to run it, and so the business had to be liquidated at a loss. In the other country, so many local entrepreneurs were eager to buy the business that the company repatriated its original investment with a substantial profit.

The chemical process and the business built on it were essentially the same in both places. But in the first country no one had asked, "What kind of people do we have available to make this decision effective? And what can they do?" As a result, the decision itself became frustrated.

This action commitment becomes doubly important when people have to change their behavior, habits, or attitudes if a decision is to become effective. Here, the executive must make sure not only that the responsibility for the action is clearly assigned, but that the people assigned are capable of carrying it out. Thus the decision maker has to make sure that the measurements, the standards for accomplishment, and the incentives of those charged with the action responsibility are changed simultaneously. Otherwise, the organization people will get caught in a paralyzing internal emotional conflict. Consider these two examples:

When Theodore Vail was president of the Bell Telephone System in the opening years of this century, he decided that its business was service. This decision explains in large part why the United States (and Canada) has today an investor-owned, rather than a nationalized, telephone system. At the same time, Vail designed yardsticks of service performance and introduced these as a means to measure, and ultimately to reward, managerial performance. The Bell managers of that time were used to being measured by the profitability (or at least by the cost) of their units. The new yardsticks resulted in the rapid acceptance of the new objectives.

In sharp contrast is the recent failure of a brilliant chairman and chief executive to make effective a new organization structure and new objectives in an old, large, and proud U.S. company. Everyone agreed that the changes were needed. The company, after many years as leader of its industry, showed definite signs of aging. In many markets newer, smaller, and more aggressive competitors were outflanking it. But contrary to the action required to gain acceptance for the new ideas, the chairman—in order to placate the opposition—promoted prominent spokesmen of the old school into the most visible and highest salaried positions—in particular into three new executive vice presidencies. This meant only one thing to the people in the company: "They don't really mean it." If the greatest rewards are given for behavior contrary to that which the new course of action requires, then everyone will conclude that this is what the people at the top really want and are going to reward.

Only the most effective executive can do what Vail did—build the execution of his decision into the decision itself. But every executive can think through what action commitments a specific decision requires, what work assignments follow from it, and what people are available to carry it out.

THE FEEDBACK

Finally, information monitoring and reporting have to be built into the decision to provide continuous testing, against actual events, of the expectations that underlie the decisions. Decisions are made by people. People are fallible; at best, their works do not last long. Even the best decision has a high probability of being wrong. Even the most effective one eventually becomes obsolete.

This surely needs no documentation. And every executive always builds organized feedback—reports, figures, studies—into his or her decision to monitor and report on it. Yet far too many decisions fail to achieve their anticipated results, or indeed ever to become effective, despite all these feedback reports. Just as the view from the Matterhorn cannot be visualized by studying a map of Switzerland (one abstraction), a decision cannot be fully and accurately evaluated by studying a report. That is because reports are, of necessity, abstractions.

Effective decision makers know this and follow a rule which the military developed long ago. The commander who makes a decision does not depend on reports to see how it is being carried out. The commander or an aide goes and looks. The reason is not that effective decision makers (or effective commanders) distrust their subordinates. Rather, they learned the hard way to distrust abstract "communications."

To go and look is also the best, if not the only way, for an executive to test whether the assumptions on which the decision has been made are still valid or whether they are becoming obsolete and need to be thought through again. And the executive always has to expect the assumptions to become obsolete sooner or later. Reality never stands still very long.

Failure to go out and look is the typical reason for persisting in a course of action long after it has ceased to be appropriate or even rational. In any business I know, failure to go out and look at customers and markets, at competitors and their products, is also a major reason for poor, ineffectual, and wrong decisions.

Decision makers need organized information for feedback. They need reports and figures. But unless they build their feedback around direct exposure to reality—unless they discipline themselves to go out and look—they condemn themselves to a sterile dogmatism.

CONCLUSION

Decision making is only one of the tasks of an executive. It usually takes but a small fraction of his or her time. But to make the important decisions is the *specific* executive task. Only an executive makes such decisions.

An *effective* executive makes these decisions as a systematic process with clearly defined elements and in a distinct sequence of steps. Indeed, to be expected (by virtue of position or knowledge) to make decisions that have significant and positive impact on the entire organization, its performance, and its results characterizes the effective executive.

DISCUSSION QUESTIONS

1. Do you agree with the author that decision making occupies only a small part of a general manager's time?
2. Recall an important decision that you have made, and analyze your decision-making process according to the steps outlined in this reading.
3. The author argues against pragmatism as a means of decision making. What are the advantages of taking a pragmatic approach to decisions?
4. Can you identify steps in the decision-making process that the author doesn't discuss?

The Human Dilemmas of Leadership 24

ABRAHAM ZALEZNIK

Though the general manager's position carries power and sometimes prestige, it is also accompanied by the inherent tensions of leadership. In particular, senior managers are susceptible to common internal conflicts: status anxiety and competition anxiety. Status anxiety stems from the distance that authority puts between leaders and subordinates. Competition anxiety can comprise the fear of success as well as the fear of failure. In this reading, Abraham Zaleznik discusses how to manage these conflicts. The general manager who is aware of his or her inner conflicts will be better able to deal with them and to manage their potential effects on behavior.

In the professional literature on the job of the executive, one seldom finds much reference to or intelligent discussion of the dilemmas posed by the exercise of power and authority. The dramatists, novelists, biographers, and journalists attempt to portray these struggles in their works, but much is left to the sensitivity and intuition of the audience. And least of all are we ever invited to consider the underlying dynamics of leadership dilemmas and the different forms open to us for their resolution.

I should like to try to lift the veil somewhat on the nature of conflicts in exercising leadership by developing these two points:

1. The main source for the dilemmas leaders face can be found within themselves, in their own inner conflicts.
2. Dealing more intelligently with knotty decisions and the inevitable conflicts of interest existing among humans in organizations presupposes that executives, at least the successful ones, are able to get their own house in order. It presupposes that executives are able to resolve or manage their inner conflicts so that their actions are strongly grounded in reality, so that they do not find themselves constantly making and then undoing decisions to the service of their own mixed feelings and to the disservice and confusion of their subordinates.

THE TENDENCY TO PROJECT

Most of us are accustomed by virtue of our training and inclinations to externalize conflicts and dilemmas. Executives who are immobilized in the face of a difficult problem are apt to look to the outside for an explanation. They might perhaps say to themselves they are unable to act because they have inadequate authority. Or they might hesitate because they feel subordinates are holding out by providing too little information, confused positions, and mixed signals. In this case, they are likely to vent their frustrations on their subordinates' incompetence.

This generalized tendency to place conflicts in the outside world is part and parcel of a well-known mechanism of the mind called *projection*. A person projects when, unknown to himself, he takes an attitude of his own and attributes it to someone else. In the example just cited, the executive who despairs because his subordinates are confused and who charges them with holding back and with indecision may well be reading his own state of mind and attributing it to others.

It is just not within us to be able consistently to separate those issues which arise from our own concerns from those issues that reside in the realities of a situation. Let me cite another example:

The president of a large company became concerned with the possibility that his organization had failed to develop executive talent. This concern of his arose in connection with his own retirement. He organized a committee composed of assistants to vice presidents to study this problem and to report to him with recommendations.

The president's forthcoming retirement was well known, and there was private speculation as to who among the vice presidents would be named as his successor. This succession obviously implied that several persons among the assistant vice presidents would be promoted. The task force met several times, but its discussions were not too productive or interesting. The group spent most of its time attempting to define what the president wanted the committee to do, instead of dealing with the issues the organization faced in attracting and developing executive talent.

In other words, they projected their own concerns and anxiety onto the president and attributed to him confused motives in undertaking the assessment of the company's needs in executive development. In reality the individuals themselves shared confused motivations. They were in intensive rivalry with one another over who among their immediate superiors would become president and how this change would affect their fate in the organization.

By centering attention on the inner conflicts of the executive, I do not mean to imply that conflicts are not based in the relations among individuals at work. The illustrations presented so far clearly indicate how vicious these relations may become. The point I am suggesting is that external conflicts in the form of power struggles and rivalry become more easily understood and subject to rational control under those conditions where the executive is able to separate internal conditions from those existing on the outside.

This process of separation is more easily said than done. Nevertheless, it is crucial for the exercise of leadership, and sometimes the separation is the very condition of survival. At the very least, by attending to the inner conditions, the executive can expect to be dealing with those situations most susceptible to rational control. It is in the long run a lot easier to control and change oneself than it is to control and change the world in which we live.

FORMS OF INNER CONFLICT

But before we examine some of the ways in which a person can learn to deal more competently with his or her inner life, we need to know something more about the nature of inner conflicts. Let us take two types that are quite prevalent among executives in organizations:

1. ***Status anxiety*** refers to those dilemmas frequently experienced by individuals at or near the top in their organizational world.
2. ***Competition anxiety*** refers to the feelings generated while climbing to the top.

These two prevalent types of anxiety, while resembling each other in a number of respects, are worth separating for further understanding.

STATUS ANXIETY

Individuals who begin to achieve some success and recognition in their work may suddenly realize that a change has occurred within themselves and in their relations with associates. Whereas they used to be in the position of the bright young executive who receives much encouragement and support, almost overnight they find themselves viewed as a contender by those who formerly acted as mentors. A similar change takes place in relations with persons who were peers. They appear cautious, somewhat distant, and constrained in their approach, where once they may have enjoyed the easy give-and-take of friendship. The individual in question is then ripe for status anxiety. He or she becomes torn between the responsibilities of a newly acquired authority and the strong need to be liked.

There is a well-established maxim in the study of human behavior that describes this situation tersely and even poetically: "love flees authority." Where one individual has the capacity to control and affect the actions of another, either by virtue of differences in their positions, knowledge, or experience, then the feeling governing the relationship tends to be one of distance and (hopefully) respect, but not one ultimately of warmth and friendliness.

I do not believe that this basic dichotomy between respect or esteem and liking is easily changed. The executive who confuses the two is bound to get into trouble. Yet in our culture today we see all too much evidence of people seeking to obscure the difference. Much of the current ethos of success equates popularity with competence and achievement. In Arthur Miller's *Death of a*

Salesman, Willie Loman, in effect, was speaking for our culture when he measured a person's achievement in the gradations of being liked, well liked, or very well liked.

REACTION AND RECOGNITION

How do executives react when they are caught in the conflict between exercising authority and being liked?

Sometimes they seek to play down their authority and play up their likability by acting out the role of the "nice guy." This is sometimes called status stripping, where the individual tries in a variety of ways to discard all the symbols of status and authority. This ranges from proclaiming the open-door policy, where everyone is free to visit the executive any time, to the more subtle and less ritualistic means such as democratizing work by proclaiming equality of knowledge, experience, and position. And yet these attempts at status stripping fail sooner or later. The executive may discover that subordinates join in gleefully by stripping status and authority to the point where the executive becomes immobilized; is prevented from making decisions; is faced with the prospect of every issue from the most trivial to the most significant being dealt with in the same serious vein. In short, problem solving and work become terrorized in the acting out of status stripping.

Executives soon become aware of another aspect of this dilemma. Much to their horror, they find that attempts to remove social distance in the interests of likability have not only reduced work effectiveness, but have aborted the intent of the behavior. They discover that their subordinates gradually come to harbor deep and unspoken feelings of contempt, because they have inadvertently been provided with a negative picture of what rewards await them for achievement—a picture unpleasant to behold. In effect, the process of status stripping helps to destroy the incentives for achievement, and in the extreme, can produce feelings of helplessness and rage.

There is yet another side to the dilemma of status anxiety which is well worth examining. This side has to do with the hidden desire to "touch the peak." Executives frequently want to be near the source of power and to be accepted and understood by their bosses. Such motivations lead to excessive and inappropriate dependency bids, and to feelings of lack of autonomy on the part of the subordinate and of being leaned on too hard on the part of the superior. Under such conditions, communication between superior and subordinate tends to break down.

So far I have discussed the problem of status anxiety as an aspect of seeking friendship, warmth, and approval from subordinates and bosses. Status anxiety is also frequently generated by the fear of aggression and retaliation on the part of persons who hold positions of authority. Executives sometimes report feeling lonely and detached in their position. A closer look at the sense of loneliness reveals a feeling that one is a target for the aggression of others.

This feeling occurs because executives are called upon to take a position on a controversial issue and to support the stand they assumed. They must be able to take aggression with a reasonably detached view, or the anxiety can become intolerable.

An executive who seems unable to take a stand on a problem, who seems to equivocate or talk out of two sides of his mouth at once is reasonably likely to be in the throes of status anxiety. Sometimes this will appear in the form of hyperactivity; the executive who flits from problem to problem or from work project to work project without really seeing an activity through to completion is utilizing the tactic of providing a shifting target so that other persons have difficulty in taking aim.

A CONSTRUCTIVE APPROACH

Now, in referring to aggression and the avoidance of aggression as aspects of status anxiety, I do not mean to imply hostile aggression. I mean to suggest instead that all work involves the release of aggressive energy. Solving problems and reaching decisions demand a kind of give-and-take where positions are at stake and where it is impossible for everyone concerned to be equally right all the time. But having to give way or to alter a position in the face of compelling argument is no loss. The executive who can develop a position, believe in it, support it to its fullest, and then back down, is a strong person.

It is just these types of people who do not suffer from status anxiety. They may love to provide a target because they know this may be a very effective catalyst for first-class work. They are secure enough to know that they have nothing to lose in reality, but much to gain in the verve and excitement of interesting work. These executives are able to take aggression, and in fact encourage it, because they have probably abandoned the magical thinking that equates authority with omnipotence. No one has the power to make everyone else conform to one's wishes, so it is no loss to learn that one has been wrong in the face of arguments aggressively put forth by others. In fact, such ability to retract a stand results in heightened respect from others.

We should not mistake the virtue of humility with executive behavior that appears modest, uncertain of a stand, and acquiescent toward others—behavior which frequently is feigned modesty to avoid becoming a target. People with true humility, in my opinion, think their way through problems, are willing to be assertive, are realistic enough to encourage assertiveness from others, and are willing to acknowledge the superiority of ideas presented by others.

COMPETITION ANXIETY

The second main pattern of inner conflict that badly needs attention is what I have termed competition anxiety, a close kin of status anxiety. It goes without saying that the world of work is essentially a competitive one. Competition exists in the give-and-take of solving problems and making decisions. It also exists in the desire to advance into the more select and fewer positions at the top of a hierarchy. An executive who has difficulty in coming to terms with a competitive environment will be relatively ineffective.

From my observations of executives and would-be executives I have found two distinct patterns of competition anxiety—fear of failure and the fear of success. Let us examine each in turn.

FEAR OF FAILURE

We may see the fear of failure operating in the activities of the child, where this type of problem generally originates. The child may seem to become quite passive and unwilling to undertake work in school or to engage in sports with children his age. No amount of prodding by parents or teachers seems to activate his interests; in fact, prodding seems to aggravate the situation and induce even greater reluctance to become engaged in an activity. When this child progresses in school, he may be found to have considerable native talent, and sooner or later becomes tabbed as an "underachiever." He gets as far as he does thanks in large measure to the high quality of his native intelligence, but he does not live up to the promise which others observe in him.

When this child grows up and enters a career, we may see the continuation of underachievement, marked by relative passivity and undistinguished performance. Where he may cast his lot is in the relative obscurity of group activity. Here he can bring his talents to bear in anonymous work. As soon as he becomes differentiated, he feels anxious and may seek to become immersed once again in group activity.

An important aspect of this pattern of response is the ingrained feeling that whatever the person undertakes is bound to fail. Such people do not feel quite whole and lack a strong sense of identity. They are short on self-esteem and tend to quit before they start in order to avoid confrontation with the fear that they might fail. Instead of risking failure they assume anonymity, hence, the sense of resignation and sometimes fatigue they communicate to those near them.

A closer study of the dilemma surrounding the fear of failure indicates that the person has not resolved concerns about competing. He or she may have adopted or "internalized" unrealistic standards of performance or may be competing internally with unreachable objects. Therefore the person resolves to avoid the game because it is lost before it starts.

If you recall James Thurber's characterization of Walter Mitty, you may get a clearer indication of the problem I am describing. Walter was a meek, shy man who seemed to have difficulty in mobilizing himself for even the simplest tasks. Yet in his inner world of fantasy, as Thurber portrays so humorously and touchingly, Walter Mitty is the grand captain of his destiny and the destiny of those who depend on him. He populates his inner world with images of himself as the pilot of an eight-engine bomber or the cool, skillful, nerveless surgeon who holds the life of his patient in his hands. Who could ever work in the world of mortals under standards that one had best leave to the gods!

You can observe from this description that fear of failure can be resolved only when the person is able to examine his or her inner competitive world, to judge its basis in reality, and to modify this structure in accordance with sensible standards.

FEAR OF SUCCESS

The fear of failure can be matched with its opposite, the fear of success. This latter pattern might be called the "Macbeth complex," since we have a ready illustration available in Shakespeare's *Macbeth*. The play can be viewed symbolically for our purposes:

Macbeth was an ambitious man. It is interesting to note that the demon ambition is projected out in the form of three witches and Macbeth's wife, who, Macbeth would lead us to believe, put the idea into his head to become king. But we do not believe for a minute that the ambition to become number one existed anywhere but within Macbeth himself. You remember that to become king, Macbeth killed Duncan, a nice old man who had nothing but feelings of admiration and gratitude for Macbeth.

As the story unfolds, we find the crown resting uneasily on a tormented head. Macbeth is wracked with feelings of guilt for the misdeed he has committed and then with uneasy suspicion. The guilt is easy enough for us to understand, but the suspicion is a bit more subtle. Macbeth presents himself to us as a character who committed a foul deed to attain an ambition and is then suspicious that others are envious of him and seek to displace him in the number one position. So, there are few lieutenants to trust. And, paradoxically, the strongest subordinates become the ones least trusted and most threatening.

The play portrays in action the morbid cycle of the hostile-aggressive act followed by guilt and retribution. In addition, if we view the play symbolically, we can say that the individual, like Macbeth, may experience in fantasy the idea that one achieves position only through displacing someone else. Success, therefore, brings with it feelings of guilt and the urge to undo or to reverse the behavior that led to the success. If such concerns are strong enough—and they exist in all of us to some degree—then we may see implemented the fear of success.

The form of this implementation will vary. One prominent pattern it takes is in striving hard to achieve a goal, but just when the goal is in sight or within reach, the person sabotages himself. The self-sabotage can be viewed as a process of undoing—to avoid the success that may generate guilt. This process of self-sabotage is sometimes called snatching defeat out of the jaws of victory.

MANAGING INNER CONFLICTS

To summarize the discussion thus far, I have called attention to the not easily accepted notion that conflicts of interest can and do exist within individuals and are not restricted to the relations among people in the ordinary conduct of affairs. I have said that the inner conflicts rooted in the emotional development of the individual are at the core of the leadership dilemma. It is misleading, in other words, to seek for causes of conflict exclusively in external forces.

Then, touching on a few of the inner conflicts of executives, I grouped them into two main types, status anxiety and competition anxiety. Both of these forms of inner conflict are rooted in the very process of human development in the strivings of individuals for some measure of autonomy and control over their environment. The forms happen to be especially crucial in the executive's world simply because executives act in the center of a network of authority and influence that at any point in time is subject to alteration. In fact, one can think of decision making and action in organizations as a continuing flow of influence interchanges where the sources of the power to influence are many. But whatever the external source through which any one person achieves power to influence, its final manifestations will reflect the inner emotional condition of the individual. I would like to suggest the following six ideas for resolving and managing inner conflicts.

1. ***Acknowledge and accept the diversity of motivations.*** The control of one's own responses and actions presupposes some accurate understanding of one's motivations. We would like to believe that our inner world is populated only by the socially nice drives and wishes. But this is not the case. It is fruitless to attempt to deny awareness of the less nice, but equally human, feelings that we all experience, such as rivalry, dislike, rebelliousness, anger, and contempt. I am not urging executives to express these feelings impulsively. I am not of the school of thought that believes the catharsis of feelings in everyday relationships at work and at home is a good thing. But the awareness of how one is reacting in a situation is beneficial and permits more flexibility in thinking and action. Unless an executive establishes a close connection between the realms of thought and feeling, the two can exist in relative isolation from one another to the detriment of managerial effectiveness. At the very least, such self-estrangement involves considerable costs in the waste of energy.

2. ***Establish a firm sense of identity.*** The exercise of leadership requires a strong sense of identity—knowing who one is and who one is not. The myth of the value of being an "all-around guy" is damaging to the strivings of an individual to locate himself in relation to others. This active location and placement of one's self prevents the individual from being defined by others in uncongenial terms. It also keeps the individual from being buffeted around in a sea of opinions. A sense of autonomy, separateness, or identity permits a freedom of action and thinking so necessary for leadership.

Not the least significant part of achieving a sense of identity is the creative integration of one's past. There is no tailor who can convert a hayseed into a big-city sophisticate, any more than a dude can become a cowboy for all the hours he spends on the range. Coming to terms with being a hayseed or a dude permits the development of a unique person who goes beyond the stereotypes offered as models.

3. ***Maintain constancy and continuity in response.*** Closely related to the need for a sense of identity is a constancy in how one represents and presents oneself to others. Constant alterations are confusing to work associates. These shifts are particularly damaging to subordinates, who are entitled to the sense of security that comes from a feeling of reasonable continuity in the responses of their boss. For instance:

I knew of one group of executives, many of whom had the practice of taking tranquilizers before a meeting with the president of the company. They claimed that they needed the tranquilizers to help them withstand the angry reactions the president demonstrated when people acted as though they had not thought through the ideas they were presenting. I think they were mistaken. They used the tranquilizers because they were very unsure as to just what he would get angry about or when. If they had had some sense of the standards of performance to which he reacted kindly or harshly, they would have been able to spend less time worrying and more time working.

4. ***Become selective in activities and relationships.*** Most executives believe that gregariousness and participation in many activities at work and in the community are of great value in their life. In a sense this belief is true. But I would urge that greater attention needs to be paid to selectivity. Without carefully selecting the matters they get involved in, executives face a drain on their emotional energy that can become quite costly. Selectivity implies the capacity to say "no" without the sense that one has lost esteem. The capacity to say "no" also implies that one is so constituted that he does not need esteem from diffuse persons and activities to enhance his self-worth.

5. ***Learn to communicate.*** Conflict resolution, both inner and external, depends on people's capacities to communicate. Communication is a complex process and one that requires careful thought and attention. To improve communication, try to develop a keen awareness of your own reactions, a point I referred to previously. And try to make your opinions and attitudes known without wasteful delays. An unexpressed reaction that simmers and then boils within is apt to explode at inappropriate times; this may lead to increased confusion and concern in the minds of listeners, to the detriment of information interchange.

6. ***Live within a cyclical life pattern.*** The effective utilization of energy seems to involve a rhythmic pattern of alternating between quite different modes or cycles of response. The prototype of alternating modes is probably best found in the comparison of wakefulness and sleep. Wakefulness suggests activity, conscious attention to problems, and the tension of concentration and action. Sleep is the epitome of passivity in the adult as well as in the child; here concerns are withdrawn from the outside world to a state of inner bliss. In this passive state, the organism is rejuvenated and made ready for a new cycle of activity.

This prototype can be applied to a wide range of events in the daily life of the executive. Building oneself into a rhythmic pattern, whether it be around work or play, talking or listening, being at work alone or in association with others, may be essential for dealing with the strains of a difficult role.

SUMMING UP

Training oneself to act and react in the ways just discussed may sound like a formidable task. Formidable it is, but perhaps the basic necessity is to overcome the sense of inertia to which we are all susceptible from time to time. While it sounds puritanical, the most elementary step necessary for achieving a mature orientation as an executive is to assume responsibility for one's own development. Basic to this responsibility is the experiencing of one's self in the active mode. (The sense of inertia referred to before is just the opposite; here life and events appear to occur apart from one's own intentions.) As soon as executives are able to assume responsibility for their own experience and in the course of doing so overcome their sense of inertia, they are on the road toward experiencing leadership as an adventure in learning.

Fortunately, increasing recognition by executives of the importance of their continuing development has made it possible for them, in conjunction with universities and institutes, to examine the dilemmas of leadership and to experiment with new approaches for their resolution.

DISCUSSION QUESTIONS

1. Are some of the "human dilemmas of leadership" already familiar to you? If so, how did you experience and deal with them?
2. Are you aware of your inner conflicts and would you know how to manage them in a business setting?
3. Does Zaleznik's description of managers' dilemmas, conflicts, and anxieties effectively challenge the view that managers are rational and unemotional?

25 Managers and Leaders: Are They Different?

ABRAHAM ZALEZNIK

Exploring and contrasting the world views of managers and leaders, Abraham Zaleznik shows that the two types are characterized by different attitudes, methods, and motivations. Managers wish to create an ordered corporate structure and are emotionally detached from their work. Leaders, in contrast, seek to introduce new approaches and ideas in the organization; they often realize their potential through relationships with mentors. General managers in largely bureaucratic organizations need to recognize and develop potential leaders and to welcome and use their gifts rather than try to make them conform to bureaucratic routine.

What is the ideal way to develop leadership? Every society provides its own answer to this question, and each, in groping for answers, defines its deepest concerns about the purposes, distributions, and uses of power. Business has contributed its answer to the leadership question by evolving a new breed called the manager. Simultaneously, business has established a new power ethic that favors collective over individual leadership, the cult of the group over that of personality. While ensuring the competence, control, and the balance of power among groups with the potential for rivalry, managerial leadership unfortunately does not necessarily ensure imagination, creativity, or ethical behavior in guiding the destinies of corporate enterprises.

Leadership inevitably requires using power to influence the thoughts and actions of other people. Power in the hands of an individual entails human risks: first, the risk of equating power with the ability to get immediate results; second, the risk of ignoring the many different ways people can legitimately accumulate power; and third, the risk of losing self-control in the desire for power. The need to hedge these risks accounts in part for the development of collective leadership and the managerial ethic. Consequently, an inherent conservatism dominates the culture of large organizations. In *The Second American Revolution,* John D. Rockefeller 3rd describes the conservatism of organizations:

> An organization is a system, with a logic of its own, and all the weight of tradition and inertia. The deck is stacked in favor of the tried and proven way of doing things and against the taking of risks and striking out in new directions.[1]

1. John D. Rockefeller 3rd, *The Second American Revolution* (New York: Harper & Row, 1973), p. 72.

Out of this conservatism and inertia, organizations provide succession to power through the development of managers rather than individual leaders. And the irony of the managerial ethic is that it fosters a bureaucratic culture in business, supposedly the last bastion protecting us from the encroachments and controls of bureaucracy in government and education. Perhaps the risks associated with power in the hands of an individual may be necessary ones for business to take if organizations are to break free of their inertia and bureaucratic conservatism.

THE MANAGER VS. LEADER PERSONALITY

Theodore Levitt has described the essential features of a managerial culture with its emphasis on rationality and control:

> Management consists of the rational assessment of a situation and the systematic selection of goals and purposes (what is to be done?); the systematic development of strategies to achieve these goals; the marshalling of the required resources; the rational design, organization, direction, and control of the activities required to attain the selected purposes; and finally, the motivating and rewarding of people to do the work.[2]

In other words, whether his or her energies are directed toward goals, resources, organization structures, or people, a manager is a problem solver. The manager asks: "What problems have to be solved, and what are the best ways to achieve results so that people will continue to contribute to this organization?" In this conception, leadership is a practical effort to direct affairs; and to fulfill their task, managers require that many people operate at different levels of status and responsibility. Our democratic society is, in fact, unique in having solved the problem of providing well-trained managers for business. The same solution stands ready to be applied to government, education, health care, and other institutions. It takes neither genius nor heroism to be a manager, but rather persistence, tough-mindedness, hard work, intelligence, analytical ability and, perhaps most important, tolerance and good will.

Another conception, however, attaches almost mystical beliefs to what leadership is and assumes that only great people are worthy of the drama of power and politics. Here, leadership is a psychodrama in which, as a precondition for control of a political structure, a lonely person must gain control of him or herself. Such an expectation of leadership contrasts sharply with the mundane, practical, and yet important conception that leadership is really managing work that other people do.

Two questions come to mind. Is this mystique of leadership merely a holdover from our collective childhood of dependency and our longing for good

---

2. Theodore Levitt, "Management and the Post-Industrial Society," *The Public Interest* (Summer 1976): 73.

and heroic parents? Or, is there a basic truth lurking behind the need for leaders that no matter how competent managers are, their leadership stagnates because of their limitations in visualizing purposes and generating value in work? Without this imaginative capacity and the ability to communicate, managers, driven by their narrow purposes, perpetuate group conflicts instead of reforming them into broader desires and goals.

If indeed problems demand greatness, then, judging by past performance, the selection and development of leaders leave a great deal to chance. There are no known ways to train "great" leaders. Furthermore, beyond what we leave to chance, there is a deeper issue in the relationship between the need for competent managers and the longing for great leaders.

What it takes to ensure the supply of people who will assume practical responsibility may inhibit the development of great leaders. Conversely, the presence of great leaders may undermine the development of managers who become very anxious in the relative disorder that leaders seem to generate. The antagonism in aim—to have many competent managers as well as great leaders—often remains obscure in stable and well-developed societies. But the antagonism surfaces during periods of stress and change, as it did in the Western countries during both the Great Depression and World War II. The tension also appears in the struggle for power between theorists and professional managers in revolutionary societies.

It is easy enough to dismiss the dilemma I pose—of training managers while we may need new leaders, or leaders at the expense of managers—by saying that the need is for people who can be *both* managers and leaders. The truth of the matter as I see it, however, is that just as a managerial culture is different from the entrepreneurial culture that develops when leaders appear in organizations, managers and leaders are very different kinds of people. They differ in motivation, personal history, and in how they think and act.

A technologically oriented and economically successful society tends to depreciate the need for great leaders. Such societies hold a deep and abiding faith in rational methods of solving problems, including problems of value, economics, and justice. Once rational methods of solving problems are broken down into elements, organized, and taught as skills, then society's faith in technique over personal qualities in leadership remains the guiding conception for a democratic society contemplating its leadership requirements. But there are times when tinkering and trial and error prove inadequate to the emerging problems of selecting goals, allocating resources, and distributing wealth and opportunity. During such times, the democratic society needs to find leaders who use themselves as the instruments of learning and acting, instead of managers who use their accumulation of collective experience to get where they are going.

The most impressive spokesperson, as well as exemplar of the managerial viewpoint, was Alfred P. Sloan, Jr. who, along with Pierre du Pont, designed the modern corporate structure. Reflecting on what makes one management successful while another fails, Sloan suggested that "good management rests on a reconciliation of centralization and decentralization, or 'decentralization with coordinated control.' "[3]

Sloan's conception of management, as well as his practice, developed by trial and error, and by the accumulation of experience. Sloan wrote:

> There is no hard-and-fast rule for sorting out the various responsibilities and the best way to assign them. The balance which is struck . . . varies according to what is being decided, the circumstances of the time, past experience, and the temperaments and skills of the executive involved.[4]

In other words, in much the same way that the inventors of the late nineteenth century tried, failed, and fitted until they hit on a product or method, managers who innovate in developing organizations are "tinkerers." They do not have a grand design or experience the intuitive flash of insight that, borrowing from modern science, we have come to call the "breakthrough."

Managers and leaders differ fundamentally in their world views. The dimensions for assessing these differences include managers' and leaders' orientations toward their goals, their work, their human relations, and their selves.

ATTITUDES TOWARD GOALS

Managers tend to adopt impersonal, if not passive, attitudes toward goals. Managerial goals arise out of necessities rather than desires, and, therefore, are deeply embedded in the history and culture of the organization.

Frederic G. Donner, chairman and chief executive officer of General Motors from 1958 to 1967, expressed this impersonal and passive attitude toward goals in defining GM's position on product development:

> To meet the challenge of the marketplace, we must recognize changes in customer needs and desires far enough ahead to have the right products in the right places at the right time and in the right quantity.
>
> We must balance trends in preference against the many compromises that are necessary to make a final product that is both reliable and good looking, that performs well and that sells at a competitive price in the necessary volume. We must design, not just the cars we would like to build, but more importantly, the cars that our customers want to buy.[5]

Nowhere in this formulation of how a product comes into being is there a notion that consumer tastes and preferences arise in part as a result of what manufacturers do. In reality, through product design, advertising, and promotion, consumers learn to like what they then say they need. Few would argue

---

3. Alfred P. Sloan, Jr., *My Years with General Motors* (New York: Doubleday & Co. 1964), p. 429.
4. Ibid., p. 429.
5. Ibid., p. 440.

that people who enjoy taking snapshots *need* a camera that also develops pictures. But in response to novelty, convenience, a shorter interval between acting (taking the snap) and gaining pleasure (seeing the shot), the Polaroid camera succeeded in the marketplace. But it is inconceivable that Edwin Land responded to impressions of consumer need. Instead, he translated a technology (polarization of light) into a product, which proliferated and stimulated consumers' desires.

The example of Polaroid and Land suggests how leaders think about goals. They are active instead of reactive, shaping ideas instead of responding to them. Leaders adopt a personal and active attitude toward goals. The influence a leader exerts in altering moods, evoking images and expectations, and in establishing specific desires and objectives determines the direction a business takes. The net result of this influence is to change the way people think about what is desirable, possible, and necessary.

CONCEPTIONS OF WORK

What do managers and leaders do? What is the nature of their respective work?

Leaders and managers differ in their conceptions. Managers tend to view work as an enabling process involving some combination of people and ideas interacting to establish strategies and make decisions. Managers help the process along by a range of skills, including calculating the interests in opposition, staging and timing the surfacing of controversial issues, and reducing tensions. In this enabling process, managers appear flexible in the use of tactics. They negotiate and bargain, on the one hand, and use rewards and punishments, and other forms of coercion, on the other. Machiavelli wrote for managers and not necessarily for leaders.

Alfred Sloan illustrated how this enabling process works in situations of conflict. The time was the early 1920s when the Ford Motor Co. still dominated the automobile industry using, as did General Motors, the conventional water-cooled engine. With the full backing of Pierre du Pont, Charles Kettering dedicated himself to the design of an air-cooled engine, which, if successful, would have been a great technical and market coup for GM. Kettering believed in his product, but the manufacturing division heads at GM remained skeptical and later opposed the new design on two grounds: first, that it was technically unreliable, and second, that the corporation was putting all its eggs in one basket by investing in a new product instead of attending to the current marketing situation.

In the summer of 1923 after a series of false starts and after its decision to recall the copper-cooled Chevrolets from dealers and customers, GM management reorganized and finally scrapped the project. When it dawned on Kettering that the company had rejected the engine, he was deeply discouraged and wrote to Sloan that without the "organized resistance" against the project it would succeed and that unless the project were saved, he would leave the company.

Alfred Sloan was all too aware of the fact that Kettering was unhappy and indeed intended to leave General Motors. Sloan was also aware of the fact that, while the manufacturing divisions strongly opposed the new engine, Pierre du Pont supported Kettering. Furthermore, Sloan had himself gone on record in a letter to Kettering less than two years earlier expressing full confidence in him. The problem Sloan now had was to make his decision stick, keep Kettering in the organization (he was much too valuable to lose), avoid alienating du Pont, and encourage the division heads to move speedily in developing product lines using conventional water-cooled engines.

The actions that Sloan took in the face of this conflict reveal much about how managers work. First, he tried to reassure Kettering by presenting the problem in a very ambiguous fashion, suggesting that he and the executive committee sided with Kettering, but that it would not be practical to force the divisions to do what they were opposed to. He presented the problem as being a question of the people, not the product. Second, he proposed to reorganize around the problem by consolidating all functions in a new division that would be responsible for the design, production, and marketing of the new car. This solution, however, appeared as ambiguous as his efforts to placate and keep Kettering in General Motors. Sloan wrote: "My plan was to create an independent pilot operation under the sole jurisdiction of Mr. Kettering, a kind of copper-cooled-car division. Mr. Kettering would designate his own chief engineer and his production staff to solve the technical problems of manufacture."[6]

While Sloan did not discuss the practical value of this solution, which included saddling an inventor with management responsibility, he in effect used this plan to limit his conflict with Pierre du Pont.

In effect, the managerial solution that Sloan arranged and pressed for adoption limited the options available to others. The structural solution narrowed choices, even limiting emotional reactions to the point where the key people could do nothing but go along, and even allowed Sloan to say in his memorandum to du Pont, "We have discussed the matter with Mr. Kettering at some length this morning and he agrees with us absolutely on every point we made. He appears to receive the suggestion enthusiastically and has every confidence that it can be put across along these lines."[7]

Having placated people who opposed his views by developing a structural solution that appeared to give something but in reality only limited options, Sloan could then authorize the car division's general manager, with whom he basically agreed, to move quickly in designing water-cooled cars for the immediate market demand.

---

6. Ibid., p. 91.
7. Ibid., p. 91.

Years later, Sloan wrote, evidently with tongue in cheek, "The copper-cooled car never came up again in a big way. It just died out, I don't know why."[8]

In order to get people to accept solutions to problems, managers need to coordinate and balance continually. Interestingly enough, this managerial work has much in common with what diplomats and mediators do. The manager aims at shifting balances of power toward solutions acceptable as a compromise among conflicting values.

What about leaders, what do they do? Where managers act to limit choices, leaders work in the opposite direction, to develop fresh approaches to long-standing problems and to open issues for new options. Stanley and Inge Hoffmann, the political scientists, liken the leader's work to that of the artist. But unlike most artists, the leader is an integral part of the aesthetic product. One cannot look at a leader's art without looking at the artist. On Charles de Gaulle as a political artist, they wrote: "And each of his major political acts, however tortuous the means or the details, has been whole, indivisible and unmistakably his own, like an artistic act."[9]

The closest one can get to a product apart from the artist is the ideas that occupy, indeed at times obsess, the leader's mental life. To be effective, however, leaders need to project their ideas into images that excite people, and only then develop choices that give the projected images substance. Consequently, leaders create excitement in work.

John F. Kennedy's brief presidency shows both the strengths and weaknesses connected with the excitement leaders generate in their work. In his inaugural address he said, "Let every nation know, whether it wishes us well or ill, that we shall pay any price, bear any burden, meet any hardship, support any friend, oppose any foe, in order to assure the survival and the success of liberty."

This much-quoted statement forced people to react beyond immediate concerns and to identify with Kennedy and with important shared ideals. But upon closer scrutiny the statement must be seen as absurd because it promises a position which if in fact adopted, as in the Vietnam war, could produce disastrous results. Yet unless expectations are aroused and mobilized, with all the dangers of frustration inherent in heightened desire, new thinking and new choice can never come to light.

Leaders work from high-risk positions, indeed often are temperamentally disposed to seek out risk and danger, especially where opportunity and reward appear high. From my observations, why one individual seeks risk while another approaches problems conservatively depends more on his or her personality and less on conscious choice. For some, especially those who become managers, the instinct for survival dominates their need for risk, and their ability

8. Ibid., p. 93.

9. Stanley and Inge Hoffmann, "The Will for Grandeur: de Gaulle as Political Artist," *Daedalus* (Summer 1968): 849.

to tolerate mundane, practical work assists their survival. The same cannot be said for leaders, who sometimes react to mundane work as to an affliction.

RELATIONS WITH OTHERS

Managers prefer to work with people; they avoid solitary activity because it makes them anxious. Several years ago, I directed studies on the psychological aspects of career. The need to seek out others with whom to work and collaborate seemed to stand out as important characteristics of managers. When asked, for example, to write imaginative stories in response to a picture showing a single figure (a boy contemplating a violin, or a man silhouetted in a state of reflection), managers populated their stories with people. The following is an example of a manager's imaginative story about the young boy contemplating a violin:

> Mom and Dad insisted that Junior take music lessons so that someday he can become a concert musician. His instrument was ordered and had just arrived. Junior is weighing the alternatives of playing football with the other kids or playing with the squeak box. He can't understand how his parents could think a violin is better than a touchdown.
>
> After four months of practicing the violin, Junior has had more than enough, Daddy is going out of his mind, and Mommy is willing to give in reluctantly to the men's wishes. Football season is now over, but a good third baseman will take the field next spring.[10]

This story illustrates two themes that clarify managerial attitudes toward human relations. The first, as I have suggested, is to seek out activity with other people, that is, the football team, and the second is to maintain a low level of emotional involvement in these relationships. The low emotional involvement appears in the writer's use of conventional metaphors, even cliches, and in the depiction of the ready transformation of potential conflict into harmonious decisions. In this case, Junior, Mommy, and Daddy agree to give up the violin for manly sports.

These two themes may seem paradoxical, but their coexistence supports what a manager does, including reconciling differences, seeking compromises, and establishing a balance of power. A further idea demonstrated by how the manager wrote the story is that managers may lack empathy, or the capacity to sense intuitively the thoughts and feelings of others. To illustrate attempts to be empathic, here is another story written to the same stimulus picture by someone considered by peers to be a leader:

---

10. Abraham Zaleznik, Gene W. Dalton, and Louis B. Barnes, *Orientation and Conflict in Career* (Boston: Division of Research, Harvard Business School, 1970): 316.

> This little boy has the appearance of being a sincere artist, one who is deeply affected by the violin, and has an intense desire to master the instrument.
>
> He seems to have just completed his normal practice session and appears to be somewhat crestfallen at his inability to produce the sounds which he is sure lie within the violin.
>
> He appears to be in the process of making a vow to himself to expend the necessary time and effort to play this instrument until he satisfies himself that he is able to bring forth the qualities of music which he feels within himself.
>
> With this type of determination and carry through, this boy became one of the great violinists of his day.[11]

Empathy is not simply a matter of paying attention to other people. It is also the capacity to take in emotional signals and to make them mean something in a relationship with an individual. People who describe another person as "deeply affected" with "intense desire," as capable of feeling "crestfallen" and as one who can "vow to himself," would seem to have an inner perceptiveness that they can use in their relationships with others.

Managers relate to people according to the role they play in a sequence of events or in a decision-making *process*, while leaders, who are concerned with ideas, relate in more intuitive and empathetic ways. The manager's orientation to people, as actors in a sequence of events, deflects his or her attention away from the substance of people's concerns and toward their roles in a process. The distinction is simply between a manager's attention to *how* things get done and a leader's to *what* the events and decisions mean to participants.

In recent years, managers have taken over from game theory the notion that decision-making events can be one of two types: the win-lose situation (or zero-sum game) or the win-win situation in which everybody in the action comes out ahead. As part of the process of reconciling differences among people and maintaining balances of power, managers strive to convert win-lose into win-win situations.

As an illustration, take the decision of how to allocate capital resources among operating divisions in a large, decentralized organization. On the face of it, the dollars available for distribution are limited at any given time. Presumably, therefore, the more one division gets, the less is available for other divisions.

Managers tend to view this situation (as it affects human relations) as a conversion issue: how to make what seems like a win-lose problem into a win-win problem. Several solutions to this situation come to mind. First, the manager focuses others' attention on procedure and not on substance. Here the actors become engrossed in the bigger problem of *how* to make decisions, not *what* decisions to make. Once committed to the bigger problem, the actors have to support the outcome since they were involved in formulating decision rules. Because the actors believe the rules they formulated, they will accept present losses in the expectation that next time they will win.

---

11. Ibid., p. 294.

Second, the manager communicates to the subordinates indirectly, using *signals* instead of *messages*. A signal has a number of possible implicit positions in it while a message clearly states a position. Signals are inconclusive and subject to reinterpretation should people become upset and angry, while messages involve the direct consequence that some people will indeed not like what they hear. The nature of messages heightens emotional response, and, as I have indicated, emotionally makes managers anxious. With signals, the question of who wins and who loses often becomes obscured.

Third, the manager plays for time. Managers seem to recognize that with the passage of time and the delay of major decisions, compromises emerge that take the sting out of win-lose situations; and the original "game" will be superseded by additional ones. Therefore, compromises may mean that one wins and loses simultaneously, depending on which of the games one evaluates.

There are undoubtedly many other tactical moves managers use to change human situations from win-lose to win-win. But the point to be made is that such tactics focus on the decision-making process itself and interest managers rather than leaders. The interest in tactics involves costs as well as benefits, including making organizations fatter in bureaucratic and political intrigue and leaner in direct, hard activity and warm human relationships. Consequently, one often hears subordinates characterize managers as inscrutable, detached, and manipulative. These adjectives arise from the subordinates' perception that they are linked together in a process whose purpose, beyond simply making decisions, is to maintain a controlled as well as rational and equitable structure. These adjectives suggest that managers need order in the face of the potential chaos that many fear in human relationships.

In contrast, one often hears leaders referred to in adjectives rich in emotional content. Leaders attract strong feelings of identity and difference, or of love and hate. Human relations in leader-dominated structures often appear turbulent, intense, and at times even disorganized. Such an atmosphere intensifies individual motivation and often produces unanticipated outcomes. Does this intense motivation lead to innovation and high performance, or does it represent wasted energy?

SENSES OF SELF

In *The Varieties of Religious Experience*, William James describes two basic personality types, "once-born" and "twice-born."[12] People of the former personality type are those for whom adjustments to life have been straightforward and whose lives have been more or less a peaceful flow from the moment of their births. The twice-borns, on the other hand, have not had an easy time of it. Their lives are marked by a continual struggle to attain some sense of order. Unlike

12. William James, *The Varieties of Religious Experience* (New York: Mentor Books, 1958).

the once-borns they cannot take things for granted. According to James, these personalities have equally different world views. For a once-born personality, the sense of self, as a guide to conduct and attitude, derives from a feeling of being at home and in harmony with one's environment. For a twice-born, the sense of self derives from a feeling of profound separateness.

A sense of belonging or of being separate has a practical significance for the kinds of investments managers and leaders make in their careers. Managers see themselves as conservators and regulators of an existing order of affairs with which they personally identify and from which they gain rewards. Perpetuating and strengthening existing institutions enhances a manager's sense of self-worth: he or she is performing in a role that harmonizes with the ideals of duty and responsibility. William James had this harmony in mind—this sense of self as flowing easily to and from the outer world—in defining a once-born personality. If one feels oneself as a member of institutions, contributing to their well-being, then one fulfills a mission in life and feels rewarded for having measured up to ideals. This reward transcends material gains and answers the more fundamental desire for personal integrity which is achieved by identifying with existing institutions.

Leaders tend to be twice-born personalities, people who feel separate from their environment, including other people. They may work in organizations, but they never belong to them. Their sense of who they are does not depend upon memberships, work roles, or other social indicators of identity. What seems to follow from this idea about separateness is some theoretical basis for explaining why certain individuals search out opportunities for change. The methods to bring about change may be technological, political, or ideological, but the object is the same: to profoundly alter human, economic, and political relationships.

Sociologists refer to the preparation individuals undergo to perform to roles as the socialization process. Where individuals experience themselves as an integral part of the social structure (their self-esteem gains strength through participation and conformity), social standards exert powerful effects in maintaining the individual's personal sense of continuity, even beyond the early years in the family. The line of development from the family to schools, then to career is cumulative and reinforcing. When the line of development is not reinforcing because of significant disruptions in relationships or other problems experienced in the family or other social institutions, the individual turns inward and struggles to establish self-esteem, identity, and order. Here the psychological dynamics center on the experience with loss and the efforts at recovery.

In considering the development of leadership, we have to examine two different courses of life history: (1) development through socialization, which prepares the individual to guide institutions and to maintain the existing balance of social relations; and (2) development through personal mastery, which impels an individual to struggle for psychological and social change. Society produces its managerial talent through the first line of development, while through the second leaders emerge.

DEVELOPMENT OF LEADERSHIP

The development of every person begins in the family. Each person experiences the traumas associated with separating from his or her parents, as well as the pain that follows such frustration. In the same vein, all individuals face the difficulties of achieving self-regulation and self-control. But for some, perhaps a majority, the fortunes of childhood provide adequate gratifications and sufficient opportunities to find substitutes for rewards no longer available. Such individuals, the "once-borns," make moderate identifications with parents and find a harmony between what they expect and what they are able to realize from life.

But suppose the pains of separation are amplified by a combination of parental demands and the individual's needs to the degree that a sense of isolation, of being special, and of wariness disrupts the bonds that attach children to parents and other authority figures? Under such conditions, and given a special aptitude, the origins of which remain mysterious, the person becomes deeply involved in his or her inner world at the expense of interest in the outer world. For such a person, self-esteem no longer depends solely upon positive attachments and real rewards. A form of self-reliance takes hold along with expectations of performance and achievement, and perhaps even the desire to do great works.

Such self-perceptions can come to nothing if the individual's talents are negligible. Even with strong talents, there are no guarantees that achievement will follow, let alone that the end result will be for good rather than evil. Other factors enter into development. For one thing, leaders are like artists and other gifted people who often struggle with neuroses; their ability to function varies considerably even over the short run, and some potential leaders may lose the struggle altogether. Also, beyond early childhood, the patterns of development that affect managers and leaders involve the selective influence of particular people. Just as they appear flexible and evenly distributed in the types of talents available for development, managers form moderate and widely distributed attachments. Leaders, on the other hand, establish, and also break off, intensive one-to-one relationships.

It is a common observation that people with great talents are often only indifferent students. No one, for example, could have predicted Einstein's great achievements on the basis of his mediocre record in school. The reason for mediocrity is obviously not the absence of ability. It may result, instead, from self-absorption and the inability to pay attention to the ordinary tasks at hand. The only sure way an individual can interrupt reverie-like preoccupation and self-absorption is to form a deep attachment to a great teacher or other benevolent person who understands and has the ability to communicate with the gifted individual.

Whether gifted individuals find what they need in one-to-one relationships depends on the availability of sensitive and intuitive mentors who have a vocation in cultivating talent. Fortunately, when the generations do meet and the self-selections occur, we learn more about how to develop leaders and how talented people of different generations influence each other.

While apparently destined for a mediocre career, people who form important one-to-one relationships are able to accelerate and intensify their development through an apprenticeship. The background for such apprenticeships, or the psychological readiness of an individual to benefit from an intensive relationship, depends upon some experience in life that forces the individual to turn inward. A case example will make this point clearer. This example comes from the life of Dwight David Eisenhower, and illustrates the transformation of a career from competent to outstanding.[13]

Dwight Eisenhower's early career in the Army foreshadowed very little about his future development. During World War I, while some of his West Point classmates were already experiencing the war first-hand in France, Eisenhower felt "embedded in the monotony and unsought safety of the Zone of the Interior . . . that was intolerable punishment."[14]

Shortly after World War I, Eisenhower, then a young officer somewhat pessimistic about his career chances, asked for a transfer to Panama to work under General Fox Connor, a senior officer whom Eisenhower admired. The army turned down Eisenhower's request. This setback was very much on Eisenhower's mind when Ikey, his first-born son, succumbed to influenza. By some sense of responsibility for its own, the army transferred Eisenhower to Panama, where he took up his duties under General Connor with the shadow of his lost son very much upon him.

In relationship with the kind of father he would have wanted to be, Eisenhower reverted to being the son he lost. In this highly charged situation, Eisenhower began to learn from his mentor. General Connor offered, and Eisenhower gladly took, a magnificent tutorial on the military. The effects of this relationship on Eisenhower cannot be measured quantitatively, but, in Eisenhower's own reflections and the unfolding of his career, one cannot overestimate its significance in the reintegration of a person shattered by grief.

As Eisenhower wrote later about Connor, "Life with General Connor was a sort of graduate school in military affairs and the humanities, leavened by a man who was experienced in his knowledge of men and their conduct. I can never adequately express my gratitude to this one gentleman. . . . In a lifetime of association with great and good men, he is the one more or less invisible figure to whom I owe an incalculable debt."[15]

Some time after his tour of duty with General Connor, Eisenhower's breakthrough occurred. He received orders to attend the Command and General Staff School at Fort Leavenworth, one of the most competitive schools in the army. It was a coveted appointment, and Eisenhower took advantage of the

---

13. This example is included in Abraham Zaleznik and Manfred F.R. Kets de Vries, *Power and the Corporate Mind* (Boston: Houghton Mifflin, 1975).

14. Dwight D. Eisenhower, *At Ease: Stories I Tell to Friends* (New York: Doubleday, 1967), p. 136.

15. Ibid., p. 187.

opportunity. Unlike his performance in high school and West Point, his work at the Command School was excellent; he was graduated first in his class.

Psychological biographies of gifted people repeatedly demonstrate the important part a mentor plays in developing an individual. Andrew Carnegie owed much to his senior, Thomas A. Scott. As head of the Western Division of the Pennsylvania Railroad, Scott recognized talent and the desire to learn in the young telegrapher assigned to him. By giving Carnegie increasing responsibility and by providing him with the opportunity to learn through close personal observation, Scott added to Carnegie's self-confidence and sense of achievement. Because of his own personal strength and achievement, Scott did not fear Carnegie's aggressiveness. Rather, he gave it full play in encouraging Carnegie's initiative.

Mentors take risks with people. They bet initially on talent they perceive in younger people. Mentors also risk emotional involvement in working closely with their juniors. The risks do not always pay off, but the willingness to take them appears crucial in developing leaders.

CAN ORGANIZATIONS DEVELOP LEADERS?

The examples I have given of how leaders develop suggest the importance of personal influence and the one-to-one relationship. For organizations to encourage consciously the development of leaders as compared with managers would mean developing one-to-one relationships between junior and senior executives and, more important, fostering a culture of individualism and possibly elitism. The elitism arises out of the desire to identify talent and other qualities suggestive of the ability to lead and not simply to manage.

A myth about how people learn and develop that seems to have taken hold in the American culture also dominates thinking in business. The myth is that people learn best from their peers. Supposedly, the threat of evaluation and even humiliation recedes in peer relations because of the tendency for mutual identification and the social restraints on authoritarian behavior among equals. Peer training in organizations occurs in various forms. The use, for example, of task forces made up of peers from several interested occupational groups (sales, production, research, and finance) supposedly removes the restraints of authority on the individual's willingness to assert and exchange ideas. As a result, so the theory goes, people interact more freely, listen more objectively to criticism and other points of view, and, finally, learn from this healthy interchange.

Another application of peer training exists in some large corporations, such as Philips, N.V. in Holland, where organization structure is built on the principle of joint responsibility of two peers, one representing the commercial end of the business and the other the technical. Formally, both hold equal responsibility for geographic operations or product groups, as the case may be. As a practical matter, it may turn out that one or the other of the peers dominates the management. Nevertheless, the main interaction is between two or more equals.

The principal question I would raise about such arrangements is whether they perpetuate the managerial orientation, and preclude the formation of one-to-one relationships between senior people and potential leaders.

Aware of the possible stifling effects of peer relationships on aggressiveness and individual initiative, another company, much smaller than Philips, utilizes joint responsibility of peers for operating units, with one important difference. The chief executive of this company encourages competition and rivalry among peers, ultimately appointing the one who comes out on top for increased responsibility. These hybrid arrangements produce some unintended consequences that can be disastrous. There is no easy way to limit rivalry. Instead, it permeates all levels of the operation and opens the way for the formation of cliques in an atmosphere of intrigue.

A large, integrated oil company has accepted the importance of developing leaders through the direct influence of senior or junior executives. One chairman and chief executive officer regularly selected one talented university graduate whom he appointed his special assistant, and with whom he would work closely for a year. At the end of the year, the junior executive would become available for assignment to one of the operating divisions, there assigned to a responsible post rather than a training position. The mentor relationship had acquainted the junior executive firsthand with the use of power, and with the important antidotes to the power disease called *hubris*—performance and integrity.

Working in one-to-one relationships, where there is a formal and recognized difference in the power of the actors, takes a great deal of tolerance for emotional interchange. This interchange, inevitable in close working arrangements, probably accounts for the reluctance of many executives to become involved in such relationships. I wonder whether a greater capacity on the part of senior officers to tolerate competitive impulses and challenging behavior of their subordinates might not be healthy for corporations. At least a greater tolerance for interchange would not favor the managerial team player at the expense of the individual who might become a leader.

I am constantly surprised at the frequency with which chief executives feel threatened by open challenges to their ideas, as though the source of their authority, rather than their specific ideas, were at issue. In one case a chief executive officer, who was troubled by the aggressive and sometimes outright rudeness of one of his talented vice presidents, used various indirect methods such as group meetings and hints from outside directors to avoid dealing with his subordinate. I advised the executive to deal head-on with what irritated him. I suggested that by direct, face-to-face confrontation, both he and his subordinate would learn to validate the distinction between the authority to be preserved and the issues to be debated.

To confront is also to tolerate aggressive interchange, and has the net effect of stripping away the veils of ambiguity and signaling so characteristic of managerial cultures, as well as encouraging the emotional relationship leaders need if they are to survive.

DISCUSSION QUESTIONS

1. Does the author favor either managers or leaders?
2. Does Zaleznik distinguish too sharply between managers and leaders? Is his description of them realistic?
3. Can managers benefit from mentoring relationships? Can they mentor leaders?
4. Are both managers and leaders essential to an organization? Do their roles ever overlap?

INDEX